Edward H. Charette
Feb. 3, 1943

THIS MAN LA GUARDIA

Mayor La Guardia at home with his family. (l. to r.) Mrs. La Guardia, Jean, the Mayor, and Eric.

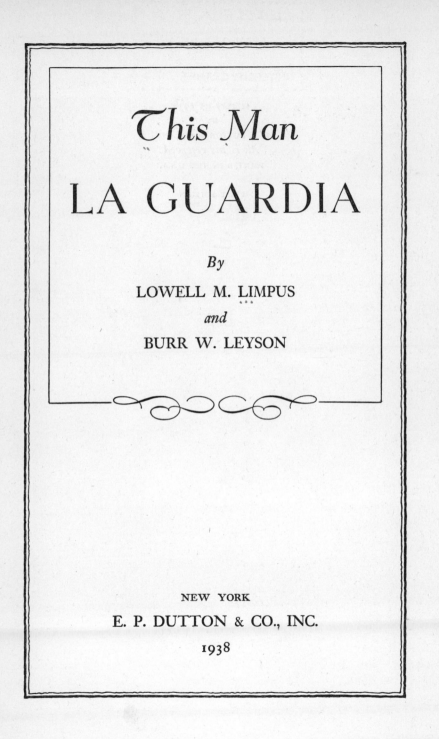

This Man
LA GUARDIA

By

LOWELL M. LIMPUS

and

BURR W. LEYSON

NEW YORK

E. P. DUTTON & CO., INC.

1938

COPYRIGHT 1938
BY
E. P. DUTTON & CO., INC.
All rights reserved
PRINTED IN THE U.S.A.

FIRST EDITION

AUTHORS' FOREWORD

IN THE belief that one's conception of a national figure, such as Fiorello H. La Guardia, is entirely a matter of personal opinion, the authors have made no attempt to present either an analysis or a critical appraisal of their subject's character, motives or politics. That is left to the reader's judgment.

Compiled from the personal files of Mr. La Guardia, the Congressional Record and other equally authentic sources, we present, up to the time of the 1937 New York City municipal elections, an authentic lifetime record of THIS MAN LA GUARDIA.

LOWELL M. LIMPUS
BURR W. LEYSON

New York, 1938

ACKNOWLEDGMENT

THE authors are exceedingly grateful to the following named persons, whose kindness and co-operation made this book possible:

Mayor La Guardia—for access to his private and official files covering the period 1916–1932, for refraining from any attempt to edit or censor the correspondence and private papers thus rendered available and for patiently answering innumerable questions;

Assistant Budget Director Lester Stone, Civil Service Commissioner Paul J. Kern and Secretaries Stanley Howe and Clendenin J. Ryan—for summaries of his record as Mayor;

Dr. Oliver Kiel, of Wichita Falls, Tex.—for his reminiscences of Major La Guardia's World War experiences.

Messrs. Attilio Piccirilli, Louis Espresso and John Gugenhan—for material concerning Major La Guardia's early New York career;

Deputy Welfare Commissioner Edward Corsi, Magistrate Harry Andrews and former Corporation Counsel Paul Windels—for information concerning his early political career;

Mr. Edward Veroneau, of Erie, Pa., former Trumpeter in the 11th U.S. Infantry Band—for a great deal of information concerning Major La Guardia's boyhood and the history of the regiment with which he was so closely identified.

CONTENTS

9

CONTENTS

CONTENTS

LIST OF ILLUSTRATIONS

13

LIST OF ILLUSTRATIONS

THIS MAN LA GUARDIA

SETTING OUT

THE United States Battleship *Maine* lay a battered hulk on the bottom of Havana Harbor and from every corner of the nation troops poured southward to avenge her loss. War with Spain had been declared. The nation was in a turmoil— rumors of battles, victories by land and sea, hummed over the telegraph wires only to be contradicted by later and wilder rumors. Harassed city editors pored over the dispatches vainly trying to sift the grain from the chaff. It was a stormy period in our history and, fittingly enough, it was at this time that Fiorello H. La Guardia's career began. It opened in the spring of 1898 in the City of St. Louis.

The city editor of the *Post-Dispatch* looked up and glowered at a youth who stood in front of his desk.

"Well?" growled the editor, "what is it?"

"I'm going to let you send me to Cuba as a war correspondent!" calmly announced the youth.

"What!" roared the editor. Then he critically examined the delicate-appearing, black-haired youngster. There was a mature self-confidence about the lad that impressed the editor. He met the latter's gaze squarely and fairly exuded a quiet determination that was not to be denied. For an instant the editor hesitated.

In that moment, with the instinctive timing that was to characterize his whole career, Fiorello La Guardia seized his opportunity, began his plea. His fiery eloquence rang with sincerity, a sincerity that later was to thrill vast audiences. It carried conviction now. Quickly and tersely the sixteen-year old boy stated his qualifications.

He had grown up in the army. His father was the bandmaster of the 11th Regiment United States Infantry, now in Mobile awaiting orders to sail for Cuba. Army life had been his life; he knew the army as no civilian could hope to know it. Wasn't he the obvious man for the position of war correspondent?

The doubting editor was so impressed that young La Guardia left St. Louis as the accredited correspondent for the *Post-Dispatch!* He had literally talked his way into his first job, appropriately enough one connected with the army.

Prior to the day when he had run away from home after the recruiting officer had refused him for service as too young, La Guardia's entire life had been connected with the 11th Infantry. His father was its bandmaster and wherever the regiment went there went also the La Guardia family.

From Fort Sully, South Dakota, to Sacketts Harbor, New York, and then to Whipple Barracks, Arizona, the family had followed the regiment. It was small wonder that young La Guardia's earliest ambition was to become a soldier.

"I guess there's military blood in my veins," mused New York's Mayor in later years. "My grandfather fought beside Garibaldi and my father gave most of his life to the American service—in fact, he gave his life *for* it."

Then he added: "Strange, isn't it, that I turned out to be a pacifist—in spite of the fact that I wore the uniform, too!"

There is, undoubtedly, warrior blood in this man who is so well qualified for the title of the most militant pacifist who ever stormed about looking for trouble. He is descended from a warrior family.

Rafael Enrico La Guardia, of Foggia, Italy, had donned the "red shirt" of Giuseppi Garibaldi and fought beside him from one end of Italy to the other. Back in the days when the great Italian patriot battled the Papal troops, Rafael became a Protestant and his family have remained so ever since. Among the children of Rafael was a son, Achille, born at Foggia who later, in the United States, became the father of Fiorello La Guardia. Achille grew up in Foggia and became a talented musician as well as a gifted composer and one of the leading cornetists of his time. Then, in 1878, he came to the United States as the arranger and accompanist for the great singer, Adelina Patti.

Achille La Guardia had met, fallen in love with and married Irene Coen Lazatti in Trieste, Italy. Born at Fiume, she was three-quarters Italian and the other Jewish, one of her grandparents being descended from a Jewish refugee who had sought sanctuary from the Spanish Inquisition by fleeing to Italy.

Settling in New York, a daughter, Gemma, was born to them in 1880. Two years later on December 11, 1882, a son was born and they christened him Fiorello Enrico. The Enrico was for his warrior grandfather and the Fiorello, translated, is "Little Flower."

Severing his connection with Patti, the elder La Guardia sought employment. Following the trend of his ancestors, he enlisted in the army and became a musician in the United States Infantry, 11th Regiment. Joining the army in September, 1885, at New York City, the elder La Guardia was assigned to the 11th Regiment then stationed at Fort Sully, South Dakota. He took his wife, daughter and three-year-old son to the Western Plains and reported for duty. There, at Fort Sully, a second son was born and christened Richard.

On August 9, 1887, the regiment was transferred to the famous old Madison Barracks at Sacketts Harbor, New York, and here the La Guardia family remained until the regiment was moved again, this time to Fort Huachuca, Arizona, where it arrived on October 16, 1891.

By this time Achille La Guardia's musical ability had won recognition and he was the bandmaster of the regiment. His first enlistment period had expired while still at Madison Barracks and when he re-enlisted in 1890 he was made chief musician, a rank he held when he enlisted for the third time at Whipple Barracks, Arizona, in 1895.

"I was too young when we left New York to remember

anything about the city," Fiorello La Guardia relates. "My earliest memories concern Sacketts Harbor and trips to Watertown with the band. I can't say that I recall very much about Sacketts Harbor. My most distinct childhood memory is that long trip to Arizona in 1891 when I was nine years old. It seemed as if we would never get there.

"We remained at Fort Huachaca, about thirty miles from the present town of Douglas, until May 4, 1892, when we were transferred to Whipple Barracks at Prescott, up near the central part of Arizona Territory. It was there that I grew up.

"Prescott was really my home town. We lived there until the Spanish-American War started the troops moving again. My sister and I went to school there, and as soon as Richard was old enough he came, too.

"It was during those days at Prescott that I first became seriously interested in music. That was quite natural. Father lived for music and he began teaching Gemma and me as soon as we could distinguish one note from another."

The La Guardias occupied an unusual social position on the boundary between officers and enlisted men. In a sense they shared the life of both—superior to the one and inferior to the other. The bandmaster's son outranked the children of the ordinary non-commissioned officers but he recognized the difference between himself and the offspring of the officer personnel. Consequently he early acquired an ability of meeting a superior on his own ground.

The Old West was already dying but here, in the shadow of Thumb Butte, it persisted for a time. Prescott, but a mile and a half from the Post, was still a frontier town and the life of its 1500-odd people was of necessity simple.

A single-track railroad line connected the town with "civilization." Ice was unknown as a refrigerant and eggs and milk were luxuries which had to be freighted in from the junction. Cowboys and Indians were a part of the scene and the saddle was a standard method of transportation. Young La Guardia learned to ride as a matter of course. As the years passed the healthy Western air and the blazing sun bronzed his skin. The outdoor life molded his frail body into a wiry frame. Here he built a physique that was to be tested to the uttermost in the years to come.

Prescott had a good school, even judged by modern standards. This six-teacher institution was the pride of the community. As the town grew it maintained its pride in its schools and by the time that La Guardia had graduated from the eighth grade there was a handsome new high school awaiting. He entered this in 1895.

As a student he was fair, not brilliant. He played and wasted his time just as all normal boys do. But at school he widened his circle of acquaintances. No longer were his playmates limited to the army children at the Post. Most of the children were civilians but as the son of an army man he always felt more or less patronizing towards them.

"Two of my friends were Tom Campbell and Ben Pope," he recalls. "I liked them both and I still remember the fight they had in Zora Morgan's barn! It was epic! It lasted from the time school was dismissed until well after dark—and then it ended in a draw! I recall how I danced around them and egged them on and I was very much disappointed the next day when they made up and failed to renew the fight according to agreement. I still think that it was one of the best fights I ever saw!"

This friendship was renewed thirty years later when Governor Thomas Campbell of Arizona visited Washington and was amazed to discover in Congressman F. H. La Guardia of New York, his old playmate from Prescott.

The La Guardia home at Prescott had little in the way of luxury. The children assisted with the housework and all of them learned to cook. It was in his mother's kitchen that Fiorello La Guardia acquired the culinary knowledge which he was so proud to exhibit in later years. Spaghetti was his forte. He mastered the difficult art of blending the sauces that make the Italian national dish so tasty. But the gustatory de-

21

lights and the music were all of the old country that Achille La Guardia permitted in his household. He barred the use of the Italian tongue and insisted that only the language of his adopted country be spoken. Fiorello La Guardia did not learn to speak Italian until he was twenty. Then, within a short period he mastered not one but several different languages.

But if Achille's mother tongue was denied, the music of his native land was not. Night after night Fiorello and his sister Gemma practiced under the strict supervision of their father. Fiorello played the cornet and his sister the violin. The La Guardia home rang with the magnificent operas of the Old Country and both children acquired a musical training that was of the finest.

Strangely, it was in this frontier town that young La Guardia first learned to hate Tammany Hall! Once each week the *New York World* came to their home—the sole connecting link with the city of his birth. As soon as his father had finished with the paper young La Guardia devoured every word printed on its pages. At that time the *World* was crusading against Tammany Hall and its editorials made a lasting impression on the youth who had never lost interest in the city of his nativity. Due to the influence The World exerted, young La Guardia grew up with a great antipathy for anything connected with Tammany. Yet at that time, little did he realize that he was to wreck the power of the New York Tiger in later years.

Such were the conditions under which young La Guardia grew to adolescence. He expected to enter the army as a matter of course as soon as he became of age. But events of national importance have a way of disrupting the best of plans. With the declaration of war against Spain went young La Guardia's hopes of a military career.

He saw his father leave for war with the regiment. He heard Bucky O'Neill, who organized an Arizona contingent for Roosevelt's Rough Riders, give a stirring talk in the High School. Later he read of the same man's death in action.

The crowning blow fell when he was rejected for service as too young! It was then he left home and started east to find the end of the trail in the office of the *St. Louis Post-Dispatch*. From there he joined his father with the regiment in Mobile. Fiorello La Guardia was an accredited war correspondent and from that time on he stood on his own feet. The fledgling had left the nest.

CHAPTER II

THE CRUSADER ARMS

THE young war correspondent never reached Cuba. He accompanied the 11th Infantry to Tampa, Fla., but his journalistic career was cut short, when his father fell a victim to the "embalmed beef" which was issued to the American Army. Bandmaster La Guardia became seriously ill. He never completely recovered from the effects of the poison. He was shipped back to Jefferson Barracks, and on August 22, 1898, honorably discharged for disability incurred in line of duty. After he emerged from the hospital, the shattered veteran was pensioned—but the responsibility for the support of the family devolved upon his son.

Fiorello accepted the burden calmly.

The boy gave up his position, and returned to St. Louis to be with his father. As soon as the latter was able to travel, they returned to New York, where they established a home and sent to Arizona for the rest of the family.

Dreary days followed. The old soldier's pension provided a portion of the family income, and it was supplemented by whatever the boy could make working at odd jobs. Achille La Guardia grew steadily weaker, and died in 1901.

His father's death made a deep impression upon young Fiorello, and sixteen years later when he entered Congress, his first bill provided the death penalty for the sale of tainted supplies to troops in time of war.

After his father's death, young La Guardia found himself in desperate straits. The family was practically penniless, and he was unable to secure a position. Grasping at the first opportunity which offered, he took the civil service examination for the United States Consular Service. He passed, and at the age of 19 received an appointment to the office at Budapest.

He entered the service the same year that his father died. For five years he remained abroad during which period he laid the foundation for his later career. He manifested unusual intellectual capacity, and a courage which was coupled with a reckless disregard for consequences.

La Guardia's brilliant mentality served him well. Learning of a vacancy in the Consulship at Fiume—then a Hungarian seaport on the Italian border—he buckled down to work for the place. He began the study of German and Italian. The boy knew nothing of the latter language because it had never been spoken at home. Now he revealed a talent for languages. He mastered the first two and then turned to Croatian. Later he was to prove equally adept at learning French, Spanish and Yiddish. Meanwhile, he learned the ways of the world in the Hungarian capital. Fiorello danced and drank and tasted the joys of Budapest's night life. Occasionally the rising sun caught him as he was homeward bound. The gay Hungarian city offered vivid temptations to the young man from Arizona! Yet he did not permit them to interfere with his career. Nor did he devote his leisure hours exclusively to cabarets. He joined an Austrian Soccer Club, and spent many an afternoon at the game. Likewise he studied.

He won the place at Fiume. One of the youngest men ever appointed to Consular Service, he was just beyond his twenty-first birthday when, in 1903, he received the appointment. His salary was increased to $800 per year.

The young consul promptly got into trouble. It was due to his democratic idealism. His first clash was with the Cunard S. S. Company.

Always eager to experiment, Consul La Guardia worked out a novel system of immigration inspection, and installed it without consulting anybody. He provided the first medical inspection center at a port of embarkation. Under this system, immigrant applicants who could not pass the medical examination, were rejected at Fiume, instead of at Ellis Island, upon their arrival in the New World.

The steamship company protested to Washington that the boy consul was exceeding his authority. La Guardia replied that the shipping magnates preferred to take the emigrants' passage money, even though compelled to return them to Europe if later rejected, pointing out that the empty ships had to return anyhow.

The basic merit of this system prevailed, and La Guardia was permitted to continue his examinations. In the next three years he personally inspected and stamped the cards of 60,000 immigrants, only eleven of whom were rejected on arrival at Ellis Island.

He is satisfied with that record today. "Twenty years later," he explains, "as a Member of Congress, I voted for a measure officially inaugurating that same system of medical inspection. I am still proud of the fact that when I was just past 21, I worked out a system which proved to be twenty years ahead of its time!"

Triumphant in his skirmish with the steamship company, he was less successful when he clashed with the Austrian Government. He denied an official request to postpone the sailing of a shipload of emigrants in order to satisfy the whim of a royal Archduchess. She wanted the ship held in port for forty-eight hours so that she might inspect those of her subjects who were bound for America.

The young consul declared that they had acquired the protection of the Stars and Stripes, and that it would be unfair to keep them sweltering below decks, even to oblige Her Royal Highness. He issued clearance papers and sent the ship on its way. When the Archduchess arrived she entered a violent protest, and the Austrian Government complained of the discourtesy to Washington. As a result, the consul was shifted to Trieste.

But already he had grown dissatisfied with the service. Consumed by a restless ambition, he observed that a consular career offered little opportunity for progress. Deciding that he was wasting his time, he resigned from the service in 1906, and returned to New York.

He soon discovered that he had arrived at an inopportune time. The panic of 1907 was just beginning, and there were few vacancies for an ambitious young man. He rejoined his family, settling down with his mother in the home at 24 Charles Street, in Greenwich Village. His younger brother was working in New Jersey.

A stranger in his home city, La Guardia plodded the streets looking for work. Nobody wanted a young man whose only assets were a useless mastery of tongues, and an ability to cut red tape! When his small savings were almost exhausted, he chanced to notice an advertisement of a business college which offered a course in stenography for $7.50. The young man enrolled in the school, and mastered shorthand within a month. It proved a valuable asset then, as well as in later years. Equipped with his new knowledge, he then secured a position typing in the office of the Society for the Prevention of Cruelty to Children. The salary was $8 a week.

As always, he was dissatisfied. He had not renounced a consular career in order to devote his life to making pothooks and curleycues! He began looking for another position. With his knowledge of stenography and his mastery of languages, he qualified for a position as interpreter at Ellis Island. By that time he spoke Italian, French, German, Serbian and Yiddish. He worked faithfully at the new job, and his winning personality brought him the friendship of his newest colleagues.

But he was still far from content. His ambition made him restless. He decided to study law, and enrolled in the New York University Law School for night sessions. During the next three years he slaved laboriously. He spent his days in the uniform of an Ellis Island interpreter, and at night he pored over his law books.

The La Guardia of those days is thus described by James I. Ellmann, a classmate, who is now a Detroit attorney:

La Guardia sat directly in front of me, and I had many opportunities for observing his characteristics. He made a very sharp impression upon me at the time because of his capacity and sure-footedness. Thin and wiry, he always seemed alert. He had the capacity for dealing intellectually with any question which came up.

He was a very quiet and unassuming student, striving sincerely to learn the intricacies of the law. We all respected him.

He completed the course in three years, received his LL.B., and passed his bar examinations. Then he hung out his shingle and prepared to practice. At that time he Anglicised his middle name to "Henry," and his shingle bore the legend:

F. H. LA GUARDIA,
Attorney-at-Law.

The next two years were uneventful. He struggled along like many another ambitious youthful attorney, getting an occasional fee and barely meeting expenses. It was a period of discouragement and despair. Clients were few and far between.

When the New York garment strike of 1912 was launched he had plenty of leisure, and he enlisted in the cause of organized labor. The young attorney volunteered his services to the strikers.

He threw himself heart and soul into the struggle, and simply *lived* garment strike during 1912 and 1913. At first he was an unnoticed recruit among the 65,000 workers involved. But gradually he won his way to leadership.

The wiry young lawyer was everywhere. He drew up briefs and argued cases, representing his penniless clients without expectation of remuneration. He worked on committees and even served on the picket line.

For the first time he won public attention. It was his initial adventure into the limelight. As a result he became a recognized leader of the garment workers, and was one of the three arbitrators ultimately chosen to settle the strike. He battled valiantly for them in committee, and helped to win a minimum wage and a fifty-hour week. The contract further provided that within a year, this was to be reduced to a forty-eight-hour week.

A picture of those days is presented in a letter which he wrote nine years later to one of the union leaders:

> You will recall the dark days of 1913 and the hopeless situation which followed the fake Union Garment Workers' Settlement. You will recall the disorganization which followed: the racial hatreds among the workers, owing to the system of exploitation which had been practiced in the shops for years; and how we all worked joyfully for the first real understanding among businesslike locals.
>
> You cannot forget how we spent night after night conferring with the Joint Board Executive Committee!
>
> You remember the examination of delegates and officers, and the numerous court cases which I conducted—not to mention that I was addressing literally hundreds of meetings during that period.

It was then that he met Miss Thea Almerigotti and fell in love with her. His was a stormy courtship. There were difficulties aplenty; not the least of which was the difference in religion. She was a devout Catholic while the grandson of the Garibaldi veteran had that same year become a Master Mason.

Miss Almerigotti already had won recognition as a dress designer for a Fifth Avenue firm. She was proud of her profession and of her Italian ancestry. Born in Trieste the girl was devoted to her native city. When Italy entered the World War in 1915 Thea's enthusiastic hope for the emancipation of Trieste from the Austrian rule kindled an answering fire in his own breast.

There was also the bitter hatred of Tammany Hall. It had been revived and intensified by the machinations of local politicians during the garment strike. He wanted to deal a blow at the organization which dominated his native city, and he went about it in the only practical manner. He joined the local Republican Club down on the lower East Side, in the district in which he resided.

Up to that time La Guardia had paid little attention to politics. Aroused by the eloquence of Theodore Roosevelt, he had voted for the latter in 1912. But he had never visualized himself in the political arena.

He seemed enlisted in a lost cause when he enrolled in the Republican organization. Tammany dominated the city. It had never lost an election in that district below Fourteenth Street with which he identified himself. The Republican organization was so weak that candidates frequently refused to run because of the certainty of defeat. The clubhouse was a lounging place for discouraged defeatists. There was no fight in them.

In mid summer of 1914 the dispirited leaders were attempting to make up a slate for the coming election. For half an hour they wrangled, trying to persuade one another to accept the thankless task of opposing Congressman Michael Farley that year. Nobody wanted the nomination. Farley was a popular saloon-keeper, the President of the National Liquor Dealers' Association, and it was regarded as political suicide to oppose him. Finally somebody noticed the black-haired lawyer, gesticulating in a corner of the room as he argued with a group of his fellow members.

"Give it to young La Guardia," a voice suggested. "Nobody wants it, anyhow."

They called him over and offered him the place. He hesitated at first, knowing as well as they that the offer was meaningless. But suddenly he remembered that it was an opportunity to fight the Tiger.

"I'll take it," he said simply.

He almost lost the nomination, even then. When the local leaders 'phoned the Republican headquarters and gave the name of their candidate, the man at the other end of the wire couldn't get it. It was spelled over and over again—but still headquarters couldn't get it straight.

"Aw, hell," headquarters interrupted at last, "give me somebody else! It doesn't matter anyhow!"

The local captain agreed, but the potential candidate, standing close by, protested so vehemently, that the switch was not made. Instead they wrote out the name carefully on a slip of paper and sent it uptown.

Early the next morning the candidate borrowed an old Ford, and began canvassing the Fourteenth Congressional District. It extended along the lower East Side—a section teeming with populous tenements, and containing great numbers of Italians and Jewish immigrants. From door to door he went, and now his knowledge of languages stood him in good stead.

Storming up and down the hallways, he exchanged sparkling repartee in Yiddish with fat Jewish matrons and bearded, skull-capped rabbis. In Italian kitchens he discussed in their own language, the best methods of making spaghetti, with homesick Neapolitans.

(He knew what he was talking about, too. Mamma Irene had taught her son to cook, and to cook well. Among his talents this was not the least.)

And always he discussed Tammany, explaining to these bewildered children of the slums, that there was an ulterior motive behind the famous "charities" of the Democratic organization. Because he spoke to all in their own tongue they listened to him. He had no money of his own and no campaign fund. The Republican organization gave him no support.

"They didn't even know I was running!" he chuckled in later years. "I remember my chagrin at one meeting when they introduced all the candidates except the candidate for Congress! I was right on the platform with a speech fairly bubbling to get out. I sat forward in my chair, always expecting to be the next candidate introduced—and then suddenly the meeting closed, without even mentioning me! It was a terrible disappointment."

Despite the enthusiastic, if disorganized, support of his garment-worker friends, nobody expected the one-man anti-Tammany crusade to get far. It was recognized as hopeless from the beginning. And it was.

Congressman Farley was re-elected by 1700 votes—but the Republican leaders sat up with a start. Never before had the Democratic majority in that district been less than 16,000 votes. The wild young radical had lured 14,000 out of the Tammany fold. That was an achievement. They regarded the young man with a kind of respectful awe. Anybody who commanded a personal following of 14,000 was worth cultivating. Some of the wiser ones decided that he *might* have a political future some day, and they agreed that it was judicious to keep him attached to the organization.

The Republican Party controlled the State, and they offered young Mr. La Guardia an appointment as a Deputy State Attorney General.

He accepted the post and settled down to a bachelor existence. His mother and sister had returned to Italy to reside with relatives, and he took a room at 39 Charles Street.

Shortly after he had taken the oath in the Spring of 1915, a slim, flaxen-haired German girl came into the Attorney General's office, seeking a job. The daughter of a staid German family, she had just graduated from Morris High School. Her stenography was not so good—but there happened to be a vacancy, and Marie Fischer was given a typewriter.

Before she had been there very long, she discovered that the other stenographers were all talking about the new deputy. The consensus of opinion seemed to be that he must be insane—he was taking his job so seriously! He was reported to be addicted to waving his arms and raving as he strode up and down his office and discussed the possibility of prosecuting certain old cases against Jersey factories that were drenching Riverside Drive with smoke and fumes. Everybody was rather

"Fiorello played the cornet. . . ." As he graduated from public school in 1895.

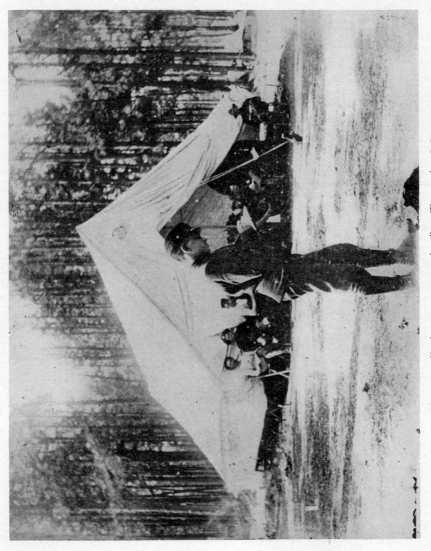

"An accredited war correspondent" at Tampa in 1898.

afraid of him; it was only natural that his work was shoved on to the new stenographer.

Miss Fischer was amazed at him. She had never seen anything quite like the exuberant vitality of this handsome young Latin. He fairly awed her. Her phlegmatic German background had never provided anything even remotely comparable. His tantrums entranced her.

She soon discovered another side of his nature. She was nervous because of her inexperience and inadequate stenographic training. When he discerned this, he became kindly and considerate. He called her to his desk and patiently taught the frightened girl what he had learned about stenography. Realizing that she was conscientious and trustworthy, he finally selected her as his personal secretary. She was to serve in that capacity for fourteen years.

The New York City branch of the State Attorney General's office had never been considered important. The real work of the department was done at Albany, where the best brains of the staff were concentrated. The New York branch served only as a clearing house for minor matters and a storeroom of forgotten cases.

Among the latter was the Riverside Drive matter. Those cases had been hanging on for years. Civic associations had repeatedly protested against the fumes that drifted across the Hudson River from New Jersey factory chimneys. Injunctions had been registered by both State and City Boards of Health. The offenders, however, were mammoth industries, and "nothing was ever done about it." Deputy Attorney General La Guardia looked over those old complaints, and immediately instituted seven different actions on behalf of the State of New York. There was only one precedent in American legal history for this course, but he took the matter straight to the United States Supreme Court.

He struck so suddenly that his opponents did not realize what was happening. He was appointed on January 1, 1915, and on February 28, the Supreme Court granted his applica-

33

tion for leave to proceed against five of the companies. The industries hastily mobilized for battle. Considerable influence was brought to bear on the young prosecutor; but he proved relentless—and he won his case. As a result, the corporations were forced to install expensive equipment and the nuisance was ended.

"It was the Long Island Scallops Case, however, that first shook my confidence in abstract justice," explained Major La Guardia. "I had not been in office very long when they sent me down there to assist in the enforcement of the laws supervised by the Long Island Game Commission. My duty was to prosecute oyster fishermen who were not observing the regulations.

"I had plenty of evidence. I prepared my cases carefully, and I prosecuted them as vigorously as I knew how—but I could not seem to get any convictions. Nobody was acquitted —the juries just disagreed! I could not understand it, and after I became better acquainted with some of the people down there, I asked what was the reason.

"I still remember the lanky Long Island fisherman who explained to me:

" 'Mr. La Guardia, all of us folks that set on these cases, know that these fellers are guilty. That's the reason we won't acquit 'em; but, at the same time, we ain't going to convict our own neighbors, when the big oyster companies are doing exactly the same thing—and getting away with murder.'

"The 'big oyster companies', I repeated. What do you mean?

"He looked at me in amazement.

" 'You mean you *really* don't know about 'em?' he asked.

"I nodded my head.

" 'Well, young feller,' he commented, 'you'd better look 'em up.'

"I did so. I found that there were three big oyster concerns that were absolutely ignoring the regulations. When I went to the Fish Wardens they expressed surprise.

" 'You don't mean you're going to prosecute them?' they demanded.

"I assured them that such was the case. The wardens were delighted. They turned over plenty of evidence, and I instituted proceedings against the three companies. Immediately I became involved in legal difficulties.

"These cases were adjourned every time they came up in court. The defense always had an excuse. I pressed for trial but I couldn't seem to get anywhere. Finally one bright morning the counsel for the oyster companies rose in court, smiled at me triumphantly, and announced that he was ready to proceed. Then he turned to the Judge and asked under what provision of the law I was prosecuting. I quoted the statute, and gleefully he slapped a telegram before the Judge.

" 'That portion of the law which applied to these corporations was repealed by the legislature yesterday!' he announced. 'Governor Whitman signed the measure last night. That law no longer applies to us!'

"I knew he was right. I stalked out of the courtroom almost bursting with anger—and I stopped the prosecution of the little fishermen.

"I have been very suspicious of big corporations ever since."

A little later Deputy Attorney General La Guardia was invited to act as one of the arbitrators in the settlement of the 1916 Shirtwaist and Dressmaker Strike. His reputation as a friend of organized labor was beginning to win wider recognition.

In the same year the young lawyer won some disdainful comment as a result of the first of his Cassandra-like prophecies. He inspired nothing but merriment when at a banquet given in honor of his friend, Jacob Panken, in July, he foretold the revolution in Russia and the downfall of the Romanoff Dynasty. He was discussing the Czar's recent order emancipating his Jewish subjects, so that they might serve in the Russian Army.

"Yes, my friends," sneered the speaker, "for the first time

in history, from the lips of a Romanoff, there came the endearing term of 'Beloved Jews.' It will turn about and end for all time the Romanoff Dynasty—thereby freeing not only themselves, but the whole of the Russian people."

These remarks, reprinted in the Yiddish press, made a deep impression on the New York ghetto. He was favorably spoken of in the synagogues as the champion of an oppressed people!

As a result, the Jewish population rallied to his support when the campaign of 1916 got under way.

La Guardia was given the nomination again because of his good showing two years before—but not without a struggle. To his assistance came Louis Espresso, an energetic young Republican leader, rising to eminence in the Greenwich Village section. Espresso was a two-fisted politician who had fought his way to the top in the hurly-burly of district politics. Quick to recognize La Guardia's worth as a candidate, Espresso vehemently insisted that the nomination should go to the man who had made such unexpected inroads on Tammany in 1914.

Nobody else, except the candidate himself, really expected that he could defeat Congressman Farley for re-election.

About him, however, gathered a group of loyal supporters. They laid their plans carefully—determined to make a mighty effort to overwhelm Tammany in one of its most impregnable strongholds. Espresso threw himself into the campaign. The friendly garment workers rallied to his standard. Harry G. Andrews, a brilliant young attorney, joined the headquarters staff, and John Gugenhan, an East Side letter carrier, who had been captivated by the La Guardia personality, mobilized his fellow postal workers. These letter carriers did yeoman service, canvassing the district as they went about their duties.

Miss Fischer, the secretary, was installed in the headquarters which he opened in a vacant store. From the first she had exhibited an amazing political acumen. She proved an able lieutenant, and was invaluable in this, as in succeeding campaigns.

Leaving headquarters in her capable hands, the candidate promptly proceeded to take the East Side apart in the first of the La Guardia whirlwind campaigns with which his native city was later to become familiar. He stormed all over the district, denouncing Tammany to his polyglot audiences in half a dozen different languages. He stood outside the saloon, beneath his rival's headquarters, shaking his fist at the windows and daring Farley to come down and debate!

The latter refused the invitation, and when Tammany plug-uglies came shouting into his meetings, to squelch the speaker, little La Guardia doubled up his fist and went for them. He was supported by a bodyguard drawn from his friends of the garment strike—and there was action all over the district.

Election day came, and still nobody thought he had a chance; it was inconceivable that Tammany should lose a rock-ribbed East Side district! Espresso, however, pulled a last-minute *coup d'état*. He mobilized his election workers at daybreak, and they concentrated on the lodginghouse vote. Inhabitants of cheap Bowery hotels were almost literally dragged from their beds, and marched off to the polls, stopping en route to breakfast at the leader's expense. Needless to say, they were urged to vote the straight Republican ticket.

When the over-confident Tammany workers descended on the lodginghouses later in the day, they were startled and dismayed to learn that that portion of the vote was already in. Still, they refused to worry.

The other Republican leaders did not share Espresso's confidence. Hopeless of success, they locked up their clubhouse and went home as soon as the polls closed. Nobody paid any attention to the Congressional race. Every one was watching the neck-and-neck contest between Woodrow Wilson and Charles Evans Hughes for the Presidency.

The Republican candidate for Congress also went home when he discovered that he could not get into his own clubhouse. And there a Tammany leader 'phoned him, to ask if he knew how large a majority he had received! It was too good to be true. Scarcely daring to believe in his victory, the exultant La Guardia hastily telephoned his Republican district leader. His hopes promptly received a dash of cold water! The leader assured him that his election was simply *impossible;* that a mistake must have been made, and that the figures would undoubtedly be corrected in the morning.

The news was true, however! La Guardia had been swept into office on a rising tide of protest, which rolled so high that, even with Tammany controlling the count, he was still certified victorious by 257 votes. He received 7,272, and Farley 6,915.

William B. Calder, of Brooklyn, had been elected to the United States Senate at the same time, and the revolt, which had begun with the Fusion victory of Mayor John Purroy Mitchel, was still growing. But La Guardia's success was the most amazing overturn of an amazing election. A Republican representative had been chosen in an East Side Tammany district! The entire State rocked with the news. La Guardia became famous overnight, and Tammany, which had been "sowing the wind" for years, awoke to discover that the harvest was at hand!

Such was Fiorello La Guardia's entrance into the political arena. Slender and handsome, eyes blazing like live coals beneath a mass of black hair, his vigor and enthusiasm made him an impressive figure upon the platform. His voice was high in pitch and constituted a minor handicap, but he learned to control it in later years.

Flushed with victory, the Congressman-elect plunged into another conflict, even before he had an opportunity to take his seat in the House. For the third time he took up the cudgels on behalf of the oppressed Garment Workers. Their employers had broken the agreement which he had helped to negotiate the preceding year, and on December 12, 1916, 60,000 of them walked out on strike.

Early the next morning, Congressman-elect La Guardia and Dr. Henry Moskowitz (who was later to win fame as the intimate of Governor Alfred E. Smith) volunteered their services on behalf of the strikers; nor was La Guardia content with merely lending them the assistance of his name.

Once more he went on the picket line, and once more he clashed with the police. Disorder marked the strike, during which 45,000 workmen engaged in mass picketing demonstrations.

La Guardia marched with them, and as the result of an affray in front of the Frank Brothers factory, at 318 East 32nd Street, on December 16 (during which gangsters attacked the strikers) the fiery attorney who had been in the thick of it, sought and obtained the assistance of the Fusion Mayor Mitchel.

He took a leading part in the negotiations that returned 25,000 strikers to work on December 19. But he did not relax his efforts on behalf of those who remained out. Christmas Day of 1916 found him on the picket line!

When the strike was finally settled he turned his attention to one more task.

War was in the air, La Guardia believed that the United States would inevitably become involved—sooner or later. He also believed in preparedness, and he decided to get ready for the coming conflict. Aviation was in its infancy; but the glamour of battle in the air appealed to him.

He went out to Mineola, Long Island, and asked his friend, Joseph Bellanca, to teach him to fly. Bellanca agreed and the Congressman devoted himself to the new art. He studied faithfully and practiced patiently, until he was at home at the controls. Before he left for Washington to take up his new duties La Guardia knew how to handle a plane.

CHAPTER III

THE FLYING CONGRESSMAN

THE Congress convened on March 4, 1917, and Fiorello La Guardia took his seat in the House of Representatives. His new colleagues eyed him askance, for he was an unknown quantity. Unknown but not unnoticed. They took stock of him carefully. He had already attained a somewhat doubtful celebrity.

The merciful oblivion which usually shrouds a new Congressman, until he has had time to find his feet, was not for La Guardia. He was in the spotlight from the beginning. Not only was he the first Representative of Italian ancestry to enter the halls of Congress, but the brand of the liberal was upon him.

Liberalism was not quite respectable in those days. The championing of organized labor was in itself enough to implant suspicion in conservative minds. It was whispered that the New Yorker had socialistic leanings—and socialism was definitely outside the pale. Furthermore, he was classed as a second-generation immigrant; and that was another cause for doubt.

Worst of all was the story of his "strike" activities! A Congressman who had marched on the picket line! You couldn't trust such a man. The socialist story must be well founded. Even before he took his seat there were men in Congress who were ready to denounce him as a radical, a pacifist and a demagogue.

His colleagues watched his every move, just as they watched those of that other newcomer, Miss Jeannette Rankin of Montana, the first member of her sex to secure a seat in the National Legislature.

Their expectations were fulfilled the very first day.

Instead of waiting to be assigned a vacant seat in the rear of the House, as was customary with new members, the new New Yorker strolled down the floor and quietly dropped into the vacant place between the eminent James Mann and another Republican leader. His fellows were scandalized; but he remained in the place he had pre-empted.

The very first act of the Congressman La Guardia was to introduce his bill providing, for the fraudulent sale of supplies, the death penalty in time of war and imprisonment in time of peace. The measure was unnoticed in the attendant turmoil.

Stirring times were at hand as the War Congress convened.

America's participation in the world conflict was recognized as inevitable. It was only a matter of time.

One month before President Wilson had severed diplomatic relations with Germany, and only seven days previously he had sought authority to use the armed forces for the protection of American rights on the seas.

War was in the air. The House was in a turmoil, and the New York legislator was in the thick of it. La Guardia refused to yield to the custom which required that a new member keep silent during his initial term. Almost from the first day, the energetic newcomer was bobbing out of his seat to discuss legislation in hand.

He divided his attention between his duties in Washington and events at home. On March 17th he rushed back to New York to speak at four big "America First" meetings on the East Side. They had been scheduled in order to give the foreign-born an opportunity to demonstrate their loyalty to their adopted country. His burning eloquence swept them off their feet. In the words of The *New York Evening World*, "Congressman La Guardia, young, enthusiastic and energetic, stirred the audience wherever he went!"

Wild applause greeted his oft-repeated "Confession of Faith": "I have no reason to believe that any considerable number among us will be found wanting in loyalty. . . . These are days when we must renew our love for our country and the flag that flies over us."

Returning to Washington, within three weeks he was called upon to vote on the declaration of war.

His was a difficult position. La Guardia knew that the Fourteenth was a predominantly pacifist district. His career was in the balance as he took his seat that 5th day of April when the declaration was introduced.

The floor was a madhouse, with the advocates of peace making their last, desperate stand. Debate waxed fervid. Congressman Kerns demanded that those Congressmen who were willing to enlist for the war they were about to declare, should identify themselves. Instantly the New York representative was on his feet. Conscious of his short stature, he stood waving his hand above his head, so that there might be no misunderstanding. And with him rose Royal Johnson of South Dakota, A. O. Gardner of Massachusetts, and Victor Heintz of Ohio.

Speaker Champ Clark ruled them out of order and the debate went on. It lasted for seventeen hours—until 3 o'clock in the morning of April 6th. Then the ballots were cast. The result was 375 to 50. America was at war—and Congressman La Guardia had voted for it!

Immediately following the declaration, La Guardia began a systematic referendum of his constituents, on the question of conscription. He sent a postal to every voter in his district, accompanied by a letter, reading: "This country is at war and needs every available man. Shall we have a volunteer army? Or an army composed of conscripted citizens of military age?" He added: "I think conscription is necessary, and I'm trying to educate people up to it. It is up to you to respond! Don't blame me if you don't like the way I vote!"

In May he paid a flying visit to New York, and addressed 1,000 Italians at the Labor Temple:

"I want to drive it home and impress it upon you, if I can," he stormed at them, "that we are in the midst of the most cruel war in the history of the world . . . and those who prefer Italy to America should return to Italy. I know there are some of you in my district who won't sacrifice themselves for *any* country—and if I thought I owed my election to that sort, I would resign."

Back in Washington he continued to play an unusually prominent part for a new member in speeding war legislation that was beginning to creep through Congress; but from the beginning he asserted his independence of thought and action.

The first of the many La Guardia battles on the floor of the House took place on May 2, 1917, when a censorship bill was under discussion. For two hours the New York representative defended the freedom of the press. The following exchange, recorded in the Congressional record is typical:

MR. STEELE. Mr. Speaker, will the gentleman yield again?

MR. LA GUARDIA. Yes.

MR. STEELE. Is the gentleman in favor of any restriction whatever on a publication that might be useful to the enemy?

MR. LA GUARDIA. No; not if it infringes on the rights guaranteed by Article I of the first amendment to the Constitution, and if it does more harm than good.

MR. HOWARD. Mr. Speaker, will the gentleman yield right there?

MR. LA GUARDIA. Yes.

MR. HOWARD. I am very much interested in this section. Do you think there is anything in section 4 that will prohibit them from lambasting the War Department for inefficiency in letting contracts, or inadequacy of food, or anything that would not be helpful to the enemy at a strategic moment?

MR. LA GUARDIA. I do; and I could so draw an indictment.

MR. HOWARD. Under this act?

MR. LA GUARDIA. Under this act.

43

Mr. Howard. The gentleman has more imagination than I have if he can do it.

Mr. La Guardia. You will find, if you pass this law, that various United States district attorneys will have a very resourceful imagination. . . .

A little later, he recalled the Spanish-American war experiences.

The people of this country are united in their demands that the scandals, abuses, graft and incompetency of 1898 are never again to be repeated and the press is their medium of detecting and exposing these abuses and crimes. It is our duty, as their Representatives, to do nothing which will impair, restrict or limit the press in the fulfillment of that duty. This alone, without considering the destruction of one of our basic fundamental principles of liberty, is sufficient justification to arouse the indignation of this House and send this bill back to the committee, where it should die in shame and neglect.

Some of the gentlemen have spoken about the protection of the American boy. We all want to protect him. It is for his protection that I oppose this bill. You have spoken about the vicious enemy. I know the enemy is vicious. We all know that, and prepare accordingly. When the American Army meets the enemy, whenever that may be, leave it to the American Army to crush him. But what more vicious, dangerous and cowardly than the friendly domestic enemy who is willing to turn American blood into gold and sell rotten corn beef, wormy beans, paper shoes, defective arms, for our American boys? And when the American press ferrets him out they will likewise crush *that* enemy. Our Army and Navy shall not be the dumping place for all the defective arms and war supplies rejected by the Allies during the past two years. On the second day of this session I introduced a bill providing death punishment for dishonest contractors. I hope the Committee on the Judiciary will report it out. I will tell you more on that subject when the time comes. I had better not get started on that now.

Do you know that American warehouses are bulging

with defective arms and ammunition that has been rejected by the Allies in the last two years? And are we
going to make our Army and our Navy a dumping
ground for these defective arms and this defective ammunition? We must keep our eyes open, so that they
will not try to put it across.

He opposed the Espionage Bill, which he considered extreme and oppressive. When it finally passed, on June 15,
1917, he voted against it. He sought to safeguard public rights
under the Enemy-Alien Property Bill, openly declaring such
legislation provided opportunities for graft and corruption.
Basing his position upon the results of his referendum, he supported the draft bill; but he flared out in open opposition to
the clause exempting Members of Congress from conscription! His colleagues eyed him askance, the prevailing opinion
being that it was the gesture of a demagogue.

He supported the War Loans to Foreign Governments, but
his was the only voice raised in a prophecy that they would
never be fully repaid. His remarks in the House at the time
were considered almost disloyal to our Allies. He declared:

> I don't share the belief of some of my colleagues who
> have expressed their complete confidence in the future
> restitution of these three billions to be loaned to For-
> eign Governments. . . . Yes, I believe that a good portion
> of it will be returned in due time; but I am certain that
> much of it will have to be entered in the loss, rather than
> the profit column in Uncle Sam's books. . . . Let us un-
> derstand that clearly now and not be surprised later. . . .
> Even so, if this brings about a happy termination of the
> war, and a permanent peace for our own country, it will
> have been a good investment.

On June 21, the New York Representative made his first
important speech in the House. It was during the discussion
of the National Food Control Bill, which was being pushed as
a war measure, that he took the floor and began:

Mr. Chairman, I am confident of the successful outcome of this bill, if it is enacted into law. It gives unheard-of powers. Yes, but necessary powers. With its proper, intelligent and impartial enforcement, I cannot see how it can possibly fail. If there is hoarding, it gives power to take the hoarded supplies away. Food may be sold at a reasonable price in order to bring down unreasonable and artificially created high prices. Speculation may be curbed, export regulated. . . . It is bound to bring about much needed relief.

Gentlemen, the passage of this bill will do more to demoralize the enemy than anything we have enacted during this session. Our declaration of war did not surprise the Kaiser. He expected it. The $7,000,000,000 bond issue did not unduly worry him. He believes we shall waste it. The conscription law caused him no immediate anxiety, for he believes that it will take a long time before its effects can be felt. But, Gentlemen, the marshaling of our food supplies, control of export, this great getting-together of the people, the taking of this drastic action, will have a telling effect upon the Kaiser— and he will know that we mean business, that thoroughness and efficiency are not his personal monopoly. When enacted by the representatives of a free people, enforced and obeyed with the true American spirit, it means success to our cause and spells peace.

Gentlemen, I am so thoroughly convinced of the need and benefit of the provisions of this bill, that I feel it is not only a war measure, but a permanent institution with us. After the war, if we are not careful, the speculators will soon be back at the old game. . . . I gave considerable attention to, and made personal investigation of, the food riots which took place in New York City a few months ago, and, Gentlemen, I give you my personal assurance that the cause of that disturbance, the action of those unhappy women, was nothing but the result of empty stomachs! Wage-earners, most of them. Others with husbands working and yet unable to provide for the proper nourishment of their families! Is not that cause for reflection? . . . As long as I live I do not wish to witness another food riot. You want and I want and every American wants everybody to get enough to eat. I realize that there is a lot to do before we can bring about such ideal conditions—but let us start *now!*

I have taken the first step toward that end. I have this day introduced a Constitutional Amendment, giving power to the National Government at all times to regulate and control the production, conservation and distribution of food supplies. This may sound extreme—perhaps radical; but under similar circumstances, the founders of this country and the framers of the Constitution, would have it so. It is the will of the American people.

The bill passed 365 to 5.

In the ensuing month the young Congressman devoted all his attention to war legislation. He had begun a careful study of parliamentary procedure, and on this subject he focused the same brilliant mentality which had so rapidly assimilated stenography and law and seven different languages. Continued in later years it transformed him into a master parliamentarian.

As a result, he was quick to detect an attempted legislative trick, which might otherwise have postponed woman suffrage. He had studied House procedure sufficiently to recognize the danger in a seemingly innocent adjournment, when a motion to discharge committees in order, was coming up. He knew that the first measure on the list was the Suffrage Amendment introduced by Jeannette Rankin. He objected, and his quick wit saved the measure!

La Guardia was an ardent believer in the cause of woman suffrage, and was directly responsible for its victory. It is not generally realized that it was his single vote, *cabled from Europe* while he was serving at the front, that provided the margin by which the amendment passed the House the following year.

The young liberal voted against increasing the membership of the Interstate Commerce Commission, and this stand, together with his opposition to the Espionage Act, and his attitude on the Alien Property Bill made him the target of bitter criticism. Whispers began to circulate that the New York

Congressman from the pacifist district, was not a loyal supporter of his country.

Some of his more vociferously patriotic colleagues were quick to join in this criticism, and he was the object of suspicious glances as he strode briskly about the floor. The gentlemen who were inclined to distrust his patriotism were soon silenced, however.

On July 25, 1917, he made good his promise. He went quietly to the old Southern Building in Washington and enlisted in the United States Army. There was no fanfare in the newspapers. He had confided his intention only to Speaker Champ Clark.

Major Benjamin D. Foulois (later Brigadier-General) was enrolling applicants.

A slight young man stepped up and offered his services. Quietly he announced that he knew how to handle planes.

"Your name?" asked the Major.

"Fiorello H. La Guardia."

"Any relation to the Congressman?"

"Not exactly." The candidate gave his secret in a whisper: "You see, I *am* the Congressman."

Naturally he was welcomed with open arms. Experienced flyers were rare in those days. He was given his examination on August 15 and passed it easily. As a result, he was commissioned a First Lieutenant on August 16, and assigned to active duty. The shortage of flying officers resulted in rapid promotion, and he received the silver bars of a Captain on September 7.

As soon as he was commissioned, his Congressional salary was discontinued, on the theory that a man cannot hold two government positions at the same time. He offered to resign from Congress, but his colleagues refused to accept his resignation. The Government then suspended his pay as an army officer, for the same reason. The young officer was soon penniless. He had no savings, and his financial situation became critical.

When he was down to his last dollar, he visited the Riggs National Bank in Washington, and explained his dilemma. To the bankers he stated that he regretted having been commissioned, since the Government would have been forced to provide his sustenance if he had remained an enlisted man. The bank arranged to advance him $100 a month on his personal note, and the Flying Congressman prepared to go overseas.

His status as a member of Congress remained in doubt, and the newly-commissioned Captain was exceedingly irked.

"Congress will have to go on record," he snapped. "I cannot think that the House will expel a member for doing just what it is advocating as the duty of every young man in the country! . . . I think I see a disposit⁀n to evade the question."

Just before he sailed, he announced that he did not propose to drop the matter. He declared that he was certainly entitled to $2500 a year as a Captain, if he could not draw his $7500 Congressional salary. "If the Germans don't get me, I'll get that pay!" he declared. "I'll take up the matter at the close of the war."

It was not until many months later that Congress decided to give him a leave of absence.

There was another matter, even closer to his heart, demanding the Captain's attention, however. As soon as he had donned his country's uniform, he hurried back to New York to exhibit it to Thea. She was manifestly proud of her suitor, and shared his delight in the silver bars on his shoulders. The girl beamed approval of his action, and was especially thrilled by the thought that he was to fight side by side with her countrymen in the struggle to reclaim her beloved Trieste from the Austrian conqueror.

She brought the matter up on the day that Captain La Guardia asked her to marry him.

"I shall never marry anybody," replied Thea, "while Trieste is Austrian territory! You may ask me again when the Italian flag once more waves over it!"

49

CHAPTER IV

SERVICE AT HOME AND ABROAD

THE evening of September 1, 1917, Captain La Guardia reported for duty at Post Headquarters, Mineola, Long Island. The foster son of the service had come home at last! In the army environment he was at home. Routine at an army post was an old story to him. He was placed in command of a detachment of flying cadets who had volunteered for special service abroad.

This was a peculiar command. His detachment was composed of men who were neither officers nor enlisted men in the strict sense of the word. They were aviation cadets and potential officers. But they were not to remain long at Mineola. La Guardia saw to that.

La Guardia received orders to take his men overseas but transportation was not available through ordinary channels. The transport service was chaotic. Nobody knew anything about sailing plans. Repeated inquiries produced no information so La Guardia solved the problem in a manner that was to become typical of him in the service. He cut red tape and went ahead!

Learning that there was a Cunard liner sailing soon, he rushed down to the line's offices. The *Carmania* was to sail on the 15th of September. He promptly bought 152 first-class passages for his men and charged them to the United States Government!

When he marched his men aboard the liner he was met by Major John E. Hunt who was in charge of the placing of the troops aboard. The Major was amazed at La Guardia's way of doing things! He objected strenuously to La Guardia's demand that his detachment be afforded first-class staterooms.

"Only officers travel first-class! Take 'em below!" insisted the Major.

La Guardia triumphantly waved a bundle of first-class tickets and his men scattered to their staterooms. Major Hunt did not learn until two years later that his argument had been with the erstwhile "radical" Congressman. Then Congressman La Guardia came unexpectedly to Hunt's assistance when charges were filed against the Major for permitting the escape of Grover Cleveland Bergdoll, the wealthy draft-dodger. At that time La Guardia declared that he knew from personal experience that Major Hunt was a conscientious officer. La Guardia remembered the incident aboard the *Carmania*.

Arriving in England, the detachment was sent to Oxford for training at the School of Military Aeronautics while a short time later La Guardia was sent to France and then Italy, leaving his command.

He had no illusions as to his flying ability.

I had been enrolled as an aviator but that did not mean that I was ready for action. There was a great deal of difference between the flying I had done at Mineola under Bellanca and that which was expected of us at the front. Consequently I was ordered to the Eighth Aviation Center School at Foggia, Italy, for training.

Foggia! The very name gave me a thrill as I stood looking at my orders. I had heard about Foggia all my life. I was returning not only to the land of my ancestors but the birthplace of my father. Generations of La Guardias had lived at Foggia—that bustling little city of Apulia, just above the "heel of the boot," a few miles from the Adriatic Sea.

I reported for duty on October 16th, and began my training under Italian instructors. As the senior American officer present I automatically took command of those Americans who were there.

I was assigned as an instructor but that meant nothing. I was simply in charge of the administrative details. When it came to flying, I was just as much a student as

any of them. We all took instruction from experienced
Italian aces.

I was officially placed on flying status on December
10, 1917.

The youthful commander got into trouble very soon. Again
his difficulties were due to red tape. He had 300 men at Foggia, and they were 1,000 miles from the nearest American
Quartermaster. Consequently, they could not obtain American Army rations, but had to share those of the Italians. The
Italian ration, while ample, aroused strong objections among
the American troops. Basically, it consisted of spaghetti seven
days a week; and meat was issued only twice a fortnight.
La Guardia solved the problem in characteristic fashion: he
marched out to a civilian contractor, and ordered the equivalent of American Army rations. He directed that the bill be
sent to the American Government.

The troops were delighted, but their commander promptly
received orders to report to headquarters of the Service of
Supply at Tours, France, in order to explain his "unprece-
dented action."

The trip itself proved a punishment. Airplanes were so
badly needed at the front, that they could not be wasted to
provide transportation for an insignificant American Captain.
He was forced to go by train, and the war-time schedules
were so disarranged, that the journey consumed three days.
There were no sleeping accommodations.

He was tired out and disgusted when they finally put him
on the carpet. Lieut.-Col. Monell of the Air Service (later
Vice President of the International Nickel Co.) sat by and
watched while a sarcastic Colonel took him in hand.

"Did you ever read the Army Regulations, Captain?" inquired the Colonel sweetly.

"I have not had time. I have been too busy," snapped the
Captain.

"Well, you will know something about them before I get
through with you!" roared the inquisitor. "Don't you know

that you are supposed to draw your food supplies from the nearest Quartermaster?"

"The nearest Quartermaster happens to be in France, sir," replied the victim. "He was too far away for me to draw rations, and I had to get proper food for my men immediately."

"You can explain all that to the Court Martial," sneered the Colonel. "*I* am going to prefer charges against you."

He then plunged into a lengthy lecture, and concluded by reading aloud a portion of the Articles of War.

When he had finished La Guardia interrupted gently:

"May I ask, sir," he began, "if you are acquainted with Article 1 of Army Regulations? The one that provides that the Secretary of War shall promulgate them?"

The Colonel nodded.

"Very well, sir," resumed the unrepentant defendant, "if the Articles we now have won't permit me to feed my men when they are hungry, I will go back to Congress and see to it that the Secretary of War makes out some new ones."

Colonel Monell, roaring with laughter, came to his defense. The other Colonel fumed for a while, but finally decided to reconsider the Court Martial. After a stinging verbal reproof, La Guardia was ordered back to Foggia.

"Incidentally," commented the latter, "this was one of only three occasions when I reminded any one during the war that I was a Member of Congress. I had to do it this time to get my boys fed. I did it a second time in order to get to the Front. And I resorted to it for a third time when we needed gasoline, while we were fighting the Austrians."

Again he took the long trip back to Foggia—but the question of the rations was still unsettled. It finally was referred to Brigadier General Charles G. Dawes, later Vice President, but then the General Purchasing Agent for the United States Army.

When the food bills were protested at headquarters, General Dawes erupted:

"Hell and Maria!" he exclaimed. "This guy La Guardia is right. I'll back him up."

The General gave instructions that the Italian Government was to be billed for the food, and that the latter should charge it to the United States. He ordered that the bills be sent to him. He paid them.

The captious Captain had scarcely emerged from this difficulty before he became involved in another.

He decided to authorize a Christmas leave for most of his command, so that the boys could enjoy the holiday in Rome. La Guardia is no prude. He was well aware that "single men in barracks don't grow into plaster saints," and he understood the dangers to which they would be exposed. He sought a practical solution of a complex social problem. The "camp followers" who, traditionally, trail the troops in the field, were kept in check in Foggia—but he realized that Rome was replete with ladies of light virtue.

In co-operation with a junior medical officer, First Lieut. Oliver Kiel, a physician of Wichita Falls, Texas, La Guardia worked out a plan for a traveling dispensary which should accompany the furloughed men. They planned to locate a mobile prophylaxis station in the Roman "red light district."

These arrangements were canceled by the senior medical officer present. The latter denounced the scheme, declaring that it would encourage immorality. When La Guardia protested, the senior surgeon advised him to keep his men in camp.

A bitter argument followed. The medical officer was adamant.

La Guardia pondered the matter in his quarters for a while; then he buckled on a pistol and went calling on the medical Major. Without the slightest vestige of authority to do so, he placed the gentleman under arrest; and locked him up in his quarters on an ostensible charge that his reports were not up to date!

La Guardia's men had their Roman holiday; but there was

utter consternation in the headquarters of the A. E. F. when the senior surgeon's written protest arrived. Staff officers stared at one another in unbelief. Such action was simply inconceivable. A peremptory order for La Guardia to report immediately to the Commander in Chief was telegraphed to Italy.

Once more the Army's stormy petrel boarded a train and jaunted halfway across Europe.

His arrival at Chaumont was an event. The commander of the American flyers in Italy had achieved a questionable notoriety. Wide-eyed Second Lieutenants gazed after him, staring at the Captain in a kind of horrified fascination. His superiors were coldly formal. He moved in an atmosphere of awe and pity. It was known that the medical corps was raging at the treatment accorded the senior surgeon, and the offender could expect no mercy.

He was ordered to report directly to Major-General Merritt W. Ireland, Surgeon General of the A. E. F. Buoyant as ever, La Guardia entered the lion's den.

The veteran received him with ominous courtesy.

"Captain, just *what* did you do to the senior medical officer at Foggia?"

"I placed him under arrest, sir."

"And *why* did you place him under arrest, Captain?"

"He refused to permit me to send our mobile prophylaxis station to Rome, sir."

The Surgeon General leaned forward with sudden interest.

" 'Mobile prophylaxis station'?" he repeated. "Why, what's that?"

Instantly La Guardia plunged into an enthusiastic description of his pet project. He explained the plan which had been worked out with Lieutenant Kiel, and told how it had been developed.

The General became more and more interested as the explanation proceeded. He interrupted again and again with technical questions: Just what materials had been taken? The quantity of each? The personnel needed to operate such a dispensary? Their training and technique?

The Captain leaned eagerly across the desk and explained each point in detail. Finally the General interrupted him:

"But how did it work out? Was it successful?"

"Entirely so, sir," came the prompt reply. "Here are the reports of its operation. I asked Lieutenant Kiel to give me copies."

General Ireland took the papers and ran through them hastily. Finally he settled back in his chair and nodded his head in approval.

"That's a great idea, Captain La Guardia," he declared at last. "You are certainly to be congratulated on evolving it. It is applicable to all rest areas in the A. E. F. I want to thank you for bringing it to my attention."

The two men parted on the best of terms. The matter of the arrest was not referred to again until just before the Captain left. Then the General brought it up, as an after-thought:

"By the way, La Guardia," he said, "would it make things any easier at Foggia if I were to transfer that medical officer?"

"Why, yes, sir, I think it would."

"Very well; he'll be gone by the time you get back."

The General was as good as his word. The transfer of the senior surgeon was ordered the same day.

La Guardia hurried back to Foggia to resume his interrupted training.

He was anxious to devote himself to his studies so that he might get to the front. Every man was needed there. Italy was facing a crisis. Her armies were still reeling from the Caporetto disaster where 180,000 men had been lost in a single week. Every man counted in the effort to bolster up the shattered lines!

Even more serious, however, was the blow to the national morale. It had become necessary to reassure the Italian populace that aid would be forthcoming from the Allies. In this crisis Ambassador Thomas Nelson Page summoned the flying

Congressman to Rome and asked him to speak at Genoa on January 13, 1918, as a representative of the American government.

He had barely returned from Chaumont when the Genoa call came. Unhesitatingly he accepted the new assignment.

La Guardia's Genoa speech proved a national sensation in Italy. Addressing a huge mass meeting, he spoke to 300,000 people, and he talked to them in their own language.

It was the greatest audience of his career, and he rose to face them with trepidation in his heart. Suddenly he felt appalled at the magnitude of the problem he faced. He realized that he was the representative of the Great Republic, wearing its uniform—and that he must deliver its message in a foreign tongue.

Never before had he doubted his ability to speak Italian. But now he was acutely aware of the great difference between his colloquial speech-making on New York's lower East Side, and that which was expected of him in the face of this tremendous audience. For the first time he became aware of the fact that every accent, every intonation, would be rigidly analyzed and harshly criticized!

Confused and embarrassed he began to express himself in hesitating Italian. The reaction was just what he had anticipated. There was a quick buzz of criticism, and occasional laughter. The discourtesy irritated him, and suddenly he lost his temper.

Then he lashed out at them with all the old vigor of the campaign days. The crowd grew suddenly silent until his flaming eloquence lifted his hearers from their seats. He promised them American assistance, yes; but he drove home the fact that Italy's salvation lay in her own soul!

The great audience was electrified. It cheered him to the echo and the newspapers devoted columns to the address. The American Flying Congressman became famous overnight and all Italy was clamoring to hear him. The government demanded other speeches. He was the tonic that the warsick Latins needed.

La Guardia, garbed in United States khaki, was visual evidence of the expected assistance from overseas. He began a whirlwind series of addresses. Night after night, when his day's drill was done, he got into a plane and flew to a distant city to address a meeting. After his address he flew back to Foggia and reported for drill as usual in the morning. This rush from city to city continued for a full six months. At Milan, on February 4th, speaking as the guest of the Italian Parliamentary Union, he spoke to another audience of 300,-000. He made a vigorous appeal for the fifth Italian war loan and assailed the "financial slackers" in a vitriolic outburst seldom equaled in Italy.

His voice rang through the great hall as he made his plea for the redemption of Trieste—and none in the wildly cheering audience realized that there danced before his eyes the vision of a girl "back home," or that there was still ringing in his ears the memory of her words: "When Trieste is under the Italian flag, *you may ask me again!*"

Two weeks later he brought a Roman audience to its feet with frantic cries of "Viva Wilson," as he paid a glowing tribute to his country's President.

Then, when he was at his busiest, devoting his days to training and his nights to speaking, there came disheartening news from home. A Pacifist-Socialist coalition had been formed in his district, with the avowed purpose of depriving him of his seat in the House of Representatives, because "he was neglecting his Congressional duties!" Petitions were being circulated for his removal, and hundreds of signatures were being secured.

His friends wrote that a special election to fill the vacancy was scheduled for March 4th, but that they would endeavor to re-elect him, despite his absence. They were fearful of the results, however, since the candidate could not be present during his campaign.

He felt a surge of utter helplessness. There was nothing he *could* do. But when a New York correspondent looked him up at the training camp, he snapped out a comment which, cabled home, demoralized the opposition.

The reporter ran up just as the aviator was climbing into his plane. He was asked for a statement concerning the move to unseat him. Stroking the big biplane, the flying Congressman responded: "Well, you can tell the folks back home, that if any signer of the petition cares to take my place in this bombing plane, I will be very glad to go back to Washington and resume my upholstered seat in Congress. It is much more comfortable!"

The New York newspapers swooped on that remark and gave it wide publicity. The public reaction was vigorous. There was a great wave of resentment against the critics and the special election was called off. The Representative from the 14th District was sure of his seat in the House until the following November.

La Guardia went on with his speaking.

He was a national celebrity now and the officials of the Italian Government grew to know him better as the weeks passed by. Out of this association grew a warm friendship with Francesco Nitti, then Minister of Finance and later Premier.

CHAPTER V

WITH THE AIR FORCES IN ITALY

EVEN in the mad turmoil of those busy days and nights, La Guardia found time to become engaged in another struggle with red tape, beside which the previous encounters paled into insignificance.

He went stark mad when that red tape caused the death of one of his most promising boys. He proceeded then and there to try to take the A. E. F. to pieces.

The background is best given in his own words:

> The American Government had, through the Inter-Allied Purchasing Commission, ordered 500 planes of an entirely new type—which were to be made in Italy. The first hundred were scheduled for delivery to my men. This plane was a purely experimental one. It had never existed except in blueprints.
>
> When we received the first plane, I looked it over carefully—and I didn't like it at all. It really was not fit to fly. It was structurally unsound, and I felt it might come apart in the air.
>
> I hurried to France and registered my protest with the Purchasing Headquarters, 45 Avenue Montaigne, Paris. I demanded that the order for these planes be canceled.
>
> My superiors stepped on me—and they stepped hard. (La Guardia smiled grimly as he recalled the interview.) They reprimanded me savagely for coming to Paris without permission. They told me in words of one syllable that I was NOT an aviation engineer, and that I did not know what I was talking about. They demanded what in hell I knew of "stresses" and "strains."
>
> I found myself in an awkward position, and my belief that the Italian manufacturers had brought pressure to bear did not relieve it at all.

It was true that I was not an engineer, and the experts with one accord assured me that I was crazy!

They had never seen the planes, but they had "every confidence" in the—*blueprints!* They reminded me that my job was to fly planes, not to criticise them! They ordered me to go back and fly them. And I went.

He had scarcely returned when an accident silenced his protests for a while. On March 14, 1918, he took a plane up for a practice flight, and was caught in a sudden storm at 15,000 feet. The plane proved underpowered, and the motor failed. He glided down through the storm, and crashed in the middle of a camp of Austrian prisoners, located near the Foggia School. He describes his experience as follows:

> Caught in a heavy gale, I was forced to go up to 15,000 feet. I was still ascending in order to avoid the clouds, when they suddenly broke. That gave me a chance to descend, and after careful maneuvering I succeeded in descending to an altitude of some 2,400 feet. Wind and rain were driving fast. So was my plane. I was strapped in good and tight—but that did not prevent my machine from making two somersaults when we crashed. I came down like a bolt from a clear sky. Fortunately, the weight of my body, pressing against the leather strap, caused it to snap, throwing me out of the machine when I was only a short distance from the ground.
>
> My plane was wrecked, and I would have been, too, had it not been for that strap breaking at the critical moment.

They dragged him out of the wreckage and carried his unconscious form to the hospital. Examination revealed an injury to the spine, and a mass of bruises. They wanted to operate, but they could not keep him in the hospital long enough to do it.

Next day he opened his eyes and gazed into the smiling face of one of his pet pupils, Lieutenant Marcus Jordan, of Washington, D. C. The latter had dropped in to visit his injured

61

commander, after being assured that the latter would recover.

La Guardia remembers that scene very well. Let him describe it.

"And what a flyer our C.O. turned out to be," laughed Jordan, "busting up planes! Why, if I couldn't do better than that——"

"Well, if I had been a better flyer, Mark, maybe it wouldn't have happened," I replied. "But at that, I don't think so much of the plane."

"Maybe so and maybe not," chuckled Mark. "Well, we'll just have to wait until those planes have been properly tested."

He kidded me for a while. He spent half an hour bucking me up, and then he took my hand and departed. "See you again, Captain," he sang out before he passed through the hospital door.

But I never saw Mark Jordan again. Two hours later they brought me word that he was dead! He had taken up one of the new planes—and it had just pulled to pieces in the air. Mark had been killed in the crash.

When they brought the news to his commanding officer that Jordan had dropped to his death, the injured Captain rose from his sick bed and went storming out. Defying doctors and nurses, he found a pair of crutches, called a car, and drove to the main office of the company which was manufacturing the experimental planes. Leaning on his crutches, he announced that he was the Commanding Officer of the American Air Forces in Italy, and then, without authority from anybody, he canceled the order for those 500 planes. And thereby precipitated one of the biggest rows of his military career.

The manufacturers did not know just what authority he possessed. They stopped production, and began burning up the wires with protests. They cabled London and Washington, and they telegraphed to Paris.

The Inter-Allied Purchasing Commission was in an uproar.

It had ordered the planes, and its members were wild over the idea that an insignificant Captain had overruled them.

La Guardia was again summoned to Paris. He arrived on crutches.

His battle with the commission was epic. He faced a tableful of Colonels and Generals, and he defied them to their faces. It was unheard of.

"*Who* canceled this order?" they thundered.

"I did."

"By what authority?"

"By the authority in me vested to take every precaution to safeguard the lives of my men!"

"Will you go back to Italy and direct the manufacturers to continue production?"

"I cannot do that."

"Well, then, will you go back to Italy and attend to your own business?"

"I don't see how I can do that either."

He presented plans and photographs. He showed them pictures of the crash that had killed Jordan. They threatened to cashier him and send him home in disgrace. He responded that he would stump the country from one end to the other, and lay the matter before the American people. He dared them to risk American lives in those man-killing planes. The experts were nonplussed. Col. Halsey Dunwoody, of the General Staff, backed him up. But when the argument was most heated, La Guardia received unexpected assistance. His lucky star prevailed.

In the interim a number of the same experimental planes had been delivered to the Italian Government. A dozen experienced Italian flyers—including some of the leading aces in their service—who had experimented with the planes, had signed a round robin of protest against them. They offered to resign their commissions rather than fly them!

The Italian Government decided to back up the aviators. It filed an official protest against the use of the condemned aircraft; and, in the twinkling of an eye, La Guardia's position was reversed. The arrival of the aviators' protest qualified him as an expert in the eyes of the commission. His reputation was made. The same men who had been denouncing him suddenly became respectful and considerate.

La Guardia was asked to remain as an advisory expert, and to recommend a plane to replace the rejected experimental ones.

He was ready with an answer. He had been studying the subject thoroughly and he urged them to adopt Caproni planes. They did so.

Returning to Italy in triumph, the doctors promptly put him to bed. His injuries were causing trouble and they wanted to operate on him but he refused to permit it. However he was held in the hospital until April 12.

La Guardia had lost so much time as a result of his speeches and his injuries in the airplane crash that he was far behind the others in his studies. His command was ready for the front and he made a quick trip to the lines to make the necessary arrangements for their transfer. On April 18 he heard for the first time the sound of enemy guns. Returning to Foggia, he received ill news from home.

The Congressman's Fourteenth District in New York City had always been strongly pacifistic. An election was due and Scott Nearing was running against La Guardia on a socialistic ticket. It was obvious that La Guardia could not campaign 2,000 miles from the scene of the election and the pacifists were optimistic. More so when word arrived that La Guardia refused to let his service at the front be used as campaign material! Writing to his friend, Harry Andrews, he said:

> If you have any campaign posters made . . . by no means use any picture of me in uniform. . . . I personally object to using the uniform for campaign purposes. I know that you will not agree with me in this . . . use the 1914 dope, adding my achievements in the 64th session.

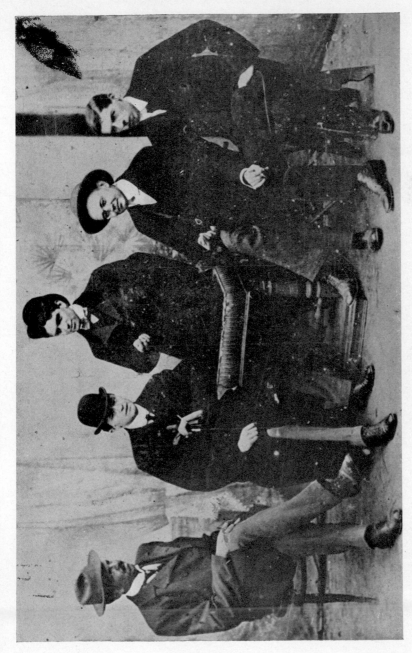

Young La Guardia (standing) as he appeared while secretary to the Consul General at Budapest in 1903.

Dinner of the senior class, New York University Law School, March 3, 1910 (La Guardia is standing third from the right.)

His military reports were the most amazing documents ever enrolled in the archives of the American Army. He criticized his superiors when he thought it justified, with a freedom which must have appalled them.

Typical is his weekly report of July 2, 1918, in which he wrote to the Chief of the Air Service in France as follows:

> I reported last week on what I considered the wasteful purchase of a Hudson 6 for the school at Foggia. Since then this car has been ordered to France. That seems reasonable. The car is being sent to France under its own power, in charge of Major ——, and is driven by an aviation cadet.
>
> I cannot refrain from stating that it seems extreme to utilize the services of a Major of the Regular Army, and on flying status, for the purpose of transferring an automobile from Foggia to Issoudon—a distance of about a thousand miles. The car left Foggia several days ago, and is at present in Rome.
>
> Judging from the stops along the road, and the time consumed for this lap of the trip, it is safe to presume that stops during the entire trip will increase in number and duration, in ratio to the attractiveness of the various resorts along the Mediterranean Riviera, so that this trip promises to be both lengthy and expensive.
>
> At this time, when there is such a great need for capable flying officers in this country, an expedition of this kind is rather embarrassing to the officers of the American Army who are here performing military duties, and who were compelled to beg the gasoline from the Italian Ministry of Munitions.
>
> I do not know who is responsible for the purchase and subsequent mission of this Hudson 6, nor what particular charm and importance it may possess to require the constant attention of a Major for its transportation.
>
> Not even a Brewster, intent upon spending his millions, could have conceived a joy ride so fantastic.

He insisted on *fighting*, and announced that he was not going to allow any more platform engagements to interfere with the completion of his training.

Despite repeated protests he stuck to his decision.

The Italian Government, not unappreciative of his services, awarded him the Commendatore, and begged him to remain on the platform. Wrote Salvatore Cortesi, from Rome:

> At the risk of displeasing you, I must repeat what I have said several times to the Ambassador: That while I am sure you will do excellent service at the front, I feel it is a great pity that you are not still here, where there is absolutely no one to replace you. You have, in no small measure, contributed to pull us together after the disaster of Caporetto, and to make us appreciate the fraternal help that America has brought us.

And Guglielmo Marconi, the inventor, scribbled a note in which he said:

> I am altogether with you in all that you are doing for us, and for winning this damn war.

The student buckled down to work with a vengeance. He was wild to rejoin his boys who were fighting at the front.

This period was saddened by the news of the death of John Purroy Mitchel, the former Mayor of New York, who had been killed in an airplane accident while undergoing training in the United States. La Guardia had always admired Mitchel, and he turned pale when a newspaper correspondent told him about the crash. He thought for an instant, and then burst out:

> I can't tell you how badly I feel! This is a great loss to the Service, for we needed men with the experience and executive ability of Mayor Mitchel. But it is a lesson—though indeed a very expensive one.
>
> I sent word to my friends months ago that Mitchel had no business flying. No man over 27 should attempt to learn at this time. It is a young man's game. I speak from personal experience. At my school I had my doctor take a man off the flying list because he was 34.

The reporter listened in amazement, and then hesitantly inquired:

"But is it not true, Captain, that you yourself are almost 36?"

La Guardia stared at his questioner for an instant. Then he nodded his head slowly, swung on his heel and marched away without another word.

Completing his preparatory training, he was transferred to the bombing school at Malpensa—where once more he nearly lost his life.

His final test before graduation was an "endurance" flight in a huge tri-motored Caproni, and he took the examination in a patched-up machine that had been wrecked in combat. The accident came after four hours in the air. It was of a sort that almost inevitably proved fatal in those wartime planes— the same type of mishap which had claimed two lives on that very field that week!

There was a sudden, rending crash—and the crankshaft splintered.

Instantly he cut the ignition, before the plane was torn apart by the flying parts of the engine. Nursing the wreck, La Guardia managed to get it to earth intact, landing in a swamp.

He had proven his ability. His Italian instructors granted him his diploma at last. He was graduated from the bombing school, and prepared to go to the front.

Then came another blow. He was detailed as a staff officer.

It was regarded as a promotion, but La Guardia did not want it. His only desire was to rejoin his boys at the front.

He hurried to Paris to protest, and was received by General Benjamin Foulois, the same officer who had enrolled him in the Air Service.

"I don't want to be 'a Brass Hat,' " La Guardia told Foulois, "I want to go to the front!"

"I fear you have nothing to say about the matter," replied the General. "The order comes from General Pershing himself. It is a great honor, and it is not possible for any officer to decline it."

He considered for a moment, and then shook his head. "I can't do anything for you, Captain. I appreciate your desire, but rejecting a personal appointment from the Commanding General is just one of those things that 'isn't done.' "

The Captain's face fell. Then he squared his shoulders and asked permission to see Major General James G. Harbord, the Chief of Staff. The request was granted, although General Foulois again assured him that it would do no good.

La Guardia pleaded in vain with General Harbord. The General could not cancel an order of Pershing's and told La Guardia he should realize that. But—he could arrange for La Guardia to have an interview with the Commander in Chief of the A. E. F. Yet he cautioned La Guardia about asking for the cancellation of the order. Such things are simply not done in the Army. Still determined, La Guardia met the Commander in Chief and when he emerged from the latter's office the order was rescinded! His eloquence had not failed him. He started back for the Italian Front facing the culmination of his great adventure at last.

Reporting for duty at Padua, he immediately took to the air. It was not, however, until September 14 that he took part in a big raid over the enemy lines. His report of the affair is terse and typical. It reads as follows:

Date	Hr. of Departure	Objective	Weather	Altitude	Result	Time
Sept. 14	11:30	Pergine	Good	3500 m.	Good	210 m.

Remarks Enemy fire intense and accurate. Plane hit twice in left wing. Right-hand Pilot.

One large bomb hit on hangar. The rest seemed to have gone to the right.

Enemy fire on return, accurate and intense.

That was all La Guardia had to say about the expedition. It remained for Donald G. Frost, now of New York City, to give greater detail. Frost was a First Lieutenant in the Air Service at the time of the raid.

" 'Plane hit twice'! Hell!" snorted Frost in discussing the report. "Why I saw it myself, and there were more than two hundred holes in it! His machine gun had a piece of shrapnel right through the magazine. It is a wonder he hadn't been blown to shreds! We were all watching when he came back to see how the C. O. acted the first time he had been under heavy fire. As I say, it had evidently been pretty hot, and he looked very serious as he climbed out of the machine. I went up to him and asked how he had liked it.

" 'It was very interesting,' he answered—and then he grinned. With that, he turned on his heel, marched into the operations office, and did something none of us had ever done: He asked to go on another flight that same afternoon—and he went.

"The Italians loved him for his guts," continued Donald Frost. "He proved he had 'em from the very beginning.

"I wouldn't say he was an artistic flyer. He was never a really finished pilot—but, boy, how he loved to try! He flew by main strength and awkwardness—but he got there just the same."

The same opinion is rendered by most of the men who flew with him. They included Kenneth Collins, Allen Bevin, Aubrey Russell, Warren Wheeler, LeRoy Kiley, Ira Galehouse, John Park, Nick Johnson, Robert F. Cutting, Jr., Paton McGilvary and Ewart Watcheon.

While he was at the front, the Captain became a Major. He was promoted to rank as from August 5, 1918. His description of the promotion is as follows:

"I shall never forget the day. It was a great occasion. I was standing in front of a hangar, talking to a visiting American Major, when an orderly brought me a letter. I opened it, and, behold, it was a notice of my promotion! I hadn't expected it, and I was considerably excited.

"I was very proud as I showed it to my visitor. He shook hands with me and congratulated me. Then he began fumbling with his shoulder straps, and, before I realized what he was doing, he had taken off his own golden Oak Leaves, and was pinning them on my shoulders! Then he stepped back, and saluted me. I protested, but he insisted he had more in his kit—and I wore his leaves during the rest of the war."

* * *

This now becomes largely the story of "The Congressional Limited," which the Austrians failed to stop. This is no figure of speech. The Congressional Limited was a big Caproni bi-plane, and it was christened by two armies. It was so called because the regular crews included the American Congress-man and a member of the Italian Parliament. It bore special insignia, which was flaunted as a gesture of defiance of the enraged Austrians as it soared over the snow-clad Alps.

La Guardia was pilot, and beside him, in the co-pilot's seat, was Captain Frederick Zapolloni, the Italian bombing ace. The Observer was Major Pietro Nigrotto, the Italian legis-lator. Private Giovanni Fiumanni was the machine gunner, and a recognized expert. All told, it was a very special plane.

The Austrians received specific orders to bring it down at any cost. They felt that two legislators (one of whom was the commander of all the American combat flyers in Italy), an enemy ace, and a famous machine gunner, constituted a prize worth capturing. Austrian prisoners, after their capture, told about the special orders to take it.

La Guardia replied with a gesture of defiance. The plane already carried Zapolloni's insignia—a flaming torch. The enemy knew it well. La Guardia placed the American shield against it. Then a note was dropped, telling the Austrians that this latter was his personal insignia, and that the two together denoted "The Congressional Limited." The enemy was free to bring it down—if they could.

They tried hard enough, but never succeeded.

In the ensuing weeks La Guardia was continuously under fire. His official reports are masterpieces of brevity.

Typical extracts from these reports made to the Commanding Officer, Air Service U. S. Army, are on file in the War Department, as follows:

Date	Hr. of Departure	Objective	Weather	Altitude	Result	Time
Sept. 15	9:30 A.M.	Bellio Runcti Buso	Good	3500	Good	120 m.

Remarks: Dropped manifestini on all three towns. Motors worked badly all the way over enemy territory, but picked up on way back, Enemy fire, wild. Right-hand Pilot.

* * *

Date	Hr. of Departure	Objective	Weather	Altitude	Result	Time
Sept. 16	9:52 P.M.	Gedega	Good	2800	Positive Excellent	153 m.

Remarks: Above aviation camp Gedega. All bombs landed in field and hangars. Bombed at 1400 metres. Enemy territory well lighted with search lights, owing to their machines being out on expedition. Saw one enemy machine, which did not give us battle; exchanged shots in passing. Enemy searchlights very efficient. Right-hand Pilot still unsatisfactory.

* * *

Date	Hr. of Departure	Objective	Weather	Altitude	Result	Time
Sept. 17	11:00 P.M.	Mansue	Very bad	3200	Fair	100 m.

Remarks: Weather made navigation extremely difficult. One of my bombs caused large fire. I doubt whether it was on the aviation field. Personally, believe it was military supplies. Flying partners and Observer contend that aviation field and hangars were hit. Enemy fire intense and well-placed. Illumination on enemy territory exceptionally good owing to large number of searchlights.

The Major's modesty is reflected in these reports. The Italian High Command exhibited much greater enthusiasm over the results achieved. It issued a special communication "To all Subordinate Commanders," in which the Italian commander praised the work of the Capronis to the skies.

La Guardia made a good record at the front. The decorations awarded him—which he could not find ten years after! —testify to that. He was the recipient of the Croce di Guerra, the Crown of Italy and the Commendatore. He was also cited by the Commanding Officer of Aviation of the Italian Army.

CHAPTER VI

THE *1918* CAMPAIGN

BACK home, America was racked by the war fever. Blase New York thrilled at the valor of her sons, and not the least of these was the Flying Congressman. The newspapers were devoting columns to his achievements, of which the following, which appeared in the *New York Times*, June 30, 1918, is typical:

> Let us not forget a soldier and a member of Congress, an orator and a patriot, an American by birth, but an Italian by origin and heart, who has shown himself to be the best mouthpiece of the White House's diplomacy, the most worthy and indefatigable herald of the Government's Democracy, who has gone to the Piave trenches with the assurance that America stands behind Italy. Let's not forget Fiorello La Guardia, the soldier-Congressman of the United States.
>
> Up to a year ago he was unknown. . . .

But he was unknown no longer, and even his old Tammany opponents joined in the tribute to his patriotism. There was a rising demand that he should not be deprived of his seat in the House because of his service at the front.

His Congressional colleagues were proud of him, and they themselves nominated him for re-election. On July 13, 1918, Republican members of the New York Delegation adopted a Resolution which read:

> Whereas, Fiorello H. La Guardia, a representative in Congress from the Fourteenth District of New York, has been serving his country as an officer in the aviation corps in Italy, and

Whereas, by his patriotism in giving his services to his country and by the splendid work he has been able to do by reason of the fact that he speaks fluently the Italian language, and also by reason of his position as a Representative in Congress of the United States, in cementing more closely the friendly relations between Italy and this country, and by reason, furthermore, of the valiant services he has rendered since he volunteered, be it unanimously

Resolved by his colleagues from the State of New York, that his course entitles him to the enthusiastic approval of all Americans, and, in our judgment, entitles him to the loyal support of the constituents he now represents in his campaign for a return to Congress at the election this fall.

Resolved, furthermore, that an engrossed copy of these Resolutions be sent to Representative La Guardia as testimonial of our appreciation.

The newspapers broke into a rash of applauding editorials, and for the first time in its history, Tammany entered a Fusion movement with the Republican party.

Leader Charles F. Murphy agreed to endorse La Guardia and Representative Isaac Segal, in return for Republican support in six other districts.

Instantly opposition flamed out against the soldier-candidate. Sentiment in the Fourteenth District had always been preponderantly pacifist, and the Socialists prepared to capitalize it. They nominated Prof. Scott Nearing, who was then under indictment for violation of the Espionage Act and facing trial for persistent interference with America's prosecution of the war. Socialist workers began a house-to-house canvass against La Guardia, and Nearing denounced him for drawing a double salary from the Government. Andrews, La Guardia's campaign manager, retorted hotly that the Major had not drawn a cent of his Congressional salary since he enlisted.

The struggle grew hotter. Again and again the Congressman was flayed for his absence from his seat, and his friends struggled desperately to vindicate him.

Even quiet little Miss Fischer, his secretary, took her pen in hand, and sat herself down to indite letters to the newspapers defending the action of her employer. She wrote:

> From the various letters which Mr. La Guardia has written, I feel free to state that he considers his present military service as an important part of his duties as a Congressman. He was many times distressed at the lack of experience and first-hand information in the House on important military matters. He gave the question of the American expedition almost constant thought, and when he finally decided to take his place in the ranks, together with the boys whom his vote on the Universal Military Law had selected for service, he did so, I know, feeling that he was acting for the best interests of his country and his constituents.

The campaign grew hotter, but La Guardia himself did not learn of the Democratic support until September 4, when he was located at the front by a *Times'* correspondent. Asked if he would return to conduct a campaign, the Major responded:

> I appreciate the compliment very much. It certainly offsets the disappointment and worry caused me last year, when an attempt was made to show that the District was un-American and not behind the President in this struggle. I cannot tell now whether I shall be back or not. That depends upon orders. Naturally, being in the military service, I cannot leave my post without proper orders.
>
> Personally, it is far more pleasant to remain here, to fight with the men trained by me, and to take a direct part in the fight. I admit it is also a source of personal pleasure to know, after a successful bombing raid, that one has played a small part in advancing the line, in hastening a victorious end to this struggle.
>
> If the people of my district desire me to resume my seat in the new Congress, I naturally shall do so. I know that they would not ask me to come back, unless convinced that my experience in the air for over a year, and the knowledge which I have necessarily acquired con-

cerning aviation matters, would be more useful to my present duties here.

The campaign waxed hotter, and it began to appear that La Guardia's seat was in danger—but the La Guardia luck prevailed. His superiors, realizing the effect which his defeat would have upon the national morale, sent him home on a special military mission, just before the campaign closed. He arrived at the strategic moment, landing on October 28. He came ashore flaming with enthusiasm and ready for another political contest. As the *New York American* expressed it the next day:

> Congressman Fiorello La Guardia, Major of Aviation in Uncle Sam's forces at the Italian Front, slipped into port last evening as quietly as if he had been gliding over the Austrian lines in his bombing plane. The subsequent effect was also a good deal like a bomb explosion!

Jubilant friends and campaign workers flocked to meet him. He bustled through their midst—a handsome figure in his army khaki, with the silver wings gleaming above the three medals on his breast, and two gold service stripes on his left arm. Reporters sought him, begging for his opinion of Scott Nearing.

"Nearing?" echoed La Guardia. "What regiment does he belong to?"

There were laughing explanations that his rival had been indicted for pacifism. Instantly the Major grew serious. He swung round and began barking orders at his campaign managers as if he were still at the front.

"That question must not be introduced into this campaign," he snapped. "Scott Nearing must have a fighting chance. I did not know that he was under indictment. But remember this: Under the laws of this country a man is innocent until he is proven guilty."

Two days later La Guardia plunged into the thick of it. He made his first speech in the Lenox Assembly Rooms on Second

Street, the night of October 30. Governor Whitman was speaking when the trim figure in khaki strode into the hall. Instantly the crowd went wild.

Ignoring the Chief Executive, men and women sprang to their feet and yelled themselves hoarse. The ovation continued for fifteen minutes. It was an affecting scene: the East Side was welcoming its own champion home from the wars— and they did it with a vengeance. There were tears in the candidate's eyes as he listened to them.

He spoke briefly, and the hall rocked with applause when he concluded. It was a cheerful omen.

He hurried from the hall to a big outdoor meeting at Stuyvesant Place and Second Avenue. There he received another ovation. Two thousand people listened to his address as he flayed the American Socialists, contrasting them with those in the Allied countries, who were supporting the war. When he concluded, members of the wildly cheering audience almost mobbed him in their enthusiasm.

No such love feast occurred on November 2, however, when he took the platform at Cooper Union to meet his opponent face to face. His first act upon his arrival had been to challenge Nearing to a public debate. The latter accepted, and the famous old building was packed to the rafters when the meeting began. It was soon evident that the Major faced a hostile audience. The Socialists were out in force.

The tumult began as soon as the two men stepped upon the stage. Upon a pillar which separated them, was a marble tablet bearing the words of La Guardia's boyhood's hero—Abraham Lincoln, who had stood upon the same platform and faced a similarly hostile audience in a crisis in his career:

> Let us have faith that right makes might, and in that faith, let us to the end do our duty, as we understand it.

Judge Jacob Panken, a Socialist himself but long a friend of La Guardia, opened the meeting and introduced the Flying Congressman.

"The issue in the Fourteenth Congressional District," began the Major, tossing his black mane defiantly, "is the same issue as that on the Western Front—and on the Austrian Front. I am personally opposed to militarism, imperialism and all manner of oppression. I am against war, and because I am against war, I went to war to fight against war!"

A storm of hisses rose in his face, and members of the audience began surging toward the platform. La Guardia repulsed them with a sweeping gesture.

"I said: I went to war to fight against war, in order to end war," he cried, his voice rising shrilly. "I don't think we can end war by merely talking against it on East Side street corners!"

Again there came a chorus of protests, but it rose to an absolute crescendo, when he turned his guns upon his opponent. He declared that Prof. Nearing in his campaign literature had commented on the many Socialists in the parliaments of our Allies, who, with but few exceptions, were supporting the war, but that he had failed to say anything about the Socialists of Germany. "Those German Socialists did not protest against the orgies of butchery to which their Government committed them!" cried La Guardia.

From the back of the hall came a hysterical scream: "That's a lie!"

It almost precipitated a riot, La Guardia's supporters, outnumbered though they were, began screaming: "Put him out!" And pandemonium ensued, until Judge Panken rushed to the floor waving frantically for order.

He waved for the speaker to continue, and instantly La Guardia precipitated another scene:

"We have before us the miserable failure of Socialism in Austria," cried the candidate. "Was the Austrian revolution accomplished by Socialists? No, it was led by Karolyi. He's no Socialist."

Another uproar followed, but La Guardia's voice rose to a

piercing scream as he hurled an ultimate defiance: "You have betrayed the Socialists of Russia by not helping us here. Do you want to know what is left of the Socialist party in America? The German who could not get back to fight for the Kaiser, has tried to do his bit, fighting under the banner of Hillquit."

This time the crowd got completely out of hand. Socialists rose to their feet, waving red banners and neckties, and screaming at the speaker. His own followers surged forward, flaunting American and Italian flags. A quarter of an hour elapsed before the audience could be quieted.

Then Nearing, the slight, boyish man of letters, took the stage. With airy, graceful gestures he made his plea for Socialism.

"I know war is on," he declared, "the war between plutocracy and the plain people. That war is now raging in every country on the face of the earth!" He continued with a fierce attack upon the profiteers.

Speaking in rebuttal, La Guardia cited his bill, providing the death penalty for such profiteers! But he closed with a typical La Guardia touch:

"I can't debate this man!" he announced. "I understood he was a Professor of Economics. It is a mistake—he is a poet!"

The return of the candidate had electrified his supporters. He dashed about the district making speech after speech, and impressive in uniform, which, as he was still in the Service, he could not discard, despite his disinclination to make any use of it in connection with campaign purposes. He received a riotous reception wherever he went. His presence revived the spirits of the oft-defeated Republican leaders, and they exerted every effort in his behalf.

Espresso, his original Republican sponsor, was especially active, and Samuel Koenig, the Republican boss of Manhattan, presently gave the La Guardia band wagon a vigorous boost.

Busy as he was, the Major found time to go outside his district and help a brother candidate. On the evening of November 3 he invaded Harlem where Congressman Isaac Siegel was opposing Morris Hillquit, the Socialist whom he had barely defeated for the seat in the Twentieth District two years before. Siegel was the second Republican to whom Tammany had granted a Democratic endorsement. This Harlem district, located on the upper East Side of Manhattan, contained a numerous Italian colony. It was to be La Guardia's principal fighting ground in the years to come. But he was a stranger to his audience when he strode on to the platform of the Institutional Synagogue at 116th Street and Fifth Avenue, that night. Siegel's Italian constituents had turned out en masse to greet their newest hero.

When he appeared in uniform, his breast covered with the medals won in the land of their ancestry, their cheers rattled the rafters. The ovation continued, and Edward Corsi, prominent Italian-born social worker, stepped forward to welcome the visitor. It was the first meeting of the two men, and the beginning of a warm friendship.

When his turn came to speak, the Major carried the fight to Hillquit almost with his opening sentence. He had been scheduled to discuss his experiences abroad.

"My experiences abroad are not important," he began. "There is a fight for Democracy being waged in this district, and I am here to help Democracy win. The Socialists of the Hillquit type have betrayed Democracy. The Socialists of Europe supported the war. Albert Thomas, the famous French Socialist, told me he knew Hillquit wasn't a real Socialist; that he wasn't worthy of the name."

There were scattered hisses from the Socialists present, but La Guardia plunged on.

"I charge Hillquit with being a tool and an ally of the Kaiser. I say Hillquit is part of the German Army. I say Hillquit is an enemy to every man in uniform," he continued. "Hillquit's god is the dollar, and his only 'Comrade' is the coupon! He has exploited and is exploiting the people he professes to champion."

There were more protests but La Guardia continued:

"And he has a past record that compares favorably with his war record. Whenever his services were required by the Labor Union, he sent in a bill. . . . When we fight Hillquit and his crowd, we are fighting the same battle that is being fought on the Western Front! And just as we must not weaken our efforts there, so we must not slacken our efforts here. We must show Europe that we are supporting our soldiers. We cannot support them by electing German tools and German supporters. We can show we are really Americans by electing those who support the President."

He left the platform amid a roar of applause—a memory of which was to influence him in the selection of a new district three years later. His first Harlem invasion had shown him that his supporters were not confined to the south end of Manhattan.

Siegel's resulting victory in the Twentieth District was largely credited to the Italian support which La Guardia had evoked in his behalf.

The Fusion cause triumphed, and when the ballots were counted on election day, the fears concerning the Major's own district proved groundless. He was elected by a substantial majority and assured of two more years in Congress.

The campaign, however, marked the birth of a legend which was to be amplified in later years. The Democratic endorsement was the basis for the accusation that he had run for office on a Tammany ticket.

Less than a week later, the Armistice was signed. The sweets of his victory were soured by the Major's realization that the actual cessation of hostilities had caught him back home—instead of at the Front! It was a disappointment which years were not able to erase. He felt no doubt that the Armistice meant the end of the war. He had studied politics too closely to believe otherwise, and he was quick to act upon his belief.

It was the morning of November 11, 1918, that the big guns ceased roaring along the Western Front, and on the morning of November 12, Major F. H. La Guardia, Air Service, U. S. A., resigned his commission and returned to civil life.

He hurried down to Washington and resumed his vacant seat in the House. His colleagues gave him an uproarious reception. They thronged about him on the floor, slapping his back and courting his notice. While the reception was in progress, one spectator leaned across a gallery rail and watched it with shining eyes. She was the little German secretary.

The Soldier-Congressman had scarcely settled back in his seat before he was again called for special duty. As a member-elect of the Sixty-Fourth Congress, which would not convene until March 4, he was certain of a seat on the Military Affairs Committee. His war record entitled him to that.

The "lame duck" session of the Sixty-Fourth Congress voted for this committee to make an investigation of conditions in the A. E. F. Waiving the customary procedure, the newly returned veteran was placed on the committee at once, and the Christmas season found him once more attired in mufti, sailing for Europe again. With his Congressional colleagues, he was soon tramping over the battlefields so recently evacuated by the struggling armies.

The group was escorted by Col. Thomas S. Hammond, Regular Army officer and West Point graduate. His quiet courtesy and quick efficiency registered a deep impression upon the Soldier-Congressman. He made a mental note of it.

Sixteen years were to pass before he recalled it. Then Mayor La Guardia sent for Colonel Hammond, and designated him Commissioner of Sanitation of the City of New York.

CHAPTER VII

THE HERO'S RETURN

THERE was a sharp rap.

"Come in."

The door opened and a uniformed American sailor stepped into the room. The Blue Jacket clicked his heels together and saluted crisply.

"Major La Guardia, sir?"

"Yes."

"Col. Edward M. House presents his compliments, sir, and he would be very grateful if you would come at once. The car is waiting, sir."

"Very well."

The Congressman slipped into his overcoat and followed his escort from the Hotel Chatham in Paris. More history was in the making.

It was early in 1919. The Peace Conference had just been shattered by the departure of the Italian Delegation. Fiume was the crux of the matter—Fiume, where La Guardia had been United States Consul sixteen years before. That was one reason he had volunteered his services.

"I just happened to be in Paris," he explains. "I had gone back to Congress, after resigning my commission, as soon as the Armistice was signed. And I had been appointed to the Military Affairs Committee by James Mann. The greatest parliamentarian of his day seemed to have taken a fancy to me.

"That committee was making a tour of inspection of the battlefields. It was a rather hard trip for some of the members who had lived on trains for ten days.

"We were on our way to the Riviera for a rest, and we

82

happened to stop in Paris the day before the Peace Conference split. I read about the affair in the papers, and decided to offer my services. I felt that I knew Fiume and its people, and I had been closely associated with the Italian Government during the war.

"I wrote a note to Secretary of State Robert Lansing, asking if there was anything I could do. No answer. After two days I sent a similiar note to Colonel House. Within an hour, a sailor, with an official car, was at my door, inviting me to confer with him."

The two men went over the Fiume situation together. La Guardia suggested that Fiume be given to Italy and Porto-Baros to Susak, in Yugo-Slavia. He also made an eloquent plea for Trieste. Colonel House approved the suggestions. They began working out a plan to bring the Italians back to Paris.

"During our conferences—for we held several of them," continues La Guardia, "I discovered that Colonel House had a very accurate knowledge of conditions in Fiume. There never would have been any trouble regarding it, if he had been able to handle the matter according to his own wishes.

"But he wasn't able to do so. He told me of his great admiration and love for President Wilson, but pointed out that, as their friendship ripened, the number of subjects which he could *not* discuss with his chief seemed to increase. Among them he listed Fiume and Mexico."

Major La Guardia explained that Signor Crespi, who had been left behind by the Italian Delegation to handle communications, was a personal friend. At Colonel House's suggestion, he was assigned to call on Crespi, telling him that the Colonel greatly regretted the break, that the Italians had made a mistake in leaving, and that the affair should not be considered closed.

La Guardia did so, and Crespi sent him back to House with the information that he had informed his Government of the message, and that he was greatly encouraged to hear of the attitude of the Colonel, because his colleagues had considered that President Wilson's stand had definitely closed the incident.

The American Congressman then transmitted the invitation of Colonel House to Premier Orlando, asking him to return and discuss the matter further. When the Premier did return, La Guardia continued to act as go-between.

"Some of the details have escaped my memory," explained the Major, "but I recall that I was the medium of exchange for three or four messages between Orlando and Colonel House. I even discussed with them the way they should dress, and the manner in which they should greet one another at their first meeting after the return.

"The last time I talked to Premier Orlando, he was in his suite at the Hotel Edward VII, busy changing his clothes, in order to pay the first formal call on Colonel House at the Hotel Crillon."

La Guardia was not present at this interview, but his Italian friends informed him later that Orlando was much disappointed that House failed to mention Fiume at that first meeting. A later conference reassured the Italian, because House then brought it up. The final settlement reached was much the same as that which the Major had outlined at his first conference with the Colonel.

Then, his work done, La Guardia rejoined his Committee.

Returning to the United States, he plunged into his legislative career.

* * *

This year (1919) was probably one of the happiest in La Guardia's entire life. It saw him establishing the foundation of his reputation; it marked his rise to real political power; and it witnessed the fruition of the first real romance of his life. In the space of a twelvemonth, fate was to offer him everything that he had desired—gifts that all too soon were to be dashed away in a whirlwind of tragedy and disaster!

He was young, brilliant and handsome. He was one of the

returned heroes over whom his countrymen were raving. He had acquired prestige, and his war record was an accolade which made him a marked man in the halls of Congress. Also—his love was returned at last.

Trieste was Italian once more! La Guardia's plea to Colonel House had been granted. Italy was awarded the city under the Peace Treaty—and Thea Amerigotti kept her word! The impetuous suitor brushed aside the religious difference almost casually. They were married in the office of Cathedral College on New York's Madison Avenue, March 8, 1919, by Mgr. Ferranti.

The bridegroom donned his uniform for the occasion. Thea was beautiful in white lace. Louis Espresso acted as best man, and the wedding party included the bride's brother, himself in the uniform of an Ensign in the United States Navy.

Followed a wedding breakfast at the Hotel Netherlands—and then they left on their honeymoon. They were supremely happy. It was a love match, pure and simple.

* * *

Even before his marriage the young husband had begun to win national notice in Congress. Although he was now serving his second term, he had spent very little time in the legislative halls. His colleagues scarcely knew him. Now they suddenly became aware of his activities.

The energetic La Guardia was not content to sink back into oblivion. He had reveled in the spotlight during the war. The adulation of the public had established his self-confidence. He was quite sure of himself—certain of the accuracy of his judgment, and prepared to demand an audience for his views.

He owed allegiance to no political boss, not even to any especial group. His conscience provided the only check upon his activities.

In the beginning the Republican leaders of the House did not realize that they had a wild man upon their hands! It so happened that his first onslaughts were directed at Democratic

Administration measures, and he consequently received the benediction of his G. O. P. colleagues. They settled back in their seats and listened complacently as he lashed out at the program of the Administration, never realizing that in the coming years they themselves were to writhe beneath the same vitriolic tongue.

For this error in judgment, the conservative Republican leadership was to pay dearly. It was glad to make use of La Guardia's military prestige and his quick pugnacity in attacks on Administration measures. The Old Guard bosses gave him opportunity to speak, because his liberal views led him to make attacks on their political foes. As a result Wisconsin dairymen and North Dakota farmers began to get acquainted with the New York City Congressman. He was establishing the foundation for his progressive reputation of the coming years.

His first successful attack was upon the preparedness program of the Administration. President Wilson and Secretary of War Newton D. Baker, had outlined a plan for a standing army of 500,000, with an additional half million men undergoing compulsory military training. Public sentiment, recognizing the lessons of the World War, was inclined to favor the measure until it aroused the determined opposition of the New York pacifist.

Denouncing all militarism, and strong in his position as one of the few members of Congress who had actually seen service, La Guardia, almost single-handed, defeated the Administration's one-million-man program. He began his fight in the Military Affairs Committee, of which he was a member. There he succeeded in striking out the compulsory training feature, and he carried his opposition to the rest of the bill on to the floor of the House. Launching a bitter verbal attack on the Democratic leaders, he led the opposition to victory. The force of 500,000 was reduced to 200,000.

The Old Guard leaders beamed with approval on their sophomore protege. Martin Madden, veteran Illinois legislator, paid him a glowing tribute. In a public declaration, he asserted that the young member from New York had, in this single-handed fight, brought about the greatest saving ever accomplished by any one man in Congress!

Flushed with this victory, the Major realigned his forces, and launched a second attack upon the Administration. This time his target was the plan to sell in Europe the surplus food supplies which had been shipped abroad for the use of the American Army.

From the floor of the House he lashed out at the Democratic leadership, bitterly criticizing the Administration for its failure to enforce the food bill while the nation was at war. He declared that the Department of Justice possessed ample power to confiscate all surplus food and regulate its distribution. He continued his attack on the Bureau of Supplies, until he forced through the adoption of a resolution compelling the War Department to bring the surplus food back home and sell it to the American people.

Already he was recognized as a thorn in the side of the Administration, but his Republican colleagues themselves began to regard him somewhat doubtfully as the Summer of 1919 wore on. He was exhibiting a variety of interest which confused them. They could not reconcile his attack on the Administration Preparedness program, with his introduction of a bill providing for the purchase of 200 bombing planes, 140 training planes, 100 pursuit planes, 50 observation planes, and 600 Hispana Suiza motors of 300 h.p. each. This bill carried an appropriation of $15,000,000, and provided that all planes purchased under the act, must be made in the United States.

When they criticized it, the Major retorted:

> "As every one knows, I have been fighting appropriations for the air service because every request that is coming from the War Department to date, has been for lump sum appropriations. . . . Mine shows how many planes are to be purchased, and also specifies the type of plane, so there can be no possibility of using these funds for other purposes, or for buying swamp lands, or giving

it to favored contractors for purchasing additional junk. . . ."

Nevertheless, he stoutly advocated a cut in the regular appropriation. On July 23 he took the floor, maintaining that the Air Service had broken down, and fiercely denouncing the attitude of the Senate, which blamed the House for reducing the appropriation.

"It is the same old story," declared La Guardia. "They want to buy more swamp lands, and dump millions into land graft! All the money spent in that way will do nothing for the progress of aviation."

At the same time he took his position as an avowed champion of a uniform Air Service.

His bitter tongue harassed his opponents from the beginning.

He first shattered the smug self-content of the conservatives, when, on February 6 he took the floor and barked at them:

> The trouble with American aviation is that it is out to make money. That was due to our mistake in the beginning. We started off with $640,000,000, and I don't know how much was appropriated afterwards—and we have less to show for it than any other country in the world. . . . The fact is, you can't build aviation motors with press agents, and you can't build up our aviation service by politics. The law of gravitation knows no politics, and if you have not a good machine, it will not fly. . . . If I told you what the airmen thought of the situation in August, September and October, it would not be couched in parliamentary language, and it could not be printed.
>
> When the appropriation of that $640,000,000 came before this House, I was still young in my legislative career. I wanted to talk about it. But the gentlemen of the House said, "Don't! Disloyal to do so! Beware of the Germans! Don't say a word about it!" And they got away with it; but what did *we* get out of that $640,-

ooo,ooo? For every American machine that went over
the lines into Germany the cost was more than the
building of a super-dreadnaught! That's what we got
out of it!

A little later when Congressman Moore of Pennsylvania protested that Congress had only performed its duty by that appropriation, La Guardia flamed back at him:

> Congress was generous. But the Packard Company
> got the fruits of that generosity.

His colleagues were further bewildered by what they regarded as the inconsistency of his attitude toward the Administration. He embarrassed the President by demanding the
withdrawal of recognition of the Mexican Carranza—which
seemed in keeping with his position as a member of the Republican opposition. Then he executed an about-face, and
loomed up as a champion of the League of Nations! The very
project which was dearest to the heart of Woodrow Wilson.
In preparing his case against Carranza, he spent weeks collecting information. He was in correspondence with various State
and city authorities along the Mexican border, and he crossed
swords with the general staff energetically.

On June 23 he wrote to Brigadier General H. Churchill,
of the Military Intelligence Division, concerning the matter:

> I desire to point out, in order that we may under-
> stand each other perfectly, that you are either not in
> possession of information concerning conditions on the
> western coast of Mexico, and in the States of Sinaloa,
> Tabasco, Colima and Jalisco; or, if you are, that this in-
> formation was purposely omitted from your report to
> me, and your statement to the press. Such action, it
> would seem, was intentional and not based upon any
> military necessity, but was taken only for political
> purposes.
> It has always been my belief that a real live, compe-
> tent military intelligence department, is not only a

necessary branch of the military establishment, but a useful government agency. One of its uses, in my opinion, is to furnish accurate and complete information to the Legislature. If a military intelligence department is not fairly and impartially conducted, it can be made a weapon for partisan or personal uses. If our military intelligence is not to be properly administered, it is better that it die in its infancy.

This was his first clash with the executive department of the government. The Churchill letter was to be the predecessor of hundreds more, written in a similar vein, during the coming years.

Washington files are full of such epistles, and in many cases proper grammatical construction is sacrificed to intensity of expression. This is usually due to the crises in which they were written. New York's stormy petrel never paused to weigh one phrase against another! Whenever any seeming abuse was called to the attention of the fiery La Guardia, he always went flaming into action without a second's delay.

Springing to his feet, he would charge up and down his office, spouting dictation in a machine-gun staccato—usually to the utter horror of his overworked stenographers. One idea, crowding upon the heels of another, would erupt from his lips, pounded home by an energetic fist, beating time to the bitter adjectives. And often sentence structure would be completely shattered in the process.

Such examples are plentiful in his correspondence, unless they were corrected by the ever-vigilant Miss Fischer. No other stenographer ever dared to change his phraseology, and the Major himself, all too frequently, would jab his illegibly-scrawled signature at the bottom, without analyzing the grammatical structure of the letter. Throughout his Congressional career, the amazing variety of his interests kept him too busy to make minor corrections.

This variety is exemplified in the subject matter with which he concerned himself, even during the first term that he actually spent in Washington. La Guardia was never an expert political marksman, concentrating his fire on a single subject! Rather he was a human fieldpiece, scattering shrapnel all over the political landscape.

He did an amazing amount of execution, however.

During the Summer of 1919, he concerned himself largely with veteran and military legislation, although he also found time to become the acknowledged spokesman of the helpless Congressional Anti-Prohibition group.

He introduced a measure providing for the Gold Star Mothers' trips abroad. The sentimental La Guardia declared he did not approve of returning the bodies of American soldiers and sailors who had been killed in France. He thought they should remain, sleeping beneath the soil, for the preservation of which they had sacrificed their lives. He took the position, instead, that the Government should provide transportation and maintenance for the parents and wives of the slain, so that they might visit the graves of their dead.

Other measures introduced at that time included the repeal of the Espionage Act, reinstatement of all men who had seen service in the Government positions they had left, and preference for war veterans in the Civil Service. He re-introduced his bill, providing the death penalty for fraudulent sales of war materials during hostilities. Finally, he sponsored the measure for the rehabilitation of cripples in industry.

Most of these bills won support in the House because the war was of such recent memory; but the early enthusiasm of the Republican leaders cooled swiftly as even more liberal measures followed.

They eyed askance his proposal to retire all Civil Service workers on pensions after thirty years. And they were plainly shocked when he introduced a resolution proposing an amendment to the Constitution, which provided that all future amendments should be ratified by a referendum of the qualified voters of three-fourths of the several States, instead of by the Legislatures of three-fourths of the States, as the present law provides.

This was considered much too radical in 1919, especially as it was recognized as a criticism of the process by which national Prohibition had been inflicted upon the nation! And Prohibition was then at the height of its popularity.

Nevertheless, La Guardia entered the lists against the triumphant Drys.

His action was regarded as political suicide at the time. Even the few conscientious opponents of Prohibition were inclined to keep very quiet about it. There was no organized opposition, and public opinion was presumed to be overwhelmingly in favor of the Great Experiment.

La Guardia had cabled his pair against the Eighteenth Amendment home from the front, and now in Washington he led the fight against the Volstead Act on the floor of the House. One of the few members who was not content with merely registering a negative vote, the New York member was on his feet throughout the fight against the measure. His clashes with Congressman Volstead were repeated. *The Congressional Record* is full of such passages as the following, which occurred on July 12, 1919:

> Mr. Volstead. Will the gentleman yield?
> Mr. La Guardia. Certainly not.
> Mr. Volstead. Just for a brief statement?
> Mr. La Guardia. Not for a statement; for a question.
> Mr. Volstead. I just want to explain—
> Mr. La Guardia. The gentleman can explain on his own time. I have only ten minutes.
> Mr. Volstead. All right—go on.
> Mr. La Guardia. I notice that the gentleman is not very generous in extending time to the opponents of his measure. . . .

On the same day he launched a fiery denunciation of the Volstead Act:

Mr. Chairman: I believe that this bill was purposely so drawn, because it is *not* the intention of the organizations guiding our committee to have this law properly enforced. With the exception of the Woman's Christian Temperance Union (whose sincerity I do not doubt) the rest of the organizations do not desire to go out of existence now. They have too much of a good thing, and want it to last as long as possible. . . .

Of course I am not able to say how much alcohol it takes to get one intoxicated, or the terrible results of the excessive use of that article. I have not had any of that in my family, or among my associates, and so I don't know. . . . I disagree with some who say that if this law is enforced, we shall have trouble because of its enforcement! *I maintain that this law will be almost impossible of enforcement. And if this law fails to be enforced—as it certainly will be, as it is drawn—it will create contempt and disregard for law all over the country.* . . . If this measure is loosely enforced, after we have adopted the Eighteenth Amendment, it will simply mean fuel to the radical element to create the disregard for and disobedience of our laws. And this measure now is humanly impossible of enforcement.

Now, I do not say that excessive drinking of whisky is good. I don't know anything about that. As I told you, none of my ancestors had that failing. I have traced them way back, and the only one I could find who drank to excess was a certain "Nero"—and he got the habit from his mother, who was born on the Rhine. (Laughter and applause.)

Is there really an honest desire to carry out the purpose of the Eighteenth Amendment? You won't do it by this bill! And I charge that you don't want to do it. You want to keep the lecture tours. You want to exploit the "drunks." (I want to reform them.) It has been profitable. It is a good thing for you—and you want to keep it up. . . .

Now, this is what you are doing here: You are absolutely increasing the use of bad alcohol! If *that* is your intention, you are going to succeed with this measure. Temperance or Prohibition is a matter of education, and not of legislation. The Woman's Christian Temperance

93

Union has been doing good work for many years along educational lines. . . . By proper education, by proper training—if you really have the interest and welfare of this country at heart you can train the people so that the next generation will not use alcohol, and will not require any law of this sort.

But, I say, with this measure as it is drawn here, we shall not do that, but we shall do exactly the contrary: we shall create a lot of whisky-drinking all through the United States!

His clashes with Congressman Upshaw were just as frequent, but less bitter. He fought with the latter to delay the vote of the special rule, which was brought in to make the Volstead Act the regular order.

Mr. UPSHAW. Will the gentleman yield?

Mr. LA GUARDIA. Yes, for a question.

Mr. UPSHAW. Did the gentleman ever know the friends of liquor to come to any time which they thought would be a good time to put them out of business?

Mr. LA GUARDIA. The gentleman knows that the moonshiners of the South are very anxious to get this bill through, because their business will increase. . . .

Mr. UPSHAW. I will give the answer to that when the time comes. . . . I will answer fully the gentleman's statement about moonshiners.

Mr. DYER. Will the gentleman claim that there are not any in Georgia?

Mr. LA GUARDIA. No doubt the gentleman is an authority on the subject.

Mr. UPSHAW. I will answer the gentleman by saying that as long as New York and Baltimore and virtuous Chicago—the same city that elected. . . .

Mr. LA GUARDIA. A question, not a statement.

Mr. UPSHAW. A question? In all good honor, the gentleman ought not to leave my answer suspended in the air like that!

Mr. LA GUARDIA. I will say to the gentleman that if the

people traveling from other states, would keep out
of New York City, we would have no drunks in
the streets.

Mr. Upshaw. Will the gentleman yield?
Does the gentleman intend to suggest that he does
not want the financial patronage of the glorious
"Dry South" in the cities that have clung on to
liquor for so long?

Mr. La Guardia. Absolutely not. It keeps our courts
congested.

That was LaGuardia—the pioneer wet champion in the midsummer of 1919.

*   *   *

Already the Drys were mobilizing against him, preparing
for the bitter twelve-year fight that was to follow. But their
opposition was offset by his increasing popularity in the ghetto.

The Major had suddenly loomed on the horizon as the leading defender of the tortured Jewry of Europe. Back home,
bearded, skull-capped rabbis nodded approval as they read in
the Yiddish papers of his newly introduced resolution, championing their co-religionists. It served stern warning upon the
lately established Republics of Poland and Russia, that they
could expect neither friendship nor aid from the United
States, unless the abuse to which their Jewish population was
being subjected, cease immediately.

The resolution attracted much attention. The Secretary of
State was summoned before the House Committee on Foreign
Affairs to testify concerning it. A monster mass meeting was
held in Madison Square Garden in New York, and there Justice Panken read the La Guardia Resolution to applauding
thousands. Its sponsor's prestige was immeasurably increased
when, in consequence, the State Department secured reassur-
ance from the countries in question, that they would guarantee
equal protection to all people regardless of race or religion.

Sam Koenig and the other Republican bosses in New York

City were studying the young Congressman critically. As they evaluated his growing strength, they began to wonder if perhaps he might not be their White Hope against Tammany Hall. The Republicans had never carried a city-wide election, but they had never presented a candidate who possessed such evident popularity among the Italian and Jewish masses.

They discussed him at length. His war record was good, and his veteran legislation had given him a following among the returned soldiery. A Republican in good standing, his liberalism would not alienate the Progressive wing of the party. The bosses could see a real future for him in the Republican ranks —and in September Sam Koenig suggested him for President of the Board of Aldermen of the City of New York.

A vacancy had been created by the election of Aldermanic President Alfred E. Smith to the Governorship of the State. The Aldermanic Presidency was an important position, and represented a definite promotion for La Guardia. A Congressman is not very impressive in New York where there are twenty-three of them in the Greater City alone. But the President of the Board of Aldermen is the second-ranking city official. He is Acting Mayor in the leader's absence, and casts three votes in the Board of Estimate—the upper house of the municipal assembly. Tammany had nominated the Honorable Robert H. Moran to succeed Smith.

Summoned from Washington and offered the Republican nomination, La Guardia demurred. He was not at all optimistic about the chances of success. "Besides, I like the House," he protested, "and I don't want to leave it."

The Republican leaders argued with him at length.

In later years he declared that Will Hays definitely promised the G. O. P. nomination for Mayor in 1921, *if* he should be elected Aldermanic President. The story of this promise was to cause the Republican leaders many a headache in ensuing years!

At last he accepted the nomination and received the benediction of the G. O. P. bosses! Paul Windels, a Conservative,

The commanding officer watches a ball game at Foggia in 1918.

Major La Guardia at the front—1918

was recalled from his Maine vacation to act as campaign manager. The tall, dignified and reserved Windels was the direct antithesis of the fiery and impulsive candidate. He was captivated immediately by the latter's charm. That meeting marked the beginning of a warm friendship, which culminated fourteen years later when Mayor La Guardia appointed his 1919 campaign manager as Corporation Counsel for the City of New York.

Senator William Calder decided to introduce the candidate to the Kings County Republican Committee at a big banquet. He sent an emissary to invite La Guardia. Half an hour later, the Senator received an excited telephone call from his emissary. "We can't have La Guardia at that meeting," babbled the messenger. "I didn't invite him. If he comes, it will ruin his chance for election."

"What do you mean?" asked Calder.

"He just had his head shaved and he looks like hell," responded the emissary. "Listen, we'll have to keep him under cover until his hair grows back."

The Senator agreed that this seemed advisable and the invitation was never extended to La Guardia. His backers made no effort to promote his candidacy until the Congressman's hair had grown long enough for him to appear in public.

When he accepted the nomination, he had exactly $35 to his name! Throughout his career he never exhibited any financial ability in his own affairs, and most of his salary was distributed in casual charities. These had been supplemented by the additional strain upon his purse as the young husband established a home in the Greenwich Village section. Nevertheless, there was nothing hesitant about his denunciation of the financial policy inaugurated by Mayor John F. Hylan. Plunging into a whirlwind campaign, the candidate stormed across the city, shouting that the 1920 budget of the Hylan Administration, "conceived in the bowels of darkness," was more than enough to stagger the public!

He denounced firetrap school buildings, and demanded the

abolition of what he termed "the useless office of the City Chamberlain." He raised Cain about the elaborate receptions which the city had given to returning veterans.

> As a soldier who fought in the Great War, I know that these heroes of the A.E.F., were more interested in getting jobs when discharged from the Army, than in costly and ornate celebrations. Under the guise of "Patriotism," the people's money was squandered, to a large extent through blunders and other wastages, and some of the items of expense are an insult to the soldiers; some of whom, as taxpayers, must bear their share of this financial burden! It was the feeling of gratitude in the hearts of the people, that thrilled the soldiers—not the showy extravagance that heaped expense upon people who were sufficiently burdened already on account of the cost of the war.

Tammany unlimbered its heavy artillery and pounded him severely because he refused to take a position on the five-cent fare—already a sore spot in New York politics. The candidate would take no stand whatever, declaring that he had been out of touch with the local situation, and could not decide so complicated an issue without further study. Later he was to become its ardent champion.

On October 13, speaking in Manhattan, he denounced "Hylan's extravagant Administration, of which Acting Aldermanic President Moran is a part. He has wasted a lot of the people's money on celebrations. More than one-half million dollars has been appropriated, and nearly all of this has already been spent. The record is a public scandal. In the Board of Estimate the affirmative vote was unanimous for these appropriations." The bulk of the money was spent on "welcoming home" celebrations and a temporary monument to the returning heroes of the A. E. F.

His denunciations of his old Tammany foes were vitriolic. On October 27, he issued a statement beginning:

Mayor Hylan runs to the Bronx and makes a political speech on the one question of which he knows absolutely nothing—that is, the traction question. The least he can do is to keep quiet and remain in hiding! The Public Service Commission belongs to the same political faith as Mr. Hylan, and is controlled by the same boss, Charles F. Murphy.

The following day he declared:

The school children are paying the penalty of the Tammany Administration's neglect of the schools, by being exposed to the peril of firetrap school buildings. . . . These firetraps are scattered throughout the city, and most of them are very old buildings, crumbling apart. The Tammany Board of Estimate has been more interested in grabbing for greater power over the school system than in making first that system adequate to the pressing needs that crowd it.

He showed unexpected strength as the campaign progressed. The Jewish and Italian sections were enthusiastic about his candidacy, and his friends of the garment strike days once again mobilized in his behalf. The Lower East Side Postal Workers enlisted their colleagues all over the city and did magnificent service. In addition, the regular Republican machine, scenting a victory for the first time in its history, moved into high gear and did its part.

Miss Fischer, the faithful secretary, had come up from Washington, and was putting into effect at headquarters the lessons she had learned during the Congressional campaigns. The girl exhibited an unexpected talent for political analysis, and her hard common sense proved a real asset in this and ensuing campaigns. Marie Fischer never occupied the spotlight, but her opinions always carried great weight at the La Guardia headquarters. She had much more to do with his success than most people realize.

The greatest handicap faced by the La Guardia forces was the lack of funds. By the time the campaign ended, they had amassed an indebtedness of $30,000. This knowledge hung like a black cloud over the headquarters where La Guardia, Espresso and Andrews put their heads together and wrestled with the problem. A nerve-racking solution was evolved: They decided to stake everything on one desperate gamble!

Espresso was approached by the late Frank Munsey, offering to bet 3 to 1 that Moran would win. Thea announced that she had $1,050 of her own money, with which she proposed to accept the wager. She suggested that her winnings could go toward the deficit.

Espresso, the acknowledged political expert of the group tried to dissuade her at first; but on the Saturday night before election, he decided that victory was in sight. He recommended that they act upon Mrs. La Guardia's proposal. The others decided to take the chance. La Guardia's supporters made a final effort, raised $9,000 more, and then calmly bet it on the election! They knew that if he won, the financial problem would be solved.

The beautiful Thea was more thrilled than the candidate himself when the returns poured in on election night. The great effort had succeeded. Her husband was elected by 1,200 votes. She was the Second Lady of New York.

CHAPTER VIII

TRIUMPH

THE Republican bosses were jubilant when Fiorello H. La Guardia took office as Aldermanic President on New Year's Day of 1920. His victory, it was felt, marked a new era for the hitherto helpless G. O. P. On the wave of his popularity even Henry H. Curran had been carried into office as Borough President of Manhattan. This gave the Republicans five of the sixteen votes in the Board of Estimate. The new Aldermanic President expounded his political philosophy upon taking office, as follows:

> My understanding of the function of the minority, is that it is to set the pace for the majority. . . . The minority must, therefore, first point out to the majority when the majority is headed in the wrong direction; and only after it has exhausted every possible means, can it possibly criticize the majority for any error committed or mistake made. . . . The minority must never be guilty of failing to support the majority, whether it is in agreement or not. It must use every effort to call the majority's attention to important matters, and then take advantage of any failure to act, afterwards.

La Guardia had submitted his resignation as a Member of Congress to Governor Smith that morning before appearing at City Hall. He was sworn in by Justice Philip McCook, the same Justice who administered the oath to him as Mayor of New York City on January 1, 1934.

Almost at once the new official was plunged into the limelight. The New York State Legislature had announced its intention of expelling five newly elected Socialist members as disloyal. Four other Socialists had been elected to the New

York City Board of Aldermen, the body of which La Guardia was presiding officer. On January 8 he took the position that they were entitled to their seats, and a week later he went on the stump in their behalf.

"In ousting the five Socialist Assemblymen," declared La Guardia, "a dangerous precedent has been created. If we deprive the Socialists of their legal rights after legitimate use of the ballot; if we deprive them of free speech and of the free press, they will be compelled to resort to the same sort of methods used in Russia." This was bad enough. But the Republican conservatives sat up and shuddered when he went on to state:

"With grain, eggs and oatmeal becoming luxuries in the average family, these Socialists, along with the general public, are right in demanding a radical change in conditions."

It was the opening gun of a fight in which he took an enthusiastic part. As presiding officer of the Board of Aldermen, he utilized his knowledge of parliamentary law, and repeatedly blocked efforts to unseat the four Socialists. As soon as he was victorious in this effort, he turned his attention to the struggle to force the reseating of the five ousted Assemblymen. Again and again he expressed himself forcibly and with vehemence, both on the platform and in the press.

"I desire to thank you," wrote Edward Cassidy, Socialist candidate for Governor, a year later, "for your repeated protests against this outrage against representative government. Your speech on the floor of the Board was splendid." . . . Referring to an article which La Guardia had written for the *New York Times,* he said: "To write such an article at that time required courage—and you displayed it."

Where the Socialist problem was out of the way, the new city official turned his attention to the Board of Estimate— the body which supervises most of New York City's financial affairs. There the feud with the Tammany Comptroller, Charles L. Craig, third ranking city officer, was born, and there it flourished like the green bay tree.

The Board of Estimate, under the old City Charter, was a most important factor in New York's government, since it controlled the purse strings. It is composed of eight members, casting a total of sixteen votes. The Mayor, Aldermanic President and Comptroller cast three votes each. The remainder is divided among the five Borough Presidents, who head the small local governments into which the Greater City is divided. They supervise city buildings, street extensions, etc. The Presidents of the Boroughs of Manhattan and Brooklyn are entitled to two votes each, while those of the Bronx, Queens and Richmond have one each.

The Republican minority, consisting of La Guardia and Borough President Curran, possessed five votes, and Tammany retained control eleven to five. This setup was disarranged, however, when Mayor John F. Hylan split with Comptroller Craig. It led to a strange alliance. Hylan hated Craig almost as bitterly as La Guardia learned to, and "Honest John" turned to the Republicans for aid and comfort. Soon he actually began to respect the sturdy opposition fighter—and an odd personal friendship ensued.

The La Guardia-Craig feud burst into flames soon after the Aldermanic President took office. Almost from the beginning, the two men fought with a ferocity which was appalling. La Guardia was a rough-and-tumble fighter. He cast dignity to the winds and screamed accusations which drove Craig (who was no mean antagonist himself) to desperation. The Board of Estimate had never seen such meetings and staid old New York was shocked to the core.

With Hylan's assistance, La Guardia killed a couple of Craig's pet projects, including a new Court House contract, and openly charged the Comptroller with dishonesty. He drove Craig to a frenzy, and once the latter, stirred to a white heat, burst out during a public meeting, addressing Mayor Hylan:

"Will you please hit that little wop over the head with the gavel!"

The feud never relaxed in the ensuing two years of La Guardia's term, and during this period the La Guardia-Hylan alliance prospered. The two men had been cold to one another in the beginning, but they soon ironed out their differences.

"He (La Guardia) showed a surprising knowledge of City affairs for a new member," declared Mayor Hylan in discussing the matter. The former Mayor later explained how they first came to an understanding. The Aldermanic President had been in office only a few weeks, when he announced that he was going to demand an investigation of the Administration.

"I was really vexed when I read his statement," explained Hylan later, "because it had been based on information that I knew was not correct. I met La Guardia that evening at the 69th Regiment Armory, at a reception which was being held for De Valera, President of the Irish Republic. La Guardia was in the reception room when I arrived and when I came in, he stood up and greeted me with, 'Good evening, Mr. Mayor.'

"I answered him very coldly, and he came up to me and asked if I was tired, or if I was not feeling well? I then told La Guardia about the statement he had given out, and that his information had been incorrect. I offered him all the records on the matter and any assistance which he might require to ascertain the facts.

"He looked surprised. I told him that night: 'La Guardia, any time you think there's anything wrong, you come to me first, and if you find that I'll not co-operate with you, or that I will stand for anything not right, you may go the limit!' "

"La Guardia asked. 'Do you mean it, Mr. Mayor?'

"I told him *I did*.

"We shook hands. From that time on, La Guardia kept his word, and I am sure that I kept mine. For the following two years, La Guardia came to me on many occasions on matters which were not right, according to his views. I stood by him in the majority of these matters—although in many instances I incurred the displeasure of the Tammany organization.

"I always found La Guardia to be entirely disinterested in

his attitude toward the matters which came before him officially. That's why I trusted him; and I'm sure that he trusted me!"

The battle over the Courthouse contracts was epic. La Guardia was in the thick of it. The part played by the new Aldermanic President in the final outcome was later described by Hylan, as follows:

Again pressure was being brought to bear from all quarters for the commencement of the new Courthouse building. A site had been selected and purchased by the previous administration. When the matter first came before the Board of Estimate, I expected unanimity of opinion on, at least, that one subject. Much to my surprise, La Guardia commenced opposing every move. In the beginning he was alone in his opposition. Later on Mr. Curran joined him. I must confess that I always was suspicious when Mr. Curran opposed anything. . . . La Guardia studied every specification for bids. He used every means he could to delay awarding the contracts. Finally the contracts were awarded for everything but the interior part of the Courthouse. La Guardia was beaten all the way through. He came to me one evening and said: "Mr. Mayor, you remember what you told me that night at the 69th Regiment Armory? Well, this Courthouse business stinks—it's ROTTEN; you can't stand for it."

I said, "What do you mean?"

He replied: "Mr. Mayor, you look into it as much as I have, and you will find that *the city is being robbed!* The price of the limestone is ridiculously high, and not only that, but the specifications call for about 300 cubic feet more than they need!"

"How do you know?" I asked the Major.

"Compare the price of the limestone with that now being paid for the same kind of stone by the Cunard Building, down on Broadway," La Guardia replied.

I said, "La Guardia, are you falling for that *New York World* stuff?"

"No," La Guardia replied. "The *New York World* is taking my stuff."

"What do you want me to do, Mr. President?"

"I want you," said the Major, "to have any one you select, look into this matter. If I am wrong in anything I have said, or off in any of the estimates I have given, I will publicly state that I have been wrong. But, on the other hand, if you find that I am right, for goodness sake, protect the city!"

I immediately ordered the Commissioner of Accounts to investigate. At the first hearing, the whole case of the limestone people collapsed. As soon as they were confronted with figures, they became panic-stricken, and walked out of the hearing! I received my own report from the Commissioner of Accounts, Hirshfield, and on my own motion, called a special meeting of the Board of Estimate. I canceled every contract that had been awarded, with the exception of the foundation contract. That could not be canceled for the reason that the contractors had already started to dig. Comptroller Craig strenuously opposed the rescinding of contracts. He not only opposed the rescinding of the contracts, but publicly advised the successful bidders to begin action against the city—advice which was followed by the contractors. The rescinding of the contracts saved the city over $3,000,000.

This was another instance in which I had to oppose, not only the powerful interests of the limestone people and the contractors, but also the wishes of the Tammany organization—which was solidly in favor of those contractors who were overcharging the city.

When the vote was taken, Mr. La Guardia said to me, "Whatever you may have done for the city of New York to date, tonight is your best day's work; you are not only saving the city millions of dollars, but you have set an example that the day of looting on public improvements is past!"

La Guardia himself said of the matter:

The New York County limestone Courthouse out-Tweeded Tweed! It was stopped in time, and nobody went to jail! I must say, in all fairness, that although I was fighting the majority after all contracts were awarded, when I still continued my fight, I placed all of the facts again before the Mayor. He then had the Commissioner of Accounts investigate, and assured me he would not sign the contracts if the facts which I complained of, and which were reported, were sustained by that investigation.

Long before it was concluded, the Mayor had given me his assurance that the matter was indeed bad, and that he would not only refuse to sign the contracts pending, but would rescind those which had already passed the Board of Estimate. In all fairness, again, it must be stated that the Mayor's decision was prior to the time that the matter was taken up by the Investigating Committee.

Some of my political friends criticized me very severely for my action in this respect. It was suggested that I might have had a great campaign issue had I waited and pointed out the terrific wastefulness of the limestone purchases.

That is the doctrine of the old school of politics. It might have been good campaign material, but it would have been far too costly to the City of New York. I considered that it was my duty to serve the city first and look for campaign issues afterward. That is the teaching of the new school of politics.

The question of increases in the salaries of city officials came up next. It was another measure sponsored by the Comptroller. La Guardia was scheduled for punishment by the Tammany organization in that the Bill increased the salary of every Aldermen except the President of the Board. The failure to boost La Guardia's salary was regarded as revenge for his protest against the ousting of the Socialist Assemblymen. The resultant fight was thus summarized by Mayor Hylan later:

The City received authority from the State legislature to increase its short-term indebtedness, which permitted us to give the city employees a sufficient increase to meet the constantly growing cost of living. Practically every politician took individual credit for obtaining the legislation. The fact is that the salaries of the city employees had not been increased since the terrible jump in the cost of living, caused by the war; and the distress of the city employees was such that the salary increases was one of the matters for which *no* individual can truthfully claim credit.

A 20 per cent increase for city employees was recommended and sponsored by the Comptroller. President La Guardia was right on the jump, and fought it. Great pressure was brought to bear by the Tammany organization. It passed through the Board of Estimates and the Board of Aldermen. President La Guardia never let up his fight. He took the matter up with me very earnestly.

It was apparent, upon examination of the pay roll, that the bulk of the available funds would go to politically appointed high officials. I considered the matter very carefully over the week end, and when I came to the office the next week, I vetoed the Aldermanic resolution, and reintroduced a new schedule of increases. We stopped *all* increases at salaries of $5000. This left several hundred thousands, which we were able to give to the lower salaried employees on a graduated scale.

The resolution and the new schedule went through. The lower salaried employees were, of course, happy—but I surely incurred the displeasure of many of the high and mighty in political circles, who were disappointed that they did not receive the $1000 and $1500 increases that the original schedule would have given them. President La Guardia co-operated with me loyally in this matter.

Craig was wild over the defeat of his projects. La Guardia continued to pour oil on his blazing wrath by hounding the Comptroller at every turn. On September 29 he made public a letter which he had just written him. It is typical of their correspondence:

Hon. Charles L. Craig,
Comptroller of the City of New York,
Municipal Building, N. Y. City.

My dear Mr. Comptroller:

I received notification yesterday that there would be a meeting of the Finance and Budget Committee today. This morning I gleaned from some of the papers, the purpose of this meeting.

I have told you repeatedly that no new matter could originate in committee, but must first be presented to the Board of Estimate and Apportionment in session, and then referred to the committee for consideration—if the Board deems necessary.

The proposed resolution which you submitted to the press, should be taken up at the next regular meeting of the Board of Estimate and Apportionment, and nothing can be done in committee today except to refer it to the Board of Estimate and Apportionment.

I am too busy with the work of the budget to play with you today.

I take this opportunity to point out that you are still unlawfully withholding payment of the 1918 teachers' refund claims, and claims for the payment of material and services to the Department of Education for the year 1918. The Board of Estimate and Apportionment has appropriated the necessary money, and it directed you to pay these claims several weeks ago. These claims, as you well know, are for payment of sick refunds of money to teachers who are in need of this money, who have waited for three years, and for claims of reputable business concerns, for furnishing materials and supplies in good faith to the Department of Education, more than three years ago.

Unfortunately, it would seem that these claimants have not that kind of political drag necessary to obtain prompt attention from you. I am asking the Mayor to take measures necessary to compel you to carry out the mandates and directions of the Board of Estimate and Apportionment. If he does not, I will.

Yours very truly,
(Signed:) F. La Guardia.

On November 19 the Aldermanic President wrote to the State Civil Service Commission, protesting against the application of Comptroller Craig to exempt over one hundred positions in his department from Civil Service examinations, thus placing them in the exempt class of the Department of Finance.

At that time La Guardia paid his compliments to the Comptroller in the following statement:

> This is a brazen attempt to discharge a large number of employees who have been in the service of the city for a good many years, and to appoint the riffraff who could not pass the civil service test. If one will stop to consider the make-up of the positions of auditors of accounts, examining inspectors, expert accountants, cashiers and statisticians in the political patronage, the danger of such procedure can be readily seen.
>
> It is a good thing for the City of New York, that the Department of Finance, under its present administration, has the large number of faithful and able employees, who really keep the work going, in spite of the Comptroller.

Craig fumed helplessly under these repeated attacks, and struck eagerly at the first opportunity.

As the year drew to a close, the Comptroller gleefully seized upon an error in the accounts of the Aldermanic President. It concerned an item of $390, which he said represented charges for personal telegrams, that La Guardia was attempting to palm off on the city! A veritable teapot tempest resulted. The Comptroller threatened to sue him for $390.24.

La Guardia admitted there had been a mix-up in the bills, but said most of them had been contracted by members of the Board of Aldermen themselves. Craig waxed eloquent in his denunciation of La Guardia for the "attempted fraud!"

He continued his attack even after William O'Connor, Legislative Secretary of the President of the Board of Aldermen, issued a statement which read in part:

President La Guardia has several times instructed me, and in my presence, instructed Miss Fischer, his personal secretary, to be very careful to see that none of his personal telegrams were charged to the city. These Western Union bills were submitted to Miss Fischer, to check up the President's personal items, and she subsequently gave me a cheque to the order of the Western Union Co. in settlement of the checked items. She also paid over in cash to the representatives of the Western Union Co., the cost of a telegram sent to Scarborough on March 26.

Whatever responsibility there is for the failure to eliminate the telegrams, set forth in the communication of the Comptroller, is chargeable to me and not to the President. President La Guardia instructed me again, after the bills had been sent to the Comptroller's office in the early part of December, to examine these bills carefully, because he was sure the Comptroller would make a personal matter of these telegraphic charges, if any of his private messages were vouched for through error!

Miss Fischer was engaged in going through her files in search of copies of all telegrams sent during the year, when the Comptroller's letter was received—in order to clear this matter up. In the meantime I had inadvertently permitted a voucher to go through! The personal telegrams not checked over by me, will amount to a very small item.

I feel this very keenly, because Mr. La Guardia had repeatedly spoken to me about the matter, and had prophesied what mean action would be taken, if I slipped up!

The controversy dragged on for weeks. On January 10, La Guardia wrote to Craig as follows:

Dear Sir:

I beg to acknowledge receipt of your letter of January 8, 1921, which reached me this morning. It bears the postmark of January 8, 9 P.M., and therefore could not reach me before, although copies of it were sent to the press last night.

Your statement to the press in connection with the

letter, that the messages amount to $390, was, of course, untrue. And you must have known it at the time you made it. One item alone amounts to $209. This was the telegraphic communication of a Resolution of the Board of Aldermen, signed jointly by the Acting President, and majority and minority leaders of the Board, in the matter of Rent Legislation, at the time that a delegation of New York City officials were in Albany. The messages on the same subject amounted to $7. Another item, which amounts to $25, was a telegraphic message calling a special meeting on August 12 of the Board of Aldermen. These two items alone, figure almost two-thirds of the total amount for the period of the voucher. I have not at yet had any opportunity to get a complete list of all messages sent.

The following day La Guardia sent a second letter:

Hon. Charles L. Craig,
Comptroller of the City of New York,
Municipal Building, New York City.

Sir:

In response to your communication of the 8th, relative to a few personal telegrams of mine which were inadvertently charged against the City of New York in a bill against the office of the President of the Board of Aldermen, I instructed Mr. O'Connor to visit your office for the purpose of examining the records in the Finance Department, with a view to ascertaining the number and the expense in connection with my personal messages.

I did this pursuant to the following excerpts from your letter:

"Your are afforded the opportunity to examine the records in your own office, in the Finance Department, and the Western Union Telegraph offices, for the purpose of picking out all telegrams sent or received by you and paid for by the City of New York, that are not a proper charge against the taxpayers of this city."

You refused to see Mr. O'Connor, and sent out word through your secretary, that you would not see any one from this office in regard to this matter, and would only permit an examination of the records under a written request from me.

I herewith make such request, and ask you to permit the bearer of this letter to have access to the records, and make copies thereof, in order that I may do now what I always intended to do—that is, pay out of my own pocket for any personal messages which may have inadvertently crept into this bill.

The matter was finally adjusted when quiet Miss Fischer stepped in and publicly took the blame for the mix-up!

As usual, the Major plunged from one battle into another. He was continually fighting with the Aldermen over whom he presided, but he was quick to come to their assistance when somebody else attempted to make them the target for an attack. Such a criticism was levelled at the Board by William H. Anderson, Superintendent of the Anti-Saloon League of New York. And the statement of *any* Prohibitionist was a red flag to the Aldermanic President! His comment was typically La Guardian:

> I am reluctant about making any reply to anything Anderson says, for the same reason I have given so many times: I don't believe in advertising Anarchists and Demagogues. As usual, this man is talking without knowing what he is talking about!
>
> I personally took the stump, urging a modification of the wording of the Resolution to which he refers, and that particular paragraph received careful consideration by the Board. No matter what I may personally believe about the wording of the Resolution, no man in this State can attack the Board of Aldermen as long as I preside over it, and get away with it.
>
> Anderson is irresponsible—knows that he is—and for that reason indulges in loose talk. He has no keen sense of honor; attacks without knowing the facts, and is so brazen that anything said about him does not affect him —but, in fact, gives him the advertisement that he craves —and needs. I know of my own personal knowledge that Anderson is a hypocrite and does not believe in temperance.

When I ran for Congress in the Fourteenth Congressional District, in 1916, Anderson supported Michael F. Farley, the President of the National Liquor Dealers Association, because, he said, he was interested in seeing Farley elected, as it would serve to aid his cause. . . .

I also know that Mr. Anderson is aware that the present enforcement laws are not capable of enforcement in a city of the size of New York, and he wants it so, in order to be able to keep up the activities of his League in this city.

It is a pity that there are so many splendid citizens in this country who are giving their good money to keep in idleness a man of the Anderson type. I took the stump in defense of the W.C.T.U. while I was in Congress. This organization is formed of some of the best women in the country—and the sooner they learn the type of man whom they are helping, indirectly, to support, the better it will be for them. The difference between Mr. Anderson and myself is that Mr. Anderson believes in the unlawful use of illegally distilled poison—whisky; and I believe in the lawful control of temperate light wines and beer!"

The flaming, fiery La Guardia of these public statements, is in violent contrast to the hesitant, unassuming Major, revealed in his correspondence with men whom he truly respected.

On January 20, 1920, he addressed a dinner, honoring Cyrus Townsend Brady. Next day he wrote the guest of honor:

My dear Mr. Brady:
I feel that I ought to apologise. I made a rotten speech —and I know it. I had had an extremely trying day, and two speeches coming before your dinner. I so wanted to make a useful speech! Please forgive me.

And he carefully preserved Brady's reply, which read as follows:

My dear Mr. President:
Frankness is a quality I have ever essayed to cultivate. As to your speech, you call the term exactly. I have

heard you speak; I know you can do it in great style; I confidently expected you would. You didn't—and you lost a great opportunity, for it is rare that a more distinguished audience is gathered in New York. Brilliant speakers had preceded you. There is no more to be said except this: I well know that you were rushed to death, that you had made several speeches before, that night, that you had not anything to eat, and that you had rushed all over the city. Therefore we all made allowances. So the matter stands.

Now, my dear Mr. President, this is not written in any captious or fault-finding spirit. But you are still a young man, and although you have accomplished much, there are many possibilities yet before you.

Permit an old man who has accomplished little, but who has spoken much, and who knows the rules of the game, to give you a little advice: *Don't* attempt too much in the way of consecutive speaking. No physique can stand it, and no brain. You should have refused me —peremptorily, if need be.

After all, the whole affair does not matter very much. We all know you: we all know what you are, what you have been, what you can do. And the failure of last night will be forgotten in no time!

I thank you very much for the generous spirit of willingness that sought to oblige.

Yours sincerely,

* * *

The variety of his interests did not lessen. He continued to be engrossed in everything that came to his attention. On January 28, 1920, he was opening a fight to oppose daylight saving, announcing that the regulation of the day, according to God's own sunshine, is bound to return, and return to stay.

On February 19, he was appealing to his friend, Senator Calder, on behalf of a longer course at West Point. "I earnestly urge that the four-year course be maintained, and that the recommendation for reducing it to three years, be rejected. . . . You will understand my interest in military matters, as a former member of the Committee on Military Affairs."

On March 2, as Acting Mayor, he was vetoing a bill for a fountain in Crotona Park, the Bronx, on the ground that, "It would be a pity to mar it by this discarded piece of work, inartistic and grotesque," and suggested an art competition, limited to natives of the Borough.

Three weeks later he was up in arms in behalf of the Direct Primary Law. Writing to Miss Lucy Timme, of the League of Women Voters: "This is the day of progress. The people are taking greater active interest in political affairs than ever before. Each year there is more interest displayed in primary elections. It is the fear of this that makes the reactionary groups insist upon a repeal of the law. The greatest need of the day is to get more of the people interested in party affairs."

In April he was mediating a strike of the Children's Shoe Workers' Union, appointing a committee to study and establish a wage scale throughout the city, and giving the workers an increase of $2 per week.

Early in May he appeared before the Connecticut Legislature, urging the ratification of the Woman's Suffrage Amendment, and declaring: "The hope of American politics is the woman's movement. We have seen in every state in which women have been enfranchized, a better political condition, progressive laws enacted and the welfare of the state guarded."

In July, he was writing to the Commissioner of Street Cleaning, suggesting that the uniforms of the "White Wings" should be laundered in the city's penal institutions.

On July 19, 1921, he was writing to Mayor Hylan, suggesting that the higher officers of the Police Department be forced to undergo the same physical tests which President Roosevelt had directed for the United States Army. There was little enthusiasm in the Police Department as he requested that all Lieutenants, Captains and Inspectors be required either to walk ten miles a day for three consecutive days, or, in certain cases, that they ride thirty miles a day for the same period.

He turned from that to the formation of an industrial art committee, headed by Charles Dana Gibson, with the object of encouraging talented high school graduates to continue their artistic studies. And followed with a proposition for a local Disarmament Conference. "Disarmament should commence at home. . . . How few realize that New York City has a little army of her own. . . . I mean, that, in keeping with all of the unjust burdens placed on New York City by the State of New York, the city's share of expense toward the National Guard is out of all proportion to that of the rest of the State. New York City pays 70% of the cost of the National Guard. . . . There are 12,250 guardsmen in the city, as against 7,596 throughout the rest of the State. The city alone, now has an army half the size of the entire regular army of the United States just prior to the Spanish War. . . . "Now is the time to consider the military burden on the city, and to have a little Disarmament Conference, all our own, right here in New York City."

On April 9, 1921, he was mediating to prevent a strike in the Housewreckers Union, and becoming very busy indeed in the study of the housing problem in the metropolis.

His idealism frequently carried him to extremes, but there was no doubt of his sincerity. On April 11, 1920, he wrote to the American League Baseball Club of New York, 30 East 42nd Street, as follows:

Dear Sirs:

I beg to acknowledge with thanks receipt of season pass No. 507, and desire to thank you for your thoughtfulness in sending it to me.

Inasmuch as I have made it an ironclad rule not to accept any passes, or favors of any kind, while in public office, I am compelled to return it to you.

I wish to make it clear that I understand fully the kind spirit in which it was sent; but, under the circumstances, I am sure that you will likewise understand my attitude in returning the same.

I hope to attend several of the games, and will do so

every time I get a chance to leave the office. I am very fond of the game, and I know of no better way of spending a disengaged afternoon.

Sincerely,

(Signed)   F. La Guardia

The same sentiment actuated him when, in October of that year, he declined the Vice-Commandership of his American Legion Post. In so doing, he insisted that "if the American Legion is to attain its potential strength, nothing should be permitted which would give the impression that the Legion is to become an instrument in the hands of politicians."

His philosophy is even more strikingly revealed in a personal letter which he wrote to a friend early in the year when Mayor Hylan and Superintendent of Schools Dr. William Ettinger, were at swords' points. La Guardia described an interview with Dr. Ettinger in which he said:

> What I have tried to point out is, simply, that neither Dr. Ettinger nor the Mayor should permit personal feelings to interfere with the exercise of their respective duties. . . . My sympathies are, of course, entirely with the Education Department. However, as a public official, it is my duty to endeavor to bring about co-operation between that Department and the City Administration. I do this solely for the purpose of expediting routine work at the Board of Estimate, relating to the Department of Education.
>
> You will readily understand that, politically, it would be to my personal advantage to play off one against the other! This I refuse to do. I look upon my position as a minority member of the Board of Estimate, and the minority representative in the city administration, as a constructive and not a destructive task. Hence my attitude and statement concerning the Department of Education.

His consideration of City affairs, however, did not reduce his interest in those of the State and Nation. He had already formed a habit, which he was to follow throughout his public career—despite the long hours at his desk, the ceaseless parade of interviewers, and the endless telephone calls: he still insisted that copies of all newspapers be placed upon his desk twice daily!

Thus he kept himself informed concerning public events, and continually he felt the pulse of public opinion; nor was he hesitant in his efforts to mould it. When on October 20, 1920, he learned that President Wilson had invited former Premier Orlando of Italy to visit the United States as a guest of the White House, La Guardia was quick to sense a political motive behind the invitation. Regarding himself as a spokesman of Italian-Americans, he promptly summoned a stenographer, and rapped out a public statement:

> The day of the hyphenate vote is past. The Italians will vote as Americans, and, as Americans, they will repudiate the policies of Woodrow Wilson. This is no time for Mr. Orlando, or anybody else, to come to this country and get mixed up in local internal affairs. The citizens of Italian extraction . . . will not tolerate Mr. Orlando, or any other distinguished person, coming to this country at this time, when the spirit or the purpose of the invitation is so doubtful.
>
> We serve notice now, to Mr. Orlando, or any other foreigner, who comes to this country and gets mixed up in politics here, that *we* can go to their countries and do the same—and we will retaliate, if there is any foreign interference.
>
> I am certain that Mr. Orlando will be more than welcome in this country, bringing with him a member of his Cabinet, Mr. Sonnino, and Gabriele d'Annunzio, and we will give them a rousing reception—*after* election!

He was quick to apply the lessons of national events to local problems.

His ardent pacifism and the memory of his recent clashes with the Administration, formed the basis of his deep-seated opposition to Woodrow Wilson, and he supported the Republican ticket in the campaign of 1920. He denounced Governor

Smith's campaign manager for seeking "to pin on to the Governor the credit of passing the Teachers' Increased Salary law, when every one knows that it was a Republican Legislature that drafted and passed that bill," and he rejoiced when the Harding landslide swept the Republican, Nathan L. Miller, into the Executive Mansion at Albany. Before many months had elapsed, however, the Major was again off the reservation, denouncing both the National and State Administrations.

On January 27, 1921, before Miller had been in office a month, the Aldermanic President broke with him completely. He bitterly opposed the latter's Transit Commission program, characterizing it as "vicious" and "likely to deprive the city of its $300,000,000 investment" in the subways. As a member of the Board of Estimate, he participated in the hearings on the petition of the New York Transit companies for modification of their contracts, permitting an increased fare. The fight was exceedingly bitter, and the Republican La Guardia backed up the Democratic Hylan with all the vigor at his command.

It was the beginning of the Major's long-drawn-out feud with the Republican Old Guard in New York State!

He now found himself in a strange position. He had swung so far to the left that he was far too radical for his own party. But the Socialists would have none of him. Soviet sympathizers booed him heartily when, on February 28, 1921, he took the platform to debate Seymour Stedman, who had been the Socialist nominee for Vice President. At that time there seemed no place in American politics for the philosophy which he enunciated.

> I admit that we need a change—but a change is going on continually. There has always been exploitation. But there is less exploitation today than fifteen or twenty years ago. We have improved. What was considered radical then is conservative now.
>
> It has been demonstrated that exploitation ceases under a Socialistic form of government; but under a So-

cialistic form of government today in Europe, there is more supervision than ever. The trouble is that every one wants to supervise, and no one wants to produce. Under such a system, you are going to have faction politics. . . .

You Socialists have gotten into bad company. You have learned everything that is bad in both the old parties.

The hisses which he evoked by his remarks were the first sign of a coming storm. The Major's hour of trial was not far off. His brief spell of happiness had ended.

CHAPTER IX

TRAGEDY

FIORELLO LA GUARDIA had been a happy man that Summer of 1920.

He was at the peak of his public career, and the future was bright with promise. He expected to become Mayor of New York City the following year—a position generally regarded as the second in importance in the United States. Already he was being courted on every hand. He would not have been human had he not enjoyed the adulation. Life was very sweet in those days—and sweetest of all was the home life. The La Guardia menage was a very happy one. The young couple were wildly in love, and Thea was expecting a baby.

Her husband was delighted at the news. A great love for children has always been one of La Guardia's most marked characteristics. He was jubilant at the prospect of enjoying the companionship of a youngster of his own.

He kept his joy to himself. He had always drawn a sharp distinction between his public and private life. The latter he regarded as his own business. It was shared only by a few close friends of long standing.

He had drawn into his circle of intimates such men as Attilio Piccirilli, Honorio Ruotolo—famous sculptors both—Albert Spalding, the violinist, and the great Enrico Caruso. Sharing this intimacy was the austere Windels, and Congressman John Morin, stalwart conservative of Pennsylvania.

Happiness reigned in the little home on Christopher Street in Greenwich Village. There, taking refuge from the storm and strife of his daily life, the young husband frequently entertained his friends. Donning a big kitchen apron, he would prepare spaghetti as Mother Irene had taught him, and revel openly in the praise of his guests. Often he would take up the battered cornet of his Arizona days, and play in a fashion that would have brought joy to the heart of Bandmaster Achille.

In November Thea gave birth to a daughter. They christened the child Fioretta Thea after both parents; but the expected joy in her presence did not materialize.

The baby was very delicate from birth, and Thea herself did not recover properly. Her health failed rapidly, and the young husband became greatly worried.

He rented a house at Huntington, far out on Long Island, hoping that the invalids would improve if removed from the roaring city. He installed his little family there, and attempted to commute, spending long hours on the train. There was no improvement. The doctors told him the truth at last—his wife had tuberculosis.

They returned to New York and placed the baby in a hospital. Then he took Thea to Saranac Lake with its crisp mountain air; but she refused to remain. She wanted to be at home with her husband and baby. He could not stay with her. His duties kept him at City Hall.

Thea insisted upon coming home. She grew fretful as the disease progressed and La Guardia was desperate. He borrowed money right and left, pawned everything he owned, and bought a house in the Bronx on University Avenue where they moved on December 3, 1920.

Craig was hounding him relentlessly, endlessly storming about those telegraph bills! There were almost daily blasts in the newspapers. La Guardia flared back at him again and again —but he could not keep his mind on the feud. His thoughts were up on University Avenue.

His career was trembling in the balance. The conservative leaders of his own party were utterly disgusted with him. No longer was the Major their "fair-haired boy." He had failed utterly to acknowledge their leadership, and gone whooping off the reservation, flourishing his tomahawk, demanding the repeal of the State Prohibition Law, and denouncing the transit problem, in the most vitriolic terms at his command.

They decided that discipline was in order. Since he could not be controlled, he should be retired to private life. Early in the Summer of 1921 word went out from Headquarters that Aldermanic President La Guardia was to be denied the mayoralty nomination! Instead, the bosses intimated that their blessing would be bestowed upon Borough President Curran of Manhattan.

La Guardia was wild over the broken promise. He discussed the matter with the invalid Thea, and then decided to fight to the finish. On June 14 he announced that he would oppose Curran for the Mayoralty nomination, and that, as far as he was concerned, it would be "a penniless primary." His private troubles had already drained his purse—but they were only beginning!

It was soon evident that there was to be a four-cornered race. County Judge Reuben L. Haskell, of Brooklyn, and ex-Senator William L. Bennett, both announced their candidacies.

La Guardia opened his campaign on June 30, with a speech in the Bronx.

> I want to make my position very clear to you. What I am trying to do is to unite the Republican Party, and to keep it alive in this city. There is a growing demand on the part of the people of this city for a change in its administration.

He amplified his position in a statement explaining his candidacy. It declared:

> I have decided to enter the Republican primaries to contest the party's nomination for Mayor. I have done so after several weeks of deliberation and consultation with Republicans all over the country. I find there is a determination on the part of Republicans in every Borough, to support me in the primaries. . . . Disapproval of

and dissatisfaction concerning the Republican State Administration in the city of New York, is universal. I hear frankly from important Republicans, and confidentially from organization leaders, that the work of the Miller Administration, admittedly, will not be endorsed by the voters of the city. Republican organization leaders are cautioning me to soft-pedal his administration. I don't intend to soft-pedal it at all. I intend to bring the issue squarely and frankly before the enrolled voters of the party, and give to thinking Republicans an opportunity to protest against reactionary legislation and the unfair action of the up-state administration.

He stormed about the city as the race grew hotter. From the beginning, the contest lay between Curran and La Guardia—and meanwhile the health of the two invalids grew worse. The candidate raced home from his meetings to walk the floor with his baby, and he sat up night after night with his wife. His days were spent at his desk in City Hall.

On August 3 he made what was probably his first major political mistake. He summarily dismissed two of his appointees, charging them with "neglect of duty," but under conditions which caused the newspapers to flay him mercilessly. Both men discharged, Charles Rathfelder and Frederick Offikofer, were District Leaders who had failed to support his candidacy.

Next day the newspapers denounced him bitterly. *The Evening Post* carried an editorial headed "La Guardia's Misstep," which declared:

> President La Guardia's dismissal of two Republican District Leaders, employed in his office, is just the kind of performance we would expect from a Tammany official! Examiner Rathfelder refused to support La Guardia in his Bronx District, and La Guardia promptly discovered that Rathfelder should be dismissed for a couple of peccadilloes which no ordinary employer would hold against an office boy. Assistant Examiner Offikofer would not promise to support La Guardia in his Coney Island District, and after an interview with his chief, "retired."

Borough President Curran is quite right in saying that these boss tactics come with bad grace from one who spends most of his time denouncing the bosses.

Mr. La Guardia's acceptance of autocracy ought not to strengthen him in a Republican primary.

The same day the *Evening Mail* carried an editorial entitled "La Guardia Rules Himself Out." It declared his action "will cost him the good opinion of scores of Republicans who have hitherto held him in esteem. Such practices are Tammany practices. They typify conditions which the anti-Tammany cause is pledged to change. . . ."

Curran joined heartily in the denunciation and there was no doubt that the incident made a deep impression on the voters. Defending himself, La Guardia said:

> I looked forward to a pleasant, intelligent campaign with my opponents on the issues but if they start anything like giving out disputive statements and engage in personalities I can assure them I'll be there. The two gentlemen who were in my office can now devote all of their time to campaigning for the organization, but, of course, not at the City's expense!

Strangely, some twelve years later this same incident was made a campaign issue by Joseph V. McKee and undoubtedly cost him a great deal of support!

The campaign came to a hectic close with La Guardia trailing after Curran, hurling challenges to debate. But Curran ignored the challenges and the two never met on the platform to cross verbal swords.

On election day the machine went crashing through to victory. When the votes were counted the totals were: Curran —103,174; La Guardia—37,880; Haskell—29,468; Bennett—4,472.

It was a crushing blow to the La Guardias. Thea suffered a relapse and had to be removed to a hospital at Croton, N. Y. Two weeks later La Guardia was seized with a sudden pain at the base of the spine. Surgeons told him they must operate. The old war injury he received when he had crashed in a plane at Foggia finally resulted in an abscess, a direct result of his refusal to permit proper treatment at the time.

Waving aside the doctors, he went to Croton to be beside Thea. There, for two days, despite intense pain, he tried to comfort her. Finally she forced him to return and on October 3 he underwent an operation at Roosevelt Hospital. The operation was a success but during the time he was in the hospital burglars had ransacked the home on University Avenue of all the family treasures.

On October 16 he went home to receive the bitterest blow of all—little Fioretta, his daughter, was dead. La Guardia nearly went mad with grief. He turned from the tiny casket to the bedside of his stricken wife. She was too weak to attend the funeral and he went to Woodlawn Cemetery alone.

After the baby's death Thea had a more serious relapse and in desperation La Guardia took her again to the mountains. But it was in vain. Within a month she died.

After the funeral, when he returned to City Hall to pick up his duties, Charles L. Craig blazed away at him as of old.

"La Guardia is not telling the truth," he shouted. "The trouble is that he wanted to be Mayor and the people gave him their answer. Now he is sore. He's the 'late lamented La Guardia'!" For the time the prophecy seemed true. La Guardia for once seemingly had lost his fire. For the first and only time in his life he turned away from a fight. He sailed for Havana on December 19, when he still had two weeks of his term to serve. With him went his friend Piccirilli and they did not return until January 1, 1922.

CHAPTER X

PRIVATE LIFE—AND PUBLIC

THE great adventure was at an end.

The crusader had been disarmed and driven from the lists. La Guardia was through politically. Every one agreed on that. The crushing defeat in the primaries meant the end of his public career. The Old Guard chuckled over the "crazy little idealist," who had presumed to defy the organization. Then it forgot about him.

His epitaph was chronicled by the *Westchester Globe*, which declared editorially:

> The prestige of a La Guardia in office has gone and will not return. A political party, in the march onward, has little use for the man who denounces the party which gave him office, when he goes out of that office. . . . The Republican Party will live on, while individuals drop out of sight.

Gone, too, was the cheering and the adulation. No longer did throngs of office-seekers and hangers-on dog his footsteps and court his attention. La Guardia was down and out!

Only John F. Hylan, who had been re-elected over Curran, remembered the broken and beaten man. On Dec. 31, 1921, the Mayor sent him a letter:

> I could not let this, your last day at City Hall, pass without writing you how sorry I am that you are leaving, and particularly that the people of this city are losing your services. I want to take this opportunity to express to you my appreciation and gratitude for your co-operation with me, and your splendid services to the people of the City of New York. . . . Your fight for the

The Aldermanic President and Mrs. La Guardia cast their ballots in the 1920 election.

"The Major made good his boast"—and produced home-made beer in a Harlem
drug store in 1926.

Five-Cent Fare, besides many other important matters in which you took such an active part, show, beyond any question, your independence and courage.

There is no office in the gift of the people that is too good for you.

His political career was ruined, true—but so poignant was the anguish of his bereavement that the beaten man never gave it a thought.

He was a tragic figure as the bells rang in the New Year of 1922. One brief twelvemonth had witnessed the collapse of his hopes and the wreck of his life. He hid himself from his friends, and night after night he paced alone those empty rooms of the little home on University Avenue.

One evening he picked up the battered old cornet, which had given so much pleasure to those whom he had greatly loved. He regarded it for a long moment and then put it gently aside. Next day he placed the instrument in a box and carried it down to the cellar.

He did not play it again.

It was necessary to earn a living, and the law was his profession. The name of La Guardia was after all an asset, and so it came about that the firm of La Guardia, Sapinsky & Amster was formed. Its first retainer came from the Free State of Fiume, for which it served as special counsel.

Toward that law office, the aged, the infirm, the weak and the unfortunate began to turn their steps in increasing numbers. There they found a hearing from a quiet, reserved, soft-voiced man with pain-seared eyes. There an ambitious Italian youth came seeking a place. He obtained it when he explained to his employer that he wanted to be a lawyer. Many nights the man remained late, advising the boy. It was the beginning of the career of Vito Marcantonio, later Congressman and a power in New York politics.

Others enlisted his aid as the weeks dragged by. Among them was the Sacco-Vanzetti Defense Committee, seeking

aid for the pair who were just beginning to become a *cause
celèbre* in American history.

Their plight appealed to the sympathetic attorney, and the
charge that they had not received a fair trial aroused his never-
long-dormant liberalism. He accepted the case and flew to
Boston to interview Vanzetti.

"I had quite a long talk with him," explained the Major,
years later.

> There was never any doubt in my mind that he was
> demented. I could not get him to discuss his case at all.
> He just paced up and down, waving his arms and shout-
> ing that he was a martyr in the 'Class War.'
> Years later, just before the two men were executed, I
> made another flying trip to Washington, trying to per-
> suade Governor Fuller, with whom I had served in Con-
> gress, to commute their sentences.
> Of course I failed.
> Fuller told me in confidence that he was absolutely
> convinced that both men were guilty.

There were other interests. He was persuaded to take up
the case of Vincent St. John, one of the many defendants who
had been convicted, along with William D. Haywood, during
the postwar "Red" hunt. La Guardia examined the evidence
and became convinced that St. John had been "framed." The
evidence indicated that, although the man had once belonged
to the I. W. W., he was no longer even a member when arrested while prospecting in New Mexico. After months of
effort, La Guardia succeeded in getting him pardoned.

Nor did the Wets forget their champion. He was offered
membership on the General Committee of the Association
against the Prohibition Amendment, and on May 17 he wrote
to Stuyvesant Fish, the Treasurer, saying:

> My dear Mr. Fish:
> I beg to acknowledge your letter of May 16, 1922.
> I would accept your kind invitation of becoming a
> member of your General Committee, were it not for the

suggestion which you make in your letter, that there will be no obligation "in any way for active work."

I am not accustomed to inactivity, and hence can not accept your invitation.

He was promptly assured that he could be as active as he wished, and on May 31 he became a member of the Committee.

During the same month he joined the Fraternal Order of Eagles, and speedily became a leader in their campaign for old age pensions. It was the beginning of a battle which he was to wage for ten years.

Gradually he was being drawn back into active life.

One day he found in his mail a letter sent by two officers who had served under him during the World War, and who were then patients in the Army Hospital at Denver, Col. They begged his support for the Bursom Bill, pending in Congress, which would provide retirement for Emergency Officers.

La Guardia began circularizing his old colleagues in the House in behalf of the legislation.

His interest in the housing problem revived. It was vital in the New York of those days when the postwar shortage of shelter worked untold hardship on teeming millions. Additional legislation was needed to protect them from the profiteering landlords. The case appealed to La Guardia, and before long the Major was back in harness, dashing about, addressing and organizing associations of tenants.

At the suggestion of his old friend, Mayor Hylan, he was appointed special counsel for the City of New York to represent it in condemnation proceedings, instituted against the Queens County Water Supply Company. His legal prestige was increased when he succeeded in reducing the award made against the City from $11,000,000 to $3,500,000. This success led to another appointment and he returned to Washington to represent New York City in its fight to obtain a 30-foot ship channel in Jamaica Bay.

Suddenly he plunged into work with a kind of bitter vehemence. He had discovered that it kept him from remembering the past. Once that realization registered, he never gave himself a moment's rest. For the next six years he drove himself almost vindictively. Few men have labored as did this man, in his endeavor to forget.

He was afraid to be alone with his thoughts and he sought out his old friends again. Once more they began to drop in at "Villa Thea." Naturally the talk was frequently about politics. Many of them were Italian and they beamed approval as their host, actuated by a fierce pride in his ancestry, eloquently discussed the glory that was Rome.

There, on March 16, 1922, the League of Italian-American Republican Clubs was born. It was evidence that his interest in things political had reawakened.

The league proved unexpectedly successful. Club after club was established in the Italian sections of the city, and soon the movement expanded into upstate communities. The Major was their inspiration. He dashed from one club to another, lecturing, explaining, organizing. The politically sagacious recalled the strength of the support which he had mobilized in Italian sections during the campaign for Aldermanic President. Then a pair of smart newspapermen remembered his feud with Miller and acted upon the inspiration.

In June the Hearst papers began to boom the little Major for Governor of New York. It is doubtful if this support was disinterested. William Randolph Hearst himself wanted to run upon the Democratic ticket and he was not averse to encouraging La Guardia to split the opposition. The Major was invited to write a series of political articles for the Hearst *Evening Journal*. He dipped his pen in vitriol and lashed out at the Republican Old Guard with all his former vigor. With plenty of old scores to settle, he leaped at the opportunity to discuss them in type. He flayed the G.O.P. organization and all its policies.

The La Guardia boom grew with amazing rapidity. By

midsummer his candidacy actually appeared to threaten Governor Miller's chances for renomination. The bosses began to be really worried. They did not relish the prospect of a La Guardia contest, with the ever-popular Al Smith looming threateningly upon the Democratic horizon.

On June 29, 1922, the Major electrified the State by tossing his hat into the ring. He announced that he would run as an Independent Republican candidate, if Governor Miller were renominated. He denounced the chief executive as the pet of the "power interests," and the Hearst backing made him a force to be reckoned with. When he began organizing "Modern Republican" clubs all over the State, things looked bad. The Italian-American clubs composed a nucleus which was expanding in every direction.

The leaders went into a hasty conference. It was all too apparent that they had written the La Guardia political obituary somewhat prematurely. They recognized his present strategic position. He could not possibly be elected but his independent candidacy would undoubtedly defeat Miller and with him the Republican ticket. Something had to be done—and Sam Koenig was delegated to do it.

The New York County leader went to the trouble-maker and offered him a chance to return to Congress. It really wasn't much of a chance—but it was the best they had to offer. Tammany had recaptured La Guardia's old district but the Republicans still held a seat on the upper East Side of Manhattan. Koenig offered it to La Guardia.

It was in the Twentieth Congressional District where he had campaigned for Isaac Siegel four years before. Siegel didn't want a renomination. The Tammany Tiger was reputed to be preparing to make one mighty effort to wipe out this last Republican stronghold on Manhattan Island and there was a growing Socialist movement to contend with. La Guardia could have the place—and welcome.

The Major considered the offer carefully. He remembered the ovation he had received on 116th Street, in 1918. He discussed the prospects with Edward Corsi, the Italian leader, and received the promise of the latter's support. La Guardia decided at last that he had a chance to win.

His political acumen was quick to realize his tactical advantage. Better than any one else, he knew he was in a position to dictate terms and he laid them down defiantly. He would accept the nomination—IF—

IF, first of all, he insisted, he was not to be bound by the party platform. He reserved the right to repudiate it *in toto*, if he so desired and to substitute for it a platform of his own making. Furthermore he would run only IF he were permitted to publish his platform and make it the leading campaign issue.

The disgusted Republican elder statesmen gagged at the mere suggestion—but their plight was desperate. After all, they knew that the man they had so ostentatiously discarded held the whip hand once more and that, if he persisted in his determination to run independently Governor Miller was inevitably doomed to defeat. They gagged, but none the less, holding their noses, they gulped it down! On August 30, he accepted the Congressional nomination.

The Republican bosses breathed a sigh of relief. They had no fear of his election, and his acceptance removed a threat to the Miller candidacy. They mobilized behind the Governor, and, incidentally, went down to defeat before the triumphant Al Smith.

Meanwhile La Guardia prepared for another under-dog struggle. Once it was launched he threw himself into it with all his heart. It provided partial oblivion for the recent tragedies. He forgot his own pain in fighting, and for the next decade he fought like a maniac. In so doing, he was to write his name in history.

*   *   *

The campaign of 1922 proved to be a bitter and dirty political fight. But it began very quietly. Harlem did not realize what was coming when the voluble Major and his quiet German secretary moved silently into the district, rented a corner store, and established headquarters. The neighborhood had never experienced a La Guardia campaign, with its accompaniment of red fire and brimstone.

The district extended from Central Park to the East River, between 99th and 120th Streets. It contained a population Italian and Jewish. Tammany appealed to the latter element by nominating Henry Frank, a Jewish lawyer, and from the beginning it attacked La Guardia as a "carpet-bagger," coming down from his home in the Bronx to run for office in a Manhattan district.

The powerful Socialists combined with the less-numerous Social Laborites and nominated William Karlin for the seat. They prepared to fight both La Guardia and Frank impartially.

The Major laid his plans carefully. He secured Benjamin Siegel, brother of the Congressman he was trying to succeed, as his campaign manager and enlisted the support of the regular Republican organization in the district.

The problem of financing the campaign was not as serious as he had feared it might be. The party organization was largely controlled by Italian-American leaders and, since the candidate was one of their own people, they promptly mobilized behind him. The usual contributions were forthcoming.

Corsi began canvassing the district and the Italian population responded enthusiastically. The Old Guardsmen decided that they had played very clever politics in clearing the way for Miller.

Then La Guardia issued his platform—and it sent shivers down conservative spines. It was utterly radical in those days. The "wild man" came out for such things as a minimum wage law, old age pensions, child labor restrictions, national maternity legislation, abolition of labor injunctions, modification of the Volstead act and legalization of light wines and beers.

He advocated the direct primary and equality of opportunity for women.

He opposed film censorship and demanded an eight-hour day, freedom of speech, unrestricted immigration and the initiative and referendum. Finally, in response to a questionnaire from the League of Women Voters, he declared himself in favor of United States leadership in the outlawry of war.

The Republican stalwarts moaned dismally when they read this program, but the moans turned into yelps of open anguish when the candidate proceeded to amplify his conception of his own party.

"I am a Republican," announced La Guardia, "but I am not running on the Republican platform. I stand for the republicanism of Abraham Lincoln; and let me tell you now that the average Republican leader East of the Mississippi doesn't know any more about Abraham Lincoln than Henry Ford knows about the Talmud.

"I may as well tell you now, for it wouldn't be fair to put it off until after I am elected, that I don't fit in at all with the average so-called 'Republican' in the East. I am a Progressive. I want to work with such men as Senator Borah, Senator Johnson, Senator Brookhart and Senator La Follette."

The very names of most of these men were anathema to the G.O.P. chieftains and unrestrained opinions were voiced in the Union League Club that the Harlem candidate was no better than a Socialist.

Only one of the leaders to whom he had announced his allegiance had any standing in the East. Hiram Johnson was fondly remembered by the Progressive element as the running mate of Theodore Roosevelt in 1912. Johnson had been partially sanctified by his association with the great T.R. and the blue-bloods hoped that he might disown La Guardia's candidacy. They were swiftly undeceived.

The Californian sent a warm endorsement to the iconoclast, enclosing it in a letter from San Francisco, dated Oct. 13, 1922, which read:

My dear Mr. La Guardia:

I am enclosing with this a note which, of course, you are at liberty to use, if you think it will be of any benefit to you. I dictated it very hastily, and it may not be what you want. My heart goes with it, however, and my prayers for your success.

(Signed)   Hiram W. Johnson.

The candidate released Johnson's endorsement on Oct. 23. It was a strong statement, which read in part:

There are many of us, three thousand miles from the scene of your campaign, who are earnestly hoping for your success. Knowing you as I do, and realizing the loyalty and courage with which you have ever served the people, I feel confident that the voters of your district will return you to the post where you have served with such honor and distinction.

In the next few years, our country will need men like you in Congress.

I wish I were on the ground, to be of some real service to you.

You will win because you deserve to win.

Between the writing of this statement and its release, La Guardia had committed himself to a proposed constitutional amendment, permitting Congress to review the decisions of the Supreme Court. The radical nature of this proposition aroused the conservatives and they were quick to make use of it in an effort to wring a disavowal of the La Guardia candidacy from the California Senator.

The same day that the Johnson endorsement appeared, the National Security League, whose query had committed the candidate to the proposal in the first place, telegraphed to the Californian:

NEW YORK PAPERS THIS MORNING PUBLISH LETTER FROM YOU ENDORSING LA GUARDIA STOP WE ASSUME THIS MEANS YOU SUPPORT HIS ADVOCACY SUPREME COURT DECISIONS STOP PLEASE WIRE ANSWER COLLECT.

The Progressive leader dismayed the opposition by the reply which he flashed back, also on Oct. 23. It read:

> I DO NOT KNOW WHAT YOU ARE TALKING ABOUT IN YOUR TELEGRAM TO ME STOP I DO KNOW LA GUARDIA AND IF I HAD ONE THOUSAND VOTES IN HIS DISTRICT I WOULD CAST THEM ALL FOR HIM.
>
> HIRAM W. JOHNSON.

The Johnson support counted heavily in La Guardia's favor and when Mayor Hylan also came out for him openly, his candidacy began to appear threatening. The Democratic Mayor declared himself in an address, delivered at Star Casino, in mid-October. In the course of his remarks he said:

> La Guardia is the type of public official that renders service for the benefit of his constituents, regardless of political affiliations. Since he left City Hall, I myself have called upon him for services for the benefit of the city.
>
> There is no office within the gift of the people that's too good for him. Now that he is running for Congress, I hope that all my friends in Harlem, regardless of party, will vote for him.

This speech, delivered on the closing day of registration, October 12, at a huge charitable festival given by an Italian benevolent society, The Sons of Columbus, proved very effective.

He also received unexpectedly strong support from the press. The *N. Y. American* flamed out in his behalf with an editorial on October 20, outlining his stand:

> He is for the Soldiers' Bonus, a Ship Subsidy . . . enforcement of Labor Laws . . . good roads, decent pay for Federal employees, public development of water power, sale of electric current at cost. . . .
>
> Such a platform is a definition of progressivism.

138

The Evening Mail, summarizing his aldermanic presidential campaign, called him a "bonny fighter."

The candidate himself was everywhere. He stormed all over the district, tossing his black mane and denouncing his Tammany opponent. He soon lost his regard for the latter whom, in September, he had referred to as "the finest sort of gentleman."

He showed no bitterness toward his Socialist opponent, and when Karlin challenged him to a public meeting, the Major responded with a letter dated September 25:

> My dear Bill:
> I have your favor of September 24, and was glad to hear from you.
> While it is true that we are both candidates for Congress, I hardly see the necessity for making your letter so cold and formal.
> Why, bless your heart, of course I'll debate with you . . . but just how interesting the debate will be, I don't know. After all, our views on Labor cannot be so far apart since we are both fighting the same battle . . . Let me hear from you soon.
> With kindest regards.
>
> F. La Guardia.

Later in the campaign he discussed his Socialist opponent with a representative of *The World.*

"Mr. Karlin," declared La Guardia, "is a conservative running on a radical ticket. I am a radical running on a conservative ticket. I know Mr. Karlin very well. We have worked together on certain labor cases. I know his sincerity. I know that he would represent to the best of his ability some of the very ideas which I represent; but, if he were elected to Congress, he would be alone. . . . As a man, Mr. Karlin is very capable. As a Congressman he would be powerless. . . .

"It has so happened in all the ages that some have labored and others have, without labor, enjoyed a large proportion of the fruits. That is wrong and should not continue. To secure to each laborer the whole product of his labor (or to do that as nearly as possible) is a worthy goal of any good government. That is my platform.

"But when the average Republican leader in the East hears it, he thinks that I am quoting from Karl Marx. It is quoted, but not from Karl Marx. I quoted it from Abraham Lincoln."

His stand on Prohibition was amplified in a telegram to the *New York Globe:*

AM FOR MODIFICATION OF VOLSTEAD ACT TO PERMIT LAWFUL SALE OF LIGHT WINES AND BEER AND IF NECESSARY CONSTITUTIONAL AMENDMENT TO PERMIT SUCH MODIFICATION. . . . HAVE CONSISTENTLY AND EFFECTIVELY FOUGHT AGAINST PRESENT INEFFICIENT HYPOCRITICAL AND DEMORALIZING LAW AM NOT IN FAVOR OF USELESS PROMISES OF REPEAL UNLESS BACKED BY INTELLIGENCE AND ABILITY TO EFFECTIVELY CARRY ON FIGHT STOP WE HAVE HAD TOO MUCH TALK OUT OF CONGRESS AND NO FIGHT IN CONGRESS ONLY PLACE WHERE REPEAL IS POSSIBLE STOP VOLSTEAD ACT MAKES IT POSSIBLE FOR RICH TO BUY AND USE IMPORTED LIQUOR OF CHOICE VINTAGE WHILE THE POOR ARE DRINKING POISON HOOCH MADE OUT OF DENATURED ALCOHOL OBTAINED ON PERMITS ISSUED BY U S GOVERNMENT.

As the campaign continued, La Guardia plunged into it with all his old vigor. He spoke on the street corners, and each night found him dashing through the East Side streets on a truck, pausing every block or two to pour out denunciations of Tammany beneath a flaming torch.

A wave of enthusiasm followed his progress—and suddenly the women of the district rose in his behalf. They flocked into his headquarters, demanding to be put to work, and little Miss Fischer found work for them to do. "The Daughters of Italy" became a permanent organization and soon 350 girls were engaging in a house-to-house canvass on behalf of the La Guardia candidacy.

Typical of the spirit aroused was a postscript, scrawled at the bottom of a letter containing a $50 contribution from a business man, one Jacob C——. It read:

> Dear Mr. La Guardia: I am Mr. C——'s private secretary, to whom Mr. C—— dictated this letter. I live in your district. This will be my first vote and I will certainly cast it for you and work for you. We have five votes in our family and I am going to see to it that every one of them votes for you.
> (Signed) Estelle K——.

Mr. C—— received the usual letter of acknowledgment, but Miss K—— had a note of her own beginning:

> "I appreciate your enthusiasm even more than I do your boss's check."

Touched by the feminine efforts in his behalf, the candidate arranged to have a box of candy distributed to each polling place on election day. It was given to the women workers, with the compliments of the La Guardia campaign committee.

Meanwhile the rising tide of enthusiasm was distinctly disturbing to the Tammany leaders. The Tiger chiefs, in council, went over the situation and decided that the Italian vote was probably lost but that it could be off-set by concentrating on the Jewish population in the district.

In mid-October Tammany began a drive for the Hebrew ballots. Frank sent Jewish New Year cards throughout the districts and the Tiger Board of Strategy closely studied the reaction to this move. It was favorable and the Tiger tacticians thereupon decided to stage a *coup-d'etat* shortly before election.

As a result, every Jewish voter in the district received a post card, which read:

The most important office in this country for Judaism is the Congressman. Our flesh and blood are united with our own on the other side of the ocean. Only through our Congressman can we go to their rescue.

There are three candidates, who are seeking your vote: One is Karlin, the atheist. The second is the Italian La Guardia, who is a pronounced anti-Semite and Jew-hater.

Be careful how you vote.

Our candidate is Henry Frank, who is a Jew with a Jewish heart, and who does good for us. Therefore it is up to you and your friends to vote for our friend and beloved one, Henry Frank, for Congressman.

(Signed)   The Jewish Committee.

The distribution of these cards created consternation in La Guardia headquarters. The Major realized that it might prove to be the turning point of the election. He called all his speakers in for instructions and prepared to do his best to counteract the trick.

Standing behind a pine board table in the back of the store, his face flushed with anger, La Guardia denounced the canard. He appealed to his supporters to go out and nail the lie. Then he handed to each of them a typewritten set of "Instructions for Speakers," that read as follows:

1. Speak, if there are only two people to speak to.
2. Adhere to the following text: "Friends, a last-moment campaign trick has been pulled by a defeated candidate. This morning in the mail, the following post cards were received by *Jewish voters only*. (Show post card.) It reads as follows: (Here was incorporated the text of the card.) Call attention to the fact that La Guardia has conducted a clean campaign. He has not resorted to personalities, and is a broad-minded, fair man. Religion was discarded in American politics twenty years ago.
   You will notice that this is an anonymous communication; that there is no address on it. There is no name attached to it. If there was, Major La Guardia

could have had the person responsible for sending it
arrested for criminal libel! It is a cowardly attempt
to create racial prejudice against Major La Guardia,
and it shows Mr. Frank is defeated, and is resorting
to any tactics.
Let the answer of the fair-minded, intelligent voters
be united, and vote for La Guardia, to resent this
un-American attack—this anonymous and monstrous
lie.

That night the streets of Harlem rang with the denunciation of the Tammany trick as La Guardia and his speakers
dashed frantically from street corner to street corner. The
backfire was not sufficient, however. The Major realized he
would be unable to reach great numbers of Jewish voters who
spoke no English.

Thereupon he decided to retaliate in his own fashion. He
cleared everybody out of his headquarters, and paced up and
down like an angry lion, while little Miss Fischer's flying pencil transcribed the words he rapped out: "An Open Letter to
Henry Frank." As soon as it was typed, he himself translated
it into Yiddish and directed that it be printed in that language.

Next morning La Guardia's girl workers flooded the District with the "Letter to Frank," printed in Yiddish. Translated, it read as follows:

My dear Mr. Frank:
    At the beginning of the campaign I announced that I
would not indulge in personalities nor in abuse of my
opponents. I have kept that pledge faithfully. . . . The
issues of the campaign are of such great importance that
the people of this district are entitled to hear them discussed intelligently by their candidates.
    You have seen fit, however, to resort to the kind of
campaigning which was discredited in American politics over twenty years ago. You, your captains and your
canvassers are making a strong, racial-religious appeal
for sympathy votes, based entirely upon religion. I regret exceedingly that this has happened. However I have

always met a fight on any issue openly. I will take combat wherever it is offered me.

Very well, then. On the issue which you have raised, I hereby challenge you to publicly and openly debate the issues of the campaign, THE DEBATE TO BE CONDUCTED BY YOU AND ME *ENTIRELY IN THE YIDDISH LANGUAGE*—the subject of the debate to be, "Who Is Best Qualified to Represent All the People of the Twentieth Congressional District . . ." We will suit your convenience in every respect.

This handbill proved to be the master-stroke of the campaign. The ghetto rocked with excitement. Its occupants insisted that the Tammany candidate accept the challenge. (La Guardia, incidentally, had been informed that Frank could not speak Yiddish, even before he issued the invitation.) The be-deviled Tammanyites went around frantically proclaiming that Frank was too ill to appear.

The explanation failed to convince the doubting Sons of Israel. They turned out en masse when the fiery Major invaded their community. He delivered three flaming speeches, "ENTIRELY IN THE YIDDISH LANGUAGE," and the rabbis themselves led the applause when he denounced his opponent for evading the challenge.

The Jewish vote was slipping—and Tammany knew it. Stung to desperation Frank sent La Guardia a letter, published on November 5. It read in part:

A challenge from you, with your well known anti-Semitic tendencies to debate in Yiddish is an insult and an affront to the Jewish electives in our community. You are certainly not qualified to represent the people, and you will know it on the day when the people send you back, bag and baggage, to your little cottage and sun-parlor on University Avenue in the Bronx.

For all of which reasons, I decline your challenge.

Now it was La Guardia who was roused to a white heat. The reference to the sun-parlor, which he had purchased for his stricken family, and where both Thea and the baby had gasped out their lives, made him almost insane with rage. He stormed through the Jewish sections, speaking upon street corners and sobbing with grief and fury:

> That letter speaks for itself. A man who could write that has sunk to the lowest possible level. For Frank to refer to the "sun-parlor" in my home is as low and unmanly an act as a man could resort to. He *knows* that I was compelled to move out of my district and purchase that house with the sun-parlor in order to try to save the life of my poor wife.

His hearers nodded sympathetic understanding. They chuckled as he continued with bitter irony:

> My Democratic opponent is making a racial appeal. He is asking the voters of this district for their votes on the ground that he is a Jew. . . . After all, is he looking for a job as a schamas * or does he want to be elected Congressman?

The day before election, Frank played his last card. He turned over to the police a "Black Hand" letter which warned him to withdraw from the campaign in La Guardia's favor. Democratic speakers eloquently denounced the threat.

That night the Major swept through the streets of Harlem, characterizing this development as a trick and an aspersion upon every voter of foreign extraction in the district. He advised Frank to discharge his press agent and denounced his rival for pretending illness.

"His is a diplomatic sickness," called the Major, from the tail end of a truck, as midnight approached and the red fire died out. "He was seen all over the district this morning! He's using this sick game to sidestep my challenge to debate in Yiddish. He was caught making an appeal on religious grounds."

Then, his throat raw and his voice rasping, he went quietly

---

* Schamas. The Yiddish term for the caretaker of a synagogue.

home to the desolate little house on University Avenue—to be alone with his thoughts.

Next day Harlem went to the polls—and when the votes were counted the Major was back in Congress.

He had beaten Frank by 254 votes.

The Democratic candidate promptly filed a protest. He charged that "bands of La Guardia's supporters intimidated the inspectors and were led by La Guardia himself. In one particular instance, one of our watchers was threatened with bodily harm by Mr. La Guardia."

The victor dismissed the charge with a shrug of the shoulders and the single word—"Silly!" But an astonished New York sat up and chuckled. *Tammany charging that it had been counted out by gangster tactics!* This was something new, indeed!

CHAPTER XI

THE CRUSADER RIDES AGAIN

THE election of La Guardia, on his own Independent-Liberal platform in the Autumn of 1922, had again focused the spotlight on New York's rebel Congressman. The Progressive revival, which was to culminate in the La Follette-Wheeler Third Party movement of 1924, was just getting under way. Progressives were thick in Wisconsin, Minnesota and Nebraska. But the discovery of one in New York was disturbing.

Conservative Republicans were of two minds; either La Guardia was a political accident, who should be ignored, or he was a menace who should be exterminated! In the ensuing ten years they were to attempt both plans of action, with a notable lack of success.

Needless to say, the Progressives welcomed the new recruit with open arms. He was invited to attend the Congressional Conference which they held in Washington on December 1 and 2, 1922, before the session began. It was called by the elder La Follette, and included Senators Borah, Brookhart, Capper, France, Frazier, Ladd, McNary, Norris, Owen, Sheppard, Shipstead, and Senator-elect Burton K. Wheeler of Montana. Of the twenty-three members of the House, only La Guardia came from east of the Mississippi. Its avowed purpose was to make trouble for the Tories of both parties.

La Guardia had not yet won his spurs as a leader of the Liberals in the House. There John Nelson of Wisconsin was in command of the political rebels. In fact, the men who were later to follow his banner, knew so little about him that he was not even named to one of the Committees which grew out of the Washington Conference.

He had enlisted, however, for the duration of the war and declared his allegiance to the cause in a public statement.

> The Progressive group in Congress," he asserted, "is under the leadership of that able Progressive and great statesman, Senator La Follette of Wisconsin. . . . There is no greater danger in this country than that of having the powers that have heretofore controlled the Government, keep control of the Courts. . . . Let's clean both parties so that the American people may be voting for decent government, instead of against it.

Returning to New York from the conference, he at once resumed his attack on the Republican Party in New York State. On December 11 he spoke at the Institutional Synagogue, on "The Awakening of the Progressive Spirit in This Country," and next morning leaders of the stalwarts began to wonder whether or not they had used good judgment in permitting the firebrand to get back into public life, even in an attempt to save the governorship! He charged:

> We have witnessed in our own State, in the past two years, a wicked and heartless government, controlled by the connivance of the privileged few, for their benefit, disregarding the rights of the many and the comfort and happiness of the population of the entire State.
> The reactionaries, receiving powerful and privileged compensations in monopolies, want to return to the date of '96. This go-back movement, deliberately calculating and cruel, started on the 12th of November, 1918, the day after the Armistice, when the reactionaries succeeded in slipping over their kind of a government on the State of New York in the confusion and excitement of a Presidential Campaign. . . .
> Their work was not completed. They had their government and a subservient, backboneless, servile Legislature. Then there sure was a return to the old days . . . taking control of monopolies, disregarding the rights of the injured working man, but looking after the interests of the insurance companies . . . letting gas and elec-

tric light companies increase their rates, and protecting their continued monopolies by preventing the proper development of water power for the benefit of the people. . . .

They knew that not one of them could survive the test of a primary, hence the abolition of the primaries. . . . The manner and purpose of the repeal of the primaries in this state will be catalogued by history as one of the most heinous and unnatural acts of the crime wave from which this country suffered, as one of the aftermaths of the war.

Four months later, speaking in Erasmus Hall in Flushing, he carried the fight to his own party in no uncertain terms. He led the attack on a pet project of the New York G.O.P., warning the leaders that they would split the party, if they supported the acquisition of the existing surface car lines by the city.

It was one of the Major's best speeches, and it made a deep impression. His voice rang with sincerity, as he tore the New York County Committee's report to shreds. He declared:

There comes a time in the life of every public official, when he must decide between right and irregularity. Of late such times have come to public officials at shorter intervals and with unusual frequency. At times it seems difficult to oppose your own political family and take issue with close political friends. In the long run, however, even in politics, right conquers; and we have seen in the last fifteen years, strong and powerful political machines entirely beaten, destroyed and put out of commission.

In 1921, I was confronted with just such a situation. I had to decide whether I would be faithful and true to my oath of office as a city official, elected by the entire city, and take a stand according to what I believed was for the best interests of the city—the protection of its resources and property and the welfare of the 6,000,000 people residing in New York—or whether I would line up with the individuals then in absolute control of the party; submit to the will and ideas of my Governor, and the wishes of the traction trust; be a "good fellow," as it were, and not cause any trouble or "agitate," but just go along with the crowd and be "a regular guy." . . . I made my choice.

As was so frequently the case, his enthusiasm ran away with his sense of grammatical construction. The ideas tumbled over one another so fast, each struggling to emerge, as he rapped out his machine-gun staccato, that subjects and predicates were constantly mislaid.

His ideas registered, however, his audience being swirled along too rapidly on the torrent of his eloquence, to analyze his sentence structures!

He concluded his address with one of his favorite platform tricks—presenting a concrete example for the benefit of his hearers. He snatched his own telephone bill from his pocket, and read to his audience a notice, which pointed out that even if fewer calls were made, the subscriber would still be required to pay for the full month's allowance; but if *more* calls were used, an extra charge would be imposed for each additional call. "In other words," he shouted, "you pay if you don't use, and you pay if you do use, and the company gets it coming and going, and the public service commission is there to give it to them."

A few days later, on April 23rd, Mayor Hylan wrote him as follows:

My dear Congressman:
I wish to thank you for coming to the meeting last Saturday evening at Erasmus Hall in Flushing, in the District of Assemblyman Clayton, and speaking there in favor of a transit law that will give the people relief.

On April 27, La Guardia replied:

Hon. John F. Hylan,
Mayor, City of New York,
City Hall, New York City.

My dear Mr. Mayor:

Just a line to tell you that I received your kind letter
of April 23, 1923.

I really do not deserve any special thanks for having
done (and continuing to do) what I consider to be my
duty as a public official.

However, a word of thanks and appreciation is indeed grateful and encouraging in these trying times.

With kind personal regards,

Sincerely,

(Signed)   F. La Guardia.

When he had finished dictating this letter, the Major looked
at Miss Fischer, and chuckled.

"That's a good line!" he observed crisply.

The secretary raised her eyebrows.

"That: 'A word of thanks and appreciation is indeed encouraging in these trying times,'" he amplified. "Must keep
that in mind. It's worth remembering. I must use it again."

And he did.

Literally dozens of times. It became the sign manual of the
La Guardia correspondence in the ensuing years.

* * *

The crusader was back in the saddle indeed. And his attention was focused on his native city.

His next tilt was with the high cost of living, and his third
with New York landlords. He won both battles, to the considerable enhancement of his national reputation.

Early in 1923 he organized the Harlem Meat Strike, which
spread over the city at large and was followed by the reduction of 5¢ to 10¢ per pound in the price of meat. Then he revived his tenants' movements to force State protection of
lower rents in the congested slum section. Night after night

was spent in organizing and addressing meetings; and finally he staged an impressive mass demonstration in the great hall of the College of the City of New York.

Governor Alfred E. Smith, himself a champion of the poverty-stricken, became interested and sent for La Guardia. He asked the Major to co-operate with his legislative Housing Commission, and the Major accepted. The latter, in consequence, personally conducted the hearings before the commission, and presented the evidence. That evidence was impressive, and for the first time an astonished nation learned that families of eight and nine were living in two-room flats, and that, in some cases, they were domiciled in cellars and coal bins! When the hearings ended, the Housing Committee reported that it was necessary to extend the existing law by re-passing it in the next Legislature. La Guardia did not rest until he had put every candidate for the Assembly and the State Senate on record concerning the measure, and so assured its passage.

In between times he found leisure to head a committee which raised funds for the relief of the sufferers from the Ward's Island Hospital fire, which occurred on February 18, 1923.

He maintained his interest in the cause of the veterans, and sponsored a meeting of disabled emergency officers at Town Hall on January 18, to back the Bursum Bill. Meanwhile he had lashed out at Col. C. R. Forbes of the Veterans' Bureau in typical La Guardia fashion, concerning the case of a war-time comrade over which he had become aroused.

Pacing up and down his office, as usual, he splutteringly dictated another of the epistolary complaints with which Washington's departmental files are jammed:

"So," he shouted, shaking his finger at the serene Miss Fischer, "after much heralding and publicity of systematizing the work of the Veterans' Bureau, we find that it has been so scientifically systematized, as not to be able to find a veteran's papers! While I am writing you, and you are writing me, and the District Manager of District No. 2 is writing you, and a corps of clerks is looking for the papers, this veteran, unable to work, and on his reduced compensation, is not able to get enough to eat!

"It's a damn shame," he roared—

"Does that go in?" asked the unruffled secretary.

"That goes in!" snapped her explosive employer, "take it down." And the dictation proceeded.

"It is a damn shame! If it was possible to locate the papers to reduce this veteran's compensation, in all fairness it ought to be possible to locate them to have the matter looked into, the veteran properly examined, and compensation awarded, in accordance with the wishes of the American people, as expressed by Congress.

"The physical condition of a veteran can't be ascertained by long-distance examination."

This letter was dated January 11.

On February 24, he was quarreling bitterly, by correspondence, with Congressman Frank W. Mondell, floor leader of the House, over the proposed immigration law. La Guardia insisted that the figures quoted in the legislation, showed a disproportionate reduction, and asserted that the basis used was "artificial and arbitrary, and solely for the purposes of excluding Italian and Jewish immigrants."

His attention was turning to national subjects as the time approached for him to resume his seat in Congress. On March 12 he announced his appointments. His secretarial staff was to consist of Mr. Patsy Bruno, Mr. Robert Levy, and of course, the faithful Miss Fischer.

Miss Fischer was at last beginning to win recognition. In commenting on the appointments, one New York paper declared: "Miss Marie Fischer is well known in Republican circles. She served with Congressman La Guardia during two terms in Congress, and was his secretary when the Congressman was President of the Board of Aldermen. Miss Fischer has earned the reputation of being a 'practical politician,' and has a host of friends among the leaders throughout the city. She is known to be more progressive than the Major himself!"

His popularity was increasing, and his star was rising rapidly, even before Congress convened. He was the guest of honor at the dinner, on March 10, given by 350 Progressive women, at the Pennsylvania Hotel, and attended by Senator and Mrs. William A. Calder and other notables. The Republican bosses decided to go along with him, and the guest list included Mr. and Mrs. Samuel Koenig and Mr. and Mrs. Jacob Livingston (these two gentlemen being the G.O.P. leaders of Manhattan and Brooklyn, respectively). Mayor Hylan was invited, but declined because of a previous engagement. He expressed warm approval of his former colleague, however, in a letter dated March 9, 1923.

There was no doubt that La Guardia's star was again in the ascendent. In his home town at least, he was recognized as a leader of the new movement, and it was no wonder that he wrote to La Follette, saying: "I am quite convinced that there will be a rush to get on the Progressive band wagon at the next session of Congress."

Already he was being boomed to run as Vice-President on the Third Party ticket, which should be headed by La Follette, Hiram Johnson, Borah or Brookhart—although, when it came to the final decision, second place was given to Wheeler.

Trouble loomed briefly in the offing when the Tammany-controlled Board of Elections granted a re-count to Henry Frank. This re-count saw the La Guardia majority reduced first to 168 votes, and finally to 11. The attempt to unseat him failed, however, and he was sure of his seat for the next two years.

On June 10 he was officially retained as counsel for the Sacco-Vanzetti Defense Committee, and plunged into the preparation of a brief to be argued before Judge Webster Thayer a few months later. In between times he found leisure to rap off a communication to the United States Shipping Board.

Mailed in mid-June, it read:

> Can't something be done to stop the proposed joy ride on the refitted *Leviathan?*
>
> Will you kindly inform me if the $10,000,000 contract for the re-fitting of this ship, did not provide that the contractor would stand the cost of the necessary tests?
>
> If advertising is really necessary—and not knowing where the advertising genius who conceived this trip may be—it occurs to me that the ship might be advertised in keeping with her tradition and the spirit of the American people. Instead of the distinguished, carefully-chosen, powerful and wealthy persons invited as special guests, invite the same persons who were passengers in 1917 and 1918, in dark, crowded, uncomfortable holds of the ship, and who are now permanently disabled and lingering in Walter Reed Hospital, but a few blocks from your offices in Washington.
>
> Make them the recipients of your engraved invitations, and give them an opportunity of enjoying a bit of change from the dreary hospital life of the past five years and the benefit of ocean air, while your experts are testing the engines.
>
> Permit me, therefore, to say—and I am sure the distinguished guests will not resent the recall of your invitations—that it might be better that 1,000 wounded American veterans in the hospitals, be invited as guests of the American government.

Next day he received a testy reply from A. D. Lester, Chairman of the Shipping Board:

> Permit me to correct your misapprehension, by stating that the *Leviathan's* trial trip was initiated by the experts, who are responsible for her re-conditioning, operation and safety . . . and was included by them in the original cost. . . .
>
> The arrangements for the *Leviathan's* trial trip, including the number of guests thereon, are proceeding entirely with the plans and demands of the experts, in the formation of which the members of the Board have

no more part than you. Not being expert ourselves in such a matter, we are following, as we should, expert advice—and shall continue to do so.

La Guardia released this letter to the press, without comment. His epistle was only one of the first of those myriad communications with which he was to haze the Administration during the ensuing ten years. Thenceforward he made the nation's business *his* business, and his demands for explanations deluged every bureau in Washington.

Before departing for the capital, he scribbled a note to Congressman Hamilton Fish, vacationing in Paris:

Dated June 13th, it read:

My dear Hamilton:
Do hope you are having a good time. Plenty of political news here.
If you want to be Governor in 1924, please tell me that you would not refuse the nomination. Now is the time to make friends.

As the session approached, he perfected his alliance with the Progressive group in Congress, and worked with them on their plans for the coming year. Nelson wrote him as follows:

Of course we know that you are strongly with us, and we rejoice to have your co-operation. Mr. Frear informs us that you desire to go on the Judiciary Committee. This being so, I suggest that you make application to the Committee on Committees. . . .

And Samuel Untermyer wrote to say:

I am delighted that you are likely to be placed on the important Judiciary Committee of the House where there is abundant opportunity for unusual public service at this time.

La Guardia was exceedingly anxious for the assignment. He loved the law and felt that a place on this committee would give him an opportunity to help mold it. That ambition was not to be realized until years later, however. The Progressives did not get good committee assignments that session; in fact, they had to fight for their very lives to preserve their standing in the party.

The Major probably killed his last chance for the assignment when he announced that on the first day of Congress he proposed to introduce in the House Senator Borah's bill providing that only seven Supreme Court judges need concur in order to hold an Act of Congress unconstitutional.

La Guardia's statement was unduly optimistic.

> We anticipate no trouble or opposition to the proposed bill. The American people all over the country are tired of one judge in the Supreme Court—when the Court is divided—being able to declare unconstitutional, Acts of Congress which are in keeping with changed conditions and changed times. Some of the most important measures of Congress were recently declared unconstitutional by the United States Supreme Court by a five to four vote. The Constitution today must necessarily be construed in the light of new conditions and the advanced age we are living in.

The Progressives knew that they held the balance of power in the coming session, but they did not realize how bitterly they were to be tested.

The twenty-three Liberals, of whom La Guardia was one, held up the organization of the House on December 13, 1923, protesting against gag rule. Under the then rules, four men were able to smother any legislation they chose by virtue of their positions as Speaker, Majority Floor Leader and the Chairmen of the Steering Committee and the Committee on Rules.

The Progressives served notice of a demand for reform.

Nicholas Longworth, the Majority Leader, announced that he would not recognize them as a group, and threatened reprisal on committee assignments. The regular Republicans became very nasty indeed, and La Guardia was unpleasantly reminded that Henry Frank was still contesting his seat, and that he might lose it if he was not a good boy!

The stubborn Major stuck to his guns, however, and so did the others. Both intimidation and browbeating failed. They held up the election of the Speaker for eight ballots. Finally the regulars surrendered. Longworth met with the committee of the rebels, consisting of Congressmen Nelson, Woodruff and La Guardia, and a compromise was worked out. Under it, the old rules were to survive for thirty days, and then be replaced by more liberal ones. As soon as the compromise was adopted William H. Gillette was elected Speaker.

The House then began to function, and before 1924 got well under way, the leaders of the Administration discovered that New York's "Little Flower" had a bumblebee concealed in its petals. The Secretary of the Treasury, Andrew W. Mellon, picked it up first.

Congressman La Guardia wrote to Secretary Mellon on January 20, asking for information concerning the amount of taxation which would be necessary to produce money enough to pay a bonus to World War Veterans.

The Secretary of the Treasury replied with a peevish letter, dated February 3, in which he said:

> I regret that unless you can present some comprehensive plan by which you propose to raise the necessary money, or in what particular you propose the taxes shall not be reduced, I am unable to give you specific figures.

It was this paragraph of the Mellon communication which infuriated the Harlem Congressman. He promptly acted upon Mellon's suggestion, and after hours of research in the Congressional Library, drew up his own plan, which he introduced as a substitute for the Mellon tax reduction scheme. The latter was the pet project of the Administration, and enjoyed the benediction of Calvin Coolidge, who had succeeded to the Presidency the preceding year.

La Guardia declared that his program would reduce the income tax of the millionaires by 25 per cent, and that of wage earners 62½ per cent, whereas, he charged that the Mellon plan gave the wealthy taxpayers a 50 per cent reduction, and awarded only a 25 per cent decrease to the wage earner. He submitted his program to the Treasury Department on February 20, and on February 21, Mellon flatly rejected it.

Fireworks followed immediately.

The dumfounded Republican leaders heard their ostensible colleague cut loose on the floor of the House with a withering attack against their own Secretary of the Treasury. He named names—and they were big names. He charged that the Mellon plan was so arranged as to give special benefit to Secretary Mellon himself, to J. P. Morgan, Charles M. Schwab, Frank Munsey, the Rockefellers and others. The attack on Mellon was regarded as political treason, and Republican leaders attempted to call him off.

They were unable to do so.

Then they attempted to muzzle him—but that effort proved futile also. La Guardia could not be silenced by the means which were ordinarily employed to discipline recalcitrant members of the House. It was useless to deny him the floor, as was the usual practice, because he knew the rules better than they. The same mind which had soaked up seven languages in sponge fashion, had mastered the intricacies of parliamentary law with equal rapidity.

The rules of the House were ironclad. Under these rules, other troublemakers had been successfully eliminated by refusing them recognition. The New York Congressman ignored such refusals and simply *took* the floor. When the presiding officers attempted to shut him off, he was eternally bobbing up with his "questions of personal privilege" and "parliamentary inquiries," "points of order" and other privileged motions. They discovered that he could rattle off an entire speech, including it as a part of his statement of a single point of order! Finally they gave it up and let him have his own way.

The Democrats whooped with glee, as he resumed his attack upon Secretary Mellon's tax plan, again and again. His Progressive colleagues mobilized behind him, and the coalition produced enough votes to defeat the Mellon tax rates.

The triumphant La Guardia then led the attack which forced the substitution of his own program.

Republican stalwarts were stunned by this flank attack upon a leading Cabinet member. Their astonishment was transformed into bitter anger by his next move.

The iconoclast wasn't through by any means.

He turned from his victory over Mellon, and launched a bolt at the occupant of the White House himself! And once more he was successful.

It looked like a hopeless fight when he began a one-man rebellion against the Administration-sponsored Muscle Shoals bill, which would have turned the Tennessee River development over to Henry Ford for the latter to operate. The Detroit motor magnate was the possessor of vast prestige at the time, and it seemed absurd for an insignificant Congressman to open a fight jointly against him and the President of the United States.

La Guardia shocked both Congress and the nation into rapt amazement when he took the floor and charged that the President's support of the measure had not been given until *after* Ford had withdrawn from the Presidential race and publicly avowed his support of Calvin Coolidge in the coming campaign. La Guardia asserted that, although the bill had been pending for months, the President had never exhibited any interest in its passage until the motor magnate's support was openly pledged!

The country was amazed at this implication of a deal between the Chief Magistrate and one of its great financial figures.

La Guardia found himself again in the spotlight, and once

"Busy as he was he did not neglect conditions at home." With President Morris Sigman of the International Ladies Garment Workers Union in Jefferson Market court during a 1926 garment strike.

"He hurried to New London and boarded the S8, sister ship of the sunken submarine."

more he made the most of it. He took advantage of the opportunity to flay Ford for his anti-Semitic activities.

It was a dramatic moment when the New Yorker strode down into the well of the House and denounced the Ku-Klux Klan as well. That organization was then at the height of its power, as demonstrated in its successful fight to prevent the nomination of Alfred E. Smith the same year. It numbered in its ranks a whole host of members and sympathizers in Congress.

La Guardia defied them to their faces. He stood on the floor of the House shaking his fist at his Klan colleagues, and screaming his denunciation of their activities, as well as those of Henry Ford. He charged them with the instigation of religious and racial hatreds, and laid the responsibility for recent Jewish pogroms in Rumania at their very feet.

Before he concluded he had stirred up a veritable hornet's nest; but again the rebellion spread, and once more the Administration went down to defeat. The Muscle Shoals bill was defeated.

La Guardia was becoming famous, or infamous, in G.O.P. circles.

After his victory he plunged on to new battles, sponsoring a bewildering array of subjects. He returned to his fight against the Ku-Klux Klan and the denunciation of Henry Ford. He demanded the release of Eamon De Valera, who was then a prisoner in Ireland. He began a fight for a child labor amendment, and another against immigration restriction. Nor did he champion any of these causes half-heartedly. Each constituted a special crusade apart from his advocacy of pacifism and his opposition to Prohibition. He carried on both those battles automatically.

The Congressional Record is full of his tart, bitter comments:

The wealth and ignorance of Henry Ford combined has made it possible for vicious men to carry on a nefarious warfare against the Jews, not only of America but of the whole world. . . . Henry Ford has done more, owing to his bigoted hatred, to create strife in this country than any other man in the United States.   (March 7)

I say to you that the leaders responsible for the Ku-Klux Klan are doing more to defeat this country than any agency that ever existed in the history of the world.
(April 8)

I say that this great leader, Eamon De Valera, will have a glorious place in history as a champion of liberty! . . . He has been incarcerated and they refused to place him on trial. . . . I say that is an outrage for any civilized country to commit against any of its subjects.
(May 21)

The plight of De Valera struck a sympathetic chord in the breast of the warm-hearted La Guardia and he carried his fight for the release of the Irish prisoner on to the floor of the House. On March 5, 1924, he introduced a resolution, which read as follows:

RESOLVED, that it is the sense of the House of Representatives of the United States that, in the absence of any specific charge of crime committed by the said Eamon De Valera, his continued imprisonment, without a trial, is against the morality, customs and policy of liberty-loving people in this advanced age; *and be it*
RESOLVED, *further*, that the Secretary of State be, and is hereby, directed to transmit this Resolution to the Government of Great Britain, as a protest against the continued imprisonment of Eamon De Valera, under the conditions hereinbefore set forth.

The resolution produced a flurry on the floor, and the busy New York Representative was soon involved in a desperate parliamentary struggle. He defended his position eloquently, declaring that this country had, officially, expressed sympathy with the Hungarian rebellion in 1848, and that two years later, it had gone on record in behalf of Louis Kossuth.

"I say that this great leader, Eamon De Valera, will have a glorious place in history as a champion of liberty," flamed

La Guardia. "He has been incarcerated. No charge has been lodged against him, no condemnation, and they have refused to release him on habeas corpus, refused to place him on trial. And I say it is an outrage for any civilized country to commit against any of its own subjects, or citizens of another country!"

"*Is* he a subject or a citizen of this country?" interrupted Congressman Vaile. "That seems to be in doubt!"

"He was born in New York State," snapped the Major. "His mother is a resident of Rochester. I am sure of that. Eamon De Valera's gallantry, courage and noble purposes in fighting for the freedom of the people of Ireland, is a guaranty that he never took an oath of allegiance to the King of England.

"I do not believe that we are in the slightest over-stepping the bounds of propriety, or in the slightest impairing the dignity of this House, when, as Representatives of the free people of America, we hail Eamon De Valera as the champion of a great cause for human liberty, and ask the Department of State to use its good efforts in seeking the liberation of this champion of liberty—to protest against his continued unlawful and unjustifiable imprisonment."

Following the introduction of this resolution (which, incidentally, failed of passage) and the subsequent debate, La Guardia was almost buried under a deluge of letters. Among them was a note from Rochester, which read as follows:

March 8, 1924

Honored Sir:

I could not let the opportunity pass without expressing my gratitude to you for the generosity you have shown in behalf of my son, Eamon De Valera. You well describe his languishing in prison. Let us hope he is not tortured as well!! Poor fellow! He has done nothing—only loved Ireland.

I hope your kind resolution will bear fruit.

I thank you with all the sincerity of a broken-hearted mother.

(Signed) Catherine T. Wheelwright.

Two days later he replied:

> My dear Mrs. Wheelwright:
> You were too good to write me in reference to my resolution. I only introduced the resolution (which I considered proper and fitting) as a Representative in the American Congress. I do hope that resolution will attract sufficient attention to force a hearing on it, and that the protest of the free men and women of America, will be heard across the sea, resulting in the liberation of one of the world's great champions of liberty.
> (Signed) F. La Guardia

Expressions of gratitude poured in from all over the country, ranging from a resolution adopted by the Manhattanville Council of The American Association for Recognition of the Irish Republic, "tendering a vote of thanks to you, as our Congressman, for the stand you have taken in the release of Eamon De Valera, President of the Irish Republic," all the way to San Francisco, where Lian Mellows Council of the A.A.R.I.R. passed similar resolutions.

He early emerged as champion of the Jews and the Italians as well as the Irish, when on April 8 he made his great fight against the restriction of immigration:

> Gentlemen: You cannot escape the responsibility of the vicious, cruel discrimination against Italians and Jews mainly—along with other countries that I have named—which you make in the bill you propose and support.

He waxed eloquent in defense of the Jewish newcomers.

> Where will you find the average Jewish immigrant? You will find him in the shop. You will find him back of the pushcart. You will find him doing the most laborious work from the moment he lands until he is laid away. What is he doing it for? He is doing it because he has come here with one great purpose, and that is to give his children the opportunity which was denied him and to his ancestors for centuries. . . .

His children know no other land, and allegiance to no other flag—love no other country but the United States. . . . The children of the Jewish immigrant will have an opportunity of an education, will take their places in the community. And in every city in which the Jewish immigrants have settled, I will show you development, progress, business industry, as the result of their labor, determination and efforts.

His fierce pride in his Italian ancestry, always a dominant characteristic, flamed out on discussing the same subject with regard to the Italian immigrant:

Where do you find him? You soon find him with the pick and shovel, building our railroads, digging our canals, boring our subways, or in the depths of our mines. He saves his money, you say? Yes, saves money so that he may send it to the other side to bring over his wife and babies.

Then he establishes his little home. . . . You show me the house of an Italian laborer, no matter how humble, and I will show you every inch of the ground of his backyard cultivated as a garden. I will show you every place where there is space enough for one seed—a beautiful flower. . . . Come to our schools in New York, and you will see hundreds of thousands of little black-headed sons of Rome, poring over their A B C's in the grade schools. In the high schools, preparing themselves for the duties and responsibilities of American citizenship.

Now, is it fair, is it manly, is it accurate, to point out an instance here and there from a population running into millions, of a crime committed—and hold such a case as typical of an entire race? . . . Aye, gentlemen, you will have to find some other justification for this law.

* * *

La Guardia's increasing opposition to Prohibition was winning him nationwide attention. Before many months elapsed, the Republican rebel emerged as the leading champion of the Wets—and even took up the cudgels for the Democratic Governor of New York.

Smith had already begun the fight which led to the bitter strife that marked the Democratic Convention of 1924. He represented Tammany Hall, which La Guardia hated. But he was also an outstanding Wet, and his fight against Prohibition commanded the Major's respect.

Consequently, when the Governor's presidential ambitions became the target of the House Prohibitionists, La Guardia came to his defense. On January 3, 1924, he again clashed with Upshaw—the old antagonists resuming the battle which they had interrupted in 1919. The *Record* shows the clash:

> MR. UPSHAW. . . . Talk about nominating a man who has always been a "Wet" and who has had a death-bed repentance? Any man who has Presidential or Vice-Presidential dreams, who opposed the Eighteenth Amendment, might as well go way back and sit down! (Applause)
>
> Talk about "Modification." The trouble with men who speak on the other side is that they are down with the complaint of not being fundamental statesmen. We read in the papers this morning about the Governor of the great State of New York calling again for his representatives here to demand modification of the present Enforcement Act. I remind him—and all of you—that the Eighteenth Amendment is organic law!
>
> MR. LA GUARDIA. Mr. Speaker, will the gentleman yield?
>
> MR. UPSHAW. I am sorry, but I can't yield now.
>
> MR. LA GUARDIA. The gentleman ought to yield when he is attacking the Governor of my State.
>
> MR. UPSHAW. I can't yield, unless the gentleman from New York wants to contradict the statement that the Governor of his State asked his Legislature yesterday to have that modification memorial sent to Congress again.
>
> MR. LA GUARDIA. Will not the gentleman yield, in all fairness?
>
> MR. UPSHAW. Very well—go ahead.
>
> MR. LA GUARDIA. Does not the gentleman believe that it is more fair and more honest for the Governor of

the State of New York to memorialize Congress as
to the viewpoint of his State, than for the Governor
of the gentleman's state to permit the manufacture
of hooch and moonshine to be sent all over the
country? (Applause)

Almost as persistent as his attacks on Prohibition were his
assaults on Public Utilities' abuses. The early part of the year
saw him opening what was to become a long-drawn-out fight
against the jurisdiction of the Federal Courts in utility rate
cases.

He appealed to Mayor Hylan and New York Corporation
Counsel George P. Nicholson for assistance in arousing public
opinion against the practice of United States Courts setting
aside by injunction the rate reductions ordered by State Public Service Commissions. He introduced his bill to end this
abuse on February 1, and two weeks later Hylan instructed
Nicholson to circularize the mayor of every city in the country on behalf of the measure.

The results were negligible, but the Harlem Congressman
returned to the attack again and again in the ensuing years.

Just as close to his heart was the cause of Child Labor.
When the Congressional Amendment prohibiting it was before the House, he wrote, on April 22, to a constituent:

> Rest assured that I will support it. It might be well for
> you to write to some of the conservative members of the
> House, who are inclined to favor the exploitation of lit-
> tle children, because of profits, dividends and coupons.
> The Progressive group, I assure you, will fight to the
> very end, and vote—every one of us—for the passage of
> this amendment, which should have been part of our
> Constitution many years ago.

Four days later he arose from a sick bed and, despite the
protests of his physician, staggered on to the floor just long
enough to cast his vote for the amendment.

167

The range of his activities was astonishing. Only by working 16 hours a day was he able to accomplish the things he did.

While the House was in session, he spent every possible moment on the floor, paying strict attention to legislation, lest somebody should slip through something dishonest in the turmoil which attends the deliberations of the National Legislature.

Every night found him in his office, racing through committee reports and dipping into the authorities he had secured from the Congressional Library. His mind, working with lightning rapidity, leaped from one subject to another, assimilating an amazing amount of information. At intervals he would spring from his chair and stride up and down, dictating as fast as he could speak while Miss Fischer's racing pencil labored to keep up with his words.

The office soon became the most untidy place in Washington. Every desk and table in the single big room was piled high with documents and reports—the objects of his study. His staff gave up all hope of keeping it in order, since nobody was permitted to touch it except the little German secretary. She, through some mysterious system of her own, was always able to produce the papers demanded by her choleric employer. "The only efficient secretary I ever saw," he snapped after she left his office.

His files expanded enormously, however. Every bit of correspondence—even hundreds of letters from insane people—had to be classified and filed away. Any information which he might conceivably need in the future met the same fate. It was almost a mania with him.

The card index included such unrelated matters as the possible future use of Governors Island in New York Harbor as an airport, the drug control program of the League of Nations, the proper method to make macaroni, possible grounds for the impeachment of various Federal Judges and the philosophical interpretation of the teachings of Jesus Christ.

(The latter was the only reference to religion. "My Masonry is my religion," he frequently declared. "A man who could live up to the teachings of the Order would need no other.")

These files constituted an ever widening index to the variety of his interests. They collected sheafs of correspondence, which indicated that he was not overly tactful in his dealings with the various branches of the Executive Departments. Typical is the following letter addressed to Secretary of War John W. Weeks.

March 7, 1924.

My dear Mr. Secretary:

I have your letter of March 7, 1924.

After I complained on the floor of the House of my inability to get the data I requested, General Patrick informed me that the information had been transmitted to you, and General Joyce, of the Ordnance Department also was good enough to tell me that the information had been prepared.

You are very busy and I am very busy. Now, what is the use of having a conference before giving me the information which I have every right to receive?

Let us be perfectly frank about this. If there is any information that is confidential, and that for strategic reasons should be kept secret, I don't want it—and I am sure that no member of the House would want it. I don't hesitate to say, however, that there is not one bit of information concerning our Coast Defense guns, and I am certain, no information concerning our planes, but what every Government in the World knows all about it.

It is just this attitude that causes lack of confidence on the part of a great many members of the House in the General Staff and the Executive Departments.

I asked for the information in time for use when the Army Appropriation Bill was under consideration, for the reason that I felt that if I could get the data I requested, I could convince my colleagues that we ought to appropriate more money for defense purposes.

If you will cause to be eliminated any part of the data collected in response to my request, which, in the opinion of the military authorities should be kept secret, I will greatly appreciate it if you will then cause the reports submitted to be forwarded to me.

Very truly yours,

(Signed)   F. La Guardia.

His avowed desire to strengthen the anti-aircraft defenses, did not, however indicate that the Militant Pacifist was weakening in his pacifism. On May 17, he introduced a Resolution for the Outlawry of War, and a few days later he wrote to the editor of the *Christian Science Monitor:*

Dear Sir:

I enclose herewith House Joint Resolution 265.

As you will notice, I patterned my resolution very much on the resolution introduced by Senator Borah in the Senate last December. His resolution is a Senate Resolution, simply expressing the view of the Senate. My resolution is a joint resolution, but goes a little bit further. I am expressing the view that war is a crime and should be outlawed. I provide for the calling of a conference for the specific purpose of outlawing war. I also provide that the invitation should call for the consideration of a code of law based upon and in keeping with the new order of civilization.

I desire to dedicate this resolution to the *Christian Science Monitor,* which has done more intelligent and constructive work for the cause of peace than all the other forces of the country put together.

Very truly yours,

(Signed)   F. La Guardia.

He had also developed a new hobby, which took up a great deal of his time. The radio was just coming into general use and the resourceful New Yorker was quick to realize its value as a means of propaganda. It provided a forum from which he was able to broadcast his stand on Prohibition, his advocacy of pacifism and the other causes in which he was most deeply interested. Eagerly he seized the opportunity to utilize the new medium and he made frequent speeches on the air beginning in the early part of 1924.

As his fame spread the matters called to his attention multiplied in number. Some of them aroused his ire.

During the Spring of 1924, he received one such letter from certain employees of a shop at the Brooklyn Navy Yard. It read in part:

> The employees of the Officers' Uniform Shop desire to procure the services of one who can direct a fight against the Purnell bill, in conjunction with their committee.
>
> They are raising funds for this purpose and, being one of the committee, I would like to ask whether you would be willing to accept this task. If not, can you suggest some one.
>
> Respectfully,
> (Signed)   Ben B——
> P.S. Your reply will be kept absolutely confidential.

When Miss Fischer laid this missive before him, the Major grew almost apoplectic. He bounced out of his chair, to the accompaniment of a flow of very forceful language.

"Tell them they can go to . . ." he snorted, then paused in mid-expletive. "Still—maybe they don't understand," he muttered, half to himself. "After all, it's not entirely their fault."

He spun around and began to dictate:

> Dear Sir:
>
> I have your letter of Feb. 9, 1924, and am sure you did not mean to be insulting. I can only attribute your offensive suggestion to your lack of understanding of the offer you suggested.
>
> You must understand, my dear boy, that money is not everything in this country. We have scoundrels here and there who accept money for doing their duty, but we also have a large number of splendid, decent, honest public officials who devote their time to their duties entirely—and nothing can influence them in any way.

171

You must never approach a decent, honest public official with a suggestion that you want to hire him to do something he *ought* to do.

Perhaps you have been unfortunate in coming in contact with officials who speak the language you suggest, but you made a very big mistake when you wrote your letter to me, suggesting that a fund be raised to help fight the Purnell bill.

I was inclined to be against that bill and told several of the boys whom I knew personally that I would fight it. But if I hear of any more letters being sent out, such as the one you mailed to me, or if I hear that there is one cent contributed to any fund, I tell you now that I will not only *support* it, but I will see that it is passed and the shop closed.

Let me repeat what I have just said so that there may be no misunderstanding.

If one cent is contributed to any fund, or any money raised to fight this bill, I will have nothing more to do with it and I will see to it that those who are responsible for raising such money will be held responsible. You must, therefore, immediately write me whether or not any money has been raised; whether you have written any such letter to any other official and at whose request or suggestion you wrote this letter to me. You have committed a very serious act, and I must know all about it.

The thoroughly frightened young Mr. B—— immediately dropped his effort to become a lobbyist and La Guardia led the fight against the bill.

The incident turned his attention to federal employees and as a result, this term marked his first appearance as the embattled champion of the postal workers, whose national idol he was to become before very long. On Feb. 9 he introduced a bill to increase their pay. Four days later he presented a measure authorizing the Postmaster General to operate an air mail service and to choose the routes to be flown.

La Guardia was thinking in national terms, visualizing himself as a representative of the entire people rather than of those who merely resided in his district. It was in that capacity that he now constituted himself the watch dog of the federal judiciary.

First of the Federal Judges to come beneath his fire was George W. English, of the Eastern Illinois District. On June 3, 1924, the New York Congressman took the floor to denounce "this disgusting report of a Federal Judge who took a plea of guilty from a war profiteer, who had stolen $1,000,000 from the Government during the war. Under the pretext of having a weak heart, he was let off with a fine of $12,500. . . .

"This man is Henry L. Joyce," announced the New York legislator. "He was Marine Superintendent of the Central Railroad of New Jersey. The two corporations that participated in the loot did not plead guilty to the crime and they were let off with a fine of $1,000 each. I consider such a fine simply disgraceful."

It was the opening gun in a conflict with United States Judges which was to be waged on half a dozen different fronts.

Having fired it, the Major prepared to return to New York and make an attempt to rehabilitate his shattered finances.

He was still deeply in debt as a result of the long illness in his family and the funerals that had occurred three years before. He was planning to go into the publishing business in an effort to recoup.

His departure was cheered by the receipt of two grateful letters from officers of the American Legion, of which organization he was a member, having joined Aviators Post in New York.

Back in New York, the Major had recourse to his typewriter. He had always enjoyed writing and now he established an Italian-American magazine, which he called *Americolo*.

La Guardia entertained high hopes for its success and placed another mortgage on the University Avenue house in order to provide funds for its establishment. He was the publisher, editor, chief contributor and most of the staff.

Despite his almost frenzied efforts, and the long hours which he put in at his desk, *Americolo* failed to prosper as the months wore on.

CHAPTER XII

OFF THE RESERVATION

AND now the campaign of 1924 was at hand and the La Follette menace, which had been no bigger than a man's hand, was covering half the Western skies. Revolutionary portents filled the air as the G. O. P. Tories mobilized behind the banner of Calvin Coolidge. The Conservatives had complete control of the Republican Party. Its leadership consisted of the very men on whom the Progressives had been concentrating their fire.

Neither was there any place for the Liberals in the Democratic ranks! Alfred E. Smith had been driven from the field by the embattled Klansmen. John W. Davis, a Conservative of the deepest dye, headed the opposition party. An attorney for the J. P. Morgan firm, his Wall Street connections made him anathema to the dissatisfied Westerners.

In such circumstances the La Follette independent candidacy materialized. Old guardsmen of both parties, quaking in their boots, watched the Progressive movement with an apprehension unequaled since 1896, when another crusader had ridden over the prairies, brandishing a "cross of gold."

Filled with misgivings, the Republican captains hurried to solidify their ranks. Endeavoring to localize the revolt as far as possible, they combined promises and threats in an effort to enforce party regularity. They anticipated little difficulty in holding their lines east of the Mississippi, with the exception of the single New York Progressive. If they could keep him in line, the East would present an unbroken front. Once more La Guardia occupied a strategic position!

The Major kept his mouth shut and said nothing. Nobody knew what was going to happen, but the atmosphere was full of dire warnings concerning the probable fate of men who might split away from the Republican Party and follow strange gods from the West!

It was known that Sam Koenig had offered La Guardia his renomination, if he would come out openly in support of the President and the national ticket.

The Star Casino was packed to the doors on the night of June 15, 1924, when Congressman La Guardia came back to Harlem to "make his annual report to his constituents." This report had become a feature of the La Guardia program. Patterned upon the New England "town meeting," it was a sort of open forum, in which he discussed past and future legislation with his constituents. Partisanship was usually barred. But rumor had gone forth that Harlem's stormy petrel would declare himself that night! His followers jammed the hall, aroused by the report that their Congressman was to be denied his nomination unless he declared his "regularity."

And La Guardia bolted with a crash that was heard all over the State.

White-faced, but determined, he stood before his people and announced his decision in words of one syllable. The silence was broken only by the rustling notepaper of the reporters, as the Major raised his hand and began:

> No one is going to read anybody out of any party!
> Any fool can antagonize the voters, but it takes a real man, with ideas and courage, to get votes. . . . I believe that every individual who steals, grafts or squanders money appropriated for disabled veterans, should be taken out and shot like a dog!
> Will they put me out of the party on that plank?

(He silenced a rising wave of applause with an eloquent gesture, and his voice rang out shrilly as he went on speaking without notes, straight from his heart.)

> Some people think they are "regular" when they are only dumb! As to my choice between loyalty to my

176

party and loyalty to my country, I am for loyalty to my country first. "My country, right or wrong," . . . Yes, but my party only when it is right. . . . Some people say I am as bad as La Follette! I only wish I were as good as La Follette!

Again there was a rumble from the crowd, and again the open palm commanded silence. Then, his voice ringing with sincerity, he continued:

If a man does that which he knows is not right, he loses his soul; but if by doing right, he becomes "irregular" and loses a nomination, he really has not lost much.

This is 1924. The world is progressing. Times are changing.

What *is* "party regularity?" It is never urged until a party asks an individual to do something which he believes is wrong.

I would rather be right than regular!

And now the applause was unleashed. It rolled across the hall in great waves of sound, while the candidate, pale and perspiring, looked on. He had made his declaration of war, and there is little doubt that La Guardia thought he was deliberately signing his political death warrant when he issued it. He was amazed and thrilled by the unexpected enthusiasm it evoked.

Following the Star Casino speech, the Republican organization concentrated its fire upon him. He had no funds and no organization with which to oppose the machine. From the very beginning he was certain that he could not capture the regular nomination and that he must run, if at all, on an independent ticket.

Nevertheless, he was astounded by the amount of support which he received from the regular channels On July 1, Hamilton Fish addressed an open letter to La Guardia's constituents, which read:

To the people of the Twentieth Congressional District:

Dear Friends:

It has been my privilege to serve in Congress with Major Fiorello La Guardia, who is seeking to represent you again in Washington.

He not only served with distinction in the World War, but I have observed that in the House of Representatives he can always be depended upon to champion the cause of Justice and Democracy. He believes in and advocates Progressive principles, and places human lives above self-interests.

I know no more effective representative in behalf of human rights and Progressive principles in all of Congress!

He is a natural-born leader and fighter for causes close to his heart, and he has earned the eternal gratitude of not only the people of Italian origin, but of Jewish as well, for his courageous and unremitting fight in opposition to the Immigration bill. He won the respect and admiration even of his opponents, by his able and fearless attacks upon this measure.

I hope he will be renominated and re-elected to continue the battle for justice and progressive principles.

Sincerely yours,
(Signed)   Hamilton Fish.

While the question of the Republican nomination was still unsettled, Fish wrote him again on August 7, 1924, saying:

Dear Major:

I am enclosing a signed letter for your use. I hope that you will not have to use it before September 16, as there might be some flareback against me.

I am honestly very glad to give you this letter, as I believe it is for the best interests of the country to have fearless advocates of human rights and Progressive principles in Congress, who will not be held back by party bonds from telling the truth and showing up corruption.

La Guardia came out openly for La Follette on August 10, at the same time announcing his own candidacy on the Third

Party ticket, and again issuing his individual platform. It contained the same liberal planks which he had espoused in 1922. He had decided not to seek the Republican nomination, but to cast in his lot with the Western rebels; and he burned his bridges with a vengeance.

He issued a statement, which read in part:

> The new party is here—and here to stay! The forces now united under the emblem of the Liberty Bell, and known as the Progressive Party, though they may differ in theory, have one great common object—which is the economic reformation of this Republic. . . .
>
> Some of us have been laboring within the old parties, hoping we could reform them, or at least gain sufficient strength in either of them, to make it the party of the *people*—the party of workers and producers. It was a long, hard, tedious, discouraging fight. . . .

This announcement brought him a surprising reinforcement, which he had neither sought nor anticipated. The very next day he received the endorsement of the Socialist Party! He first learned of it when he received the following letter from Norman Thomas:

August 11, 1924.

My dear Mr. La Guardia:

> I take pleasure in enclosing a copy of a release which I am just giving out to the press. Please consider that it bears my sincere congratulations. I speak not merely as Socialist candidate for Governor, endorsed by various Progressive groups, but as one who earnestly desires a new Labor Party in America. By your act, you have taken a creditable pioneer part, looking to the formation of such a party—an act which I don't think Progressives, by whatever name they may call themselves, will forget.

Sincerely yours,
(Signed)   Norman Thomas.

Two days later the Major replied:

August 13, 1924.

My dear Mr. Thomas:

Thanks so much for your kind letter of August 11,
1924. It was so nice of you to write to me in the midst
of your many duties.

I look forward to the pleasure of meeting you personally very soon.

You were too generous in your praise of me. I only
did what was right. I do hope we may get together real
soon for a talk!

With kindest personal regards,

Sincerely yours,

(Signed)   F. La Guardia

This Socialist endorsement, while it proved of great value
to him in the 1924 campaign, was to reappear to plague him
in later years. Despite the fact that it was unsought, it, together with his Fusion race of 1918, gave color to widespread
reports that La Guardia had joined four different parties, and
at various times had run for office as a Republican, a Democrat, a Socialist and a Progressive!

Following the Socialist endorsement, the Republican machine disowned their former protege and nominated Isaac
Siegel for his seat. Tammany renominated Henry Frank, his
opponent of 1922—and the three-cornered race got under
way. From the beginning the district was torn to shreds by
the contending factions. Benjamin Siegel, who had been La
Guardia's campaign manager in 1922, now became the manager of his brother's campaign. A great deal of bitterness ensued.

Once more the Major established his headquarters in a vacant store at 106th Street and Madison Avenue, and again the
little German secretary installed herself therein. By this time
she was a master of politics, and she ran the headquarters while
the Major stumped the district.

He took up arms for the new party at once, and blazed away impartially at both Democrats and Republicans. The latter were fighting desperately for Coolidge, but their opponents faced a rather hopeless campaign.

The Klan issue had split the Democratic Party wide open, as a result of the famous Madison Square Garden deadlock between Alfred E. Smith and William G. McAdoo. After weeks of fighting, the delegates had finally compromised on a ticket headed by John W. Davis, the Morgan attorney, with Governor Charles W. Bryan, of Nebraska, in second place.

When this slate was announced, La Guardia telegraphed his friend, Congressman Nelson in Chicago:

> Democrats have finally nominated a ticket that not even a brother can support—no, not even William Jennings can make it Progressive, and how will he explain its impossible political biology?

New York's political rebel was definitely off the reservation at last! He took his departure enthusiastically—whooping off on the warpath, with his tomahawk striking in every direction. There was nothing hesitant in the stand he took. On October 24, 1924, he issued an open letter, which read:

> My dear Friends:
>
> After twenty years of public service, I am convinced that the welfare and happiness of the American people, as well as the perpetuation of our Republic, requires a new party, and with it, a change in our political system. The Progressive Party, of which I am one of the founders, is based upon the theory of representative government, and believes that the working men and women of America should have a voice in the affairs of their government.
>
> Both old parties have degenerated into mere agencies to carry out the will of the privileged, and for the continuance of legalized exploitation.
>
> Senator Robert M. La Follette, our candidate for Pres-

ident, and Senator Burton K. Wheeler, Vice-Presidential candidate, typify in every way this new movement.

Six years have I served with Senator Robert M. La Follette in Congress. He has been my inspiration and ideal, and I am proud to be with him as one of the founders of the new party.

To cast a vote for the Progressive ticket is to take part in a new political era in our country. I, therefore, ask you not only to vote for Senator La Follette for President, but to do all you can from now until election day to bring the message of freedom to all your friends, and help in every way you can.

With kind personal regards, I am,

Sincerely,

(Signed)   F. La Guardia.

Political wiseacres regarded this open endorsement of La Follette as equivalent to political suicide. The Wisconsin states-man was in distinctly bad odor in the East. Even New York Progressives eyed him askance, and the organized opposition of the American Legion was regarded as fatal.

La Guardia's opponents were quick to strike at this apparent chink in the armor of the rebel Congressman, and they dug up a summary of La Follette's war record which had been widely reprinted six years before.

It was an article in the *New York Evening Telegram*, published January 19, 1918, which had been exceedingly embarrassing to the Major at the time. It was headed "Reward of Loyalty," and read as follows:

Washington, D. C., Tuesday.

For the sixth time, investigation of Senator La Follette's alleged disloyal speech of last September, at St. Paul, was postponed today by the Senate Elections Committee.

Rome, Tuesday.

Fiorello H. La Guardia, who represents the Fourteenth Congressional District of New York in the House of Representatives, may have to face the alternative of resigning from Congress, or from the American Flying Corps.

Which would you rather be: Representative La Guardia, loyally undergoing the discomforts of war at the front, and being stabbed in the back at home by politicians who want his seat? or Senator La Follette, whose fealty is tainted, held in power by his fellows through Senatorial courtesy?

The contrast between La Guardia and La Follette is strong.

For the Representative to resign would be quitting in the face of the enemy—something he will never do.

As for La Follette, he should go—and not alone. He should be accompanied by the fellows who are protecting him.

This attack proved a veritable boomerang, however. In the effort to discredit La Follette by arousing the opposition of the Veterans, the opposition also succeeded in calling attention to La Guardia's war record, and the fact that he was a comrade of the man to whom the appeal was made. As a result, his position was probably improved.

The concentration of both Republican and Democratic fire upon the Major again focused national attention upon him. The Progressives regarded him as a tower of strength in the East, and their standard bearer wrote him as follows:

Dear Congressman:

I sincerely hope that the situation in your district is such as would justify you in making some speeches for us outside of New York.

Niles informs me that the demand for you is very great, and I know that you could be of inestimable value in such states as Massachusetts, Connecticut, Rhode Island and New Jersey.

Of course you realize that I would not ask you to make speeches outside of your district unless you were satisfied that the situation is such there that you would be justified in giving time elsewhere.

With kind personal regards,

(Signed) Robert La Follette.

The situation in Harlem, however, was far from satisfactory. The joint attack of his enemies proved effective, and La Guardia was soon fighting for his very political life. Instead of giving assistance he was badly in need of it, and La Follette himself came to the rescue.

Speaking in Madison Square Garden on September 18, the Progressive candidate declared:

> I want to take this opportunity to tell the people of New York of the splendid service rendered by Congressman F. H. La Guardia in Washington. There is not a better legislator, nor a more progressive one than La Guardia, in the whole country. It is an honor to commend him to you. Do all you can to send La Guardia back to Congress. Not only the people of New York, but the people of the country, need him there.

The La Follettte sponsorship enraged the opposition, and both parties renewed their attacks bitterly:

"In plain, political English, La Guardia is a 'carpet-bagger' who maintains a mansion in the University Heights section of the Bronx, and expects the good people of the upper East Side to consider him for Congress," ran one news story in an evening paper.

He did find time, however, to go to Brooklyn to campaign in behalf of Congressman Loring Black, a Democrat. The latter's Republican opponent, William T. Simpson, issued a public statement which reflects the feeling that was aroused by the Major's turning against his own party.

"Let him come," said Simpson. "He may liven up the fight a bit. I am sure the people in my district will be interested to hear him speak. La Guardia crawled in at one end of the political tent, and came out at the other end a La Follette man! He has had his finger in every pie and party."

Leaders of the Ku-Klux Klan thought they saw an opportunity to repay him for his defiance on the floor of the House, and the sheeted brethren entered the Harlem campaign. They flooded the district with a special edition of the *Fellowship*

Forum (the Klan paper) containing an article from which excerpts follow:

> Protestant Americans have proven in the recent primaries that they do place Americanism before their party, and will do it in the November election.
>
> Americans should vote for Americans in every race—from village constable up to the President. . . . Out of 323 Congressmen who voted against the 1890 quota bill, 298 were renominated. This means that 298 restrictionists are up for re-election, and should receive your support. . . .
>
> Fiorello H. La Guardia was one of the most active hyphenates in the fight against the 1890 bill. He is a member of The Sons of Italy, and boasts of his friendship for the Jewish immigrant. He seems to think more of keeping the bars down for the Jews and Italians to come in, than to keep America for Americans. He bolted the Republican Party, and has cast his lot with the Socialists.

VOTE AGAINST LA GUARDIA

As the campaign proceeded and the fight grew more bitter, La Guardia's prospects waned. Competent observers were of the opinion that Frank would probably win another Tammany victory. And then the Ghibonnes came into being.**

In the ensuing years the Ghibonnes were to increase in number until they had 1800 members on their rolls—1800 idealistic hero-worshipers, led by the brilliant Marcantonio. They were all young men and all Italian, all madly devoted to La Guardia. They gathered from the tenements of Little Italy to do battle for their idol, and each of them took a secret oath of allegiance, promising to follow his leadership unswervingly,

---

** Ghibonne: An Italian word difficult of translation, but approximating the English "swashbuckler." Composed of young Italian-Americans, they mobilized around La Guardia—and they were true to him ever after.

This organization, of which most New Yorkers never heard, was a secret fraternity, the members of which took an oath of personal allegiance to Major La Guardia. (Ever since that 1924 campaign they have formed the backbone of the well-oiled political machine that has kept him in office.)

and to support him without reservation. This secret fraternity, unknown except in Harlem, was composed of a cross-section of Italian-American life. It included young lawyers, professional men, World War veterans and youngsters just out of college. They were crusaders, and they followed their leader blindly.

The Ghibonnes proved a mighty asset. They were the vanguard of a youth movement which swept the district. Bands of girls took possession of the street corners, singing La Guardia songs to the accompaniment of guitar, mandolin and ukulele. The most popular was one written by Curtis Koehler and Miss Ann Carbone, well-known organizer. It went to an adaptation of *Mandalay*, and ran as follows:

> Fiorello H. La Guardia,
>> We're with you——
>> And we'll be with you to the end!

> Fiorello H. La Guardia,
>> Harlem needs a man like you in Congress:
>> You voted for the Soldiers' Bonus,
>> Helped the Immigrants,
>> And fought in Congress for us!

> Fiorello H. La Guardia,
>> With a record like yours,
>> Harlem needs you!

Enthusiasm swept the district and even spread outside its borders. Little Miss Fischer even handed the reporters a telegram from Kineo Station, Maine:

HON. FIORELLO H. LA GUARDIA,
CONGRESSMAN, TWENTIETH DISTRICT,
233 BROADWAY, NEW YORK, N. Y.

LETTER FORWARDED ME HERE TODAY. VERY SORRY UNABLE TO BE WITH YOU AT ST. LUCY'S CLUB TONIGHT. WILL GET TOGETHER WITH YOU WHEN RETURN. BEST WISHES FOR A BIG VICTORY.

(SIGNED) GENE TUNNEY.

The flaming enthusiasm spurred the volatile La Guardia to a white heat. He flew about the district as of old, fighting his opponents with a vigor which gave him the first joy in years.

Early in October he went storming into New York County Supreme Court and secured a show-cause order, demanding that an election board reconvene in the district in order to register one Charles Lipschitz, of 8 East 108th Street. The candidate was fighting for every vote.

In court, he declared: "Mr. Charles Lipschitz is an American citizen and has been living at the same address for over five years, and on four previous occasions has voted from that address. He happens to be a Progressive, and the board refused to enroll him because he did not have his citizen's papers with him. Whereas the law explicitly provides that a citizen who has previously voted, need not exhibit his citizenship papers."

Mr. Lipschitz was registered and permitted to vote.

The candidate was determined to prevent Tammany from stealing the election. Just before election day he wrote to Mayor Hylan:

> My dear Mr. Mayor:
>
> I know that you stand for representative government, and are a firm believer that the will of the people shall not be thwarted by the agents of corrupt interests who thrive on legalized exploitation, and who are in a position to control the conduct of men who are willing to stoop to anything for their masters.
>
> I desire to appeal to you for proper police protection in the Twentieth Congressional District on election night.
>
> As you know, I am a candidate for Congress on the Progressive ticket. It has been an open boast in this district that efforts would be made to count me out. In other words—the wishes of the voters are to be disregarded, and returns falsely made, based on a fraudulent count. On behalf of the sanctity of the ballot and repre-

sentative government, I request that an extra and fresh detail of police be assigned to the polling places just before the opening of the ballot boxes, with specific instructions to enforce the provisions of the election law.

His friend Mayor Hylan granted the request and directed Police Commissioner Richard Enright to furnish the desired detail.

The campaign closed on a crashing crescendo. The night before election the Ghibonnes staged an old-fashioned parade through the streets of Harlem, the torches dripping red fire, while fireworks exploded all around. Enthusiasm rose to a high peak.

Next day Harlem went to the polls—and Mayor Hylan's police swarmed in to see that all ballots were counted. When the returns were in, the vote stood:

La Guardia 10,756
Frank 7,141
Siegel 7,099

La Follette had gone down to a crushing defeat, carrying only his own Wisconsin. Coolidge was swept back into office on a landslide, and the victory of the New Yorker remained as the sole monument to the Progressive cause in the East!

There was a flood of congratulatory letters next day, and among them one from Richard, the baby brother of the Arizona days, now Acting Principal of the School of Letters in the New Jersey Prison at Trenton. It read:

Dear Brother:
    Mary and the children join me in extending to you our most sincere congratulations on your victorious result.
    While none of us are personally in favor of the party which you now are a member of, we realize, however, the special handicap you had in succeeding as well as you did.

(Signed)   Richard La Guardia.

Before returning to Washington the victorious candidate filed his financial statement for the campaign. It showed that he had expended $3,828.98. He had received contributions amounting to $3,764.25. Of this amount, the largest contribution was a $500 donation from the Amalgamated Clothing Workers of America. Most of the balance came in the form of $5 and $10 contributions.

The Major had financed his successful fight on a "shoe string."

CHAPTER XIII

THE MILITANT MINORITY

THE Representative of the Twentieth New York District found himself in an unenviable position when he returned to Washington after the Coolidge landslide in 1924. His opponents were in the saddle, and not unwilling to let him feel the spur. The Prohibitionists were the dominant force in an Administration which had but little use for the man usually referred to as "that damn little demagogue from New York."

He had read himself out of the Republican Party, of which the Conservatives were in absolute control. They no longer depended upon the little Progressive bloc for the balance of power, and they were quick to retaliate upon the man who had held them up two years before.

Returning to Washington, La Guardia was informed that stern discipline was in prospect for the supporters of the defeated La Follette. He was to be barred from all party caucuses, and deprived of his important committee assignments. Sympathetic correspondents with whom he had already attained great popularity, brought him the news.

"I don't care," replied the New York rebel. "They can't keep me off the Committee of the Whole."

This body, composed of the entire House membership, is essential to the work of Congress, and there La Guardia continued to function as of old. He became especially obnoxious on "Calendar Monday" as he bobbed up repeatedly to hamstring pet personal measures of his colleagues, which were dependent upon unanimous consent. He sat up nights studying these bills, and he frequently knew more about the proposed fish dam in Salt Creek, Ala., or the theft of 17¢ in stamps from the Podunk, Mich., Post Office, than the Representatives who introduced the bills concerning them.

For the next eight years he was to make such matters the subject of his personal attention, and things finally came to such a pass that other Congressmen found it necessary to call at his office to explain their cases in detail, if they hoped to avoid his persistent "I object."

He was in a hopeless minority, but he carried on against his old foes with unflagging zeal. He could always find sufficient time to do battle with them—and in December he filed suit against the *New York Tribune*, which had opposed him during the campaign, for libel. He based his suit on a story which had stated:

> La Guardia startled the voters throughout his district by electioneering in a battered, rusty, old automobile, and, it is said, he goes without a collar.

The Major branded this statement as "false, and maliciously published, to hold him up to ridicule and scorn," and he struck back in a fashion calculated to make the editors of the eminent Republican journal wince. Declaring that "said malicious article was published and sold by the defendant in the City of New York and throughout the State of New York *to the extent of its limited circulation*," he fixed his damages at 6¢. He won his case—and collected the damages!

The ensuing session found him working like a beaver. He devoted most of his attention to Prohibition, aviation and the income tax, although he meddled with almost everything that came to his notice. It was never possible to prophesy where La Guardia would strike next.

On January 13, 1925, he wrote to Secretary of Labor James J. Davis, demanding that the Archduke Boris of Russia be inspected on his arrival in the United States to determine whether or not he was likely to become a public charge—as was the custom with immigrants of lesser social status. His letter caused a sensation in both official and social circles because of its scathing references to the manner in which the élite of New York and Washington were reputed to pay admission in order to bow before, and kiss the hand of, "these repudiated Royalists."

A month later he was introducing a bill for the relief of the "wage slaves" of organized baseball, and demanding that clubs which "sold" players to other teams, be taxed 90% of the proceeds, when they exceeded $5,000. He also sponsored a measure to render campaign contributions unavailable outside the State in which they were made; re-introduced his Outlawry of War bill; and, finally, swooped down on Tammany Hall, with an appeal to Leader Olvany to take the New York City Comptrollership out of politics.

None of these measures got anywhere, but they kept his opponents busy killing them off.

He also took a fall out of the New York Life Insurance Company, which had threatened to withdraw its investments from certain property in the District of Columbia, if a pending rent law were passed by Congress. Writing to Harry H. Bottome, its General Counsel, on January 28, 1925, the ubiquitous Harlem Congressman said:

> I have your letter of January 28, 1925, relative to the Senate Bill 376, known as the "Rent Act of the District of Columbia."
>
> You state that upon examination of this bill, "I am of the opinion that, should it be enacted, it would be unwise for this company to continue to make investments secured by mortgages on residential property within the District."
>
> Permit me to say that *I* am "of the opinion" that you will do nothing of the kind!
>
> Insurance companies are simply handling public funds. If any company, or group of companies, conspire to sabotage against any Federal Statute, does it occur to you that such company, or companies, may be prevented from doing business in the District of Columbia?

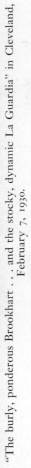

"The burly, ponderous Brookhart . . . and the stocky, dynamic La Guardia" in Cleveland, February 7, 1930.

"It proved to be another stormy campaign." Congressman La Guardia speaking in Madison Square, October 3, 1930.

There is not the remotest possibility of the Rent Law impairing present or future investment of your funds . . . unless the company indulges in speculation and profiteering ventures, which the law specifically prohibits. You cannot be at any disadvantage through the passage of any regulative bill.

You have permitted yourself to become part of a vicious, unwarranted and organized propaganda, carried on throughout the country where rent laws have become necessary.

Doggedly, the liberal New Yorker continued his seemingly hopeless fight. They were dark days for liberals everywhere. During the Summer he was bombarded by letters from his friend, Nitti. The former Italian premier had fled to Zurich when the Fascisti seized his country. From there he begged for La Guardia's support, painting brief word pictures of his own tragedy. "My house has been invaded and sacked. Everything has been destroyed by pistol shots and grenades."

Nitti frankly admitted the danger of revolution. "I desire with all my energy to avoid it," he wrote on June 14. "Much as I detest Fascism, I am even disposed to assist it if it will renounce its violence. In order to avoid a revolution, I am disposed to yield everything." By August 7, however, Nitti had decided that Mussolini's regime was thoroughly bad and generally opposed. "I am positive that Fascism will end in a few months," he wrote.

The Major had no inclination to dabble in Italian politics, however. He ignored Nitti's flattering postscript in which the latter explained that he had asked for help only from a few trusted "Italians or sons of Italians." La Guardia was too busy in America to concern himself with European events.

And he had one major interest which took precedence over all others. That was the fight against Prohibition, into which he threw himself heart and soul. It aroused his greatest enthusiasm—and so began the active campaign during which he was to emerge as the nationally recognized leader of the Congressional Wets.

As 1924 drew to a close, he discovered that he could really embarrass the Drys by insisting on larger appropriations for Prohibition enforcement, "in order to give you every chance to attempt to enforce this impossible law." Gleefully he pressed more and more money upon them, at the same time calling attention to every breakdown in enforcement which he could locate in any part of the country.

As these tactics began to be better understood, in the following years, his Prohibition mail assumed mountainous proportions. Wets in every State in the Union supplied him with ammunition, which he used on the floor of the House.

La Guardia was a conscientious Wet and yet, paradoxically, advocated temperance. Although he always drank freely, he has never been seen under the influence of any intoxicant. Declaring firmly that "liquor never did anybody any good," and that "temperance should be secured by education," he never hesitated to indulge himself in the "cup that cheers," being especially fond of Italian wines.

He expressed his philosophy in a letter to a Pelham, N. Y., correspondent, who wrote him under date of December 30, 1924:

Hon. Fiorello H. La Guardia,
233 Broadway,
New York City.

Dear Sir:

You are quoted in this morning's *Tribune* as speaking in favor of a large appropriation for the enforcement of Prohibition.

As this has not been your reported position in the past, I hasten to assure you that thousands of well-wishers for our country's good, are rejoicing in this, your apparent new attitude on this issue. We are with you at all times when you speak for the advancement of the United States.

Most sincerely,
(Signed)   H. L. H———.

In reply the Congressman wrote:

January 7, 1925.

Mr. H. L. H.———,
Pelham,
New York.

My dear Mr. H———

I have your letter of December 30, 1924.

I do not believe it would be fair to you were I to knowingly permit a misapprehension to be entertained concerning my attitude on Prohibition.

I believe that a modification of the law is necessary. However, as long as the law is on the statute books, it must be enforced. I am not in sympathy with the policy of partial enforcement, or, even worse, utter disregard of the law.

In representing my District (which is overwhelmingly wet in sentiment) I feel it is my duty to seek a modification of the law—but only in a proper legislative manner. I do not consider that I am expected to countenance a disregard of the law or to wink at it, thus facilitating the activities of bootleggers.

The present situation in regard to the Government's attitude, and the activities of organized bootlegging, is nothing short of scandalous!

Sincerely yours,
(Signed)   F. La Guardia.

The Prohibitionists attempted to ignore his tactics but he hazed them unmercifully. On December 1, 1924, he introduced a resolution asking the Secretary of the Treasury to submit a report on the dismissal of Prohibition Agent Robert J. Owens, and the restitution of liquor seized by Owens from the home of Hugo Gilbert de Fritsch of 142 East 54th Street, New York City. The liquor had been seized on August 1, and the raid created a sensation owing to the social position of the de Fritsch family.

"I want to determine whether there is to be one sort of enforcement for the rich and another for the poor," he shouted on the floor. "Whether it is necessary for an enforcement agent to carry a Social Register along with the Statutes of the United States in enforcing the law in New York City? I am informed that the liquor was returned with apologies, and without even asking the form of a hearing before a proper United States official."

He concentrated his fire on the Treasury Department. A letter written October 11, 1924, to Secretary Mellon, began as follows:

> My dear Mr. Secretary:
>   Inasmuch as there is so much talking these days concerning law enforcement, and actual conditions being so far from it, I take the liberty to bring to your attention certain facts which (if true) reveal a tendency on the part of high enforcement officials to brook disregard, rather than compel strict enforcement of the law.
>   Contemplated changes at points of concentration would indicate that a bootlegging conspiracy is soon to be firmly entrenched in the good graces of the Department.

His letter continued, making specific charges concerning gross irregularities in the supervision of a Pittsburgh distillery, and also concerning conditions in Cincinnati.

On October 16, the harried Mellon replied with a long four-page letter discussing and denying each of La Guardia's charges in detail.

He had no illusions concerning the prospect of any form of modification at that time, although he kept pounding away and introducing, and re-introducing, various wet measures. Writing to a constituent on December 17, 1924, he said:

> Frankly, I do not think there are 125 members in the House who would stand up and vote for modification. The trouble is, there are too many politicians and others, making money out of Prohibition, and selling poor people poison—and I am trying to show up these conditions.

And nearly a year later he declared:

> My latest bill, to amend the Prohibition Law, is simply
> what is known as the "Beer Bill." I do not believe there
> is a chance in the world of getting any action in this
> Congress. There have been many statements sent out by
> enthusiastic members and the prospective candidate for
> nomination of Senator in Maryland, but the vote is not
> here—and that's all there is to it.

Undiscouraged by this lack of support, he redoubled his efforts against Prohibition, and for the first time succeeded in
seriously embarrassing the Dry stalwarts. They were thrown
on the defensive by his repeated charges that enforcement had
broken down. The Wet press played up these charges vigorously, and La Guardia returned to the assault again and again.
The Drys fought back fiercely. They slowed him up at times
but never stopped him. The resilient New Yorker was always
hopping to his feet to harass them. The following exchange,
which took place on the floor of the House, March 10, 1926,
is typical of his repeated snipings:

> MR. LA GUARDIA. Will the gentleman yield?
> MR. BLANTON. Yes.
> MR. LA GUARDIA. The gentleman is defining and char-
> acterizing the duty of members under the Evasion
> Clause of the oath which we have taken. Who is the
> member who is guilty of evasion? The outstanding
> Wet, who seeks to modify the law by proper con-
> stitutional or legislative means? Or the advocate of
> the Drys, who violates the law every day of his life,
> here and in his own community?
> MR. BLANTON. I think we ought to run that kind of
> Dry out of the public service of the United States.
> No officer in the Army or Navy should violate the
> law, no officer of the United States should violate
> the law, no Senator or Congressman should violate
> the fundamental law of his country, which he is
> under oath to uphold and obey. And whenever they
> break the law, we ought to put them out of the
> service.

Mr. La Guardia. Then we wouldn't have a quorum here. (Laughter)

Mr. Celler. Will the gentleman yield?

Mr. Blanton. In just a moment I will yield. I want first to answer the gentleman from New York (Mr. La Guardia). I think this is an unfair accusation against his colleagues. I have been here nearly ten years, and I can count on the fingers of my two hands the colleagues during that time upon whose breath I have smelled liquor.

Mr. La Guardia. That's not the only test, I will say to the gentleman.

Mr. Blanton. Oh, it's the acid test. When you see smoke, there is always some fire; and when there's whisky around, the telltale fumes are easily detected.

Mr. La Guardia. Does the gentleman go round every morning after the call for a quorum has been made, and smell every member's breath as he comes into the Chamber?

Mr. Blanton. No, I don't; but I mingle freely with my colleagues. Whisky is one thing which you cannot conceal. When a man drinks liquor, you can always smell it upon his breath.

On June 10 he made a prepared speech which attracted wide attention in the House. Taking the floor, he described General Lincoln C. Andrews, the Prohibition Administrator, as a "distinguished and gallant soldier with a record for courage, gallantry, loyalty and intelligence, second to none who ever wore the uniform."

He continued, "But what has happened to this man? It is a different man entirely who appears before the Appropriation Committee. General Andrews would sooner have been shot than to make the statements and the promises which he made to the Committee on Appropriations to a superior military or staff officer. Instead of the gallant, brilliant cavalry officer, studying his problems and terrain, calculating the forces required for his mission, and reporting the facts as fully and truthfully as he would as a soldier, we find the typical cringing office-holder, seeking to please his boss, the Administration, the Budget Lord, the Committee on Appropriations, the Drys and the Wets. He strives for law enforcement without unduly disturbing the law-breakers."

During the discussion, a brisk exchange followed.

MR. GREEN.   Let me say to the gentleman that we enforced the law in Iowa when the States around us were against it, so that we did not need the men you are speaking of. The gentleman has talked about "being frank," but he has not made a frank statement.

MR. LA GUARDIA.   Will the gentleman from Iowa say there is no liquor consumed in Iowa?

MR. GREEN.   No, no.

MR. LA GUARDIA.   There is your answer.

MR. GREEN.   But let me say to the gentleman that we are getting along pretty well.

MR. LA GUARDIA.   But the gentleman admits that liquor is consumed in Iowa?

MR. GREEN.   Yes—and always will be. Gentlemen are all the time talking about liquor, and saying that the liberty of the people is being taken from them because they cannot have wine and beer.

MR. LA GUARDIA.   Let me say to the gentleman that the per capita consumption of alcohol in the State of Iowa is equal to that of the per capita consumption in any other part of the country.

*   *   *

MR. FISH.   My understanding is that the last dozen or so of agents who were appointed in New York were appointed on the recommendation of the Wet district leaders. Can the gentleman answer as to whether that is true?

MR. LA GUARDIA.   Well, you can expect anything from the Treasury Department. Let me say this to the gentleman: What can you expect when the Secretary of the Treasury was formerly a whisky distiller himself?

The Harlem Congressman took the cue for his next attack from Madden's statement that the enforcement officials had received all the money they requested. He promptly began his efforts to force more money upon the harried Drys. On June 29, he tried to amend their enforcement appropriation by increasing it from $2,686,760 to $102,686,760. The embarrassed Prohibitionists finally succeeded in defeating the amendment.

Not content with harassing the Drys on the floor of the House, La Guardia continued to pester the Treasury Department unflaggingly with reports of violations of the Volstead act, demanding an investigation of each one. Scarcely a week passed without the forwarding of some such letter as the following, sent to General Lincoln C. Andrews on May 13, 1926:

> It seems to be common knowledge about the city of Pittsburgh that the Hazlewood Brewing Company is running full blast, and that real beer is flowing from the vats as fast as mature brewing and the law of gravitation will permit.
>
> I am sure that if the Honorable, the Secretary of the Treasury, who, I understand, will be in Pittsburgh tomorrow, will make inquiry, he too will learn of the prosperous activities of this particular brewery. A mere casual inquiry, perhaps among some of the very gentlemen who may have been on the platform or in reserved seats at the meeting on Friday, may disclose information valuable for the proper enforcement of the law entrusted to the Treasury Department.

Of course, such letters did not bring any action other than, as in this case, a routine acknowledgment that the matter would be referred to the proper officials in the field.

They did, however, constitute splendid ammunition for the anti-Prohibition press, to which the Major always furnished copies.

Nor did he limit his activities to letter-writing alone. He demanded the impeachment of Federal Judge Frank Cooper, of the Northern District of New York, on a charge of lending himself to entrapment by co-operating with Dry agents, when the latter permitted violations in order to secure evidence. La Guardia pressed the case against Judge Cooper before a hostile House Committee. Its members treated the New York Congressman almost as if *he* were on trial himself—and the case naturally made no progress!

He exposed conditions in Indianapolis, and ripped the cover off the famous Remus case in Cincinnati, over which the Drys had been congratulating themselves as a splendid example of enforcement. The Indiana officials, who were notorious Drys, promptly subpoenaed him to appear before a grand jury there. But the Major was too clever to be caught in such a trap.

He knew the best way to appeal to his colleagues. Taking the floor on a question of high Constitutional Privilege, he ridiculed the subpoena, and submitted an appalling array of facts to prove that some of the officials had sold the liquor *seized by themselves*. He even gave the voucher numbers of the barrels to which he referred.

The House, which has always been very sensitive concerning the privileges of its members, instructed him to disregard the subpoena, and directed the Department of Justice to investigate the charges. Indictments and convictions followed.

Next he exposed a system used in Pittsburgh in which Post Office workers were employed to investigate prospective jurors for Prohibition cases. This created more scandal, and he received the assurance of the Post Office Department that the practice would be discontinued.

This Wet crusade resulted in an astonishing change in the status of the Major. It brought him out of the rut and into the limelight again. Following the Progressive political catastrophe of 1924, he had gone into an almost total eclipse. The Liberal bloc in Congress had been disarmed and discarded; but La Guardia, the nonentity of 1925, was transformed into La Guardia the national figure of 1926. His assumption of leadership in the anti-Prohibition fight had made him the target of a storm of criticism. But there was a mounting tide of support.

By his advocacy of a seemingly lost cause, he had placed himself in the van of a steadily growing movement. There were Wets in both Houses of Congress during this period, but most of them were keeping quiet about their convictions. Colleagues who were essentially conservative and yet conscientiously opposed to Prohibition, began to rally to the support of the very man whom they had ostracized because of his La Follette connection. Ere long he was their acknowledged spokesman.

La Guardia had emerged as one of the outstanding Wet leaders of the nation, and with his usual flair for publicity, promptly proceeded to capitalize his position. What his enemies denounced as his "demagogy" his friends referred to as a talent for the spectacular! He utilized this talent to point out another flaw in the Prohibition law, when he proceeded to make home brew and drink it on the steps of the Capitol! The Drys raged at the sacrilege and denounced him frantically for "taking advantage of his Congressional immunity!" He, thereupon, announced that he would go home and repeat the performance at the corner of 106th Street and Lexington Avenue, in his own district to which his immunity did not extend. And he notified the New York Prohibition agents in advance of his intention to do so.

On June 22, 1926, he issued a public statement:

> My attention has been called to an announcement from Prohibition headquarters at Albany, that any one found making beer under the La Guardia formula (by mixing near beer with Malt Tonic) would be arrested for violation of the Volstead act.
>
> I accept the challenge, and upon my next visit to New York, I will walk up to a soda fountain counter in a drug store in my district and order a bottle of malt tonic and one of near beer, and will drink it right then and there. If the Prohibition Department desires to test the law, I will give them the opportunity.

It is silly to hold that the malt extract which I used, or any other duly authorized brew, sold under a permit, cannot be lawfully purchased!

Of course, if the Prohibition unit in Albany was attending to its business honestly, they would not have time to issue such silly statements. Bootleg whisky, hooch, moonshine and other poisonous beverages are sold within a stone's throw of the very Prohibition Headquarters in Albany. Everybody but the Prohibition unit knows that Albany is "wide open," and that all the hooch desired, can be obtained by simply going up and asking for it! Of course, certain officials, and the Anti-Saloon League, are always seemingly enraged when the people can obtain anything lawful, which naturally hurts the bootleg trade—if you get what I mean?

The Major made good his boast and quaffed the beverage, as he had promised, while cameras clicked. He was not even arrested, however—which denouement disappointed him greatly. He was sincerely anxious to become a martyr to the cause.

He explained his attitude in the matter to a correspondent in Madison, Wis., as follows:

I am sure you realize that the purpose of my demonstration was to show, first, the absurdity of the law; second, that any mild beer is not harmful; third, the absurd position of the Department in issuing permits; fourth, the possibility of getting something like beer by taking two mild beverages and mixing them; and, fifth, to drive into the minds of the public, the fact that if it is possible to do so indirectly, the reasonable demand for beer ought to be granted by a proper modification of the law. . . .

I am about to send out a statement, in reply to the Department's official statement, that these extracts are not fit to drink. *If* they are not fit to drink, I am going to ask why are permits given for them as a medical drink, and approved by the Department for "Loss of Appetite, Nursing Mothers, and Convalescents"?

Prohibition was not occupying all his thought, however. It was merely one phase of a versatile campaign. He devoted almost as much time to the defense of General William Mitchell, former Chief of the Air Service, under whom he had served during the World War. Mitchell had been court-martialed for disobedience of orders, in a spectacular military trial. The case grew out of the General's advocacy, in a series of magazine articles, of a unified air service.

This happened to be a hobby of La Guardia's, and he plunged into the fight with alacrity. He testified in Mitchell's behalf, and received some exceedingly caustic criticism from the prosecution, which even endeavored to question the extent of La Guardia's own service at the Front! Major La Guardia writhed beneath the sarcasm of Major Gullion, who closed for the prosecution.

Referring to Congressman Frank Reed, General Mitchell's Counsel, Gullion sneered: "It is regrettable that he has not called to his assistance that courtly colleague of his—that eminent strategist, Mr. La Guardia. . . . Our reason for qualifying our witnesses in this way is to show the difference between a real expert and some of these petty, so-called experts introduced by the defense."

Though a lawyer himself, and a master of sarcasm, the Major did not relish it when *he* was the target. He protested Gullion's tactics to the Secretary of War in a letter dated January 7, 1926, insisting that the Assistant Judge Advocate made misstatements in his summation, and gave it out to the press before it was presented. The Secretary of War stood squarely behind his subordinate, and left La Guardia fuming. It remained a sore subject with him for years.

He rendered yeoman service for Mitchell, however, introducing a whole series of bills in Congress for the protection and vindication of the General, and even tried to secure the passage of a measure remitting his punishment after the conviction. Mitchell expressed his gratitude in a letter written March 22, 1926, in which he stated:

The aid you gave me is duly appreciated. I feel that you have assisted in bringing to the people a realization of facts relating to the national defense of our country, which will undoubtedly lead to its improvement.

With grateful thanks for your help and support, etc.

La Guardia continued to be a thorn in the side of the Administration during this term and taking advantage of his reviving prestige, he led another attack on Secretary Mellon's newest income tax program. On March 25, 1925, at his "town meeting," he had declared war on it, as follows:

President Coolidge has adopted as his slogan and seemingly nailed to the door of the White House, the fourteenth verse of the fifteenth chapter of St. John: "Ye are my friends if ye do whatsoever I command you"; while the Secretary of the Treasury, in his studies and recommendations for modification of the Income Tax law, seems to be guided entirely by the precepts of the twenty-fifth verse of the fourth chapter of St. Mark: "For he that hath, to him shall be given; and he that hath not, from him shall be taken away even that he hath."

He fought the bill bitterly in the House, taking issue with both Democrats and Republicans. On December 10, 1925, he took the floor to explain:

Unless the Income Tax schedule is amended, I shall vote against this bill, if I am the only member of the House to do so. . . .

A great deal has been said about the non-partisan agreement on the bill under discussion. There seems to be no opposition, although the bill changes the very policy of the taxation system of this Republic. When the United States Congress arrives at a point where it acts with unanimity for the people . . . then God help the people of America!

I was startled to hear the distinguished gentleman from Texas (Mr. Garner) state his approval of the bill. This bill contradicts everything which Mr. Garner has stood for in his long years of useful service in this

205

House. I cannot reconcile his attitude on this bill with his fight on the Mellon plan in 1924. Yet Mr. Garner takes the floor, scolds and berates the Ways and Means Committee, seeks to reform the Republican members of their habits, and yet will share in the fruits of their sin! One is reminded of the Reverend Davidson, trying to convert and save Sadie Thompson. . . .*

Here and now you come in with a unanimous report, and change the policy entirely. This is not only a bill for the reduction of taxes, but it is a bill that abolishes entirely the very purpose and spirit of an income tax law.

I don't want to destroy wealth, but I do want to abolish poverty. Something is wrong with the economic system of a country where the Chief Executive of that country in his Message, asks for *charity* for dependent widows and orphans; and his Secretary of the Treasury asks for a bill to repeal taxes on incomes of $5,000,000 a year. . . . The Democrats have a duty to fulfill. It is a duty of the minority party to check the greed and ruthlessness of a majority.

He was winning a reputation by his brilliance in debate. His repartee attracted attention, and the Capitol guides were frequently asked by visitors to point out "La Guardia of New York." They saw a short, rather stout man with snapping black eyes, moving restlessly about the floor. He was usually munching peanuts, since he refused to leave the House even for lunch. His attention was always concentrated upon the business in hand. And frequently they were rewarded by hearing his high-pitched voice pipe out one of the tart comments which were a continual trial to the party leaders.

On one such occasion when a bill for the establishment of public shooting grounds in connection with migratory bird refuges was before the House—April 29, 1926—he shot to his feet announcing:

I am for the conservation of bird life; but when I want advice on the subject, I refuse to take it from a

---

* The reference was to a current play, *Rain*, in which the Rev. Mr. Davidson endeavored to save the soul of the prostitute, Sadie Thompson.

paid agent of ammunition and gun makers! If this bill is to pass, gentlemen, let there be no hypocrisy about it. Let it be known as "The Bird Slaughter bill," and at the entrance to this bird slaughtering precinct, let us replace the figure of the chaste Diana, the goddess of the hunt, with a monument of Peggy Joyce as "queen of the chase."

His colleagues feared to engage in repartee with him.

They expunged his retort to the good-looking Wingo—the Adonis of Arkansas, who was reputed to be very proud of his personal appearance—from the *Congressional Record* of February 22, 1926, but crowded galleries heard the exchange:

> Mr. Wingo. Mr. Chairman, it is always interesting to find one of these pork barrel gentlemen, like the gentleman from New York, who voted for the biggest and worst and most ridiculous pork barrel bill that ever disgraced Congress—the one that was passed here the other day.
>
> Mr. La Guardia. Does the gentleman designate that as "a pork barrel" bill?
>
> Mr. Wingo. Pork barrel?
>
> Mr. La Guardia. Yes.
>
> Mr. Wingo. If the gentleman does not know that is a pork barrel bill, he has not enough sense to get in out of the rain. Everybody else but the gentleman from New York knew it was a pork barrel bill, and in private admitted it.
>
> Mr. La Guardia. If the gentleman designates that as a "pork barrel" bill, he is *still* out in the rain!
>
> Mr. Wingo. That may be; but I have enough sense to keep out of the rain, and I know something about my own country.
>
> Mr. La Guardia. But, apparently, you know nothing about the *bill*.
>
> Mr. Wingo. Yes, I know about that bill. I know exactly how it was put through the House. Everybody apologizes for it, but everybody is saying, "Well, I have got to be for it because I have a ham in it!" That's what one member said to me when I jumped

upon him about it. And if the gentleman is in the
same attitude as that member was, I will say to him
now what I said to that member: "You think you're
going to get some of that pork? You say you're
going to get a *ham?* But unless I miss my guess, the
only part of that pork you will get will be the pig's
tail! (Laughter) And I hope they will!

MR. LA GUARDIA.   Will the gentleman yield now in all
fairness?

MR. WINGO.   I am not surprised at these artistic comments coming from the gentleman from New York.
I remember quite well one of the first "pork barrels" that came before the House, after I came to
Congress, was a bill to increase the appropriation
for the Assay Building. I believe it was in New
York City. They came in here and wanted $385,000
for the adornment of the façade. Does the gentleman from New York know what a façade is?

MR. LA GUARDIA.   Of course he does. Does the gentleman from Arkansas?

MR. WINGO.   Yes. That is the same thing to a building
that a snout is to a hog. It is the front part of it.
And a porkeater ought to know what the façade
is. . . .

That is all the *Record* shows, and posterity is thereby deprived of La Guardia's weary reply (which electrified the
House:)

MR. LA GUARDIA.   If the gentleman from Arkansas
were *less* interested in his own façade, and more in
the *inside* of the head, he would be a better legislator!

The same weary sarcasm breathed through a letter which
he sent to Secretary Davis on January 12, 1926, after the
Countess Vera Cathcart had been excluded from the country:

Honorable James J. Davis,
Secretary of Labor,
Washington, D. C.

My dear Mr. Secretary:

My attention has just been called to the fact that an alien by the name of Vera Cathcart, is now detained at Ellis Island, and ordered excluded as a person belonging to a class of aliens excluded under Section 3 of the Act of February 5, 1917.

According to information which I have before me, it would appear that the said alien has been excluded as a person who has been convicted of, or admits having committed, a felony, or other crime or misdemeanor, involving moral turpitude. It so happens, I am informed, that the exclusion is based upon the fact that this alien committed adultery with one William George Bradley, 5th Earl of Craven, who arrived in the United States on the S.S. *Belgenland*, November 20, 1925, now living in New York City. Clearly, if the Countess Vera Cathcart, is excluded as a person having committed an act involving moral turpitude, so must be the said William George Bradley, with whom she is charged with misconduct.

Under our law, both parties committing such act are equally guilty. If one is excluded on that ground, surely the other is here in violation of the law.

We are not concerned with what the law, or custom, may be in other countries; we do know that we have but one standard of morals in this country, and the law is applicable to both the man and the woman in such cases. Under the circumstances, nothing is left for the Department to do but issue a regular warrant for the apprehension and deportation of the person equally guilty with the alien now under order of exclusion.

I know that the Earl's social connections in this city will not prevent a miscarriage of equal justice.

Likewise when Judge English finally resigned under the relentless fire of La Guardia's demands for his impeachment, as a result of his handling of bankruptcy cases, the Major returned to the attack:

What is there in this resignation that removes this Judge from the consideration of the high court of impeachment. (A demand made in the House on December 11, 1926, after the impeachment managers had recommended the discontinuance of the proceeding, saying that it would be improper to place the burden of a trial on the United States Treasury.)

Were that rule followed, we would have absolutely no system of jurisprudence, or ever bring to trial big offenders. Why, the Doheny-Fall trial is costing the United States hundreds of thousands of dollars. Should that case have been *nolle prossed* because of the expense involved? Should the trial be discontinued and Congress vote the defendants the Congressional Medal of Honor? There is precedent to proceed with the trial, the resignation to the contrary notwithstanding. Since when does the American Congress take the easiest way, for the sake of saving a few paltry dollars, and permit a venal, brutal, unscrupulous judge to avoid trial by handing in his resignation? . . . The fact that this man usurped the power of a Federal Judge, the fact that he permitted improper administrations in bankruptcy cases, the fact that he improperly called State and County officials before him, abused them and read the riot act to them, and interfered with their duties, improperly and illegally— are these things to be removed from the question of impropriety by our conduct today? . . . What is there in this resignation that removes the vicious acts of this Judge from the consideration of the high court of impeachment? . . .

Let the Senate hale the impeached Judge before it and then take such action as may be proper. . . . If he is not guilty, the man is entitled to that verdict, and I think he owes it to the gentleman in this House who took the step in his defense, to stand trial! If he is not guilty, then why does he not proceed to trial? Why did he resign?

A fierce parliamentary battle ensued, with La Guardia fighting desperately, but without success, for the impeachment.

It is impossible to chronicle the full scope of the New York Representative's activities. Yet, busy as he was in Washington, he did not neglect conditions at home. During the Winter of 1925–26, he became aroused over the high cost of living and organized a city-wide meat strike in New York. He circularized the entire country to obtain price comparisons, went to Chicago to confer with the representatives of the great packing houses, and finally took his battle to the floor of the House. There he forced attention by one of his typical gestures. His colleagues sat up and took notice when he began drawing lamb chops from his pocket and waving them in the air.

The *Record* for January 30, 1926, tells the story:

MR. LA GUARDIA. The Department of Agriculture wanted to aid in our fight against the high prices of meat, and they sent me this pamphlet, *Lamb and Mutton, and Their Uses in the Diet!*
Never mind the diet, say we to the Department; our appetites are all right. We know all about lamb, but, as I told you the other day, 90 per cent of the people of New York City cannot afford to eat lamb chops! Why, I have right here with me now—where is it? Oh, yes, here it is in my vest pocket (indicating) 30¢ worth of lamb. Here's one lamb chop (indicating) which is sold in New York City for 30¢ —and they want to instruct us in the economical use of meat! (Laughter)
No, let me show you a steak. Here (exhibiting) is $1.75 worth of steak. How much, I wonder, did Brother Hudspeth's cattle-raisers get for that?
MR. TIMBERLAKE. It looks like a pretty good steak.
MR. LA GUARDIA. It *is* a pretty good steak.
MR. COOPER (of Wisconsin). How much does it weigh?
MR. LA GUARDIA. About two and one-half pounds; it is selling at 75¢ and 80¢ a pound.
Now, here is a roast (exhibiting). Three dollars worth of roast. What workman's family can afford to pay three dollars for a roast of this size? What are we coming to? I believe it is high time that this matter of price-fixing be stopped, and a better system of distribution created. . . .

Again I repeat, if we take the packers' own figures as to his profits, plus the freight rate, which we have authenticated, plus retail profit, we would still be able to buy meat in New York City for 40 per cent less than we are paying for it. We would be willing to divide this 40 per cent with the cattle raiser, if we were only sure that he would get it. . . .

Now, gentlemen, we simply have to eat. We have formed the habit. Whether it is a good or a bad habit I need not discuss. We want the people in the city to live up to the American standard. That standard is easily definable, and it includes good and sufficient nourishment. I remember when I was a kid, out in Arizona, we enjoyed an American breakfast; ham and eggs, bread and butter. These are luxuries in New York City today. The American breakfast has almost disappeared. If we continue along these lines, we shall not only be on the meatless diet of the Russian peasant, but we shall soon go on the rice diet of the Chinese coolie . . . unless something is done, I will say that the people of New York will stop eating meat. It will be no difficulty at all to arrange a city-wide meat strike in twenty-four hours. Civic organizations, community councils, tenants' organizations, social centers, church clubs—all will respond and co-operate; and I will say right now that any time our friends, the cattle-raisers, want us to do it, we are ready to go ahead. We want to stop this exploitation. We want a readjustment of the present system. We want to restore the American breakfast to the children of this age! (Applause).

This speech brought a wail from the packers. The Major received a number of letters from Norman Draper, Washington representative of the Institute of American Meat Packers —one of which flayed him for presenting "extremely inaccurate information concerning the price of meat." This letter went on to say:

The comparison between 75¢ steak and 3¢ a pound Texas bulls, is absurd on its face. In the first place, 75¢ a pound does not represent the average retail price of steak in New York last September. *The Monthly Labor Review* of the United States Bureau of Labor Statistics for November 25, page 45, gives the average retail price of sirloin steak in New York for September as 47.8¢ per pound, chuck roast, average, 25.2¢, plate beef, 19.8¢.

We are not questioning your statement that steak was selling for 75¢ in New York. In fact, it is undoubtedly a perfectly reasonable price for a certain class of beef-steak. But it does not come from 3¢ Texas bulls. It comes from corn-fed steers, which cost the packers about 12¢ a pound, live weight in Chicago.

The Major went through the correspondence, and on March 26, he dictated an explosive reply to Draper:

Dear Sir:

I beg to acknowledge your letter of February 22, 1926, and your letter of March 20, 1926.

I know of no better source of obtaining retail prices of meat than by going into the New York City butchers' shops and buying the meat. That is what I do. Do you deny the cost of meat in New York City, as stated by me on the floor of the House? I will be glad to take you, or your representative, on a tour of New York City on any day, to learn the retail prices of meat.

I am not concerned with bulletins, reports or statistics. You know we cannot feed the people of New York on ticker tape or statistics. We are up against the practical proposition of buying meat every day. We know the excessive and exorbitant prices we are paying for meat. That is my source of information. . . . Both of your letters display the arrogant attitude of the packers. Instead of seeking to co-operate with us, instead of trying to help the situation, you simply arrogate to yourselves the only source of accurate information—and then demand that your version be taken as the Gospel truth, and end it there. What care I whether you present your figures through other channels or not!

Despite all the money that the packers are spending for propaganda, publicity or otherwise, the people are not fooled. We are paying the prices in New York City. I maintain now, as I told your people in Chicago, that the packers have it within their power to reduce the retail cost of meat in New York City from 25 per cent to 33⅓ per cent. Some of these days we will simply stop eating meat in New York City, and perhaps then we may arrive at a fair level of prices.

The packers' representative did not accept La Guardia's challenge to make a round of New York's butcher shops, and the Major proceeded to demonstrate that he had not been bluffing about calling a meat strike. He made a personal appeal to the city editor of every New York newspaper, asking for co-operation. The papers responded, giving the movement wide publicity, and the strike proved a rousing success. The price of meat came down immediately.

CHAPTER XIV

IN NEW YORK

GLOOM shrouded the outer office where a handful of people sat in dismal silence. It was even deeper in the inner office. There a short, plump man paced up and down in nervous desperation. Publisher La Guardia was facing a crisis. The magazine from which he had hoped so much was on the verge of failure. Into it he had poured every cent he could raise—all of his salary, and the proceeds of the mortgage on the University Avenue home. Now he knew that the sacrifice had been in vain.

He had secured subscribers, but he had expended more on each copy than he had received for it when sold. Advertising, relied on to make up the deficit, had not materialized. Now the day of reckoning was at hand.

Fiorello La Guardia paced up and down his office and faced an unpleasant truth. He had no more money. He could not pay the cost of another issue. He couldn't even pay the interest on the mortgage on his home.

It was a bitter realization and rendered even more so by the knowledge that he had been so near success. If only he could have survived a few months more!

His friends had been busy in his behalf. They had evolved a plan for the rescue of the publication. It had been decided to capitalize his popularity with his Italian following.

His enthusiastic countrymen had elected him Commander of the Sons of Italy a short time before. The organization was large and prosperous. His friends had sponsored a program by which the magazine should be adopted as the national organ of the fraternity by the next convention. If he could only keep the publication in existence until then, but——

215

The Congressman shrugged his shoulders and turned toward the door. After all, there was no use in torturing himself with reflections of what "might have been." All that remained now was to pay off the staff, and suspend publication.

And then—the door flew open. *Americolo's* advertising manager came charging into the room with a shout of triumph. He hurled his hat at the ceiling, and threw his arms about the startled publisher in a transport of pure ecstasy.

"We're saved, F. H. We're saved!" shouted the triumphant newcomer.

He slapped a paper down upon the desk with a resounding smack and struck a Napoleonic attitude, while the Major regarded him in puzzled bewilderment.

"I have here, Major La Guardia," he began dramatically, "a contract, signed, sealed and delivered—a contract from an advertiser, if you please; a contract calling for a page in *Americolo*, to run in every issue for the next year!" He beamed upon his chief. "How's *that?*"

And now it was the Major who began a war dance of delight. He fairly shouted with glee as the possibilities unfolded before his eyes.

The office fairly glowed with the atmosphere of triumph. Dramatically the happy publisher produced a bottle of wine and glasses from his desk. The two men drank to the success of *Americolo*.

Then the Major settled back in his chair and called for the contract. "Let's see this advertising," he demanded.

Proudly his colleague extended the copy.

La Guardia glanced over it—and the light died in the shining black eyes.

He studied the copy long and carefully.

It proved to be an advertisement for a certain *Doctor-Yourself-at-Home-by-Looking-up-the-Symptoms-in-the-Index* variety of medical book.

The Major stared at the ceiling reflectively. In his inmost soul he was waging the most desperate battle of his career!

And when he came to a decision at last, he regarded the Advertising Manager sympathetically.

He knew that the latter's small son was under the care of a specialist.

"Satisfied with your doctor?" barked the Major.

The eyes of the advertising man widened in astonishment. Then he nodded understandingly. Association with the Major had already taught him the speed with which the latter's mind flicked from one subject to another.

"How's the baby getting along, anyhow?" persisted his superior.

The other's heart quickened at the thought of his own child. He became expansive at once.

"Why, he's getting along fine. Thanks a lot, Major. The new treatment seems to be doing him a lot of good. We expect to see him fully recovered in a month or so."

La Guardia's ultimatum cracked like a whip.

"All right," he snapped. "Fire your specialist—and doctor the baby out of this book. If *you* will do that, I will accept the advertising!"

The other's jaw dropped. He stared at the Major in frank bewilderment. The latter went on kindly:

"You see, it's this way. I appreciate all that you have done, and I am really grateful to you for it. But there are hundreds of poor Italian immigrants who subscribe for this magazine because they have confidence in me. For that reason, and that reason alone, they regard everything in its pages as gospel!

"And for that reason also, my boy, everything we print has to be good enough for you and me!

"If it's not good enough for us—then it's not good enough for *them*. That's all there is to it."

Protests were useless. The Major stuck to his decision. He was adamant.

The results were quick and crushing. *Americolo* was discontinued at once. The mortgage on the house at 1852 University Avenue, was foreclosed, and once more La Guardia faced the world without a cent.

It was a quixotic gesture—but typically La Guardian.

His friends have always known that the Major could no more resist the dramatic *beau geste*, than he could cease breathing. They insist that he is *not* theatrical, but rather that he *thinks* in terms of the dramatic.

One result of the fiasco, however, was that he gave up his residence in the Bronx, and moved into his district, thereby putting an end to the oft-repeated cry of "carpet-bagger." He rented a simple flat at 109th Street and Madison Avenue.

His popularity was still growing. His constituents, who had always respected his courage, were beginning to appreciate the warmth that was so typical of the man himself. He made himself available to *anyone* in times of trouble. Significant is the letter written at this time to a friend in the Tombs who was waiting to be sentenced to Sing Sing after conviction in a bankruptcy case. La Guardia scribbled him a note, which read as follows:

> My dear Harry:
>
> I have your letter.
>
> I think you got yourself into this mess, and I say now what I have always said, that I think you were dumb, and that it was your stupidity and not your viciousness that got you into the mess.
>
> Unless something unexpected should happen here, I will leave Thursday at midnight, to appear as a character witness, Friday, as you request. By this time I believe the Judge will have made up his mind, and everything be settled. It strikes me that you are still susceptible to kidding—as you have been ever since I have known you. Your character witnesses are not going to help you a bit; but when you appeal to me, as you have, I will respond.
>
> But, for goodness sake, stop believing all the politicians, fakirs, shysters and the rest of the bums whom you have always believed, and who have gotten you into the difficulty you are now in.

Please tell your attorney to keep away from me. I don't want any suggestions from him at all.

Wishing you the best of luck, I am,

Sincerely,

(Signed)   F. La Guardia.

Equally relevant is a letter which he sent to a brilliant young protege, for whom he had secured a position in a New York law firm. Under date of January 23, 1925, he wrote:

My dear Boy:

Your conduct when I was in the city last, was not at all what I had expected. You are young, you have a lot to learn, and a long way to go before you will be a lawyer, in the real sense of the word.

I am fond of you and want to help you. Were I not interested I would not have planned as I did—looking far into the future.

You simply must learn that you don't know it all, and that others in this world have some brains. Both Mr. C—— and Mr. F—— are splendid gentlemen and able lawyers, and I shall expect a courteous, respectful, obedient attitude toward them at all times.

You have an opportunity presented to you such as very few boys have, other than those who can step into their own fathers' office, knowing that one day it will be theirs. This is what I am offering you. You must make up your mind and be fair with me. You either are going to be a politician, a social worker or a lawyer. If you are satisfied, as I told you, to make a living from the Magistrate and Municipal Courts, with General Sessions as the possible limit, you can keep up your social and political activities.

But if you love your profession and want to be proficient, and intend to follow it, then you have got to change your attitude and your whole mode of living. You have to cut out your evening appointments, your dances, and your midnight philandering, for the next five years, and devote yourself to the serious study of the Law. From 1907 to 1912 I did it. . . .

Be careful of your personal appearance. Get a Gillette

razor, and keep yourself well groomed at all times. Be always respectful and courteous to all—the humble as well as the high. And, for goodness sake, keep your ears and eyes open, and keep your mouth closed for at least the next twenty years!

Sincerely,
(Signed)   F. La Guardia.

As the election of 1926 drew near, his confidence in his ability to retain his seat increased. He was aware of the growth of his popularity aforesaid—and he knew the value of the Ghibonnes. The one great problem confronting him was whether or not he should return to the Republican ranks, or continue as a Progressive.

His decision was undoubtedly influenced by the fact that he was disappointed in the calibre of the men who had enrolled beneath the Progressive banner in New York. Writing to a friend in Brooklyn, he said:

> Candidates who ran under the Progressive emblem last year received more funds than their fitness for office and standing as Progressives, merited. Just because a man cannot get a political job with one of the two old parties does not necessarily make him a Progressive—just as, because one calls himself by a military title and claims to be a hero of the World War, that does not necessarily make him an ex-service man.

In response to a letter from Gilson Gardiner of the Scripps-Howard newspapers in reference to a Progressive dinner, he wrote:

> Before accepting your kind invitation, I would want to look over the list of names. There are some fakirs in New York City calling themselves "Progressives" whom I do not care to be embarrassed by any close contact with. The last election was a living example of the disgraceful and dishonest conditions in New York.

Earlier he had written to Nelson, with reference to the Progressive Convention, saying:

> As you know, personally, I am not in favor of the formation of a party from the top down. I feel very strongly that our party should be built from the bottom up.
>
> I shall refuse to sign a call for a convention. I have not yet decided whether I shall attend.

The militancy of the Progressive movement, as exemplified in an independent party, having faded away, La Guardia finally determined to re-enter the Republican fold, and endeavor to recapture the G. O. P. Harlem organization. Backed by the Ghibonnes, he simply walked in and took charge of it. The Old Guard surrendered without a struggle.

Lacking any real opposition he secured his renomination on the Republican ticket. The Democrats named Samuel Dickheiser to oppose him, and the Harlem Congressman entered the least dramatic of all his campaigns. Again he established headquarters at 106th Street and Madison Avenue, and again little Miss Fischer presided behind the scenes.

Over-confidence almost proved his undoing. He did not indulge in any of the spectacular performances of preceding years, and the Tammany organization polled an unexpectedly large vote. The Ghibonnes saved him with a last-minute canvass on election day, and La Guardia won out by the slight margin of fifty-four votes!

The victory contributed to his prestige, however. The La Guardia legend was growing. He had defeated Tammany six times in succession, and he seemed to be the only man in New York who was able to do it consistently. The "silk-stocking" Republicans, controlling the inefficient New York City machine, had very little use for him—but they reflected that, after all, he seemed to constitute their only certainty of Congressional representation. After this victory they accepted him —with a touch of tolerance.

If the "Silk Stockings" thought, however, that La Guardia's return to the Republican ranks implied that he was growing more conservative they were shortly undeceived. Almost before he had had time to settle down in his seat for his sixth Congressional term, he again plunged his native city into turmoil—this time as the champion of the Civil Liberties Union. He clashed with thirteen leading patriotic organizations, including the Daughters of the American Revolution, the Daughters of the Confederacy, the American Legion, the Reserve Officers Association, the Military Order of Foreign Wars, and the State Chamber of Commerce. The Board of Education was caught between two fires.

These patriotic organizations had protested vigorously when permission was granted, early in 1927, to the Civil Liberties Union to hold a meeting in Stuyvesant High School. They maintained that the union was a radical and disloyal organization. Although it had been refused the preceding year, the permit was finally issued by the Board of Education, but not until several postponements had occurred. The board was cautious, and imposed severe restrictions on the meeting, including directions that the topic to be discussed at the meeting should be limited to "The Growth of New York Since 1900," that the board be furnished with copies of all addresses two days in advance, that the speakers confine themselves to their subjects, and, finally, that the meeting be opened with patriotic exercises.

The Civil Liberties Union complied with these terms, and then called a mass meeting, announcing that Congressman La Guardia had been invited to deliver the principal address. The right of free speech had always been close to his heart, and the busy legislator accepted gladly. He came up from Washington and addressed the meeting on the night of June 9. The Congressman was in fine fettle, but his remarks did not attract much attention until nine days later. Then, on June 18, Chairman George L. Darte, of the patriotic committee of the Military Order of the World War, filed an official protest against him, with the Board of Education. The newspapers took it up, and La Guardia soon became a *cause celebre*. The protest was enclosed in a letter signed by Darte, which read in part:

> Please find enclosed stenographic record of the meeting held by the American Civil Liberties Union at the Stuyvesant High School, New York City, June 9. While this is a stenographic report, it does not attempt to cover *all* that was said by the various speakers, but only those points that could be clearly recorded and considered important to report.
>
> You will note in several places in the record that we have endeavored to interpret the meaning of the words of several of the speakers, but have referred not at all to the sneering and sarcastic voice and manner used with some verbal statements, particularly in the case of Congressman La Guardia.
>
> It is believed that, in view of the requirements laid down by the Board of Education, the American Civil Liberties Union went far afield that evening in a number of instances.
>
> It *did* comply with the display of the flag; but the reading of the Bill of Rights could hardly be interpreted as being "patriotic exercises" within the *intent* of the Board of Education.
>
> It should have been clear to any one (sympathetic or otherwise) who was present, that the subject, "The Growth of New York City since 1900" was a camouflage, with the ulterior motive of breaking down the so-called ban against the American Civil Liberties Union, and to build its foundation for future demands. That subject entered but little into any of the talks, and it is believed that the reports of representatives of the Board of Education present, will support this assertion.
>
> Irrespective of the fact that the occasion was not to be a "free speech meeting," the subject of "free speech," as interpreted by the American Civil Liberties Union, was referred to more or less, directly and indirectly, by practically all the speakers. The tenets of *Socialism* were the resounding note through practically all of the talks.

Congressman La Guardia's speech was an attack upon the Supreme Court and the Constitution. There was much criticism of the local judiciary, and, all in all, the meeting was one wholly characteristic of the American Civil Liberties Union, but was, in a degree of course, softer than what it would naturally have put on had it not been in the position they were. . . .

If consistent, will you be so good as to advise us as to what further steps are to be taken by the Board of Education in this matter.

The report proper was devoted almost exclusively to criticizing the remarks of La Guardia, although the patriotic society was almost equally disturbed by those of Nelson S. Spencer, President of the Civil Service Reform Association, and Dean Charles N. Lathrop, Executive Secretary of the National Council of the Protestant Episcopal Church.

A section of the report follows:

Mr. Ward: (Rev. Harry F. Ward)

Our next speaker is one who is always willing to involve himself in the issues of the Civil Liberties Union. Congressman La Guardia has already done what he could for freedom of speech.

La Guardia: *Political Issues in New York City.*

Well, I am here to fight—where is the militia? I see you have a Red sign on the wall (smiling and referring to a red placard on the platform wall.) It's a great game, politics! You have to play the game according to the rules. If you don't play the game according to the rules, you are characterized as "radical," "not dependable," etc. . . .

The previous speaker said that the type of Judges depends upon whether the people want that type of Judge —and this is applicable to politics in general. You simply can't go out and fight if the people don't want to fight with you! I tried it in 1924, and got a good deal of "moral support," and a great deal of encouragement— and didn't get the votes!

"A satisfactory victory." The winner poses in his Headquarters at 106th Street and Madison Avenue on the night of November 5, 1930.

"They smiled at one another as the glad tidings rolled in." La Guardia and
Seabury on election night.

One of the greatest issues, strange as it may seem even to some of my own colleagues (and it is going to come back to us some day), and that is whether or not the people have the right to say what the law of the land shall be. *When the constitutionality of the law is tested,* Congress ought to have the right to over-rule the decision of the Supreme Court—and I firmly believe it. And yet you will find people going along and saying that you will the eby destroy the whole structure of the Constitutio

There is nothing in the Constitution which says that the Supreme Court has the power to set aside the Acts of Congress; there's nothing in any document to indicate that it was in the mind of the framers to give that power. It was first brought about as a policy of expediency.

(He eulogized La Follette as a great American, and praised his progressive work.)

I think since 1924, that the Supreme Court has looked at things in a broader light. Thank God we still have Justice Holmes and Justice Brandeis. But Justice Holmes and Justice Brandeis may retire some day, and we will have an era of *prosperity* and *contentment.* But that issue is coming back, and when it does come back, it will be in the form of a Constitutional Amendment. . . .

The common law was made by landowners for landowners, so when we were confronted with the real housing problem (and I know), they took this great "Constitution" of ours, and we could not carry it out.

. . . After all, the Constitution must be read and interpreted in the light of the age in which we live—and changed times and conditions bring about changed interpretation. If the Courts refuse to supply it the people will have to apply it. There are imperfections in our form of government. But I would sooner have the specific, and even bad, politics of representative government in the hands of the people, than the best dictatorship in the world.

Where are we going to end if the present tendency of intolerance continues? It will indeed be a sad day if men

and women cannot express themselves freely in any public or private place in the United States! There is no
honest man, or honest Administration, who really fears
criticism. . . . I don't know of any infallibility in the
Senate, the House, or—the Board of Education. What is
all this fuss about? To stop people from thinking? But
they thought about it, didn't they? *We believe that if
we could have a commission form of government, these
men would say: "We would have better government!"
If it was intended to stop people from thinking about
changing the government to meet conditions, they should
never have put into the Constitution the means of amend-
ing it. You cannot expect the people to submit to such
a condition. . . .*

(Emphasis and under-scoring—ours.)

NOTE ATTACK ON SUPREME COURT, THE
CONSTITUTION, AND THE APPEAL FOR FREE
SPEECH; AND, PARTICULARLY, THE REFER-
ENCE TO "COMMISSION FORM OF GOVERN-
MENT," WHICH BORDERS CLOSELY UPON THE
SOVIET IDEA OF GOVERNMENT BY COM-
MITTEES.

There was much more in the same tenor.

Reverberations of the Darte protest and the accompanying
charges persisted for months. They resulted in a letter addressed to the Congressman on November 17, by Morris
Ernst, of the Civil Liberties Union, which read as follows:

F. H. La Guardia, Esq.,
220 Broadway,
New York City.

Re: American Civil Liberties Union—Board
of Education.

My dear Mr. La Guardia:

As you no doubt were informed, a public hearing was
held before the Board of Education in the above matter
on October 14, 1927. At that hearing Mr. Gibney, Director of Extension Activities, attacked the American

Civil Liberties Union, because of what he claimed occurred at the meeting at the Stuyvesant High School, June 9, 1927.

We have not sufficient copies of the stenographic reports of the hearing to send them to all interested parties, but we believe the enclosed memo. will be amusing, exciting and irritating to you. It was submitted by the Military Order of the World War, to the Board of Education, as evidence in this case.

You will find reference in the latter part of the report to remarks made by you. This is only part of the attack which will be made upon you. If it were not for the fact that there is a danger that the Board of Education might be misled by this silly kind of stuff, the entire situation might well be passed over as a bit of "Governmental humor."

Within a week, on November 25, the disgusted La Guardia replied:

Thanks for your letter of November 17, 1927.

No, I am not amused, or even irritated, as you suggest. I have gotten accustomed to the annoyance of cooties, and they do not get a rise out of me any more.

I believe that some of the quotations concerning my reference to the Courts, are substantially correct. They are all, however, disconnected, and fail to show the point that I was making, or trying to make.

As to the last paragraph, that is so graveled and disconnected that it could only be presented in that shape intentionally.

I was sustaining a representative form of government, and showing how some of our conservative friends were urgently expressing the desirability of abolishing parliamentary government. A commission consisting of Mellon, Hoover and Gary, would be to their liking—that was substantially what I stated. So the person who drafted and compiled my remarks, with the deductions which he draws, is not only an artistic liar, but, in good plain military language (if I may be permitted to state in all candor and frankness,) he is also an everyday, ordinary son of a bitch.

I hope I have made myself sufficiently clear.

The affair dragged on until the Spring of 1928, when,—on March 9—Forest Bailey of the Union wrote to La Guardia:

Honorable F. H. La Guardia,
220 Broadway,
New York City.

Dear Congressman:

I think you will be interested in learning that the long-delayed hearing of our controversy with the Board of Education, has been set for next Monday evening, the 12th, at 8 o'clock at the Board Rooms.

You are already informed that a part of our difficulty with the Board is the accusation, on the part of Mr. Gibney, that we violated the terms of our agreement at the meeting in June, when you addressed the vast throng. You were a very special offender, according to Mr. Gibney. Mr. Ernst showed me your written comment, and I thoroughly concur. If anything, you were guilty of under-statement. But the fact remains that we are represented as having shown bad faith in allowing our speakers to digress into other fields than the thrilling subject of "The Growth of New York City since 1900."

The Major shrugged his shoulders and attempted to ignore the entire affair. It proved a real drawback in the mayoralty campaign of 1929, however, when he was unable to shake off the charge of radicalism, and completely lost the support of the conservative wing of the Republican Party. The charges were revived four years later by Joseph V. McKee, but by that time they had lost their force, and failed to stick.

The split with the Conservative wing was further widened when he opposed the appointment of Charles H. Tuttle as United States Attorney for the Southern District of New York. Tuttle had the backing of the "Silk Stockings," but La Guardia minced no words when, on April 2, 1927, he wrote to Sam Koenig:

Lest there be any misunderstanding later, I want to state now that the appointment of Charles H. Tuttle does not meet with my approval. . . . The manner of the selection was indeed a bad beginning for the declared efforts to unite all factions of the Republican Party in this State. The appointee can do nothing toward restoring the confidence of the great masses of the people in this city. He typifies no particular school of thought within the party. It is true that the gentleman may have rendered great services in the fight for city parks—but such services were rendered on the wrong side of the case.

If his great legal services in the Long Island Park Case are to be rewarded, the gentleman might properly be the recipient of the Order of the Garter, from the lords of the Long Island manors. The boastful array of the gentleman's church connections, glare in irreconcilable contrast with his professional connections with bootlegging cases in the Federal Court.

Desirous as I am of co-operating with you, I must reserve the right to carry on the fight for the great mass of the people of this city who have confidence in me, and who look to me to represent them in such cases, as well as in obtaining proper and useful legislation.

His unvarnished opinion of the Republican leaders in New York was further expressed in a letter to Ogden Mills, dated August 11:

Everything along the Hudson is quiet. Your friends of the party are keeping up their batting average of errors and blunders. Tammany has succeeded in trading a perfectly good, upright, approachless Judge for five out-and-out useful Tammany politicians. Svengali Untermyer has sent Trilby Lockwood to find out if Charlie Hughes will run. Otherwise, nothing new.

A further estimate of the Republican Party in New York was shown by his response to William W. Pellett, a candidate for Justice of the City Court who had requested his support. On September 13 he wrote Pellett as follows:

> If you are out to win, and will wage a real honest-to-goodness campaign, I will be glad to go on your committee. If, on the other hand, you are going to wage the usual Republican campaign, of sitting down and letting Tammany win by default . . . count me out.

And on October 22, he replied to Abraham Menin, also the recipient of a Republican nomination, who had made a similar request for support:

> Of course I know you well, and know all about the Court for which you have been nominated. But I don't know much about this party which you say nominated you. You ought to tell me more about it. In the meantime, let me know what I can do to help you.

* * *

The friendly tone of the correspondence with Ogden Mills reveals a new note in the La Guardia personality. His sincerity had begun to command the respect of his political opponents, while his vibrant personality won their admiration and affectionate regard. They knew that he would show no mercy in political combat; but he was friendly and likable when outside of the lists. This resulted in some strange friendships.

The Major's opponents were divided into two distinct classifications: those whom he liked personally and whose friendship he valued outside the arena; and those whose sincerity he did not respect and whom he could not tolerate under any circumstances. Among the latter were President Coolidge, Secretary Mellon and the Secretary of Commerce, Herbert Hoover. The friendly enemies included Nicholas Longworth, John Nance Garner, John M. Morin, Ogden Mills and Hamilton Fish. Garner, as the Democratic leader of the House, was less frequently opposed to the liberal La Guardia than the others—ostensibly the members of his own party, but bitter opponents of the things he stood for.

The passing years had softened the memory of his poignant tragedy. He still worked long hours, but he no longer buried himself in his labors. He was finding time to cultivate a little social life.

He occupied a small apartment in New York and another in Washington. There he frequently entertained his friends. He loved to cook for them—and invitations to his spaghetti dinners were eagerly sought by his colleagues and the Washington correspondents.

Gradually the little circle of intimates widened. Frequent visitors to the Washington apartment—in addition to his friendly enemies—were Congressman O. J. Kvale, the Wisconsin Farmer-Laborite, an ordained Lutheran minister; the brilliant Paul Y. Anderson, of the *St. Louis Post Despatch*, and Ray Tucker, of the Scripps-Howard organization.

Miss Duff Gilfond, a frequent contributor to the *Nation*, dropped into his office to interview him, and in time became a close friend of the Major as well as of Miss Fischer. The little German girl had become a mature and charming woman. She was invaluable to the Congressman, carefully supervising both the Washington office, and affairs in the home district. It was known that she enjoyed his implicit confidence, and her prestige in the political field had increased immeasurably.

The circle of his New York friends was just as varied. It included the conservative Paul Windels, whose home was frequently visited, and with whose children the jovial Congressman was a great favorite. His love for all children was intense, and his arrival at the Madison Avenue apartment house in which he lived, was usually marked by wild excitement among the youngsters of the neighborhood. They clustered about him in droves, and escorted him to his very door.

Other members of the New York circle included Piccirilli, Ruotolo and Spalding, who shared his artistic tastes. He loved to slip off to a concert in such congenial company, or simply to spend the evening listening to classical music on the radio. Very frequently the music-loving Major was to be found crouched in the upper balcony of the Metropolitan Opera House, reveling in the performance of the artists whom he fairly worshiped. Other evenings were spent in company with friends who were prominent among New York liberals. These included Ernest Gruening, the journalist, and Morris Ernst and Jacob Panken, both leading attorneys.

He was literally the idol of the New York Italian colony, and always received an uproarious ovation from its members. The entrance of the short, sturdy man in the big black, slouch hat into an Italian speakeasy was the advent of royalty. Waiters, bartenders and patrons thronged about him, chatting in their native language and whooping with glee at his repartee. He was deluged with invitations to drink, which were always rejected. He made it a point to pay for his own, though he was exceedingly generous with his invitations.

This generosity was also responsible for a multitude of private charities, which he concealed as carefully as if they constituted activities wholly reprehensible. He seemed incapable of refusing any appeal from the unfortunate, and his salary was dissipated to the last cent in consequence. As a result, the man was always in financial straits.

He had acquired a number of proteges whom he guided in fatherly fashion. Chief among these was young Marcantonio, on whom the Major lavished his attention. Marcantonio was now practicing law on his own account, and La Guardia was patently proud of the boy's success.

Assuming an almost paternal attitude, he carefully supervised Marcantonio's legal training, and worked him into the well-oiled little political machine which was gradually evolving in Harlem. Afterward he founded a law firm, admitting his protege to partnership; and seven years later he had the satisfaction of seeing Marcantonio take the very seat he had occupied in the House. (The support of Mayor La Guardia was a valuable asset to Congressman Marcantonio in the bitter campaign of 1934.)

CHAPTER XV

WASHINGTON

To THE Ogden Mills letter of August 11, 1927, La Guardia added a postscript: "Has Seymour Lowman any sense of humor?" Mills responded: "You will be interested to know that Seymour has a most *decided* sense of humor."

The Lowman sense of humor underwent a real trial in the ensuing months as the leading Wet Congressman settled back to the task of undermining the Prohibition bulwarks in earnest. With the usual La Guardia profuseness, he scattered his fire all over the field, but reserved his fiercest volleys for Major Chester P. Mills, Prohibition Administrator of New York City. He preferred so many official charges against Mills that the latter's superiors grew dizzy. He flayed the gentleman on the floor of the House, precipitating a fierce controversy, and he besieged United States Attorney Emory R. Buckner with dozens of letters, demanding the prosecution of some of Mills' subordinates.

The Major enjoyed his Prohibition "field day," however, when he discovered the Government itself in the liquor business! He took the floor on January 5, 1927, and revealed conditions which won the attention of the entire nation. He had spent weeks preparing his evidence, and required two days for its presentation before the House Ways and Means Committee on February 23-24, 1927. La Guardia told the Committee about a Government-operated speakeasy, the Bridge-Whist Club in New York. He discussed the work of A. Bruce Bielaski, and the "piece-work purchase of information." He startled the Committee by charging that the Government agents had been distributing poisoned alcohol *on permits*, for beverage purposes, and he revealed that the Government had

had recourse to wire-tapping in Prohibition cases. More than that, he charged that the Dry agents had tapped the wires of their own superiors—and then used the information so obtained for blackmail purposes! His bitter eloquence stunned his hearers.

> Please do not think, gentlemen, that I am making insinuations or indulging in innuendoes. I make the specific charge that these under-cover men *stole* the Government's money. They *stole* it, they thieved it, they bootlegged with Government money, under the guise of Government authority! They procured profits and obtained no beneficial results.

The Major got results that time. As an outcome of his investigations during these months, Bielaski lost his job; the approval of $44,000 of undercover expense money was held up; wire-tapping was discontinued; the Government went out of the speakeasy business; and the use of entrapment methods in Prohibition cases was specifically disallowed.

Fourteen formal charges against Mills were filed on January 10, 1927, charging laxity, and blaming that official for everything from diversion of denatured alcohol, to "paying for liquor with rubber checks."

"Regardless of the merits of the transaction," wrote La Guardia, "concerning the latter charge, or whether it was bad liquor or bad checks, the fact remains that such conduct is a bad example to the force, and not conducive to good discipline. While not justifying in any way the conduct of the bootlegger, and *not* sympathizing with his plight, yet his plaint is not unreasonable, considering the fact that bootleggers' dealings with officials are generally on a cash basis!"

The Major enjoyed the situation hugely when he found himself in a strategic position from which he was able to embarrass the superiors of Prohibition.

On January 13, 1927, he wrote to Buckner, demanding the indictment of Mills, Bielaski and Ralph W. Bickle, for violating the law, by operating the Bridge-Whist Club at 14 East 44th Street, New York City. The be-deviled Prohibitionists were already sick over that fiasco, and were plainly disconcerted when La Guardia returned to the subject concerning which he had raised such a row that preceding week.

"Obviously, you have no choice in the matter," he told Buckner. "The overt acts of Chester P. Mills, A. Bruce Bielaski and Ralph W. Bickle, make up as clear and perfect a case of conspiracy to violate the provisions of the Prohibition law, as well as the overt act of unlawfully selling liquor, as ever came to the attention of any District Attorney anywhere, any time." He warned Buckner that pressure would be brought to bear in behalf of the three, "under the pretext of law enforcement," but denied the validity of this argument, "the law being clear that Government officials dare not violate the law."

Two days later Chief Assistant United States Attorney Robert E. Manley responded that Buckner, who was recovering from an operation, had left that day for Florida. "I am sending your letter to him," concluded Manley. "He will answer it shortly."

La Guardia snapped back a telegram on January 17, which declared:

YOUR LETTER JANUARY FIFTEENTH MOST UNSATIS-
FACTORY. REALIZE NECESSITY MR. BUCKNER TAKE VA-
CATION TO RECUPERATE, BUT THAT DOESN'T MEAN
OFFICIAL BUSINESS MUST STOP. . . . OURS IS A GOVERN-
MENT OF LAW AND NOT OF MEN. HENCE DURING MR.
BUCKNER'S NECESSARY AND UNAVOIDABLE ABSENCE,
OFFICE MUST FUNCTION. SECTION 178 OF REVISED
STATUTE ACT OF JULY 23, 1868, SPECIFICALLY PRO-
VIDES THAT, IN EVENT OF ABSENCE OR SICKNESS OF
HEAD OF ANY BUREAU, ASSISTANT OR DEPUTY OF SUCH
CHIEF SHALL PERFORM THE DUTIES. . . . YOU ARE,
THEREFORE, CLOTHED WITH AUTHORITY, AND MUST

ASSUME RESPONSIBILITY AS LONG AS YOU ARE IN
CHARGE OF THE OFFICE. MATTER IS OF SUCH IMPOR-
TANCE, I CAN'T PERMIT IT TO GO VACATIONING, AND
MUST HAVE PROMPT ACTION. PLEASE WIRE ME WHEN
YOU INTEND TO DO SO. I MAY TAKE THE MATTER UP
WITH THE DEPARTMENT OF JUSTICE, SHOULD YOU DE-
CIDE TO AWAIT MR. BUCKNER'S RETURN.

The same day Manley wired La Guardia in Washington:

BEFORE MR. BUCKNER WENT SOUTH, I TOLD HIM
ABOUT YOUR LETTER. HE ASKED ME TO SEND IT DOWN
TO HIM AND TO WRITE YOU ACKNOWLEDGING ITS RE-
CEIPT AND TELLING YOU HE WOULD ANSWER.

On January 20 La Guardia carried the matter to the floor
of the House. The *Record* shows that he amplified it considerably:

MR. LA GUARDIA: I charged here a few days ago that
the United States Government, through its agents, designated as "undercover men," was violating the law in the
City of New York, in that they unlawfully operated a
club known as the "Bridge-Whist Club," where liquor
was unlawfully purchased and sold; that United States
agents unlawfully purchased liquor, caused the unlawful
transportation of liquor, and unlawfully sold liquor over
a bar for six months.

I now add to those charges, and I charge that the
United States Government, through its agents, unlawfully operated a pool room on Chapel Street in Nor-
folk, Va., and unlawfully sold liquor there, through its
undercover agents.

I now charge that the United States Government,
through its agents, unlawfully operated a distillery at
Elizabeth City in North Carolina, purchased and operated
by government agents with government funds, and sold
liquor there.

That is public business. Congress is entitled to know
to what extent the Government is engaged in the opera-

tion of unlawful distilleries. We want to know just how many pool rooms and dives the Government is operating. We want to know how much is being spent for these unlawful purposes. Yet the Secretary of the Treasury gets the chairman of the Committee on the Judiciary to report on these resolutions. If he thinks that is going to keep me from giving the country the information which I have, he is sorely mistaken. The undercover system has created such a situation in a few months that high officers are at the mercy of these undercover men. No one dare move. The undercover system has got the Treasury Department at its mercy and stalemated. I asked for the dismissal of Chester P. Mills on charges that I have filed. Mr. Andrews dare not dismiss Mr. Mills, because if he does, Mr. Mills may bring certain cases to trial that Mr. Andrews does not *want* tried. Mr. Mills dare not dismiss Mr. Bruce Bielaski, because if he does, Mr. Bielaski may use some of the undercover information which he obtained, which may be very unpleasant for Mr. Mills.

I know now that the Treasury Department is preparing a good supply of whitewash, and expects to give three or four coats; but even that is not enough for Mr. Bielaski and Mr. Mills. I have filed specific charges. Most of the matters contained in my charges are matters of record. Yet the plan is to brush them aside!

. . . I filed charges against these officials. I have even brought the matter to the attention of the United States Attorney in New York City, because there has been a flagrant and vicious violation of the law. . . .

Mr. Blanton.   Mr. Speaker, will the gentleman yield?

Mr. La Guardia.   Yes.

Mr. Blanton.   As I understand, the gentleman from New York is in favor of a strict enforcement of the Prohibition Law in New York City?

Mr. La Guardia.   Yes; as long as it is a law; and I don't want the Government Departments to violate it.

Mr. Blanton.   And you want them to enforce it?

Mr. La Guardia.   Yes. I know that the minute they start to enforce it in my State, in the State of New Jersey, and in the gentleman's State of Texas, and in the State of Maine, and in the State of Pennsylvania, you gentlemen will join us and seek a change in existing conditions. . . .

MR. SCHAFER. Mr. Speaker, and Gentlemen of the House, I have listened to the arguments of the two preceding speakers with a great deal of interest. Personally I have not gone into the evidence which our colleague from New York (Mr. La Guardia) has on the matter, which he has just presented to the House; but, knowing the gentleman from New York as I do, I know he would not take the step and make the charges he has made, if they were not sustained. . . .

MR. BLANTON. Mr. Speaker, will the gentleman yield?

MR. SCHAFER. Yes.

MR. BLANTON. Then, if I correctly understand the gentleman from Wisconsin, he is joining the gentleman from New York (Mr. La Guardia) in demanding that the Prohibition Law be strictly enforced in New York and in Milwaukee?

MR. LA GUARDIA. And in Texas, too. (Laughter)

MR. BULWINKLE. I was wondering if the gentleman from New York construed the remarks of his Wet leader to mean that his fight on Prohibition did not amount to anything! (Laughter)

MR. LA GUARDIA. Well, I will tell you. I don't think it does just now, do you? (Laughter) I refuse to fool myself. I absolutely consider that the Drys are in an overwhelming majority in this House, and what I am seeking to do is to carry on a campaign of education. I don't believe your folks back home know what's going on! And the people of this country don't know the farce, the crime, the hypocrisy, the graft, in the very department that is entrusted with the enforcement of this law. When they do, they will realize that there is something in the fight which we are waging here!

The Major did not slacken his attack on the Prohibition officials. On March 19, 1927, he wrote to Mr. Andrews:

Your continued fulsome praise of your Prohibition administrator in New York City, and the alleged results obtained by him, are so far from the facts that you are simply making yourself ridiculous. Your support of this incompetent administrator, and the deliberate misstatements of facts you are publicly making to protect him, are placing you either in the position of sharing the responsibility of his misconduct, or else to be qualified in the category with him. . . . When you and your administrator, Major Mills, state that there is no beer available in New York, you are deliberately stating a fact that you know is not true. Beer is flowing from the vats in and around New York as fast as the law of gravitation will permit. . . . If the present conditions in New York City are permitted to continue, I will hold you personally responsible—and, I can assure you, I have the evidence.

One week later, the Congressman wired the *New York Daily News:*

YOU MAY QUOTE ME . . . AS FOLLOWS:

PRAISE OF MILLS BY GENERAL ANDREWS IS CONTRARY TO VIEWS EXPRESSED BY HIM TO ME AND OTHERS HERE IN WASHINGTON. ANDREWS ADMITTED TO ME PERSONALLY THAT HE REALIZED CONDITIONS IN NEW YORK WERE ROTTEN, AND THAT MILLS DID NOT UNDERSTAND AND DID NOT HAVE THE SITUATION UNDER CONTROL. I DEFY HIM TO CONTRADICT THIS STATEMENT, MADE TO ME IN THE PRESENCE OF A HIGHER OFFICIAL OF HIS OWN DEPARTMENT.

The Major returned to his seemingly hopeless battle with dogged persistence. He coined one pet phrase, which he used in the House, and which concluded most of his letters to the Treasury Department. It resounded as monotonously as the "Delenda est Carthago" of Cato in the Roman Senate. La Guardia's slogan, endlessly repeated as long as Prohibition was on the statue books, was: "Let it be enforced."

He again took up the attack on Judge Cooper, and forced the consideration of the impeachment charges after as bitter a fight as the House had ever witnessed. The *Record* of January 28, 1927, fairly reeks with vitriolic exchanges.

MR. LA GUARDIA. Mr. Speaker I am not at all surprised at the very technical objection that has been raised in order to prevent a discussion of the facts upon which my charges are based, and the reason why they should be referred to the Committee on the Judiciary.

Typical of that opposition is the fact that the gentlemen themselves used the time, and claim that it should be taken out of my time. The gentleman from Missouri (Mr. Dyer) joined in that kind of tactics.

MR. DYER. Will the gentleman yield?

MR. LA GUARDIA. No.

MR. DYER. The gentleman from New York ought not to make a statement of that kind.

MR. LA GUARDIA. I do; and I repeat it. The gentleman from Missouri joined in taking me off my feet in the presentation of these facts.

MR. CRAMPTON. Mr. Speaker, I make the point of order that the gentleman is not discussing facts for the justification of the presentation of his charges, which the speaker has already decided is the only subject he is entitled to discuss.

MR. LA GUARDIA. I make the point of order that the the gentleman from Michigan should not address the Chair with his hands in his pockets. (Laughter)

MR. BLANTON. Mr. Speaker, I make the further point of order that the gentleman from New York (Mr. La Guardia) is out of order when he impugns the motives of the gentleman from Missouri (Mr. Dyer) and the gentleman from Michigan (Mr. Crampton).

MR. DYER. And refuses to yield.

MR. CRAMPTON. And I make the point of order that in the consideration of impeachment charges against a Federal Judge of the United States, it is a matter not only of the highest privilege, but ought to be a serious affair in this House, and not an occasion for levity.

Mr. La Guardia. The gentleman from Michigan is making it an occasion for levity. Now let me say for the purpose of the *Record*, that some gentlemen seem to be very much, and unduly, exercised as to the facts I am about to bring out. Now, gentlemen, interrupt me as much as you please, I am not going to stop. I am a member of this House just as much as any other member is.

Mr. Rankin. And the gentleman represents two parties.

Mr. La Guardia. Now, Mr. Speaker, with the permission of the gentleman from Michigan, and the gentleman from Missouri (Mr. Dyer) I want to say that there are very grave reasons and important public necessities why these charges should be preferred to the Committee on the Judiciary for their immediate action. But before referring to these charges, of course, it is necessary to point out that a *prima facie* case is presented, and that there is reasonable ground to believe that the committee will sustain these charges and bring in a proper Resolution of Impeachment. . . .

Mr. Blanton. Now, will the gentleman yield?

Mr. La Guardia. In a moment. I continue with the letter. (Reads letter.)

Mr. Blanton. Will the gentleman yield there?

Mr. La Guardia. No, not just yet. I helped the gentleman when he was in the same predicament in which I am now, not so very long ago. I helped him to overcome some points of order that were raised.

Mr. Blanton. I would like the gentleman in fairness to yield to me.

Mr. La Guardia. Not just yet. I shall give the gentleman an opportunity in just a few moments. Now, get this picture. . . .

Mr. Blanton. Mr. Speaker, will the gentleman yield there?

Mr. La Guardia. Not yet.

Mr. Blanton. The gentleman is not afraid of his case, is he?

Mr. La Guardia. Not a bit.

Mr. Blanton. Then, why will he not yield to his friend—even though his friend is a Prohibitionist?

Mr. La Guardia.   Because I have no confidence in the gentleman's judgment in a matter of this kind.

Mr. Blanton.   May I ask the gentleman one question?

Mr. La Guardia.   No, not yet. But I am going to yield to the gentleman before I get through.

Mr. Blanton.   I thought the gentleman would be fair enough to do that.

Mr. La Guardia.   . . . I ask any member of the House, is that American justice?

Mr. Blanton.   Now, will he yield for me to answer the question?

Mr. La Guardia.   In just a moment.

Mr. Blanton.   Will the gentleman yield for a question?

Mr. La Guardia.   Yes, for a question.

Mr. Blanton.   If I understand what this Judge did. . . .

Mr. La Guardia.   I said a "question."

Mr. Blanton.   I want to ask the gentleman if this Judge did more than tell—

Mr. Sabath.   Mr. Speaker, I make the point of order the gentleman from New York has refused to yield.

Mr. La Guardia.   Oh, I yielded for a "question." Did he do more than what?

Mr. Blanton.   Did the Judge do more than to suggest to the Prohibition Commission that the higher-ups would be brought to justice, as well as the lower-downs?

Mr. La Guardia.   Yes.

Mr. Blanton.   I want to ask the gentleman this question: I notice that his speech is printed in galley proof. Is that for giving it out to the newspapers over the country?

Mr. La Guardia.   Mr. Speaker, that is just about as fair—that is just about as sporting as the gentleman from Texas can ever be! In other words, he judges others by himself. Why, Mr. Speaker, this (indicating) is not my speech. This is a Senate document. *That* is not going into the *Record*. It is a public document. Now, who is talking for the newspapers, I, or the gentleman from Texas? (Applause) Has the gentleman any other question that he wants to ask?

Mr. Blanton.   After the applause by his Wet friends

here, I would like to ask this question: Does the gentleman not approve of a Judge who insists on enforcing the law against the higher-ups, as well as against the lower-downs?

Mr. La Guardia. I do not approve of a Judge who will enter into a conspiracy with agents of the government to entice and entrap people to commit a crime, so that these people can be brought before him, and he be able to send them to jail. No, I do not approve of that—and there is not an impartial man in the House who approves of it. (Applause)

Now, gentlemen, you can sneer about some of these things—as some of you do. You do not like to hear about these things, and I will tell you why. You show me a Judge—you show me a prohibition agent——

Mr. Crampton. Mr. Speaker, I make the point of order that there is no quorum present.

Speaker. The gentleman from Michigan makes the point of order that there is no quorum present. The Chair will count. 220 members represent a quorum. . . .

Mr. Stalker. Will the gentleman yield?

Mr. La Guardia. Yes.

Mr. Stalker. I am endeavoring to arrive at the gentleman's motive. Does the gentleman object to the fact that Judge Cooper imposes jail sentences upon practically every bootlegger brought before him?

Mr. La Guardia. Properly brought before him?

Mr. Stalker. Brought before him?

Mr. La Guardia. Properly brought before him.

Mr. Stalker. Does the gentleman realize that Judge Cooper is one of the most effective and efficient Judges in the State of New York? (Applause)

Mr. La Guardia. That applause comes from the gentleman from Texas, who does not know a thing about the Northern District of New York!

On February 11, when La Guardia's resolution came up again, there was a bitter fight with Blanton, leading the Dry forces:

Mr. Blanton. The Chairman of this Committee is working right in with the Tammany bunch and with the gentleman from New York (Mr. La Guardia)—with this holy alliance that has been formed between the Socialist member from New York and the Wet Tammany bunch, to discredit a man because he has done his duty.

* * *

Although he fought the case to the end, the odds proved too great, and the crusading Congressman lost his battle against Judge Cooper. He was unable to force the impeachment resolution on the floor, but he did secure a statement condemning the practice of entrapment. Concerning this practical victory he wrote to a Connecticut correspondent on March 2, 1927:

> The Committee decided not to proceed in the impeachment case, but administered a rebuke of the Judge's activities.

He continued to be a thorn in the side of the Republican Party, and his feud with the Administration became more bitter when he introduced an embarrassing resolution concerning our policy in Nicaragua and Central America. The Liberal La Guardia bitterly opposed American intervention. He outlined his position in a telegram to the *St. Louis Post-Dispatch*, dated August 4:

> REFERENCE TELEGRAM 2ND, OUR CONDUCT IN NICARAGUA CANNOT BE JUSTIFIED IN LAW, REASON, MORALS OR NECESSITY. WE HAVE NO MORE RIGHT TO POLICE NICARAGUA, AS WE ARE DOING, THAN LIBERIA HAS TO POLICE ANY OF OUR STATES INDULGING IN LYNCHING OF NEGROES, EXCEPT THAT WE HAVE THE BRUTE FORCE TO DO IT. BUT BRUTE FORCE HAS NEVER BEEN INVOKED AS A JUSTIFICATION OF THIS COUNTRY'S ATTITUDE! OF COURSE, WE ARE LOSING FRIENDS; AND NOT ONLY FRIENDS, BUT THE CONFIDENCE OF THE SISTER REPUB-

LICS OF THE WESTERN HEMISPHERE. MACHINE GUNS
MAY COLLECT INTEREST ON BONDS, BUT THEY WILL
NEVER MAKE FRIENDS. . . . YOU ASK IF POLICY OF
JOINING FORCES WITH SISTER REPUBLICS WOULD NOT
BE BETTER? OF COURSE IT WOULD—BUT WHY ASK
MERE MEMBERS OF CONGRESS SUCH QUESTION? ASK
THE BANKERS WHO CAUSED THE EXPEDITION TO BE
SENT DOWN THERE! THEY KNOW.

(SIGNED)   F. LA GUARDIA.

He was becoming steadily more unpopular in his own
party. Administration leaders attempted to ignore his eternal
harping on Prohibition and such matters as the Nicaraguan
affair, but their patience was about exhausted. He was like a
mosquito, everlastingly buzzing about their ears, shrilling his
incessant warnings, and occasionally swooping down to draw
blood!

The Washington correspondents loved him, because his
continuous attacks inevitably made good copy. Republican
leaders read the resultant stories and ardently cursed "the
damn little demagogue."

The Capitol breathed a sigh of relief when Congress adjourned and he returned to New York. That rejoicing was
premature, however. He continued to make headlines at home.

The G. O. P. chieftains writhed when the press services
transmitted his remarks of March 17 at The Star Casino. Making his annual report to his constituents, in the course of his
town meeting, he issued another blast at his own party, taking
as his text the uncertainty regarding President Coolidge's desire for another term.

"The figure three will play an important part in determin-
ing who the next President of the United States may be," announced the stormy petrel of Harlem. "It will not, however,
resolve itself, as many now believe, around the question of a
third term, but whether or not the farmers of this country are
going to be rebuffed for a third time! The East simply can-

not, or will not, understand the crisis of the farmers and the critical situation in which they find themselves."

After campaigning enthusiastically for his friend, Jacob Panken, who was running on the Socialistic ticket—and seeing the latter go down to defeat—the Major came grimly back to his pet subject—PROHIBITION. He had discovered a new means of pestering the Treasury Department. Gleefully he pressed his demands for investigation of the permits given to medicated liquor. Because of his official status, the harried Prohibition officials were forced to investigate—or, at least, reply to each of his myriad communications. A sample exchange is as follows:

July 29, 1927.

My dear Secretary Mellon:

I enclose herewith photostat of an order sheet, sent out by the Banfi Products Corporation, 273 Bleecker Street, New York City, and also advertisement contained on reverse side of the said order sheet.

I desire to call your attention to the articles advertised and described in No. 1 and No. 4. Either the products are in violation of the law, or the advertisement is misleading. If it is the former, your Department should take action; if it is the latter, it should be referred to the proper department having jurisdiction over such matters, for *their* attention.

The first article, "Marsela Florio," is the name of a well-known wine, of the nature of sherry. The name "Marsela Florio" is as typical of a certain kind of wine as is "Gordon Gin" or "Martell Cognac." There can be no mistake as to what "Marsela Florio" means, or is intended to mean. The same applies to the product described as No. 4.

As long as Prohibition is on the statute books, let it be enforced.

(Signed)   F. La Guardia,
Member of Congress.

This brought a reply, dated August 5, from Alf. Oftdhahl, Acting Commissioner:

> I have the honor of acknowledging the receipt of your letter of July 29, 1927, addressed to the Honorable Andrew W. Mellon, Secretary of the Treasury, regarding certain advertising matter which is being distributed by the Banfi Products Corporation, at 273 Bleecker Street, New York City, and calling attention to two of the articles named in the circular which you enclose.
>
> After examining the record of this Permittee to import all of the products described in the circular, since they have been examined and found to be unfit for beverage purposes, it appears that approval was granted for the importation of "Marsala Florio Chinato," and "Vermouth Corasala Florio," or "Vermouth Cora."
>
> The firm has deviated from the names under which the products were heretofore approved, and their attention will be immediately called to this matter.
>
> The most recent analyses of all of the products referred to by you, indicate that they are made in accordance with the formulae upon which approval for their importation was based, and that they are unfit for beverage purposes.

Instantly La Guardia returned to the attack, with a communication declaring:

> The facts as contained in your letter, agree in every respect as I find them, and as reported in my letter to you. There is, therefore, no difference in the facts. I am somewhat surprised, however, that you treat the matter rather lightly. As far as I know, there has been no amendment or repeal of the provisions under Section 3 or Sections 18 and 19 of title 2 of the National Prohibition Act, covering misrepresentation, and the offering for sale of alcoholic beverages. The omission of part of the name, "Chinato," (which indicates the presence of quinine in these beverages) with the absence of the quinine flavor or taste, coupled with the boastful and brazen advertisements of their 18 per cent alcohol content, strikes me as a flagrant violation of the law.

The widespread propaganda sent out by manufacturers and distributors of so-called "medicated liquor," concerning their political influence and power of obtaining special permits, is part of their advertising campaign.

Unless this permit, and similar permits which I am investigating and shall bring to your attention, are immediately revoked, I am going to hold a public demonstration and show the flagrant manner in which the law is being violated—seemingly with the knowledge of the Department.

I shall bring each of these individual cases to your attention first, even at the risk of becoming unduly annoying and boring to you.

As long as the Prohibition Law is in effect, let us have the law enforced.

> (Signed)   F. La Guardia,
> Member of Congress.

He never missed an opportunity to stir up trouble for the Drys, and he spent hours scanning the daily papers for clues which might put him on the trail of violators.

He found one such lead in the *New York Times* of September 28, in a story quoting Joseph S. Wise, Jr., a prominent attorney at 20 Broad Street, as having said:

> I have drunk liquor with Justices of the United States Court, and I have seen them drink liquor furnished by United States Marshals, in their chambers.

The Major dropped the sheet with a howl of delight. He shouted for a stenographer, and plunged into the dictation of a letter to the lawyer:

"This is indeed a most startling and shocking charge," began La Guardia. "If the drinking was subsequent to the adoption of the Eighteenth Amendment and the enactment of the enforcement laws, I demand the names, places, dates and full particulars against the parties concerned, before the Congress convenes in December."

Next day the embarrassed attorney replied:

I have yours of today. I did not mean to be understood to say that I have seen Judges drinking liquor in their official chambers, furnished by United States Marshals since Prohibition. You are rather hasty in your demands for particulars, under the idea that I implied knowledge that would support you in impeachment proceedings.

To which the Congressman rejoined on September 30th:

There could have been no question as to the meaning of your statement, as quoted in the press of this city. My demands, therefore, were not "hasty," but quite timely. Aside from all of that, I believe you owe it to the profession as well as to the Bench, to make public announcement that you were misunderstood, misquoted, or that you overstated yourself.

In an article which he wrote for the Smokers' Campaign during the Summer, La Guardia declared:

It is impossible to tell whether Prohibition is a good thing or a bad thing. It has never been enforced in this country. . . . I am for temperance, and that is why I am for modification. . . . I am ready to concede the absolute good faith and sincerity of a great many Dry leaders in this country. I do not believe they are hypocrites or insincere, any more than I believe that every advocate of modification is a rum-hound and a drunkard. There are a few rascals and scoundrels among the Drys just as there are among the Wets. Why not take inventory and ascertain the true conditions? . . . Let the American people know what is going on.

This article proved the beginning of a new interest for the dynamic Congressman. He suddenly realized that he could write for newspapers and magazines, thereby securing a wider hearing for the various causes which were dear to him. Eagerly he swung back to the typewriter which he had neglected since the Spanish-American War days and after a lapse of thirty years the La Guardia "by-line" was revived.

During the Autumn of 1927 Congressman La Guardia began to appear in print with considerable frequency. An article published in the *New York American* on August 15 fairly bristled with pride in his Italian ancestry. It traced the history of Italian success in this country, paying a graceful tribute to his friends Ruotolo and the Piccirilli brothers. He listed judges, lawyers, surgeons and actors and devoted a special paragraph to Tony Lazzeri, the baseball star.

"There are no monkeys and no bananas in Italy," continued La Guardia, "yet in the earliest days of immigration the Italian was attracted to both monkeys and bananas. Many of the older immigrants are somewhat ashamed of the organ-grinding and banana-peddling Italian. Different is the generation of today. We are quite proud of those honest and hard-working immigrants."

"If the Italian went about grinding out music his organ was in tune and its music good. He brought music to places where music was necessary. We are not at all ashamed of him today—and the banana pushcarts have developed into enormous fruit companies of national importance."

The following month he produced an article entitled "Give Aviation a Chance" which appeared in the Sunday Magazine Section of the *New York Times*. It was based on the theory that "Aviation has developed in this country in spite of the Government. . . . Our past experience in blundering can well be of service now in keeping the Government's hands off development, construction and design of airplanes."

Discussing the clamor for a Government ban on transoceanic flights, he pointed out that the development of transportation has always been accompanied by accidents, fatalities and resultant progress. Referring to a "foolish and childlike demand for the prohibition of automobiles only twenty-five years ago," he quoted headlines from New York newspapers, such as "Automobiles Spread Death," "Massacre by Automobile," "Paris-Madrid Horror" (this last named describing a cross-country race). Coming to the defense of the airmail service he told of the same criticism which the railroads experienced a century earlier. He cited a letter written to a Philadelphia paper in 1835, complaining that the mail from New York to the Quaker City, when transported by railroad, was usually late, requiring more than thirteen hours to make the trip from Jersey City.

His most conclusive parallel was a quotation from the official report of the Post Office Department for the same year, which read: "From the experience we have had the adaptation of the railroad to the question of mail transportation is becoming every day more and more questionable. It is very apparent that the railroad cannot be relied upon to any degree of certainty—which is all important in the transportation of mail."

CHAPTER XVI

AFLOAT AND ASHORE

TWELVE days of dreary desperation. With bated breath the nation watched and waited while grim-faced officers gambled human lives against odds amid the raging waters off Cape Cod.

The submarine *S-4* lay at the bottom of the sea and its doomed occupants still signaled feebly for the help that could never reach them.

Aboard the U. S. S. *Bushnell* crack divers went over the side again and again under the eye of Admiral F. H. Brumby. There was frenzied desperation at the scene of the disaster and a kind of horrible tension in Washington. It centered in the Navy Department but cast its blight as far as Capitol Hill. Government officials and Members of Congress paced up and down their offices and asked—"Can't *something* be done?" That question beat upon the brain of one member of the House ceaselessly.

Congressman La Guardia could not sleep at night. He lay awake thinking of the boys penned in the wrecked vessel! He felt responsible for them. It was their Government that had sent them to sea in an unsafe craft—and he was a part of that Government!

It grew to be almost an obsession. The responsibility was his. He had sent them out to die.

And with it there developed a rising anger against the ineffectuality of the rescue party. It broadened to include the entire Navy. Congressman La Guardia dropped down at his desk and began to consider a speech—denouncing the naval authorities.

It was never completed. He could not concentrate. Men were dying off the New England coast and he was not certain how much the responsibility was his. He had to go and see. He had to know what those boys were up against before he could finish that speech. He snatched up another sheet of paper and scribbled a telegram:

S-4 CERTAIN TO CREATE CONSIDERABLE DISCUSSION
IN CONGRESS, A GREAT DEAL OF WHICH NO DOUBT
BASED UPON MISAPPREHENSION. I AM SEEKING TO GET
ALL POSSIBLE ACCURATE SUBMARINE INFORMATION.
. . . I DESIRE TO OBSERVE SUBMARINE IN ACTION. IS IT
POSSIBLE TO BOARD ANY SHIP . . . WITHIN FEW DAYS?
I COULD GO TO NEW LONDON OR NEAR-BY PORT. IT IS
MY DESIRE TO MAKE SUBMARINE TRIP.

The naval authorities gladly gave him the permission he sought. On January 1, 1928, he hurried to New London and boarded the *S-8*, sister ship to the sunken submarine. He spent thirty-six hours on the ocean bottom and when he returned his hair was grayer than before.

La Guardia went out to investigate submarine accidents. He got his wish. For the sake of public morale, he co-operated with the naval authorities in keeping secret the fact that the *S-8* broke down while he was aboard. For six hours it lay helpless on the ocean floor, while officers and crew struggled desperately to repair the mechanism—and the Congressman again looked death in the face.

It taught him a lesson. From the destroyer that brought him back to Boston, he radioed as follows:

10:02   Admiral F. H. Brumby, U. S. S. *Bushnell*.

I can now realize the unfavorable conditions under which you are operating. There certainly is a great deal about submarines which the laymen don't know.

Signed—F. La Guardia.

When he returned to Washington on January 4, the Congressman delivered one of the most famous speeches he ever made in the House. His graphic description of what he had witnessed held his colleagues spellbound.

As he took the floor he became the target for sniping by the Tammany delegates, members of which attempted to criticize him for his spectacular performance.

La Guardia snapped back at them, calling Congressman O'Connor the "self-appointed leader of the Tammany delegation in this House," and paying his respects to Representative Anthony J. G. Griffin as follows:

> Mr. Chairman, the difference between my colleague and myself from New York is that I *know* I am not an expert on submarines. As for his criticism and the mild rebuke directed toward me for going to Provincetown and looking around, I thought the House was entitled to more constructive and certainly more accurate information from the submarine experts. As to my being lavishly entertained, let me tell the gentleman that if he will spend thirty-six hours on a submarine on the North Atlantic on a cold Winter night, he will disabuse his mind concerning any "elaborate entertainment." If going to the spot and talking with men who know their business was a wrong thing for a member to to, then I plead guilty.

He plunged into a detailed description of the disaster and the attempts at rescue, which enthused the House. He told how the divers risked their lives in establishing communication with the submarine; how Fred G. Michaels became entangled in the wreckage and how Thomas Eadie worked for forty-five minutes with a hacksaw, 100 feet under the water, to release him.

The Associated Press commented upon the rapt attention given to his address which required additional time, unanimously voted to him by the House. Instead of denouncing the Naval Service, as he had originally planned to do, the Congressman concluded his speech as follows:

Living conditions on a submarine are not exactly comparable to the Ritz-Carlton, or to any other hotel. I believe that both officers and crews should receive additional pay such as we are now allowing for flying service. Quarters for the officers and men should be provided for when the submarines are at their base. Insurance should be provided by the Government for the dependents of men who lose their lives in line of duty. Now, let the House of Representatives send word down to Provincetown that we have confidence and faith in these men who are working night and day and we know that they are doing everything which is humanly possible under the circumstances. (Applause)

Next day the postman in the House of Representatives staggered in under a load of letters. The deluge was on. He had not anticipated the result of his adventure. He was appalled at the hundreds of communications which poured in, enclosing plans for submarine safety devices. Some of them were exceedingly elaborate and manifestly impracticable. The Congressman threw up his hands and referred the whole business to the Navy Department.

Early in 1928 he began his Cassandra prophecies concerning the uncertainty of the "Prosperity" which the country was enjoying. It was almost indecent in those days, and La Guardia's unemployment warning in the House, like that of Robert F. Wagner in the Senate, was a muted voice crying in the wilderness! Nevertheless, he went definitely on the record:

> Whatever may be said about "Prosperity" today, and personally I believe that a great deal of that "Prosperity" is simply stock-ticker prosperity, the fact remains that we have considerable unemployment.

His warnings were ignored—nor did he add to his popularity in the article discussing the patron saints of Wall Street which he wrote in the *Graphic* and in which he said:

255

Mr. Andrew Mellon, who made a fortune for himself, a fortune perhaps never equaled before in the history of the world, is invariably described as one of the financial giants of the world. As a matter of fact, just how many of America's millionaires are claiming the title of "financial giants"? It is true that Messrs. Mellon, Ford, Rockefeller, Schwab, Morgan and a great many others increased their fortunes every year.

The writer will not dispute the financial genius of any of these gentlemen. But can any of them improve upon the financial genius of Mrs. Marie Esposito, or Mrs. Rebecca Epstein, or Mrs. Maggie Flynn, while keeping house in a city tenement, raising six children on a weekly envelope containing $30, trying to send the children to school warmly clad and properly clad, paying exorbitant gas and electric light bills, and endeavoring to provide meat at least once a day for the family? *That's* financial genius of the highest order . . . let some of our greatest financial geniuses try housekeeping in a New York tenement under these conditions and get a real test of their financial wizardry! How about trying to make the lot of the American family better as a real test of real public service—rather than the individual accumulation of personal fortunes?

Neither did his popularity in Republican circles improve as a result of the embarrassing questionnaires with which he began canvassing all potential candidates early in the year. He wrote to the Secretary of Commerce, Herbert Hoover, and Senators Charles Curtis and Frank B. Willis, asking each of them whether, if elected President, he would, (1) enforce Prohibition equally in all States and (2) if necessary, employ 100,-000 men to spend $200,000,000 a year to enforce it; and (3) if enforcement failed under these circumstances would he advocate repeal?

Curtis and Willis both replied rather indefinitely—but Hoover ignored the questionnaire—and thereby began a feud with the New York Congressman which was to grow more and more bitter during the ensuing four years.

"The Mayor-elect cleared the decks for action." La Guardia at his desk the day after election.

"Such appointments were unorthodox." The Mayor-elect confers with some of his designees. (rear row) Welfare Commissioner Hodson, Corporation Counsel Windels, Commissioner of Accounts Blanshard, Special Counsel Irving Ben Cooper. (front) Police Commissioner O'Ryan, La Guardia, Fire Commissioner McElligott. Photo taken December 15, 1933.

The amazing variety of his interests continued. On January 31 he introduced a Federal Stolen Property measure which became known as the National Fence Bill. He prepared it and the very extensive correspondence with Louis McHenry Howe, Assistant to the Chairman of the National Union Commission. The latter body, whose executive committee included Franklin D. Roosevelt, Norman Davis, Charles E. Hughes and Frank O. Lowden, backed the bill energetically, and enlisted the aid of newspapers in forty-four States in its behalf.

On February 3, he boarded a train and dashed off to Pittsburgh to investigate personally conditions resulting from the Pennsylvania Coal Strike. After a whirlwind tour of the coal fields he telegraphed Senator Hiram Johnson, pledging his support in the investigation which the latter demanded. His message read:

HAVE JUST MADE TOUR OF MINING DISTRICT AND HAVE INTERVIEWED SEVERAL PEOPLE. I HAVE NEVER WITNESSED SUCH DISTRESSING CONDITIONS . . . SUFFERING AND HUMILIATION. THE LOT OF THE STRIKERS AND THEIR FAMILIES SIMPLY BEYOND DESCRIPTION. THE BODY OF PRIVATE POLICE AND MINE OWNERS AND UTTER DISREGARD OF LAW SHOCKING AND AMAZING. THE POOR AND UNHAPPY AND MISERABLE STRIKEBREAKERS ARE VERITABLE PRISONERS. THEY ARE NOT ONLY EXPLOITED BUT DEBAUCHED, AND DEPRIVED BY THEIR OWN EMPLOYERS. A CREW OF THESE STRIKEBREAKERS, CRAZED WITH HOOCH, WERE ARMED WITH SHOTGUNS YESTERDAY AND TOLD TO SHOOT INTO THE BARRACKS WHERE THE FAMILIES OF THE MINERS WERE LIVING! THEY EVEN DELIBERATELY SHOT INTO THE SCHOOL WHILE IN SESSION. PERSONALLY SEEN SIGNED CONFESSION OF ONE OF THESE GUNMEN, ADMITTING BEING INSTRUCTED AND PAID BY PRIVATE POLICE TO COMMIT THESE OUTRAGEOUS ACTS. MINEOWNERS NOT ONLY MAINTAIN PRIVATE POLICE FORCE BUT HAVE

PROVIDED JAILS WHERE MINERS ARE UNLAWFULLY DE-
TAINED AND VICIOUSLY ASSAULTED. PLEASE PRESS THE
RESOLUTION TO A VOTE. AN INVESTIGATION SHOULD
COMMENCE AT ONCE.

He made a statement for the Pittsburgh papers in which he said: "I have never seen such thorough deliberate cruelty in my life as there displayed against the unfortunate strikers by the coal operators and their army of coal and iron police . . . imagine, gentlemen, a private army with its private jails where miners are unlawfully detained and assaulted! Surely such flagrant abuse of men's constitutional rights brings this affair clearly in the province of a Senatorial investigation. Saturday I shall hear the operator's side of the case, if they will talk to me—but it will take a hell of a lot of explaining to account for men walking along a ridge, as at Brewsters the other day, and firing into barracks of these suffering miners!"

His files contain notes he jotted down on the spot. Some of them are as follows:

> Saw thousands of shot holes on wall, and even inside of store window, easily borne out by gunshot. Old ladies extremely nervous and on verge of hysterics. Spoke to several of the wives of miners who described how they escaped gun raid and how they rushed out to save the children playing in front of barracks.

Returning to Washington, he took the floor on February 8, and denounced the coal companies (including that of Andrew W. Mellon), for breaking their contract with the strikers.

> Oh, I have heard it said many times that we should not bring any child into it. You can't keep the child *out* of it! The mine operatives have taken away the miner's homes; they have taken away their jobs; they have taken away the very bread from their mouths. I appeal to you gentlemen to put aside statistics, to put aside returns, and to rally behind a resolution to give these people some help and the assurance of a square deal.

His burning enthusiasm enlisted the support of his liberal colleagues and Congressmen John Casey and Clyde Kelly, of Pennsylvania. Both took the floor in his support.

The flare-up in the House proved to be of great assistance to Johnson in the other end of the Capitol and helped to make possible the Senate Committee of Investigation.

Writing on the same subject in the *Nation* of April 4, La Guardia said:

> These monopolies are becoming more powerful, more brazen, more greedy and more defiant of constitutional law when it stands in their way. It will not be long before the plain people will realize that something is fundamentally wrong and they will then be less impressed by our favoritism, coal economics and powerful trust combines.

When the Coal Strike Investigation spotlight shifted to the Senate, the crusader turned his attention to another type of corporation. He joined hands with the veteran Norris for another attack upon the power companies. Early in 1928 they launched their attack upon the public utilities, each introducing a resolution providing for government operation of Muscle Shoals. The patient Nebraska Senator finally pushed it through the Upper House while the peppery New Yorker battled desperately at the other end of the Capitol.

La Guardia's testimony before the Affairs Committee on February 17 is significant in that it reveals once more his length of vision. He foretold the ultimate victory even as he had done so often in the case of Prohibition. The record shows his stand in the matter.

His Joint Resolution 105 provided for the completion of Dam No. 2 and steam plant at Nitrate Plant No. 1. He began by discussing the offers made to purchase the plant.

> Mr. La Guardia. Let's be perfectly frank about it, Mr. Chairman. Muscle Shoals is the greatest power plant in the country and that is what makes it at-

tractive. All this talk about a keen desire to help the farmer is simply window-dressing. If you offer Muscle Shoals to any one and tell them that you will give them all the help, all the *power* they need to make *fertilizer* and limit them to that alone, they will not give you five cents for it!

That being so, why should the Government part with this priceless possession? And why should any group of individuals be picked out, and this plant turned over to them for the purpose of running it as a power plant?

I am not afraid of this talk of the Government going into business, or of the Government being paternalistic, or of the Government depriving private industry of what it should have. There is nothing to that.

I remember the time, and you do, too, when it was considered Socialistic for a municipality to own its own water supply. . . . Gentlemen, times are changing and so it is going to be in the case of power.

MR. BOYLAN.   You think then that it is their underlying purpose to get this development for power purposes only?

MR. LA GUARDIA.   Certainly, because while good sound business men may try to kid this committee and Congress, they are not kidding themselves. That is the language of the city that you and I come from. We must face this proposition, and face it truthfully. My resolution would provide for the Government to keep that plant and it would be a model power plant for the whole United States and would start a new era in this country.

Members of the committee deluged him with inquiries, asking him if he would agree to a plan by which the power would be sold to power companies instead of to municipalities?

MR. LA GUARDIA.   No; that's Al Smith's plan. That's a compromise. I have no misgivings about this proposition. I know that I can't convince this committee.

. . . I know that neither this committee, nor Congress, nor the country is prepared for the broad scope of Section 2; but just as sure as we are here this morning, conditions are going to be such in this country that we shall have to come to that—just as we did when we took over the supply of fresh water!

MR. BOYLAN. Does the gentleman mean to say that he is so far ahead of Congress and the country that we cannot keep up with him?

MR. LA GUARDIA. No. I will say this, however. There is a school of thought that *is* ahead of them!

MR. BOYLAN. Then you are the leader of this new school of thought, are you?

MR. LA GUARDIA. No. I am one of the obscure young pupils in this new school of thought. . . . This resolution, gentlemen, is the same resolution introduced in the Senate by Senator Norris. . . . This is the greatest Government plan now conceived—unless you authorize the Boulder Dam plant and the same things apply to Boulder Dam as apply to this.

Norris and La Guardia won a meaningless victory. Their resolution passed the Senate 48 to 25 and La Guardia forced it through the House 211 to 116, but President Coolidge killed it by a pocket veto. The legislation was not to become law until the New Deal made it so.

Despite the fact that he seemed to make no progress, he renewed his battle against the public utilities a week later, concentrating on the power of the Federal Courts. On February 23 he warned the House that the New York transportation companies would seek to avoid State regulation which was endeavoring to force them to fulfill their own contracts by resort to the Federal Courts. This marked the renewal of his fight to deprive the United States Courts of jurisdiction in such cases. He introduced the same bill which he had brought forward on February 21, 1924 and on Dec. 5, 1927.

On April 13, 1928, he again addressed the House on the same subject. He declared that in that interval the New York

transit companies had sneaked into the Federal Courts seeking to restrain the Transit Commission and stated:

> Gentlemen: This is an outrageous condition. Do you
> wonder that millions of people in this country are losing
> confidence in the Federal Courts?

"That is a strong statement," interjected Congressman
Celler.

"You bet it is a strong statement!" snapped the Major. "I
will say to my colleague from New York that it is a *very*
strong statement! Federal judges have become messenger boys,
and, to use an Army term, they are becoming 'dog robbers'
for the public service companies. How can you explain *that*
to the average citizen?"

Week after week he bobbed up on the floor, singing the
same old song. On May 8 he resumed his fight in the House
by pointing out that the Federal Courts had set aside the contract solemnly entered into between the municipality and a
public service corporation! "As a matter of fact," he declared,
"the Interborough can operate a 5¢ fare under the contract of
the City of New York and make money. Everybody in New
York knows it—except the three judges who sat upon the
case!"

During the Spring he also found time to participate in the
struggle for Philippine independence, to lead a fight for higher
wages for postal employees and to back the bill for the retirement of emergency officers.

He also clashed with his Southern colleagues on the race
question when he took the floor on March 29:

> La Guardia. Mr. Chairman, this is a matter that I want
> to call to the attention of my colleagues from New
> York. When you come up to my district and tell
> my people that Congressman La Guardia does not
> get along with his own party, just be reminded that
> today you are not getting along with *your* party.
> Today we had quite a bit of discussion on the Pro-

hibition and Immigration questions and now the color question bobs up and I see many of my colleagues not in complete harmony with their party! The gentleman from Mississippi (Mr. Busby) raised the question of the constitutionality of the bill now under consideration. I want to suggest to the gentleman that when the Constitution was amended, giving the Negroes citizenship and equal rights, that amendment carried with it an obligation to give the Negroes an equal opportunity for education in this country. (Applause) A republican and a representative government canot endure without education. If the State of Mississippi is doing so much for the higher education of the Negro, I should think that it would welcome this movement to relieve it of a part of the burden placed upon that State.

Mr. Busby. Mr. Chairman, will the gentleman yield?

Mr. La Guardia. No, I have only a few minutes.

Mr. Busby. I will give you the one minute you took away from me.

Mr. La Guardia. Oh. That's like giving the Negro the right to buy a Pullman car ticket in your State. (Laughter)

Mr. Greene (of Florida). Can they ride with you?

Mr. La Guardia. Surely they can. Mr. Chairman, it seems strange in this day and age that there should be an objection to joining a university of this kind. I would do more for it. This government can well afford to spend money in this way. The purpose of this bill is simply to avoid kicking Howard University around every year when we have under consideration the appropriation bill. In New York City our colored boys can enter the College of the City of New York and the colored girls are entering Hunter College. We provide for their education whether they come from the South or elsewhere; and we believe in making the Fourteenth Amendment something real. (Applause)

His stand on Philippine independence is illustrated by a letter which he wrote to his friend Quezon, thanking him for the gift of a straw hat:

June 22, '28.

Hon. Manuel L. Quezon, President,
The Philippine Senate,
Manila, Philippines.

My dear Senator:

Thanks so much for your kind letter of June 12, 1928. I was so happy to hear from you. The sombrero arrived and it was indeed a pleasant surprise. I shall display this gift with a great deal of pride. . . . I fear, however, that its very fine workmanship and stylish cut will show in striking contrast to my shabby clothes and disproportionate figure! I do hope that this will find you fully recovered.

I am sure that you will be amused to hear about the chat I had with young Aguinaldo a few months ago. As you know, he resigned from the Military Academy and has held a position with the Harriman Bank. He is now returning to the Philippines as Secretary of one of the bank's subsidiary corporations. The youngster, out of caution I believe, tried to appear very conservative; but by the end of the evening I had him rooting for complete Philippine independence. I impressed upon him the necessity of setting a good example to his people and the danger of ever appearing to compromise on a great cause of complete independence.

I do hope to see you real soon.

With kind personal regards, I am
Sincerely,
(Signed)   F. La Guardia.

He again interested himself in the question of immigration restriction which lay close to his heart when he learned of a Department of Labor regulation requiring identification cards for incoming aliens. After wiring William Green, President of the American Federation of Labor, calling his attention to the matter and characterizing it as "the entering wedge for a vicious regulation law which would submit every worker to an inquisition," he telegraphed to Secretary of Labor Davis:

I DESIRE TO CALL YOUR ATTENTION TO OFFENSIVE
STATEMENT ISSUED BY ONE GEORGE G. HARRIS, WHO
CALLS HIMSELF "ACTING COMMISSIONER OF IMMIGRA-
TION." THIS DULL AND STUPID EMPLOYEE, ACTUATED
BY THE SPIRIT OF THE KU-KLUX KLAN, ISSUED A PUB-
LIC STATEMENT WHICH APPEARED IN THE NEW YORK
TIMES OF JUNE 15, 1928, AND IS OFFENSIVE IN EVERY
DETAIL STOP I HAVE LONG KNOWN OF THE PREJUDICE
AND HATRED OF THIS MAN HARRIS, AND I TELL YOU
FRANKLY THAT UNLESS YOU TAKE STEPS TO REMOVE
HARRIS AND CLARIFY THIS SITUATION, THIS QUESTION
WILL BECOME AN ISSUE IN CAMPAIGNS . . . I SPEAK
THUS FRANKLY BECAUSE I KNOW YOUR VIEWS AND
FAIRMINDEDNESS STOP YOU CANNOT INCLUDE JEWS,
ITALIANS AND OTHER IMMIGRANTS WITH CHINESE
COOLIES. I DEMAND IMMEDIATE EXPLANATION STOP
MOREOVER, I DOUBT THE RIGHT OF DEPARTMENT TO
COMPEL THIS YELLOW TICKET OF SO-CALLED INSPEC-
TION FROM IMMIGRANTS STOP HOW DO WE STAND STOP
EXPECT REPLY BEFORE I PUBLISH THIS TELEGRAM AND
CHARGE DEPARTMENT WITH RACIAL PREJUDICE.

Two days later, on June 20, Secretary Davis replied by
wire:

FEEL THAT YOU MISUNDERSTAND SITUATION. HARRIS
WOULD NOT IN ANY WAY CAST REFLECTION UPON MEN
OF FOREIGN BIRTH—IF HE DID HE WOULD BE REMOVED
—NO DISCRIMINATION HERE SO LONG AS I AM SECRE-
TARY. WRITING.

La Guardia again telegraphed Davis on June 26:

YOUR TELEGRAM AND LETTER RECEIVED. BOTH UN-
SATISFACTORY REGRET YOU HAVE TO RESORT TO MIS-
STATEMENT OF FACTS TO JUSTIFY OUTRAGEOUS INDE-
CENT ORDER STOP THIS ORDER MARKING IMMIGRANTS

FOR LIFE IS THE RESULT OF THE INSISTENCE OF THE
KU-KLUX KLAN. I CHALLENGE YOU TO DISPROVE THIS
STATEMENT STOP YOU WOULD NOT DARE TO ISSUE THE
ORDER YOURSELF SO YOU WAITED UNTIL YOU WERE
OUT OF THE CITY TO HAVE AN EMPLOYEE DO IT STOP
YOUR ISSUING THIS ORDER AT THIS TIME IS NOT ONLY
CONTRARY TO LAW BUT SOME ONE IN YOUR DEPART-
MENT IS BETRAYING THE PARTY WHICH YOU ARE SUP-
POSED TO REPRESENT. THIS DOUBLE-CROSSING DOUBLE-
DEALING MUST BE EXPOSED STOP I TRIED TO ADJUST
THIS MATTER QUIETLY AND PRIVATELY WITH YOU STOP
YOU HAVE MADE IT AN ISSUE WITH 500,000 AMERICAN
CITIZENS IN THIS CITY STOP WILL ACCEPT THE ISSUE
AND EXPOSE THIS.

Following which La Guardia made public the correspondence.

Davis was not the only recipient of La Guardia's letters. As
usual, he never relaxed his persistent hammering on the Prohibition question. On June 10, he wrote to Seymour Lowman,
Assistant Secretary of the Treasury, saying that he had been
startled to hear that a medical certificate had been filed with
the police of Atlantic City in the matter of the death of John
M. Phillips, alleged head of the Queens County sewer ring, in
which the examining physician stated that he had found him
"in a state of alcoholic intoxication," and that "he continued
to drink every day until the fatal one." Wrote La Guardia:

> It is apparent that this liquor was not prescribed by
> the physician and therefore its transportation into the
> possession and use of the hospital property was unlaw-
> ful. I am reliably informed that no permit was issued to
> transport any legally possessed liquor from his home to
> Atlantic City.
> This bald statement of free and unlimited use of
> liquor by a man under indictment and under supposed
> surveillance by your own department seems to have

266

been accepted as a matter of course by the department without the slightest attempt to follow up the case. Can it be said that a Bradstreet rating gives a person immunity from prosecution for violation of the Prohibition law? I know now and I state that no action will be taken against this million dollar property, and that no million dollar property will be padlocked as long as it is financed through a bond issue or its mortgages held by influencial financial interests.

Kindly advise me what action you expect to take in this matter.

Three days later Lowman reported that the matter had been referred to the Prohibition Bureau.

He interrupted his correspondence long enough to make a brief campaign trip as a delegate to the Inter-Parliamentary Union where he represented the United States at Berlin in August of that year.

Returning home the following month, he arrived just before the Puerto Rican hurricane disaster. On September 13 the Congressman telegraphed the American Red Cross:

OFFERING MY SERVICES AS VOLUNTEER IN CONNECTION WITH RELIEF WORK IN PUERTO RICO. AM READY TO START IMMEDIATELY EITHER BY BOAT OR PLANE. HAVE HAD SUFFICIENT EXPERIENCE TO HANDLE ANY TASK ASSIGNED.

His offer was not accepted but in December he led a winning fight in the House to appropriate $18,000,000 for relief in the island. His action increased his popularity in his own district where a rapidly-growing Puerto Rican colony had secured a foothold.

Two months later he plunged into an investigation of the *Vestris* disaster and at his request the Steamboat Inspection Service made exhaustive tests of the *Vauban*, a sister ship of the lost liner. He used this story as a basis for corrective legislation which he introduced in December.

267

Busy as he was, he found time to inaugurate a feud with Major Philip B. Fleming, Graduate Manager of Athletics at West Point. The row was precipitated by an argument over football tickets. La Guardia was roused when he received poor seats for a game. On November 8 he telegraphed Fleming:

> HAVE RECEIVED FOUR TICKETS FOR $16 IN THE UPPER STAND. THE WAY YOU ARE HANDLING THESE TICKETS IS SIMPLY DISGRACEFUL. TICKET SPECULATORS HAVE BETTER TICKETS ON SALE. I AM GOING TO HOLD YOU PERSONALLY RESPONSIBLE FOR EVERY TICKET SOLD BY THE SPECULATORS.

The Major did not receive any better tickets and he was unimpressed by the explanation that seats assigned to owners of the stadium in which the game was played might have found their way into the hands of the agents. For the next three years he hounded the unfortunate Major Fleming with a persistence worthy of a better cause. He bombarded the War Department with protests and complaints, demanding full investigation concerning Fleming's expense accounts, his troop duty stations and his accounting for athletic funds. Major Fleming, a popular officer with an excellent reputation, submitted repeated explanations and was backed up enthusiastically by his superiors in the War Department. The feud finally expired when the officer's term of duty expired at West Point.

But La Guardia was interested in more worthy causes as well. Close to his heart was the Child Labor Amendment, as shown by a letter which he wrote to Mrs. Franklin D. Roosevelt, June 23, 1928, in reply to a communication from her:

> I can think of nothing that has surprised and disappointed me more than the defeat of the Child Labor Amendment; that this matter was misrepresented to the public has been most discouraging. The question of the

protection of childhood is not a political one. It is not even an American question. It is simply a humane problem in which all decent folk should be interested.

Discussing the defeat of the Amendment in a speech before the Children's Welfare Committee of America at 730 Fifth Avenue, New York City, he said:

> Do you realize that you are living in a country that spends 70 per cent of its entire expenditures for past, present and future wars? . . . Would it not be far better, regardless of cost, to build up a childhood, wholesome and happy, and to use our efforts and our moral influence to bring up the same kind of child in other countries, so that when they grow up they will understand each other? Thus we can prevent this waste of millions of dollars for war! I suppose that some one will cry "He's a Pacifist!" You will not offend me at all by saying that I am a Pacifist. Any one who has dropped as many bombs as I have and any one who has fired as many shots as I have, can be called a Pacifist, if you wish. But I am not proud of any of the bombs I have dropped. When I went abroad and came back they called me a "hero" because I had dropped bombs; but when I went down to City Hall and tried to appropriate more money for milk and better homes for these children—then they called me a "Radical"! When the history of this city is written the year 1924 will stand out as a black spot because it was the year in which the intelligent people of the United States first defeated a Child Labor Amendment.
>
> And there is no sound and honest reason why that amendment was defeated.

His stanch pacifism is illustrated in a letter which he wrote at that time to a friend in Englewood, N. J.:

> My father went through one war and I went through the World War. I think I know something about war. It is so easy to love mankind and practice the doctrine of brotherly love that one wonders what exactly is back of this desire for war.

These varied interests took up so much of his time that he did not participate in the national political campaign although he again ran for Congress on the Republican ticket. He had no enthusiasm for Herbert Hoover, his ostensible standard bearer, and he proceeded to issue his own platform again. Tammany redoubled its efforts for his defeat, this time opposing him with Warren Hubbard who was a powerful district leader in his own right. It was the first time that La Guardia had clashed with one of the official chieftains of the hated Hall. The Ghibonnes mobilized behind him once more and his own well-oiled little political machine functioned perfectly, largely because of the personal attention he devoted to it. The practical aspects of his political philosophy are revealed in a letter which he wrote on October 5 to John Q. Tilson who had requested him to speak in New Jersey:

> My dear Colleague:
>
> I have yours of the first. Damn it, I want to do what I can but a lot of sons of feminine dogs in Washington are going out of their way to make things difficult for us here in New York. You have been in the game long enough to know that the captains of the districts are the top sergeants of politics. I must get two or three things straightened out, all within the realm of reason—or else my organization is going to pieces.

Nevertheless, he did not permit his political opposition to interfere with his idealism. A week later he wrote to George Harvey, whom he had warmly endorsed for Borough President of Queens, saying:

> I regret exceedingly that I cannot see my way clear to endorsing the candidacy of your friend, Irving Klein, who is running for Congress. Mr. Klein elaborated quite extensively upon his activities in collecting old clothes for Italian children. While this, of itself, may be laudable, it could not necessarily constitute all the required qualifications for a member of the House of Representatives.

What I am interested in knowing about Mr. Klein is where he stands on the power trust, railroad legislation, inheritance taxes, unemployment insurance and kindred measures.

During the same month he wrote to Congressman Fred Davenport who had asked him to speak up-State because of the Italian population there, saying:

Dear Fred:

Permit me to say with all frankness that I am sorry to note that you too feel that I have influence with only a small racial group of our population. I assure you, Fred, that if for a moment I felt that my continuance in public service depended largely upon sentimental affection from any one racial group in this city I would get out of politics in a minute. . . . As a Wet Member of the New York Delegation I am quite willing to publicly endorse your candidacy and ask support of the same for I know that you are sincere personally and politically and one whom I have never seen violate the law—and that's much more than I can say for many Dry leaders!

Before taking any chance of my spilling the beans in your district, I will say that should I speak, it would be upon the following conditions: (1) The meeting must be general and not limited to one group or race of people; (2) I shall stress my Wet attitude in contrast to your Dry—but speak of your sincerity and splendid personal and political record on the subject; (3) I shall express my dissatisfaction with the power plank in the New York State platform but point out and acknowledge your knowledge of the job and your usefulness as a Member of Congress for that reason. I suppose that you think that I am acting like a prima donna in imposing these conditions but that is the result of twenty years of uphill fighting.

Davenport responded that he wanted him under *any* conditions and La Guardia addressed a meeting in Rome, N. Y., on October 18. Two weeks later, discussing a report of his remarks at that time, he wrote to Paul Windels:

It is not true that I attacked Mr. Hoover. It *is* true that I was silent on the subject. If my attack on the power industry and the water power situation was so construed, I will say that from what I know of the gang, I can readily see how they would interpret my attack in the way you describe it to me. This is a gang that will ruin the Republican Party.

Nothing in this letter need be considered confidential.

The La Guardia organization won an impressive victory over Hubbard. It was a crushing blow to Tammany when the triumphant La Guardia sent one of its leaders crashing down to defeat. The victory served to enhance the tradition of his invulnerability when opposed to Tammany Hall—especially as it was secured without the co-operation of the State party leaders.

They had no use for him and he did not trust them. His conviction is reflected in a letter he wrote to Sam Koenig after the election, referring to a bill for occasional Federal Judges and discussing an eminent jurist who still ornamented the Bench:

I see no reason why you should take Judge —— into your confidence concerning this procedure. While he has pretended to be for more judges I have accurate information that he is encouraging the Tammany delegation to block its passage until "a deal could be made." All of which goes to show that it takes more than a Presidential appointment and Senatorial confirmation to make a judge out of a laundryman.

CHAPTER XVII

EVENTFUL 1929

THEY bent across the littered table; so close that the two heads almost touched. Together they tunneled through the mass of documents.

"Where in hell are those Canadian figures?" his voice rasped irritably. "I've GOT to have them."

"They're here somewhere," she replied. She was patient as a mother with an erring child. "You laid them down a moment ago and——"

"There's no system in this office," he snapped angrily. "How in the devil am I going to debate Brookhart if I can't quote facts? You can't bluff the radio audience. If you'd put them back in the files——"

"I thought you might want them again." Her patience was astonishing. "I laid them aside before you went to supper and——"

"And when I came back," he growled. Suddenly he stopped short and glared at her accusingly. "Have *you* eaten yet?"

She smiled wearily. "I had a sandwich," she rejoined. "Let's finish up and——"

His regret was breath-taking. "Good Lord. I've kept you here until almost midnight. You had that sandwich early in the afternoon." He turned away decisively. "You go home right now. We'll finish this tomorrow." Her half-voiced protest died at his gesture. Obediently she tripped across to the coatrack. He gazed at her reflectively.

"It's brutal—the way I make her work," he mused, half aloud. "Nobody else would stand for it. . . . Nobody else. . . . And the way she's stuck by me. . . ."

He watched as she donned her coat and hat, and suddenly

273

he started as from a galvanic shock. Congressman La Guardia was really SEEING his secretary for the first time in fifteen years. Seeing her as woman rather than a machine. Reacting to the charm and loveliness he had never noticed before.

"Why, she's—WONDERFUL," he whispered to himself. "And what a life I've led her. Worked her like a slave. No home life. No social life. No——"

She threw him her quick smile. "Good night, Major." The door closed behind her.

Instantly he was on his feet. No hesitation now. With him, to think was to act. His mind was made up in a flash.

"Muh-REE!" He ran after her in a panic. The sound of the footfalls in the empty corridor outside reassured him before the door opened. He met her in the portal. Again that ready smile.

"Yes, Major. What is it? Forget something?"

He nodded solemnly.

She waited expectantly.

"Marie, you're FIRED!"

The smile died instantly. She knew him too well not to realize his serious moods. And he was serious now.

She reeled as from a blow. The years rolled back miraculously. She was just Marie Fischer, from Morris High School again. Uncertain of her stenography and afraid of her employer. But there was a catch in her throat now. Not to be with him any more. Not to share his work. Not. . . .

"Why, Major." Her voice was trembling. "You don't mean——"

His tones were low and earnest.

"I mean it," he said. "How can I court a girl that works for me?"

There was an instant of utter silence. He broke it at last, and his voice was trembling now.

"Miss Fischer," he began, hesitantly. "May I see you home —and maybe—call on you tomorrow evening?"

It was a whirlwind courtship. He literally swept her off her feet. They were married on February 28, with the Reverend Congressman Kvale officiating. And so began the greatest happiness he had ever known; a happiness in a perfect home life from which the public was to be forever barred.

It was the most important event of a very eventful year; 1929—the twelvemonth that was to be the most tumultuous of his life. A year that was marked by vast increase in his Congressional prestige; by his first crushing political defeat and by the beginning of a domestic joy which brought peace to his battered soul.

His second marriage was, easily, the most important of this trio of events. It was to exert the least recognized but certainly the most powerful influence that affected his subsequent career.

They were so wildly happy from the very beginning. Their home life was delightful; with both of them acting like a pair of carefree youngsters, instead of a sedate married couple. The cares of public life vanished at their door.

Night after night he came prancing in like a schoolboy, bursting with unleashed mischief. "Yoo-hoo, Skin-nay!" he would shout as he burst into the room, and she, matching his mood, would respond with a laughing, "O. K., Colonel!" and melt into his arms.

A turn or two about the room, to the music of the ever sounding radio, and then he would seat her solemnly in a big chair and doff his coat and vest for a big kitchen apron. There she remained, "by order," while he prepared dinner and conversation rippled through the kitchen door. That procedure never varied in the years to come.

Of course, they had no money. Mrs. La Guardia did her own housework from the beginning, assisted sometimes by a part-time maid. They took a tiny apartment in Washington and their New York home was in a dingy tenement house at 109th Street and Madison Ave. They stored their furniture during Congressional sessions. They couldn't afford two establishments, what with his continual charities. But Marie La Guardia didn't mind. Her dream had come true—at last.

His friends beamed approval of the match. All of them had known Marie for years. She welcomed them with charming grace and an invitation to their home became a prize worth while.

Thursday nights were "their" nights, however. No visitors then. It was music night as well. She shared his tastes and the La Guardias dedicated Thursday night to their love of music. They could usually be found, perched in cheap seats at the opera in season or struggling with the crowds at the City College stadium concerts.

Always between the acts he vanished to mingle with the musicians behind the scenes. They hailed him as a brother and discussed technical aspects of the performance with gusto.

If there was no concert, the Major and Marie sat quietly at home each Thursday evening, tuning the radio from one classical program to another. For hours at a time they never spoke, just drinking in the music with shining eyes.

From the day of their marriage, Marie Fischer vanished out of the political picture. She seldom visited her husband's office. She never voiced an opinion on public affairs. She specifically disclaimed all knowledge of the Congressman's actions—but, in the eyes of the initiated she remained a mighty power behind the scenes.

For years she had shared his confidence and he had learned to respect her judgment. His career remained her chief interest in life. She was the only person in the world to whose advice he would always listen—though it was often disregarded in the whirlwind days to come.

They came swiftly. His new romance had reawakened the consuming ambition of the early years. Again he was thinking in terms of the New York mayoralty—the second highest office in the country. Already he was sharpening his blade and preparing for another tilt with Tammany as well as the reactionaries of his own party. He hoped to bestow on Marie the honors which Thea had missed.

Before invading the New York area, he consolidated his position in the national field, and thereby vastly increased his prestige in his home city. In one brief campaign, he refocused attention on himself as the Wet leader of Congress.

He pressed his charges against Federal Judge Francis P. Winslow, of the Southern District of New York, fervently demanding his impeachment. On February 18, the House Committee on the Judiciary voted to investigate the charges, but the jurist resigned while the matter was still pending. La Guardia promptly took the case to United States Attorney Tuttle, insisting on a Federal prosecution.

Tuttle wrote the Congressman on April 16, asking for facts which might serve as a basis for criminal charges against the judge. Four days later the legislator replied:

> My duties as a Representative, in reference to the impeachment of Judges, are well defined in the Constitution of the United States. Your duties as a prosecutor are well defined in the laws of the United States. I performed my duty and brought about the removal of an undesirable judge from the bench. I stand behind every single charge I have made.

In the same letter, he stated: "It required a great deal of time, effort and patience to get my facts into shape . . . and in spite of the Department of Justice, rather than with its help. I begged the Attorney General for help and was bluntly refused. . . . I worked for a long time, single-handed in this matter, when I should have had the help of the entire Department of Justice."

Meanwhile he continued attempting to force extra appropriations on the Prohibitionists. On January 31, he took the floor to say:

Why, it was stated here that we should not embarrass the President-elect. It was stated that this measure was intended to embarrass him. Are you afraid to trust Herbert Hoover with twenty-four millions? I am not. I have so much confidence in the honesty and ability of Herbert Hoover that I am not afraid to trust him with this $24,000,000.

I know that Herbert Hoover is big enough, so that, after we have given him this money and after he will have tried this "noble experiment," he will come back to Congress and say: "I can't enforce this law. . . . The next best thing is to deal with it constructively and bring about the necessary modification."

He created a scene on April 26, when, white with rage, he took the floor, after Dry members of the House had applauded the shooting of a bootlegger by a Prohibition Agent. The *Record* shows the exchange:

> MR. LA GUARDIA. Mr. Speaker, I can't gloat, or join in the applause over the shooting of any human being, even though that human being may have been transporting liquor for prominent people in the District of Columbia. . . . I submit that under the law he was *not* justified in shooting the driver of that car.
>
> MR. DICKINSON. How about a bank robber?
>
> MR. LA GUARDIA. I accept the suggestion made by the gentleman from Iowa that the police could better direct their weapons against bank robbers and bank wreckers. There is nothing inherently wrong in the transportation of liquor. . . .
>
> If by your cheers and applause you desire to approve of the murder of this boy, suspected of a violation of the Prohibition laws, then a novel method of enforcement, incompatible with a civilized people, is indeed suggested. . . . Sooner or later you'll have to face this Prohibition question seriously and modify it in accordance with the real desire of the American people.
>
> MR. DICKINSON. We faced it last November.
>
> MR. LA GUARDIA. We did *not* face it last November at all.

MR. DICKINSON.   Oh, sure we did.

MR. LA GUARDIA.   Oh, no, we didn't, because I and many thousands of others took the stump on the assurance of our standard-bearer that it was an experiment and that he would give it a fair trial, and if it didn't work out, then he would himself suggest a remedy——

MR. SUMMERS.   Give it a fair trial.

MR. LA GUARDIA.   You are giving it a fair trial? Well, murder, corruption, graft, disregard of and contempt for law follow it.

The following day he wired Amster Spiro of the *New York Evening Journal*, as follows:

REPLYING YOUR TELEGRAM I WITNESSED SCENE IN HOUSE YESTERDAY AND PERSONALLY EXPRESSED MYSELF THEN AND THERE STOP I CONSIDER OUTBURST OF APPLAUSE AFTER DRAMATIC DESCRIPTION OF BULLET ENTERING BACK OF BOY'S HEAD MOST UNBECOMING UNCHRISTIAN DISGRACEFUL ACT OF PROHIBITION DEPRAVITY STOP . . . PEOPLE MAY BE FOUND NO DOUBT WHO WILL JOIN IN APPLAUSE OF THIS AND OTHER UNJUSTIFIABLE KILLINGS BUT IF THE ADMONITION OF THE PRINCE OF PEACE WERE FOLLOWED DASH LET HIM WHO OBEYS THE LAW NOW APPLAUD COMMA THERE WOULD BE A MORGUE-LIKE SILENCE THROUGHOUT THE COUNTRY.

The eternal sniping continued. When Drys praised Capt. Robert Dollar, on May 9, for announcing that Dollar Line ships would serve no liquor, the obnoxious New Yorker bobbed up with the suggestion that the line might begin its law observance by paying more attention to the La Follette Seaman's Act and the anti-narcotic laws. He spoke of Chinese sailors and doubted the efficacy of the Captain's pledge. There was the usual exchange:

Mr. Crampton.   There are no bars on the Dollar ships.
Mr. La Guardia.   But there's liquor.
Mr. Crampton.   He can't regulate what his passengers do.
Mr. La Guardia.   Then let him keep quiet about law enforcement.

He swung his guns in every direction. On April 23 he sent a radiogram to Bishop James J. Cannon, Jr., the prominent Prohibition leader, en route to the Holy Land, which provoked guffaws from an irreverent Wet press:

BISHOP CANNON

S.S. OLYMPIC

I DESIRE INFORMATION FOR MY FILES AS TO WHY YOU TOOK PASSAGE ON RUM SOAKED BRITISH SHIP INSTEAD OF DRY AMERICAN SHIP STOP SEVERAL FIRST CLASS BONE DRY AMERICAN SHIPS WERE AVAILABLE TO YOU STOP IF IT IS WRONG FOR OTHER AMERICANS TO PATRONIZE RUM SOAKED SHIPS HOW DO YOU JUSTIFY YOUR ACTION STOP DO YOU REALLY PRACTICE WHAT YOU PREACH STOP I CRAVE INFORMATION.

F. LA GUARDIA.

Such actions were frequently misinterpreted and the Major minced no words in rebuking those who presumed that he opposed Temperance as well as Prohibition. Such an error was made by a young West Point cadet, the son of one of La Guardia's most intimate friends.

One of the young man's class-mates had been court-martialed by the authorities at the Military Academy, for intoxication, and ordered discharged. The son of the friend wrote a bitter letter to Congressman La Guardia, explaining that a great injustice was being perpetrated because clemency had been extended in five previous cases, in some of which the accused cadets had possessed political connections.

On January 23, the youthful correspondent received his reply. It was probably not what he expected but ran as follows:

> Dear Bill: Received your letter on behalf of your classmate, O——.
>
> What do you mean by saying he has no friends? When I called on the Judge-Advocate General, I found that a Senator, a Congressman and an army officer had already interceded in his behalf—so I guess you won't need my help any more.
>
> Were it not for the discrimination that you attempted to point out, I don't think I would have any sympathy for him whatever. Frankly, I believe that *any* Cadet who drinks should be kicked out of the Academy. I am really hard-boiled about that. I don't think much of any young man who can't get along without booze.
>
> There is a great deal in what you say about discrimination. But although I have not a great deal of sympathy with some of the officers at the Point, individually, I can certainly understand their attitude.
>
> The mere fact that the Cadets were not good enough sports to appreciate leniency in five separate and distinct cases and continued to be smart and drink liquor, seems to me to indicate that an example *had* to be made. Of course it was pretty tough on O——, or any one else who happened to be that example, but I do not know of any law or any kind of coercion that compelled O—— or any other Cadet to go out and lick up liquor.
>
> It is manifestly unfair for you and O—— to criticize the other cases and invoke political aid. In the first place, you are not sure that they did so and in the second place it appears to me that O—— is not the poor, lonesome, forsaken and friendless chap that you describe. I think he is rather resourceful to have a Senator, a Representative and an army officer all rush to his defense within a few hours after he was tried.
>
> You criticized the Cadet whose mother, a Republican National Committee-woman, helped him out of his troubles. Did it ever occur to you that she might have gone to her boy's defense as a mother, rather than as a politician?

I repeat that I think the Academy authorities have been exceedingly lenient with the boys, having given them no less than five separate and distinct warnings. The Corps should have played the game, instead of abusing the considerate and generous attitude shown them by their officers.

I am always sympathetic toward young men, but I haven't much hope for a youngster who is training himself in a highly specialized profession and has not sufficient self control to refrain from drinking liquor, when, under the regulations and upon his honor, he is expected *not* to drink—and I don't think much of a youngster, who having failed to play fair and being caught, then plays the baby act.

Just because I happen to be opposing Prohibition, I hope neither you nor any one else gets the idea that I am in favor of young people drinking liquor.

I may or may not continue my interest in O——'s case.

I suppose you consider this letter a lecture. It is.

With kindest personal regards to you and the rest of the boys, I am,

Sincerely,
F. LA GUARDIA.

The Major was really fond of the Military Academy, despite his feud with Fleming, and took especial pride in the career of Cadet Harry Wilson, the West Point football star, whom he had himself appointed. Shortly after his marriage, Major-Gen. William R. Smith, Superintendent of the Academy, invited the newly-weds to visit the institution. On March 4, La Guardia responded:

The reason that I don't want to come up is that I don't care to be entertained at all. Please don't misunderstand this seeming rudeness. I have so little time and there is so much I would like to see that I can not afford any time for any thing else. I surely don't "rank" a review and would not think of having one especially for me.

I had planned to come up one day and had arranged to have luncheon with the Cadets, when some one spoiled it all. I was informed that there would be an automobile waiting to take me places and all that sort of thing.

If I can come up . . . and be left alone to go around as I please . . . and be permitted to just talk with the boys and perhaps mess with them, I would like that.

Now when you talk about the organ and the chapel, you have hit my weakness. I know of nothing that would be more delightful than, after a day of tramping and nosing about, to sit in that beautiful, restful chapel and listen to beautiful organ music. Thanks so much for your kindness and courtesy.

Two days later, General Smith replied, assuring him that he would be welcome to do just as he pleased and the Major accepted the invitation.

He was too busy to go then, however, as the Prohibition struggle was occupying every spare moment. The acknowledged spokesman of the Wet forces, he was kept busy, dashing around the country and presenting his case over the radio.

On June 15, he met Dr. Clarence True Wilson, chairman of the Board of Temperance, Prohibition and Public Morals of the Methodist Episcopal Church in a public debate at Atlantic City, New Jersey. Their subject was "Prohibition" and the contestants went at each other hammer and tongs, while a huge audience sat enraptured.

At the conclusion a vote was taken and both the official judges and the audience at large gave their decision in favor of the fiery lawyer-legislator. It was the first time that Dr. Wilson had ever been defeated in a Prohibition debate.

La Guardia then accepted a challenge to meet Senator Smith W. Brookhart of Iowa, his personal friend but Prohibition foe, in a debate on the same subject before a monster mass meeting at Cleveland, Ohio. He spent a great deal of time preparing for that.

A little later, the liberal New Yorker came to the assistance of Chicago's newly-elected colored Congressman, Oscar De Priest. Some of the latter's Southern white colleagues had protested against his being granted space adjoining them in the

House Office Building. On April 8, La Guardia telegraphed his friend, Speaker Nicholas Longworth:

> HAVE NOTICED IN PRESS AGITATION AMONG SOME MEMBERS AGAINST ALLOTMENT OF OFFICE TO OUR COLLEAGUE THE GENTLEMAN FROM ILLINOIS MISTER DE PRIEST STOP I WILL BE GLAD TO HAVE HIM NEXT TO MY OFFICE STOP IT IS MANIFESTLY UNFAIR TO EMBARRASS A NEW MEMBER I BELIEVE IT IS OUR DUTY TO ASSIST NEW MEMBERS RATHER THAN HUMILIATE THEM
>
> F. H. LA GUARDIA, M.C.

This incident brought a flood of correspondence, both critical and laudatory. The colored Congressman wired immediately:

> CONGRESSMAN LA GUARDIA,
> 220 BROADWAY, NEW YORK CITY.
> I HAVE READ IN THE PUBLIC PRESS YOUR TELEGRAM TO SPEAKER LONGWORTH AND WISH TO THANK YOU FOR EXPRESSION THEREIN ALTHOUGH I SHALL KEEP MY PRESENT OFFICE IN THE HOUSE OFFICE BUILDING THOSE WHO DO NOT LIKE TO BE NEAR ME CAN MOVE I HAVE NO OBJECTION TO ANY MEMBER MAKING A FOOL OF HIMSELF IF HE WANTS TO AS EACH MEMBER IS RESPONSIBLE FOR HIS OWN CONDUCT AGAIN THANKING YOU
>
> OSCAR DE PRIEST.

The colored people generally applauded his action and he received an official endorsement from George P. Davis Post No. 116, of the American Legion, the only Negro post in Brooklyn. Four years later, when he ran for Mayor of New York, Congressman De Priest came east and spoke in his behalf and the Harlem vote proved that the bread cast upon the waters was bobbing back.

The Major also advocated Congressional reapportionment and fought against the Hoover tariff. He had no illusions about the import of either measure. On June 8, he declared in the House:

> Mr. Chairman. Stripped of all the flag waving and the camouflaged opposition, the case of every Member who is opposed to this bill boils down to the fact that in the proposed reapportionment his State will lose one or two Members. Let us be perfectly frank about it.
>
> According to the same estimate, my State will lose one Member. I have absolutely no doubt that if my State loses one Member, it will be my District that will be eliminated. I know that there are Powers in both parties in my State that will agree to that.
>
> However, I am willing to take my chance and go into another District. They will not get rid of me as easily as that.

He dramatized his fight on the tariff in typical La Guardia fashion, producing "Tariff Menus" in the House to show the cost to the consumer of each meal. "A tariff is imposed for a purpose," he declared, "and any tariff on an article which is not imported into this country is surely reflected in the cost to the consumer or else there would be no tariff schedule on that commodity. The difference in the price does not come out of the air. The producer does not pay it and it requires no financial wizard to know that the ultimate consumer pays."

Taking the case of a family of five, he presented his menus, to include two pounds of meat, two pounds of fresh vegetables and one pound each of raw tomatoes and stewed figs, with tariff duties of 26 cents. "We will assume that father took his lunch from the left-overs of the previous day," continued the New York legislator, "but we will also assume that father smoked six cigarettes in one day and we will add salt and pepper for lunch and dinner." This ran the total up to 31½ cents.

In the silence that followed the presentation of his figures, La Guardia observed dryly:

> If anyone is interested, I shall be glad to prepare a similar menu of caviar, lobster, guinea hen, tropical fruit and other delicacies.

The strain of the recent years had affected even his iron physique and his health was beginning to trouble him. Marie insisted that he take a vacation and on June 17 they left for Hot Springs, Ark. There he spent a fortnight in the Army and Navy General Hospital.

Returning to New York in midsummer, the stormy petrel immediately plunged into the maelstrom of city politics. He prepared to steal the Republican nomination for Mayor from beneath the very noses of an astonished Old Guard, already united in support of Congresswoman Ruth Pratt, who represented the Park Avenue District and probably the wealthiest constituency in the country.

He had been sounding out his friends concerning Mayoralty prospects ever since the first of the year, as evidenced by a letter to Cortlandt Nicoll, dated February 14:

> My dear Courty: Thanks for your letter of Feb. 2, 1929. It surely contains some wholesome political advice. I guess I am not much of a politician. I always worry about people voting for me under a misapprehension or a belief that I am something I am not. That's why I have always stressed my platform and even gone out of my way to declare my position on controversial matters. It may be poor politics but I assure you it is good for the soul.
>
> I agree partially with what you say about people generally understanding issues. Some issues they do understand and grasp and it is on some of these issues that elections are won. For instance, the issue of graft will be readily understood if properly presented. Another very important issue which has given me a great deal of concern is the financial condition of the city.

I simply dread to contemplate what the next administration will have to meet. The debt service, which includes the interest and sinking fund requirements, is increasing to an alarming degree. True, there is some slight relief in the fact that a great deal of tax exempt property will be subject to full taxation in 1930 and 1931.

Through his Harlem organization he kept his finger on the local political pulse. There was indecision as to whether or not Mayor Jimmy Walker, Tammany's pampered pet, was to run again and progressive elements in the Democratic party were pushing Aldermanic President Joseph V. McKee, who had acquired a certain reputation as a liberal. On June 4, La Guardia wrote to Edward Corsi:

My dear Eddie: I received your interesting letter of June 1, 1929, and was glad to hear from you. Taking up your letter, seriatim, I would say:

(1) Mr. Fox is apparently under an entire misapprehension as to my independent strength. I have more groups back of me than any one who has been mentioned to date. These groups will all be marshaled and brought into the battle.

(2) Very much interested in what you have to say about McKee. He fits into an anti-Tammany picture about as much as the Pope of Rome would fit into a Ku-Klux Klan Konklave.

As soon as he returned from Hot Springs, the Major began his fight to mobilize independent support for his candidacy. Speaking before the Young Republican Club of Brooklyn, on July 18, he said: "It is simply unbelievable that a greater number of citizens don't take a more active part and interest in the coming municipal campaign." He went on to demand an aggressive set of candidates, including a well-equipped Comptroller, and gave the Republican business men just 48 hours to produce one who measured up.

The same day Jimmy Walker entered the race. August Heckscher, venerable philanthropist, headed a "non-partisan committee" of 700 members, which begged the chief executive to run again, telling him that it would be a calamity for the city if he refused.

Walker replied in a long speech, reviewing the humanitarian aspects of the Tammany Administration and telling of his own great love for the city. He concluded: "To have you say in your eloquent words that you, too, as well as my own Party leaders, want me to carry on; if it is the will of the people of this City, to have me in this office of the Mayor of the City of New York for another four years, this is the answer: 'Who could say No?' "

Next day La Guardia tossed his own hat into the ring, a few hours after the Walker announcement. He denounced the circumstances attending the City Hall love feast, when he addressed the Republican Club in Town Hall.

"Any candidate has a right to have his friends call on him and ask him to run again," sneered the Major. "But the only man convinced that the membership of *that* committee was 'non-partisan' was the venerable August Heckscher, who introduced it as such.

"Now, any man who has been in office four years can get a committee of that many persons to ask him to run again. But the only persons who could be gotten on that committee, outside of a few who had received favors from the Administration and a few others, were members of Tammany Hall. However, they wanted to give it a touch of nobility, so they scouted around and finally added a French Count and an English peeress. I am indeed surprised that Grover * couldn't manage to get Queen Marie on it, too."

Next day the Republican leaders began a wild scramble to unite on a candidate to head off La Guardia. They didn't want him at any price. A special emissary was dispatched to Europe

---

* Evidently referring to the Hon. Grover Whalen, chairman of Mayor Walker's Committee on the Reception of Distinguished Guests, who had charge of the greeting of Queen Marie of Roumania, on her arrival in New York.

At "the home of the city government." Mayor La Guardia and his new cabinet at City Hall. (l. to r.: standing) Commissioners Delaney, McKenzie; Budget Director McGahen; Secretary Dunham; Commissioners Kracke, Moss, Muller, Forbes, Finegan, Moses and Davidson. (seated) Morgan, McCormack, Hammond, Rice, O'Ryan, the Mayor, Corporation Counsel Windels, Commissioners McElligott, Hodson, Goldwater, Post, and Blanshard.

"New York could not keep up with its spectacular Chief Executive." With Bronx Borough President Lyons (left) and Colonel Jacob Ruppert, owner of the New York Yankees, (right) at the opening game of the 1934 baseball season.

to try to persuade Supreme Court Justice Harry E. Lewis, of Brooklyn, then on vacation, to accept the nomination. They finally combined in support of Ruth Pratt, however.

The real maneuvering and the final decision was reached behind the scenes. It has been frequently said that La Guardia forced his nomination by threatening to bolt and split the Republican Party in New York. The truth is quite otherwise. He did force his nomination, but he did it by threatening NOT to bolt. Foregathering with the G.O.P. leaders before the City Convention, which was scheduled for August 1, Harlem's Congressman talked turkey to them in words of one syllable.

"I am refusing to be the goat," he told them. "You intend to nominate Mrs. Pratt. You expect that I will then split the Party and so provide you with an alibi for a defeat which you all know is certain. You think that you will then blame it all on La Guardia. Well, you can't.

"If you go ahead with your plans, I will not say a word. I will not bolt. I'll simply go to Bermuda and remain there during the campaign.

"You can stew in your own juice this year. But next year, when you nominate a candidate for Governor, I will go into the rural Republican districts upstate and challenge your sincerity. I will then tell the voters how you refused to give the nomination to the only man who has ever been successful in defeating Tammany on a straight ticket. And I'll lick your Governor for you.

"Now, choose."

Fearing for the Governorship and the State ticket, they surrendered. There was little enthusiasm in the organization ranks, however. On July 29, President Nicholas Murray Butler of Columbia University, a power in the party, wrote La Guardia as follows:

My dear Congressman: I am very much obliged for your kind note which comes this morning. The leaders of the organization had been kind enough to suggest that

I should preside at the City Convention on Thursday night and personally I was quite willing to do so. When my doctor heard of it, however, he put his foot down and said that, what with the crowd, the excitement, the heat and the nervous strain, it would be foolish for me to undertake this labor at this moment. Therefore I had to say that I could take no public part in the convention proceedings.

I confess I do not know how to answer your question about the outlook. We are in so hopeless a minority that little short of a revolution would give us a chance to elect a Mayor. Walker has so attractive a personality and has made himself so agreeable to the general public and to many influential individuals that I suspect he will poll a very large vote. One thing that distresses me, both locally and nationally, is the absence of any deep concern for principles of government or for good government. Your excellent article on the Eighteenth Amendment, which I read yesterday, offered several illustrations.

Of course it remains true that, whether we can win or not, we should put our best foot forward and try to build up the morale of our party and its organization.

This letter, with its defeatist spirit and the absence of Butler at the convention, was typical of the entire Republican attitude. In the words of *The New Yorker:*

On the night of August 1, the party assembled in the ornate Mecca Temple and bowed to the inevitable. With fixed smiles and synthetic cheers the delegates told this maverick of the herd that he might go forth against Tammany Hall. In their hearts there can have been little cheer, however.

Half of them viewed La Guardia as, in the language of the Silk Stocking District, "impossible." The rest knew him as a Socialist, a foe of Prohibition, a menace to Americanism, common, vulgar and undisciplined. They had applauded a suggestion by Emory Buckner that Walker be branded as "Jimmy the Jester" for campaign purposes, but the respectables of Republicanism asked themselves whether this Italian-American Congressman was not even more of a clown.

The Convention was certainly cut and dried. Major-Gen. James G. Harbord presided and Emory R. Buckner delivered the keynote address. La Guardia was nominated by Former State Senator Nicoll, who referred to him as "the man whose first appointment to public office was made by Theodore Roosevelt and Theodore Roosevelt made few mistakes." His old friend, Ex-Senator Calder, seconded the nomination. Justice Lewis withdrew the name of Mrs. Pratt and the nomination was practically unanimous.

The candidate appeared and addressed the convention. His radiant charm impressed even these half-hearted supporters as he began:

> I accept the nomination.
> Your remarks generally are most flattering. I appreciate the many nice things you have said about me. Thanks. Now let's get down to business. No man can be a good mayor merely by being a good fellow. My plan . . .

and he began a discussion of his hopes.

He plunged into a typical whirlwind campaign at once—but the Silk Stockings exacted their revenge. He was left high and dry from the beginning. Without funds and without assistance, he was left to wage his hopeless fight against the debonaire and popular Jimmy Walker. Yet he made a valiant effort.

Vainly he attempted to expand his little Congressional District organization into a machine covering the twenty-two other districts in the Greater City. He asked too much of the Ghibonnes, however. There were not enough of them. The lack of funds was a terrible handicap. Headquarters was crowded into a tiny little suite in the Hotel Cadillac. There was no reserve; few campaign posters and fewer leaflets.

Since the convention was purely unofficial, it was necessary to hold the regular primaries on Sept. 17. His old foe, William M. Bennett opposed him, but the organization kept its word.

La Guardia was an easy winner, although his own wife couldn't vote for him. (Marie hadn't resided in the district long enough to qualify.)

In October she came down to the Cadillac and took charge of Headquarters, thereby releasing him for his campaigning. His old followers rallied to the call; Paul Windels, Harry Andrews, Louis Espresso and the rest. Keyes Winter, Silk Stocking leader of the Fifteenth Assembly District, acted as campaign manager and worked conscientiously. Frederic Coudert Jr., another scion of the elite, brought additional reinforcements when he accepted the nomination for District Attorney of New York County.

Spasmodic efforts in his behalf, coming from other quarters began to raise the candidate's hopes. On Sept. 26 there was an unsolicited letter from Commander Spafford of the American Legion. It read:

> Dear Major: In yesterday's paper I saw that "Veterans Line Up to Battle for Walker." According to this press notice, Commissioner Deegan is leading this lineup. No other names were mentioned in the article that I saw. . . .
>
> What can I do to be of assistance to you?
>
> You do not need any Veterans' organization to work for you for you are known to every one of us. You were not only unafraid when your Country called; you were eager to serve. You left your seat in Congress and went to the Colors. You did not seek a position behind the lines; you went straight to the combat and flew over the enemy lines.
>
> Your record of service to your Country in war and in peace is clean as a hound's tooth.
>
> Many of my friends in Congress have said that you were the most popular man in Congress. We are proud of you and your service record.
>
> With best wishes for your success,
>
> Sincerely yours,
> (Signed)   Edward E. Spafford.

Spafford's chief service to the campaign proved to be smashing of a canard circulated to the effect that the Major had never seen any actual fighting during the war. This item of Tammany propaganda was nailed by the Legion commander in a statement issued Oct. 11, in which he stated:

> A whispering campaign derogatory to the military record of Major La Guardia is under way, to the surprise of every intelligent citizen. Knowing that F. H. La Guardia has definitely stated that he is not running for the office of Mayor of New York City on his war record but is running on the proposition that he can and will give to the citizens of this community an efficient, businesslike administration, I feel called upon to refute the aspersions being used and to set forth the military record of Fiorello H. La Guardia as I know it to be true.

He then summarized the Major's accomplishments on the Italian front.

As always, the candidate staged an aggressive and spectacular campaign. He made literally dozens of speeches every day, dashing frantically from one meeting to another. He twisted the Tiger's tail in each of the five boroughs, while Mrs. La Guardia, with quiet efficiency kept the Headquarters staff working.

Tammany practically ignored him, and the "wise-cracking" Walker scarcely bothered to recognize the existence of an opponent. Nobody even faintly suspected at that time that the charges which La Guardia was shouting from the housetops were to spell the ultimate doom of the Tammany Tiger. Even the wisest political sages failed to envision the possibilities when he produced a check signed by Arnold Rothstein, notorious murdered gambler, to prove the link between gangsters and the Democratic organization.

It made little impression at the time and most observers thought the Republican candidate had made a mistake by involving Magistrate Albert Vitale, a compatriot, and thereby forfeiting a portion of his Italian support.

In fact, he seemed to be alienating support at every turn. On October 22, he wrote a letter to Mrs. Violet S. Weitzman, secretary of the Bronx Young Republicans, attacking the party leaders in that county; a letter which certainly did not serve to unite the shattered ranks.

"I will be glad to help the Bronx Young Republicans," wrote the candidate, "in any way within my power. I can't, however, take any part in their campaign as long as the unfortunate people of the Bronx suffer under the present Republican leadership. I have no confidence in that leadership. I don't believe the Regular Republican organization in the Bronx is on the level. . . . The first thing to do is to demand a complete change in the leadership.

"When you are ready to do that, rest assured I will be glad to coöperate with you in any way."

This letter, in the hands of his opponents, was used to plague him for years to come. It could always be depended upon to arraign the Bronx County organization against him. It was even used by Joseph V. McKee in the 1933 campaign, four years later.

McKee was running for Aldermanic President on the Walker ticket. He joined in the La Guardia attack and the Major deliberately held his fire, although he had in his possession at that time evidence which proved fatally effective against McKee four years later.

La Guardia had learned that McKee had written an article for the *Catholic World* back in 1915 in which he made what were generally regarded as slighting references to Jewish school children. Such information was dynamite, in New York, with its large Jewish population. La Guardia wrote to the Congressional Library and secured a copy of the magazine in which the article was printed. He copied it and placed it in his files, but made no use of it until 1933. Then it provided the backfire for anti-Jewish charges made by McKee, by that time a candidate for Mayor in his own right.

Just before the campaign closed, the Republican candidate

summarized his case in a public statement. Issued on November 2, it began:

> The campaign has been fought on the proposition that this community is entitled to honesty, efficiency and competency in the administration of its affairs. Tammany has been in absolute control for 12 years. The result has been graft, corruption, waste and neglect.
>
> I have charged the Walker-Tammany administration with specific acts of favoritism, racketeering, inefficiency and waste—with a total disregard of the taxpayers' interests. I have sustained every charge. Tammany cannot deny them. I now present my Bill of Particulars to the voters of this City:

He listed a long line of abuses ranging from tax racketeering, through failure to increase assessments on favored properties (and quoting such instances as Wanamaker's Department Store and the plant of the New York Sun) to speculation in school sites, license graft and sale of inferior meats to city hospitals.

Tammany ignored the charges—and so did the voters. By election day Fiorello La Guardia was probably the only person in New York who really expected that he would win. Nervous and unstrung he roundly denounced a close friend who told him, just before the polls closed, that he had no chance of election.

Consequently it was a terrible blow when the returns came in. Walker had won a sweeping victory, receiving the greatest majority ever given a candidate in a municipal election. La Guardia was beaten by more than 500,000 votes in a total of less than 1,200,000.

The volatile Major suffered keenly, but Marie comforted him as if he had been a disappointed youngster—and within a month he had recovered his self-confidence and was ready to resume the fight against the Tiger.

The silk stocking Republicans evinced a great deal of tongue-in-cheek regret over the disaster. The conservative

Herald-Tribune analyzed the situation editorially on November 7: .

> In spite of a campaign which was vigorous and aggressive, Major La Guardia polled a relatively small vote in his race for the Mayoralty. His defeat primarily was due to the overwhelming desire of the main body of voters for four years more of Tammany. But the small vote which he received must be attributed to other factors.
>
> One of these was the quality of the Republican organization, in such places as there was any Republican organization at all. The other was the fact that Major La Guardia's honesty, courage and capacity for dramatizing public questions did not counterbalance the fixed belief of many, based on his earlier career, that he was a volatile and uncertain quantity.
>
> The *Herald Tribune* supported Major La Guardia because it was convinced that he had matured and attained a stature which he did not have when the City knew him on the Board of Estimate and when he first went to Congress, and because it hoped that he would throw the Republican deadwood overboard, and because of the obvious fact that he offered the only chance of rebuking Tammany. The rebuke failed and the deadwood is still on board. But Major La Guardia is certainly to be commended for having waged a vigorous campaign without using destructive personalities. He also deserves credit for having accepted his defeat with a smile and without rancor or hard feeling.
>
> Fortunately his period of public usefulness is by no means ended. He is still a young man and he is still a Member of Congress. We shall watch his career with interest, hoping that he will justify the promise which his record already shows.

A week later he received a telegram concerning a statement made by Jacob Livingston, Republican leader of Kings County. It read:

HON. FIORELLO H. LA GUARDIA,
HOUSE OF REPRESENTATIVES, WASHINGTON, D. C.

LIVINGSTON OF BROOKLYN SAYS YOU WERE DE-
FEATED BY REPUBLICANS WHO DESERTED YOU BECAUSE
OF YOUR WET STAND AND FOREIGN EXTRACTION. REC-
OMMENDS NOMINATION OF INDEPENDENT DEMOCRATS
FOR MAYOR. ALSO ELECTION OF COUNTY LEADERS AT
PRIMARIES BY ENROLLED VOTERS. SUGGEST REPUBLI-
CAN ADVISORY COMMITTEE AND CHANGES IN MUNICI-
PAL GOVERNMENT TO ALLOW BIPARTISAN PUBLIC EDU-
CATION AND MAGISTRATES BOARD GOVERNOR TO PICK
SUPREME COURT JUSTICE WITH APPROVAL STATE SEN-
ATE WOULD APPRECIATE YOUR REACTION TO THIS
STATEMENT.

BROOKLYN EAGLE.

Instantly the Congressman rapped back his telegraphic reply:

BROOKLYN EAGLE,
BROOKLYN, NEW YORK.

REPLYING YOUR TELEGRAM DO NOT UNDERSTAND IN-
NUENDO MADE AS TO MY QUOTE FOREIGN EXTRACTION
UNQUOTE AS A NATIVE AMERICAN MY STATUS IS NO
DIFFERENT FROM THAT OF PRESENT MAYOR OR PAST
MAYORS CITY OF NEW YORK STOP MY STAND ON PRO-
HIBITION WELL KNOWN I DO NOT BELIEVE LAW IS EN-
FORCEABLE AND HONESTLY SO STATED STOP IF REPUB-
LICANS OF NEW YORK CITY DECIDE TO ADOPT BONE DRY
PLANK IN THEIR PLATFORM THEY CAN DO SO BUT IT
WILL DRIVE GREAT MANY SINCERE REPUBLICANS OUT OF
PARTY IN CITY STOP IT IS TOO EARLY NOW TO TALK
ABOUT SELECTION OF NOMINEE FOR MAYOR FOUR
YEARS HENCE STOP REPUBLICANS VOTED WITH EYES
OPEN AND REFUSED TO TAKE OPPORTUNITY TO DEFEAT
TAMMANY STOP AT PROPER TIME WE WILL ALL HAVE

SOMETHING TO SAY ABOUT CANDIDATE FOR MAYOR . . .
HAD I BEEN ELECTED MAYOR I WOULD HAVE CAUSED
REMOVAL OF SEVERAL MAGISTRATES AND WOULD HAVE
APPOINTED HIGHSTANDING COMPETENT CLEAN HON-
EST MEN IN THEIR PLACES STOP SAME TRUE BOARD OF
EDUCATION THESE WERE PLANKS IN MY PLATFORM I
AM STRONGLY AGAINST APPOINTIVE JUDICIARY THERE-
FORE DO NOT APPROVE SUGGESTION . . . I HAVE NO RE-
SENTMENT OR RANCOR AGAINST ANY ONE WHO VOTED
AGAINST ME AS I BELIEVE IN UNIVERSAL SUFFRAGE AND
FUNDAMENTAL PRINCIPLES OF DEMOCRACY STOP I OF-
FERED CONSTRUCTIVE PLATFORM AND EXPOSED CONDI-
TIONS WHICH WERE SHOCKING TO SAY THE LEAST STOP
THE VOTERS HAVE DECIDED AND I ABIDE BY THAT DECI-
SION BUT I RESENT NASTY OR BIGOTED INNUENDOES
AND AM CERTAIN MR. LIVINGSTON DID NOT INTEND IT
THAT WAY.

F. H. LA GUARDIA.

He could not resist a brief "I told you so," when inter-
viewed in Washington a few days before Congress convened.
Already the fuse was sputtering along the mine he had laid.
The Vitale charges were to be investigated by the Appellate
Division of the New York County Supreme Court and
Former Justice Samuel Seabury was being mentioned for ref-
eree in the case.

"Although less than two weeks since election day," snapped
the Congressman, "several of the charges which I made during
the campaign and which Tammany and some of the Republican intelligentsia termed mud-slinging have already been
sustained." He went on to say that the people of the city
might soon realize the cost of the Tammany victory, pointing
out that the Merchants Association had since vindicated his
exposé of conditions in the public markets.

When a representative of the *Evening Post* visited him in
Washington on December 4, and asked for a comment on a

statement made by Col. William Hayward concerning election frauds and intimidation, La Guardia replied:

> Col. Hayward states the case mildly. There was intimidation in various parts of the city on last election day. Many were prevented from voting and an enormous number of voters were compelled to vote in the presence of Tammany officials or Tammany politicians. It is also true, as Col. Hayward states, that in many cases election officials were not permitted to check the final vote from the back of the machine.
>
> But what I would like to know is simply this; where was the Republican Party when all this was taking place? What were the Republican election officials doing when these criminal acts were being committed? Why did the Republican election officials sign the returns in the face of such conduct and acts, openly, flagrantly and publicly committed?

This was his last word on the ill-fated effort of 1929. The Congressman had no talent for post-mortems, and already he was turning his attention back to national problems. The depression was less than two months old and he was keenly alive to the need for quick and desperate remedies.

He had warned of its approach for months and now the panic was at hand. La Guardia had no confidence in the graveyard whistling of the national leaders who were spouting assurances that the trouble was merely temporary; that American business was fundamentally sound and that the unemployment bugaboo was an unfounded fear.

Even as the old year died, the rebel New York legislator was up in arms, screaming his futile warning to his countrymen and demanding the action that was to be so long postponed. On December 29, making his first address in New York since the election, at the Eighteenth Assembly District Republican Club on East 116th Street, he declared:

> We might as well face the actual situation. There is at present unemployment in every industrial center of the

East. I am informed that this is also true of industrial centers throughout the country. While there has been a great effort to precipitate public improvements, that all takes time. . . .

I believe it is necessary, under our present ecnomic system, which makes unemployment possible, that the real causes of unemployment should be studied. Labor conditions, terms of employment, relations between employer and employee; these cannot stand still while science, mechanics, electricity, chemistry and education rapidly forge forward. No one can stop progress. . . .

With it all we are not to be discouraged. Let us keep up the fight—from within as well as against the enemy. Some of us are not satisfied with being a meek, ineffective minority. We want to make our party kindly and human as well as militant.

Uniform labor laws throughout all the States, unemployment insurance, old age pensions, a shorter work week, these must all be hurriedly pressed into reality to save this country from a real crisis. We have the anomalous situation of excess profits and unemployment.

The two are inconsistent.

It was his valedictory to the mingled triumphs and defeats of 1929. It was his war cry as he went forward into 1930.

CHAPTER XVIII

THE DRY ROAD GROWS SLIPPERY

THE beginning of the depression spelled the doom of Prohibition, and New York's ubiquitous trouble-maker was quick to realize it. Scenting victory, at last, he began a systematic drive upon the Drys. He organized the Congressional Wet bloc and was duly elected its leader. In that capacity he became a national figure of growing importance. Invitations for him to speak began to pour in from all over the country. He accepted as many of them as possible. The Wet band-wagon had begun to roll and Fiorello La Guardia occupied the driver's seat.

This anti-Prohibition campaign developed into the chief interest of his last three years in Congress—even though he took time to dabble in a number of other matters. He managed to break, finally and conclusively, with President Hoover and the leaders of his own party as he pressed for the impeachment of additional Federal Judges, led the successful fight which defeated the sales tax and joined in the campaign for unemployment relief. But it was Prohibition that mattered most to him. Before he left the House, in 1932, the triumph of the cause for which he had fought so long was certain, although the leader was unhorsed in the very moment of victory.

His debate with Brookhart, on February 7, 1930, took on the aspects of a national event, when it was broadcast over a nation-wide hookup. The two men met in Cleveland, Ohio, and 2,500 people packed the Public Music Hall. The subject was announced as "Can Prohibition Be Enforced," with the Iowa Senator supporting the affirmative, and the Harlem Congressman in opposition.

They presented a compelling contrast; the burly and ponderous Brookhart of the slow and forceful speech and the stocky, dynamic La Guardia whose staccato delivery was accompanied by dramatic gestures. Senator Brookhart based his case upon the claim that the Eighteenth Amendment could be enforced efficiently if jurisdiction was transferred from the Treasury to the Department of Justice and $240,000,000 a year appropriated for the work.

The audience proved restive under the Iowan's lecturing and Wet sympathizers began to heckle the speaker. The first questions brought the New Yorker to his feet in a flash. He rushed to the front of the platform and announced heatedly:

"If Senator Brookhart does not get a respectful and attentive hearing, without any more interruptions, I am going to walk off this stage and I'll not come back." There was an instant of complete silence, and La Guardia resumed: "I represent the spirit of tolerance. Don't you understand that? I won't stand for intolerance of any kind."

Leaning across the footlights, he shook his fist at his unwelcome supporters and fairly screamed at them: "I'm ashamed of you. Why, that's what brought Prohibition to this country —INTOLERANCE! Remember, there are some very sincere Drys—and Senator Brookhart is one of them."

He strode back to his seat and there was no more heckling. When his turn came, he proceeded to take his opponent's arguments apart. He insisted that the people did not want Prohibition and would not stand for it, suggesting that the Canadian system of government control of liquor sales offered a solution of the problem. A wave of applause followed his declaration that: "It would take 75,000 Coast Guardsmen to protect the Florida coastline alone—and then we'd need 75,000 more to watch *them*."

Amid rising enthusiasm, he raced on to his peroration:

> Have you any other law that requires the machine gun and the cannon of the Coast Guard for its enforcement? Do you need machine guns to get the counterfeiter? For that matter, do you associate with counterfeiters?

Do you ever go down the streets of Cleveland and see in your jewelry and sporting goods stores little hypodermic needles, for use in taking narcotics? Of course, you don't. But if you go into your sporting goods stores, your jewelry stores and your department stores, you will find little flasks, little curved flasks, little straight flasks and all other kinds of little flasks. And are you shocked?

Why, not at all.

Well, it is no different from Ohio in New York—or Iowa.

When the debate was concluded, members of the audience were asked to vote for the winner. One fifth responded and the ballots stood:

> Brookhart 110
> La Guardia 355

Ten weeks later, on April 28, the restless iconoclast managed to get himself into a position where the newspapers of Kansas rose en masse and howled for his scalp. This followed the payment of his respects to that arid area during an address at Symphony Hall, Boston, Mass., wherein he discussed the failure of the Dry law along the Kaw.

The Prohibitionists were already up in arms and attempting to backfire his attacks as he swung around the country. The day before the Boston meeting, he received the following telegram from the chairman of the committee in charge:

APRIL 23, 1930

HON. F. H. LA GUARDIA,
WASHINGTON, D. C.

DRYS HERE TRYING TO OFFSET YOUR APPEARANCE SUNDAY BY WIDE SPREAD ALLEGATIONS YOU ARE RED COMMUNIST STOP WE HAVE ATTACKED THEIR BOYCOTT PROPAGANDA IN STATEMENT TO ALL PAPERS TONIGHT STOP WISH YOU WOULD WIRE A FIGHTING MESSAGE ON

THIS POINT FOR USE PRESS TOMORROW AFTERNOON
STOP DRY ATTITUDE TYPICAL REACTION YOUR EFFEC-
TIVE ANTI-PROHIBITION WORK IN CONGRESS STOP AM
INVITING TINKHAM DOUGLAS MC CORMICK FOR SUNDAY
MEETING.

C.W. CROOKER.

For once, the volcano failed to spit fire. The Boston press
received no "fighting message." The Major simply wired
Crooker in reply:

STATEMENT ALLEGED TO HAVE BEEN MADE BY DRYS
AGAINST ME TOO SILLY TO TAKE ANY NOTICE STOP
WOULD NOT EVEN DIGNIFY SUCH ATTACK BY REPLY
STOP MY RECORD OF TWENTY-FIVE YEARS OF PUBLIC
SERVICE SPEAKS FOR ITSELF

F. H. LA GUARDIA.

The Boston speech aroused the Kansas papers to a fighting
pitch, however, when he flatly charged that Prohibition had
failed in the dryest State in the Union. He backed up his statement by reading an affidavit from a member of the staff of the
Wichita Eagle and painted a dramatic word picture of the
plight of the victims of the "jake paralysis" epidemic, which
had followed the drinking of Jamaica ginger.

He went on to charge both the old parties with dodging
the Prohibition issue, pointing out that the Congressional Drys
voted as a unit, while the Wets had so far observed their party
lines. This was followed by a demand that 1930 candidates
must be forced to declare their attitude toward repeal of the
Amendment.

The Wet champion expressed little hope for the results of
the report of the Wickersham Commission, appointed by
President Hoover to make a survey of law enforcement, including the Prohibition situation.

As soon as he saw the report, he snapped to the reporters
who had brought it to him:

"Behold—'the mountain has labored,' and here is the mouse."
They pressed him for a statement and he rapped out the following:

> For months the Wickersham Commission has labored,
> groaned and toiled, and all we have now is this legal
> abortion—this legislative monstrosity. In a desperate attempt to do something, an entirely new system of criminal procedure has been hastily, ill-advisedly and most
> unscientifically slapped together. The entire Anglo-Saxon
> idea of trial by jury is abruptly brushed aside.

Referring to the provisions for trial before United States
Commissioners, he went on:

> Under the guise of seeking to relieve congestion in the
> Federal courts, they have provided a rubber-stamp justice, long-distance testimony and trial by correspondence.

On June 2, he submitted his minority report, protesting
against the Judiciary Committee's approval, in which he
stated:

> The bill provides an entirely new system of criminal
> procedure. It is destructive of every fundamental precedent and custom in our Federal practice.
> The bill is a slipshod, ill-advised, impractical system
> for turning out stereotyped justice in quantity production, regardless of the merits and circumstances attending each individual case.

The prominence he had achieved on the Prohibition front
made him the target of attacks from all over the country.
Typical of many communications is the telegram received
from a resident of a Western town:

> IF IT IS BLOODY MURDER TO DEFEND THE CONSTITUTION AND MAJESTY OF AMERICAN LAW AGAINST LAW
> BREAKING LIARS WHO SPIT ON THE FLAG THEN YOU

WERE GUILTY OF MURDER WHEN YOU LEFT CONGRESS
TO HELP ITALY AND THE ALLIES KILL AUSTRIANS AND
GERMANS I DARE YOU TO DEBATE THE WHOLE PROHI-
BITION QUESTION IN WASHINGTON NEW YORK OR ANY-
WHERE ELSE ON EARTH

This argument, frequently repeated by the Drys, drew a reply from the House Wet leader, in a public statement, issued on January 21:

> In view of the statement made by Commissioner Doran, who holds a high and responsible position under the Federal Government, and a like statement made by a distinguished and eminent Senator, indicating by innuendo that the recent acts of violence growing out of the resistance to and attempted enforcement of the Prohibition laws are due entirely to so-called inflammatory statements made, I deem it necessary to state my position and I believe that of others opposed to the Eighteenth Amendment and seeking its repeal:
>
> If there is violence—if there is murder—it is not the fault of any statement made in opposition to the Eighteenth Amendment, but it is due entirely to Prohibition itself. There is no other law on the statute books of our country that has created so much trouble. There is no other law that compels the use of armed forces, of semi-military organization of the Government; of machine guns and cannon to attempt its enforcement. . . .
>
> History is simply repeating itself. Ridicule, abuse and violence against William Lloyd Garrison did not stop that great man in his efforts to abolish slavery. He, too, was charged with making inflammatory statements. But the names of the little group who rallied around Garrison—the Lovejoys, James G. Binney, Benjamin Lundy, Arthur Tappen, Gerrit Smith, John Greenleaf Whittier, Wendell Phillips, Gamaliel Bailey and Harriet Beecher Stowe—will live long in the memory of men and in history; while the names of their traducers—the selfish and narrow-minded—who heaped abuse and violence upon them, have long since been forgotten, even despite the comparatively short time that has elapsed.

No matter what is said, we shall not submit to the suppression of free speech, to the exercise of every Constitutional right to amend the Constitution as it has been amended heretofore, nor shall we refrain from invoking every proper parliamentary strategy and from appealing to the American people to recognize the danger to the rest of the Constitution and, in our devotion and loyalty to the Constitution, seeking to repeal the one amendment which endangers the entire sacred document.

The Drys were attacking from all sides and he fought back vigorously. He clashed with leader after leader, usually making burning counter-attacks of which the following is typical:

February 10, 1930.

Honorable W. L. Jones,
Senate Office Building,
Washington, D. C.

My dear Senator:

I have your letter of February 10, in which you take exception to the statements made by me on the floor of the House during the discussion of the bill providing for the transfer of the Prohibition Bureau to the Department of Justice.

May I in return quote you in saying that a cause must be in desperate straits when its sponsors resort to blanket denials instead of referring to the proper sources for the facts or to the record. You state that you are reminded of the methods used in the old saloon days. I, too, am reminded of the old saloon days when I contemplate conditions in your State.

Every one knows that Puget Sound is the receiving point for wholesale liquor in such enormous quantities, and in daily shipments to such an extent that such conditions could not exist without the knowledge if not the connivance of the very officials entrusted with the enforcement of the law.

Surely you cannot plead surprise at the conditions I describe as existing in your State. These conditions have been a matter of official record for a long time. . . .

May I suggest that you take advantage of the inquisi-

307

torial tendencies of the Senate and have a select committee appointed to investigate prohibition conditions in the
State of Washington?

Very truly yours,

F. La Guardia.

Early in March he renewed his attack on Henry Ford, in a
letter dated the 10th of that month. It read as follows:

My dear Mr. Ford:
Your telegram endorsing Prohibition was submitted
to the Committee on the Judiciary of the House of Representatives in the course of the hearing now being held
on several bills and resolutions pending for the repeal of
the Eighteenth Amendment. Your name has been mentioned by several of the ladies and gentlemen appearing
before the committee as one of the outstanding indus-
trialists of the country favoring Prohibition.

Inasmuch as you have taken an active part in the cause
of Prohibition, I would greatly appreciate a word from
you reconciling statements made directly by you in two
articles purporting to have been written by you, appearing, one, in the *Forbes Magazine* of September, 1929,
and the other in the *Pictorial Review* of September,
1929.

In the *Pictorial Review*, in the article entitled "Let
Prohibition Begin at Home," bearing your name as the
author, it is stated:

> For myself, if booze ever comes back to the
> United States, I am through with manufacturing. I
> would not be bothered with the problem of han-
> dling over two hundred thousand men and trying to
> pay them wages, which the saloons would take away
> from them. I wouldn't be interested in putting auto-
> mobiles into the hands of a generation, soggy with
> drink.

In the *Forbes Magazine* article entitled "My Supreme
Mission," bearing your name as author, you state:

> As you know, we have arranged to build all our
> tractors in Ireland, even those to be sold in this

308

country—we are allowed to bring them in free. Ireland needs industry. It so happens that we will be able to make our tractors as cheaply in Ireland as anywhere else. Ireland, indeed, is better located as a base for supplying the world with tractors than we are here in Detroit. We can ship from Ireland by water to all parts of the world, whereas we have to ship a thousand miles by rail.

It may interest you to know that tractors have already begun to come from Ireland and that they are better than we ever made here. I was examining two of them out on my farm this morning.

These conflicting statements seemingly are not the result of additional consideration or the outcome of changed conditions. They both appear in the same month. Quite true, the two publications are published for different classes of readers in this country.

When you talk about automobile manufacturing, every one in this country feels that you know your subject. If you threaten to close all your factories (as stated in the *Pictorial Review* article) if Prohibition is repealed, then how do you justify your factories in Ireland, England, Canada, Germany and other countries, where they have no Prohibition? . . .

How do you explain the fact that your tractors built in Ireland according to your *Forbes Magazine* article are better than the tractors built in the United States? Has Prohibition anything to do with that? We have Prohibition here.

Inasmuch as you have been featured so greatly in this Prohibition controversy, I feel justified in making this inquiry.

Very truly yours,

F. La Guardia.

One after another, the Dry leaders shivered lances with the Wet champion. Their challenges were never ignored. On March 14, 1930, he secured a copy of a telegram, sent by Captain Robert Dollar, the head of the shipping concern, to which he had previously paid his respects. The telegram referred to one of La Guardia's declarations:

STATEMENT THAT WE SELL LIQUOR ON OUR SHIPS IS
A VILLAINOUS FALSEHOOD AND ON NO ACCOUNT WOULD
I PERMIT IT EVEN IF THERE WERE NO PROHIBITION
STOP BOOTLEGGERS MAY HAVE SOLD LIQUOR BUT I HAVE
NO KNOWLEDGE OF IT AND WILL USE EXTREME MEAS-
URES TO STOP IT IF I HEAR OF IT.

Instantly La Guardia went whooping to the attack. Glee-
fully he produced a summons issued by the District Court of
Singapore some six years previously to prove that the Dollar
Steamship Line was at that time suing one William Bals, of
Singapore, and quoting from the document:

> The plaintiff's claim is for $203.70, being the equiv-
> alent of $101.85 American gold currency, amount due
> for liquor and goods supplied on board their steamship,
> the *President Van Buren*, as per particulars already ren-
> dered to the defendant.

He backed this up with a two-page winelist, used on the
Dollar steamers, which listed champagne, clarets, whiskies,
beers, wines and mixed drinks.

That his attack registered is shown in a letter which he
wrote to the president of a Washington, D. C., life insurance
company, on March 27, 1930:

> Thanks for your letter of March 27, 1930. It sure hits
> the bull's-eye. Please permit me to read it into the
> *Record*. I am getting impatient with the way Captain
> Dollar carries on. When I first exposed conditions on the
> Dollar ships about a year ago or so, Dollar got Senator
> Copeland of New York to beg me to "lay off." The
> Senator, at that time, told me that young Dollar said
> that if they had to make repeated denials of liquor on
> their ships, that it would ruin their passenger business.
> While they go the very limit to prevent truthful state-
> ments being made, old Captain Dollar jumps into print
> with his Prohibition stuff at every opportunity. . . .
> You can better understand my attitude when I tell

you that Captain Dollar referred to my statement as a "villainous falsehood." That telegram is in the *Record*.

Nor did he relax his time-tried tactics of harassing his arid opponents both by letter and on the floor. Nothing was too trifling for him to snatch up and use as ammunition. He bombarded the authorities with everything that came to hand, as witness the following communication from the Treasury Department, dated March 31, 1930:

> My dear Mr. La Guardia:
>
> Receipt is acknowledged of an anonymous letter addressed to you and referred by you to this office, in which it is alleged that Prohibition Administrator Maurice Campbell of New York City, is protecting violators of the National Prohibition Act. This will be given prompt attention by field officers of the Bureau. We appreciate your calling the matter to our notice.
>
> J. M. DORAN,
Commissioner.

Next day he was up in arms, protesting against a bill sponsored by the Department of Justice requesting additional appropriations for enforcement expenses. He bobbed to his feet waving a packet of Dry Agents' expense accounts and sputtered into the *Record:*

> MR. LA GUARDIA. I want to call the attention of the House to the way the public funds are being spent. It does not happen to refer to the Department of Justice but directly connects with so-called Prohibition enforcement.
>
> In a little over a month, a special agent of the Department, a woman by the name of Kitty Costello, expended in the City of Washington, $523.91, and received in payment for her services rendered in spending this money, $430.00. She was working with an agent by the name of Yates. Let me read you some of the expenditures of Agent Yates.

(He then read a number of items from the expense accounts, including: "Jan. 5—Whisky for 6, $20; Jan. 6—Whisky for 9, $15; Jan. 7—Dinner party for 10, $22, Whisky, $25; Jan. 8—Dinner party for 6, $10, Whisky, $10.)

> Mr. LA GUARDIA. Now this is in addition to the $523.00 paid Kitty Costello and the $430.00 she received. . . .
>
> Mr. CLARK (of New York). Does the Gentleman have a picture of Kitty with him? (Laughter)
>
> Mr. LA GUARDIA. I submit that the very nature of these expenditures reveals extravagance and waste of the public funds under the ostensible purpose of obtaining evidence. . . . Why these dinner parties of six and ten, guzzling whisky? The Gentlemen know that one sale and one drink is sufficient. There is no need for these wild whoopee parties. . . .
>
> Mr. SCHAFER (of Wisconsin). This is another example of the way the Federal funds are thrown down the sewer of Prohibition. They spent thousands of dollars to obtain the conviction of one little bootlegger.
>
> Mr. LA GUARDIA. I think it was thrown down the gullets of the Dry agents.

As the Prohibition fight waxed more and more bitter, the Harlem Congressman literally sat up nights, evolving plans for the further embarrassment of his opponents. On one such night he conceived a scheme which evoked wails of anguish from the enforcement officials. He borrowed the idea from the Department of Agriculture's Bulletin on "Unfermented Grape Juice and How to Make It in the Home."

It served as the model for his own "Rules for the Making of Lawful Wine and Beer in the Home," a leaflet which he began mailing to his constituents, accompanied by a copy of the Department of Agriculture Bulletin, on June 9. His legal mind had located another hole in the law and he plunged through it by calling his products "non-intoxicating." The leaflet concerned itself more with the laws of the land than those of fermentation.

As the fame of the leaflet spread among home brew-masters,

it was given a wide circulation. La Guardia had announced its preparation for circulation among his constituents with his tongue in his cheek. It was plainly intended as a national text-book on the means of taking advantage of the faults of the law.

He joined hands with other anti-Prohibition leaders in an attempt to recapture the Republican Party from the Drys. It was the beginning of a struggle which was to increase in intensity during the next two years. On August 23, 1930, La Guardia wrote to Nicholas Murray Butler:

> My dear Dr. Butler:
>
> I have your letter of August 21. I agree with you that the time has come for the Republican Party of the State of New York to declare itself either for or against the Eighteenth Amendment. This must be done at the next State Convention. It is not necessary for the platform to go into details on a substitute system, as suggested in the Brooklyn formula. An eight word declaration, "We favor the repeal of the Eighteenth Amendment," will bring the issue squarely before the Convention. . . .
>
> At this time I also declare that I will join others taking the same stand, to bring the issue squarely before the National Republican Convention in 1932. We must not permit such an association of bigotry as is now being formed in the State of Alabama to receive the sanction or acquiescence of the National Republican Party.
>
> If this declaration does not meet with the approval of the Republicans of my district, I am willing to decline the nomination and run as an Independent, as I did in 1924.
>
> I am entirely in accord with you that the repeal of the Eighteenth Amendment is quite apart from the liquor question. There are so many important and vital problems to be solved in this country in the immediate future. We simply cannot get to them as long as splendid Progressives are divided on this vexing subject of Prohibition.
>
> I want to take this opportunity to state that I have no quarrel with many sincere Dry advocates, whom I

know and who have not yet realized that National Prohibition is a failure. But we cannot continue in the same Party. I am disgusted and impatient with political leaders, particularly in our State, who know conditions, who are convinced of the necessity of the repeal of the Eighteenth Amendment, and yet have not the courage to declare themselves. If they continue in their timidity and insist upon seeking to play both ends, I shall without any regret, part company with them as above indicated.

> Very truly yours,
> F. La Guardia.

He precipitated another political storm, when, on September 8, 1930, in an effort to force the Republican leaders to take a definite stand on the subject, he released a list of "Republicans Who Know That Prohibition Is a Failure." Angry Drys protested that he was hitting below the belt when they read:

> With all due deference, but without any hesitancy, I submit a partial list of men prominent in the Republican Party, both in the Nation and in the State of New York, whom I dare include in this category. I want to make it clear that I have not been authorized by any of these gentlemen to use their names. I do not intend to speak for them. Some will surely resent my action. Those who do will have an opportunity unequivocally to state their stand. I am very eager to hear what they have to say.
>
> Here is a partial list of distinguished Republicans who, in one way or another, have had an opportunity of observing national Prohibition and who, I say, know that Prohibition is a failure, but have not yet so publicly declared:
>
> Hon Andrew W. Mellon, Secretary of the Treasury.
> Hon. Ogden L. Mills, Under-secretary of the Treasury.
> Hon. Henry L. Stimson, Secretary of State.
> Hon. James J. Davis, Secretary of Labor and Republican candidate for the Senate from Pennsylvania.

Hon. Nicholas Longworth, Speaker of the House of Representatives.

Hon. George H. Moses, United States Senator from New Hampshire.

Hon. Wesley L. Jones, United States Senator from Washington.

Hon. Frederick Hale, United States Senator from Maine.

Hon. Will Wood, Chairman of the Committee on Appropriations of the House.

Mr. George Wickersham of New York.

Hon. John Q. Tilson, Majority Floor Leader of the House of Representatives.

Dr. James Doran, former Commissioner of Prohibition.

In the autumn, the Drys retaliated by hurling a set of questions at him. So firmly established was his position as the acknowledged leader of the Anti-Prohibition forces in the House, that he was one of the seven outstanding Wets in the nation to whom the advocates of aridity submitted their questionnaire entitled "What Practical Substitute for Prohibition Have the Wets to Offer?" The communication was endorsed and signed by fifteen prominent Dry Leaders, including Mrs. Ella Boole, President of the Women's Christian Temperance Union; Dr. F. Scott McBride, of the Anti-Saloon League; Dr. Daniel Poling of the International Society of Christian Endeavor and Colonel Raymond Robbins of the Citizens Committee of One Thousand for Law Enforcement.

Extracts from the New York Congressman's replies are as follows:

1. What plan for the regulation and control of the liquor traffic do you propose as a substitute for the Eighteenth Amendment?

> Answer. Repeal the Eighteenth Amendment. The several States will then be enabled to enact such regulatory laws as the needs, conditions and desires of the people within each State may demand. The Federal Government should retain jurisdiction over inter-State

shipments of liquor. The importation of liquor into States retaining Prohibition would be forbidden. Alcoholic beverages would be taxed at the source by the Federal Government. The revenue from this source should be kept separate and such part of it as may be required allotted to bone dry States having Prohibition. The plan would relieve these bone dry States from the expense of enforcing Prohibition by reason of importation or infiltration from Wet States. The State would have complete jurisdiction and control of the enforcement and would have its own force and personnel but at no cost to itself. The supervision and personnel of the Federal Government would be limited to interstate shipments. This would relieve the Federal Government of local police duties, and at the same time permit the Dry States to enforce Prohibition to their hearts' content without any cost to the State itself.

4. Do you favor a return of the saloon? If not, how under your plan can its return be prevented?

Answer. The saloon can be prevented only by the attitude, customs and wishes of the people. A Constitutional amendment and rigid enforcement laws did not abolish the saloon. I hope that, after the repeal of the Eighteenth Amendment, there will be fewer saloons than there are operating today.

6. If the Eighteenth Amendment were repealed, would you be in favor of a nation-wide program of temperance education?

Answer. Yes.

7. Specifically, what kind of a program of temperance education would you favor?

Answer. Primarily, in the schools, through a proper and well-considered course in physiology on the evils of the excessive use of alcohol. Encouraging abstinence by making it one of the conditions for participation in collegiate sports. Re-establishing the social and moral code which existed prior to Prohibition—that chronic

316

drunkenness or sporadic intoxication is degrading and repulsive instead of being considered "smart" and "socially proper." Once liquor is deprived of its "forbidden fruit character," it will lose its charm for the youth of the next generation. A tolerant and sympathetic understanding for the other fellow's viewpoint.

8. Do you believe that the Prohibition laws, until they can be modified or repealed, should be enforced? Do you believe that, until then, they should be observed?

> Answer. Yes, if the American people so desire, and if the American people are willing to spend $400,000,000 a year to do so. No one has yet submitted a plan to provide for the physical detention or punishment of all the violators who would be brought in under a system of rigid enforcement.

10. Pending the repeal or modification of the Eighteenth Amendment and its supporting legislation, do you favor an educational program designed, in the immediate interests of temperance, to decrease the use of liquor?

> Answer. Yes, but it must be so carefully planned and executed in such a way as to avoid the remotest suspicion of hypocrisy.

These replies, made public on October 17, 1930, aroused a great deal of editorial comment throughout the country. The Major was the spear-head of a growing opposition, and already he sensed the ultimate victory. With uncanny accuracy, so often reflected in his political forecasts, he predicted the very year of Prohibition's defeat.

On December 14, 1930, he wrote an article, published in the *New York Herald Tribune*, entitled, "Drys Can't Win in '32 Against a Wet on Repeal Plank." Therein he indulged in a voluminous analysis, predicting that the voters would support Wet Democrats, even against Independent Republicans at the next election. He concluded: "Will the Republican

Party sacrifice Prohibition for victory? Whatever happens the end of Prohibition is near."

And now, as the Drys gave ground, he began to devote more attention to the economic crisis. He felt certain that Prohibition was doomed, but in the ensuing two years, he did not concentrate on his pet crusade as exclusively as before. Except for his famous radio debate with Brookhart in 1931 and a savage, final, death-dealing attack in 1932, he relaxed his eternal sniping at the Drys. He sensed victory and had no more time to waste on a retreating foe.

The depression was another matter. La Guardia settled down to work on that problem in earnest early in 1930. He secured quantities of material and began an exhaustive study of unemployment insurance legislation in various foreign countries, with especial stress on that of England, France and Spain. As he dug through it, once more his mastery of languages proved a great convenience.

Of course, there were the usual side issues. His mind was always wandering off on tangents and this period was no exception. He spent weeks working on a scheme to obtain reduced railroad rates for college student trips to the National Parks, and expanded this idea into a program for Yellowstone Park excursions for the denizens of the New York slums. Neither plan accomplished anything more than to fill his files with timetables and correspondence. The railroads failed to co-operate.

He secured better results when he returned to his attack on the interference of Federal Courts in public utility rate cases. After ten years of harping on the subject, he was beginning to win a hearing from an influential audience. Early in the year he wrote letters to all the Governors and the Mayors of most of the country's leading cities, begging for support of his measure. An amazing number of replies were received:

"My dear Major:" wrote Governor Franklin D. Roosevelt of New York, on March 10, "Thanks for your nice letter. It was good to get that glimpse of you at the Inner Circle dinner.

I assume that your Committee in the House will let us know in Albany when the hearings are held on the bill to limit the jurisdiction of the Federal Courts."

"We are in thorough sympathy and accord with the provisions of the bill," declared Corporation Counsel Sam Ettelson of Chicago, in a letter dated February 18. "When there will be a committee hearing, I shall be pleased to appear in Washington myself."

On the same day came a letter from Attorney General John Dunbar, of Washington, which read: "This State is very much interested in this bill and I request that you notify us of the date of the hearing." Next day it received the approval of Attorney General James Morris of North Dakota, "It meets with my approval and I hope it will be enacted into law."

On March 3, the corporation counsel of Seattle endorsed it. "We believe this legislation is desirable from every standpoint," and three days later New York's Attorney General Hamilton Ward notified La Guardia of his desire to appear before the committee. Other officials rallied to its support, including Corporation Counsel Arthur J. W. Hilly of the Major's home town, but the measure was anathema to the G. O. P. stalwarts of the Hoover Administration and it went down to defeat again.

Similarly, he participated in the futile fight on the Hoover tariff. Writing to a constituent, La Guardia explained: "I voted against the tariff when it left the House for the Senate. I voted against the conference report when it returned from the Senate. I opposed every unconscionable feature of that tariff. My record on the tariff, therefore, is in keeping with the best interests of the country, the city and the district which I represent."

He seemed in disagreement with the Administration on practically every measure that President Hoover brought forward. Already it was understood that the Italian Congressman was *persona non grata* at the White House. He was pointedly ignored when Congressional leaders were invited there for conferences, and he bitterly resented it.

During the Hoover term of office, the New York Congressman darkened the doors of Number 1600 Pennsylvania Avenue just once. That was on the occasion of the official visit of a minister of the Italian Government. The La Guardias were invited to the White House reception in the visitor's honor. They went.

"I can't say we received an excessively cordial reception," laughed the Major afterward, "but, boy, didn't we create a sensation when we left? We certainly established an historical precedent.

"After the affair was over, the guests gradually withdrew to the door. The flunkies were falling all over themselves ordering up limousines. 'Ambassador This's car!' 'Senator That's car!' 'General Somebody Else's car!' And all the high hats strutting into their equipages and rolling off in state.

"Then Marie and I came strolling out and one of the doormen rushed at me. 'May I get your car, Congressman?' He nearly fainted when I answered:

'We haven't any car. We'll have to walk.' There was a kind of hush, as he repeated it aloud, and then Marie and I hoofed it away from the White House toward our apartment, while the big limousines rolled by. They acted like it was the first time anybody ever had *walked* out of there."

It wasn't parsimony that left the La Guardias on foot. The poor in the Harlem district were still getting every cent he could spare. The Major simply couldn't afford a machine. In fact, he couldn't even afford the new rug for the living room floor, which was already beginning to trouble Marie. Four years were to elapse before it could be replaced.

To the national finances, however, he directed an attention which his own never received. Early in the year he dragged the Postal Shipping Subsidy skeleton out of its economic closet. A stream of criticism was instantly directed at him.

"I have just read the newspaper reports of your denuncia-

"His first major engagement." Speaking from City Hall, the Mayor makes use of the radio during the 1934 fight with the legislature.

"An undeniable talent for the spectacular." Snatching up his little daughter, the Mayor hustles for his car after reviewing a parade. Mrs. La Guardia follows while Chief Inspector Valentine smilingly clears the way.

tion of the Hoover Administration in its awards to the United States Lines of mail contracts in preference to certain foreign lines," wrote John H. Lambert, from New York, on March 5, 1930. "I fail to appreciate your apparent representation of New York citizens, *i.e.*, Americans, and yet flagrant opposition to preferential awards made to our native shipping.

"I and my family are normally Republicans, but it is this intolerant attitude which won for you an overwhelming defeat in New York's last mayoralty campaign. I will not venture to predict what the voters will do when confronted with such tactics as those just demonstrated by you in the last Congress."

As usual, the Congressman's reply was prompt. Dated March 7, it read:

> You have either not read my statement or, having read it, misunderstood it—or else you have purposely ignored my attitude in order to make an unwarranted criticism.
>
> The point which I made was based on actual facts of favored United States companies receiving foreign mail contracts, but not actually carrying mail because their ships are too slow, and the first class mail is actually carried by foreign steamships to the same point of destination.
>
> Another point was that one contractor chartered ships from the Government at one-third of the amount which he, in turn, received for mail contracts from the same Government—and then, in fact, carries no mail.
>
> The United States Lines, to which you refer, carry first class mail and they are being paid for the same, but have not yet received a mail contract.
>
> It seems to me that before you resort to denunciation such as is contained in the letter before me, you should get your facts straight.

The peppery iconoclast never hesitated to lift a sacrilegious hand against the economic idols of his generation. He turned from one gigantic corporation to another, as he selected the targets for his puny bolts. Barely had he ended his

protest against the shipping concerns, when he took the field
against the Steel Trust.

On April 1, he introduced a resolution in the House calling
upon the Attorney General of the United States to take immediate action to prevent the pending merger of the Bethle-
hem Steel Corporation and the Youngstown Sheet and Tube
Company. From the floor, he warned that this was the first
step in the formation of a gigantic steel trust. He pointed out
that a director of the United States Steel Corporation was
then actively engaged in the negotiations between the other
two firms. He shrilled at his colleagues:

> At this very moment, the Bethlehem Steel Corpora-
> tion is seeking to absorb the Youngstown Sheet and
> Tube Company. The suave, genial Mr. Charles M.
> Schwab was in Youngstown a few days ago seeking to
> expedite what he calls the merger—but what is actually
> more than that—the absorption of the Youngstown
> Company. . . .
> Now, what is there about this proposed merger that
> makes it a matter of public interest? First, the very
> negotiations disclose that it is being carried on in viola-
> tion of the provisions of the anti-trust laws. Its purpose
> is to create a combination in restraint of trade, and when
> the Bethlehem Company absorbs the Youngstown Com-
> pany, the largest independent producer is eliminated,
> and that with the co-operation of the interests of the
> United States Steel Corporation through one of its own
> directors, Mr. Samuel Mather.
> It is clear that this deal is being carried on with the
> knowledge and approval, if not in the direct interest of
> the United States Steel Corporation. It can readily be
> seen that after this deal is consummated, the few remain-
> ing steel companies will be at the mercy of the United
> States Steel-Bethlehem Corporation combination.

His fight was, of course, useless, but he achieved considerable more success when he appeared before the House Committee on Immigration, June 9, and proceeded to demolish
Grover Whalen's famous "Red Scare." The dapper Police

Commissioner of New York had made public a series of alleged "official documents," involving the Soviet Government in an anti-American conspiracy.

The New York Congressman bobbed up with proof that "a printer in New York City had printed the letter-heads on each of these alleged Russian documents." At his own expense he had retained the services of a photostat expert to check the copies furnished to the press by Whalen, and, when he concluded, the great conspiracy vanished in a gale of laughter.

A little later he wrote to C. D. Atkins, Director of the Brooklyn Institute, refusing to debate with Professor Jerome Davis, who desired to support the proposition that Soviet Russia should be recognized. "We are both on the same side of that question," commented La Guardia. "I would suggest the Honorable Hamilton Fish Jr., who admits being an authority on the subject."

These were all side issues, however. The subjects nearest his heart were Prohibition and unemployment, and from the middle of 1930 on he gave unsparingly of his time and energy to the effort to solve the problem of the jobless.

It was but natural that he extended a helping hand toward Robert Wagner in the Senate. Most of the national leaders were engaged in bombastically discounting the serious nature of the crisis. They privately denounced and publicly sneered at the men who sought to provide remedial measures. Wagner and La Guardia were favorite targets.

Both men had warned of the coming storm back in the days of prosperity and both had been ignored. Now that it was at hand, Wagner in the Senate and La Guardia in the House insisted that something must be done at once. They faced an impregnable opposition during the Hoover era, but they stretched their hands across the Capitol and gave aid and comfort to one another.

It was a strange alliance—as strange as that earlier one between the volatile Latin and the stubbornly honest "Red Mike" Hylan. Now it was the dignified and judicial Bob

Wagner, of the phlegmatic German temperament, the statesman and idealist—strange product of Tammany Hall—who fought shoulder to shoulder with the excitable Harlem spitfire.

Senator Wagner was the acknowledged leader in the two-man crusade but Congressman La Guardia proved a loyal and devoted follower. When Wagner, the Tammany Senator, chose a Republican Representative to guide his bills through the House, instead of one of the twenty-one Tiger Congressmen in the New York delegation, it excited considerable comment. The choice proved a happy one, however. La Guardia threw himself into the fight with a zeal that ripped the paint off the Capitol dome.

Wagner's trio of Unemployment Relief bills had finally passed the Senate, due principally to the unswerving support of the American Federation of Labor, which rejected the substitute measures sponsored by Secretary of Labor Doak. The Administration was bitterly opposed to them, however, and they were marked for slaughter in the House. Then it was that Wagner turned to La Guardia for help.

Valiantly the Major responded. On June 10, 1930, he took the floor and began to fight for the measures, "sponsored by the Junior Senator from my State. He has given the subject a great deal of thought and attention. This bill is a step in the right direction."

His Republican colleagues, already organized against the first Wagner measure, which provided for the planning of emergency measures in advance of the depression, were astonished. They moved swiftly to the attack as La Guardia began a discussion of technological unemployment, and the usual cat-and-dog fight resulted. It was finally referred to the Committee on the Judiciary of which the New Yorker was a member.

Next day, Senator Wagner himself appeared as a witness before the committee, on behalf of his proposals, and the two men exhibited splendid teamwork as they developed testimony in its behalf. They made up an excellent case, backed up as it was, by such witnesses as William Green, President of the American Federation of Labor, and Miss Frances Perkins, then Industrial Commissioner of New York State.

The committee slaughtered some of the New York Senator's pet provisions, however, and on June 23, La Guardia filed a minority report and prepared to carry the battle to the floor. "The committee amendments take the very life right out of the bill," he snorted, as he urged its passage in the original form approved by the Senate. "The committee amendments cripple and destroy the purpose of the bill."

His minority report amplified his position and minced no words.

> I denounce the action of the committee in eliminating from Senator Wagner's Advance Planning bill sections which are necessary and vital to make the plan effective. . . . National legislators must have the vision to see ahead. One who does must contemplate with horror what will happen if we fail to provide by uniform labor laws a shorter working day, the five-day week and legislation for unemployment, child labor and old age pensions. I expect to devote the greater part of my energies to bringing about constructive legislation, and changed conditions in industry and commerce. . . .
>
> The Wagner bill (S.3059) should be passed by the House in substantially the same form as it passed the Senate. The section above discussed should not be eliminated from the bill.

He carried the fight into the House, and, on July 1, 1930, made a fiery speech, in which he denounced his opponents bitterly.

> There is a school of thought which believes that unemployment is a condition to be taken advantage of, to drag down wages and to lower labor conditions. This school is based on sordid selfishness and lack of vision.

He won a partial victory, only to see it wiped out when President Hoover vetoed the Wagner measures later.

The La Guardia bags were already packed, when he rose to deliver his final appeal for the bill, and that night the Major and Marie rushed back to New York. Next day they sailed on the S. S. *America*, for a belated honeymoon. The Major had been selected as a delegate to the Inter-Parliamentary Union again. Its meetings were held in London, where they arrived on July 10.

It was the 26th conference of the Union, which convened in the Royal Gallery of the Parliament Building on July 16, and remained in session until July 22. The fiery American delegate was assigned to membership on the Commission of Ethnic and Colonial Questions (National Minorities). On July 18, he made his principal address at the Conference—a plea for pacifism.

The American delegate had followed the proceedings closely, and benefited by his linguistic ability as representative of the various nations, spoke in their own languages. When his turn came, he rose and began:

> So many beautiful expressions of mutual admiration have heretofore been made in the course of the debate, that, may I be permitted to eliminate all oratorical embellishments and get right down to the business in hand. . . .
>
> The continuance and usefulness of the Inter-Parliamentary Union now lies in the task of using its tremendous moral force in seeing to it that the principles of peace are strictly observed and put into every day practice. . . . It is now up to the Parliaments of the Nations, not necessarily awaiting any further international agreements to give life to this principle by curtailing weapons of war. Renunciation of war and disarmament are so closely related that the one is meaningless without the other. . . .
>
> We have learned by sad experience that the promotion of peace, and I say this with all due respect and

deference, cannot be left to professional diplomats. . . . We have learned that the security of human life cannot be left to old school diplomacy and ambitious admirals. . . . Let us stop talking about over-production and stress more the lack of ability to purchase the necessities of life. Let us be frank enough to say that this lack of ability to purchase could be in a great measure decreased if nations would have the good sense to devote to useful and beneficial purposes a portion of the enormous sums expended annually for armies, navies and preparations for future wars. . . .

The Inter-Parliamentary Union must put these principles into every day practice and Parliaments must give them life by curtailing the weapons of war. All peoples of the world are in agreement upon this question; there is no need to crystalize public opinion in favor of world peace for it already exists.

The elected representatives of the peoples must carry out their wishes and put them into practical effect. The problems of peace must no longer be left to professional diplomats.

The address was well received, and the adoring Marie beamed approval as her husband received round after round of applause. After a brief visit to Dublin and a short trip through Ireland, they sailed for home on the S. S. *Roosevelt*, arriving at the end of July.

A letter was waiting, mailed by John Q. Tilson at Sunapee, New Hampshire, on July 25. It read:

My dear Fiorello: Now that the long-drawn-out session is finally over and I am taking a little rest here in the New Hampshire woods before the next battle begins, I am utilizing this opportunity to write you a word of personal appreciation for your uniform kindness, good will and such help as you were able to give me in my work as Floor Leader. I congratulate you upon the splendid public service rendered by you during the Session.

Wishing you a delightful vacation with no more

troubles than you can handle successfully and hoping to see you in the best of health next December, I remain,
Very sincerely yours,

Soon there came a letter from William Green. The American Federation of Labor chief wrote:

> I wish to express to you my deep appreciation of the valuable support you gave to the legislative measures supported by the American Federation of Labor and in which Labor was deeply interested all during the time you have served as a Member of Congress. You have been steadfast in your support of remedial legislation proposed and supported by Labor. There are many outstanding instances to which I could refer wherein you rendered very valuable service to Labor and to the masses of the people. From a Labor standpoint your record as a Member of Congress is most satisfactory indeed.

He was deeply interested in the cause of the working man, and early in October he wrote to Secretary Davis urging "a plan of rotation of employment." Davis endorsed it in a letter dated October 6, and others were not slow to express appreciation of it.

Hamilton Ward wired on October 24:

> HEARTILY ENDORSE YOUR PLAN OF ROTATION OF EMPLOYMENT AS SALVATION OF WORKERS IN PRESENT BUSINESS DEPRESSION

and three days later Matthew Woll, Vice-President of the American Federation of Labor, wrote him a letter calling it "a great contributive factor in meeting the present emergency," and expressed "appreciation for your deep concern in the unemployment problem and your anxiety to contribute toward the helpful solution of this tremendous task."

La Guardia had little time to devote to his idea, however, because another election was at hand, and again he was forced

"He pushed the almost bankrupt city toward solvency." The Mayor urges his tax program before a joint meeting of the Aldermen and the Board of Estimate during the spring of 1934.

"The quiet little lady beaming proudly on the sidelines." Mrs. La Guardia with her husband and the late Colonel Hammond at the 1934 Army-Navy football game in Philadelphia.

to struggle for his political life. This time Tammany decided to fight fire with fire and they named an Italian to oppose him, in the hope of splitting the Italian vote. The candidate was Vincent Auletta.

It proved to be another stormy campaign. The Major's political machine was in good order, however. His idealism had never blinded him to the practical aspects of politics. He had been very busy that Spring, but not too busy to remember that election was coming and to look after his fences.

All through February and March, the Congressman had kept up a heavy correspondence with his friend Corsi, insisting that the latter should see to it that residents of La Guardia's district were given jobs as census enumerators. On February 17, he wrote: "You will consult me on my appointments for enumerators in the Twelfth, Fourteenth, Sixteenth and Seventeenth Assembly Districts. I trust you will have no trouble about that." And on March 21, he complained: "I was sorely disappointed that there were no Puerto Ricans; Shilling told me he had a lot. I have seen some of the captains who were not worth a damn."

Now this attention to detail bore fruit. His little organization closed ranks and resisted all attempts of Auletta and the Tammany cohorts to disrupt it. One charge of the Democratic candidate, however, sent the choleric Major into paroxysms of fury. The Tiger standard-bearers charged that he had been giving his appointments to the Military and Naval Academies to boys residing outside the district.

La Guardia saw red, because he had appointed Auletta's own son, Albert, to Annapolis on the 20 of the preceding February. The boy had failed to pass the examination, but his appointment had been duly acknowledged by the Bureau of Navigation on February 24. For months afterward, the Major could not discuss the incident without choking from rage.

As usual, Marie took charge of the headquarters, which were installed in the vacant store on one of the "lucky corners" at 106th Street and Madison Avenue. She functioned exactly as before her marriage, handling the strings behind the scenes with deft, feminine touches, while her husband stormed about the district. She supervised the "window display" which fascinated the residents of the neighborhood, with its pictures of the Major visiting the coal fields, his trip on the submarine, etc.

The Ghibonnes did their work well, and their idol again achieved a satisfactory victory, defeating Auletta by approximately 1,000 votes. It began to appear that he was absolutely impregnable to the Tammany assaults in his own bailiwick.

"My dear Fiorello:" wrote Ogden Mills, on November 12, "let me take this occasion to send you my congratulations on your very fine 'win.' It was really quite an extraordinary performance."

CHAPTER XIX

MANY THINGS TO BE DONE

THERE were so many things to do.

And now, spitting fire and sizzling blue sparks, New York's little dynamo went into action. His seventh term in the House coincided with the last two years of the Hoover Administration, during which he proceeded to make himself thoroughly obnoxious to the leaders of his Party, to generate an additional set of feuds, and to short-circuit a number of the G. O. P.'s pet plans and projects.

This period was marked by a renewal of his campaign against Federal Judges, three of whom came under his sarcastic fire; a spectacular and successful one-man revolt against the Sales Tax, and his strange transformation into the leading Congressional apostle of the New Deal, during the dying days of a "Lame Duck" session. Nor did the variety of interests, so characteristic of the man and his career, flag.

They were exemplified in his activities as the old year closed. The election returns of 1930 were scarcely tabulated before the Major and Marie packed their bags and rushed back to Washington. There were so many things to do. His voice was still hoarse from campaigning when he plunged again into the legislative fray, championing a change in the copyright laws, and his own measure for the control of narcotics.

The copyright bill precipitated a desperate struggle, with the nation's leading department stores arrayed on one side and a polyglot opposition on the other. It included various authors and writers, the American Federation of Labor, the Artists' League and a number of book and magazine publishers. Known as the Vestal Design Copyright bill, the measure

331

sought to protect the property rights of creative artists in their productions.

The Major early emerged as one of the leading champions of the reform. As a result he was deluged with mail presenting both sides of the case. Much of the material came from department stores, and his attitude is reflected in his reply to a communication, dated November 3, 1930, from Abraham & Straus, one of the largest concerns in Brooklyn. The firm had protested that passage of the measure would restrict the sale of certain types of merchandise. La Guardia wrote:

> It is only fair for me to state that I heartily approve of this bill and will help its passage through the House at every parliamentary stage. . . .
>
> The provisions to which you object are the very things necessary to give it vitality. . . . I can readily understand the opposition to this bill coming from department stores. We in Washington can also understand the arrogance of the department store lobbyists in Washington, as displayed by representatives of the Retail Dry Goods Association.
>
> The department stores are so accustomed to having their way and to disregarding ordinances and regulations, by reason of their participation in and contributions to dirty politics, I feel that you and other department stores rely too much on influence, which might be brought to bear on the press because of the large advertising space used.

He did not relax his efforts, as shown by a grateful letter, written on January 16, 1931, by Gene Buck, President of the American Society of Composers and Authors, which read:

> Dear Major: A thousand thanks for all you have done . . . for the authors, artists and composers of America . . . for your valuable assistance in helping pass the Vestal bill. . . . Mere words inadequately express how much they are indebted to you for your sympathy and understanding in the interests of culture in America.

These campaigns were comparatively minor matters, however. His first vital concern, after the return to Congress, lay in the drive on the Federal Judiciary, and in mid-October he went after the scalp of Judge H. B. Anderson in earnest, although still working on the cases of Judges Moskowitz and Lauderback.

He had demanded the impeachment of Judge Anderson because of the latter's activities in his Memphis (Tenn.) district. The case was referred to the Judiciary Committee, of which La Guardia was a member. He submitted his evidence to four of his colleagues, who, with him, constituted a special sub-committee, and acted as the jurist's prosecutor. The New Yorker cross-examined every defense witness except one.

That refusal illustrated his legal acumen. The wife of Judge Anderson had just finished her testimony, when W. E. Armstrong, the jurist's counsel, submitted her to the brow-beating lawyer-Congressman's cross-examination. The woman tensed herself for the ordeal, as the stenographer's pencil recorded the exchange:

> MR. ARMSTRONG. Major, I submit the witness to your care.
> MR. LA GUARDIA. You may step down, Mrs. Anderson.
> MR. ARMSTRONG. What! No cross-examination!
> MR. LA GUARDIA. No.
> THE CHAIRMAN. Sir?
> MR. ARMSTRONG. The Major does not desire to cross-examine Mrs. Anderson.

He showed no such tenderness with the lady's husband, though, when he got the jurist into the witness chair. During the latter's cross-examination Judge Anderson branded the testimony of Herbert Harper, a preceding witness, as untrue. With deceptive sweetness, the New Yorker interjected into the *Record:*

MR. LA GUARDIA. Had not Mr. Harper always conducted his official business before you in an able,
lawyer-like, skillful manner?

JUDGE ANDERSON. Well, by comparison with others,
perhaps so, but I could not sit here and say that Mr.
Harper is a great trial lawyer or a great lawyer.
He does the best he knows how.

The New Yorker smiled sweetly and promptly produced
two letters both signed by Judge Anderson. One of them,
dated December 1, 1926, asked Congressman Will Taylor, as
a personal favor to him, to see to it that Herbert L. Harper
was retained as Second Assistant United States Attorney in
Memphis. The second, under date of October 21, 1927, addressed to the Attorney General, recommended that Harper's
salary be increased to the maximum possible. Drily, La
Guardia read extracts from the communications:

> Harper is a very remarkable man, with the best edu-
> cational qualifications of any one who has ever been
> connected in any capacity with the Government Build-
> ing in Memphis. In addition to that, he is a horse for
> work and will be very valuable to Phillips in relieving
> him of a vast amount of detailed labor. . . . Harper has
> the highest social connections here and stands well with
> the best elements of our people. . . .
>
> He has been successful and his ability and merit en-
> title him to a larger salary. . . .

Then the cross-examination went on:

MR. LA GUARDIA. Did you write this letter?
JUDGE ANDERSON. I imagine I wrote that letter.
MR. LA GUARDIA. Examine it.
JUDGE ANDERSON. Yes, that's my letter.
MR. LA GUARDIA. You knew Mr. Harper before he was
appointed, did you not?
JUDGE ANDERSON. Yes, sir.
MR. LA GUARDIA. And you endorsed him at the time of
his appointment?
JUDGE ANDERSON. I did.

The Major thereupon waved him aside with an eloquent gesture.

There were so many things to do, and, as usual, New York's tireless Congressman attempted to do them all.

His agile mind flitted from one subject to another with a speed which left his secretaries dizzy. The record of his activities for those mid-depression days of the Hoover Administration constitutes a virtual encyclopedia of newspaper headlines.

The crusader was never idle for an instant. Every story of misery and abuse was a summons to battle. He never failed to respond, and for months he stormed madly about Washington, championing one cause after another.

Even his friends realized that the resultant lack of concentration handicapped his efficiency—but their protests fell on deaf ears. There was so much to do.

New Year's Day of 1931 found him busily engaged in collecting affidavits from Italian laborers who had been forced to make contributions in order to secure work on a Federal project on Governor's Island, New York. La Guardia flew to the War Department with his evidence, and refunds were promptly forthcoming.

As soon as the Stobbs act, reducing the penalties for Prohibition violations, was signed on January 16, the Wet Congressman descended upon the Attorney General of the United States, demanding a complete list of all persons sentenced under the Jones act, who would have been entitled to less severe punishment under the new legislation. He announced that he intended to ask pardons for them from the President. This project collapsed when the Department of Justice reported, two weeks later, that it was impossible to compute the statistics desired.

Meanwhile, he was not oblivious to the events transpiring in his home town. The mines, which he had laid during the 1929 campaign, were beginning to explode, one by one, and an investigation of the practices prevalent in the Magistrates Courts was under way. Congressman La Guardia followed its progress eagerly in the newspapers, and occasionally contributed his bit toward the embarrassment of his ancient Tammany foes. He was enraged by the failure of the late Magistrate Abraham Rosenbluth to appear before the Seabury Inquiry, and on January 19, 1931, he telegraphed the late Judge Joseph E. Corrigan, then Chief Magistrate:

CONTINUED ARROGANT DEFIANCE OF CERTAIN MAG-ISTRATE REFUSING TO APPEAR FOR QUESTIONING UNDER PRETEXT OF BEING ILL WHILE BASKING IN SUN OF SOUTHERN WINTER RESORTS COMMENCING TO GET UN-DER SKIN OF PEOPLE STOP MAY I RESPECTFULLY SUG-GEST THAT YOU REFUSE TO CERTIFY PAY ROLLS OF ALL MAGISTRATES UNDER INVESTIGATION WHO ARE ABSENT AND HAVE NOT RESPONDED TO SUMMONS FROM SEA-BURY INQUIRY STOP CUT OFF THEIR PAY AND SUMMON THEM BACK TO NEW YORK STOP HOW CAN WE EXPECT CRIMINALS TO ANSWER SUBPOENAS IN COURTS IF SOME OF THE MAGISTRATES GIVE SUCH AN EXAMPLE OF DE-FIANCE AND INDIFFERENCE TO CONSTITUTED AUTHOR-ITY STOP YOU MAY ADD FOR ME THAT THE WIDESPREAD CORRUPTION IN THE MAGISTRATES COURTS REQUIRES MORE THAN THE SIMPLE ACCEPTANCE OF RESIGNA-TIONS STOP IT IS JUST AS NECESSARY TO RUN DOWN ALL RAMIFICATIONS AND ALL PERSONS CONSPIRING AND CONNIVING WITH RESIGNING MAGISTRATES AS TO RE-MOVE THE INDIVIDUAL MAGISTRATE HIMSELF STOP THE SAME APPLIES TO THE PURCHASE OF JUDICIAL OFFICE STOP CONDUCT OF MAGISTRATES IN DEFYING SUMMONS AND THUMBING THEIR NOSES AT INQUIRY IS NOTHING SHORT OF DISGRACEFUL STOP HOPE PEOPLE WILL JOIN IN COMPELLING THE STOPPAGE OF SALARY UNTIL THESE MEN RESPOND AND TESTIFY.

The same week he clashed with Will Hays, the czar of the Motion Picture Industry, over the film *Little Caesar* which he maintained was a reflection upon American citizens of Italian descent. In response to his protest, Hays wrote him that, "No complaint from any sources regarding it have been received by this office, and I therefore cannot personally express an opinion upon the merit of the complaint. However, will try to see the picture right away."

To this La Guardia responded in a telegram dated January 26:

> I STILL CONSIDER THE FILM LITTLE CAESAR MOST
> UNFAIR AND OBJECTIONABLE IN MANY RESPECTS STOP
> I STILL BELIEVE THAT THE PEOPLE THEMSELVES ARE
> THE BEST CENSORS STOP I AGREE THAT LEGISLATION
> CANNOT TAKE GREED FROM PRODUCERS OR COMPEL
> ORDINARY COMMON DECENCY IN CONSIDERATION OF
> PEOPLES FEELINGS STOP I UNDERSTAND THIS IS A FIRST
> NATIONAL PICTURE THAT BEING SO I SHALL MAKE A
> PUBLIC APPEAL TO THE PEOPLE OF MY CITY TO RE-
> MEMBER THESE PRODUCERS AND BE GUIDED ACCORD-
> INGLY IN THE FUTURE STOP THERE IS NO USE DISCUSS-
> ING THE MATTER WHILE THE PICTURE IS ON THE
> SCREEN STOP I HEARD COMMENTS OF THE AUDIENCE
> AND KNOW THE EFFECT IT IS PRODUCING.

On February 4, 1931, the whirlwind was checked for a space when an airplane in which he was returning from Erie, Pa., where he had been the principal speaker and guest of honor at the annual banquet of the Uplift Society (a charitable organization) crashed, and La Guardia was slightly injured. Confined to his bed as a result, he busied himself with his correspondence. Significant was the bitter confession which he dictated on February 6 to an Italian minister in New Rochelle:

> I have for years been trying to protect unskilled labor in New York City . . . but I seem to be simply helpless in the matter.

337

The same sense of futility is evidenced in a letter written to Norman Thomas three days later:

> Please don't talk repeal of the Espionage Act to me. I introduced a bill for its repeal in 1919, and in every Congress thereafter. We just cannot get anywhere with it. It is most discouraging. . . . It may interest you to know that, although a new member at the time of the enactment of the Espionage Act, I protested against its passage and voted against it. In the light of what has happened, I feel I was correct in my attitude and justified in my vote. Frankly, I do not believe we can get any action on its repeal at this session of Congress.

There was so much to do—so many battles to fight. At every turn something stirred him to new action. While he lay in bed, recuperating from the accident, Marie turned on the radio for his amusement. A deep voice came from the loud speaker, and a few minutes later Fiorello was frantically demanding his clothes! Marie soothed him to silence, but next morning he insisted on going to the Capitol.

He rushed up to the press gallery, summoned the reporters, and took them down on to the steps in front of the big building. There he registered his angry defiance of what was at that time one of the most powerful public utility corporations in America. He was thoroughly aroused and began:

> Mr. Martin J. Insull made an address over the National Broadcasting Company network last evening. He attempted to appear in the role of an important person, making an address for the good of the public. The name "Insull" is so closely associated with greedy power companies that no one should be deceived. Mr. Insull insinuated that a small group of political aspirants, and some radical newspapers and college professors, are, for selfish purposes, creating the general opinion that there is a "Power Trust." Then he adds that "They are able to bring all kinds of charges against the thing called the 'Power Trust' without assuming any legal responsibility."

The Congressman shook his black locks in the Winter wind and snapped:

> Well, *I* am not afraid to assume legal responsibility for saying that there is a vicious association of various power and electric companies. In order that this powerful power magnate may not have the opportunity of claiming that I am making this charge under the protection of my Congressional immunity, I am making it, not on the floor of the House but out here, on a public street in the City of Washington.

Such was La Guardia's challenge to the Insull interests on February 14, 1931.

Two weeks later he was the center of a scene of turmoil in the House. The occasion was the consideration of an immigration bill which would have tightened existing restrictions. The blackhaired Manhattan Congressman was the spearhead of the opposition, and he became half mad with rage when deserted by the Tammany delegation on whose support he had relied. La Guardia precipitated a row under unusual circumstances. It was late in the evening when the bill was called up. The New Yorker made a point of "No quorum" in order to block its consideration at that time. Speaker Longworth counted 238 members of the House on the floor, even as Tammany delegates raced for the door. He announced that the required majority constituting a quorum was present.

Instantly La Guardia bounced to his feet, repeating his cry of "No quorum." Still the Speaker counted a sufficient number. La Guardia, wild with rage over a broken agreement to postpone consideration of the bill, ran over the Democratic side of the House, screaming, "All right, all right! You're out for blood—and you're going to get it. There is no use talking on the bill when you are acting like this. It carries no credit to you to stand there and gloat over human misery. This bill deals with families which might be separated, and you come in here with tactics that are a shame and a disgrace."

His voice was trembling as he wheeled to the dais:

"I say to you, Mr. Speaker," he shrilled, "that this proceeding is a blot on the history of the American Congress. And to you on the Republican side, I say it will be a different story next October when you come to me on your knees begging, Come into my district, Mr. La Guardia, and tell my people what a good Congressman I am!

"Now I see how you stand—whose friends you are! When you members of the Agricultural Committee would not bring in a bill dealing with pigs, under this procedure at this late hour. But you are not going to get this bill by."

Nor did they.

The New York Congressman stood screaming in the well of the House until he forced an adjustment. Later he defended his tactics energetically in response to a letter from a constituent who flayed him bitterly, saying:

> One expects this sort of nonsense from the ignorant Jew, the worst Jew, a Polish Jew, but I had credited you with more intelligence. If it is a vote-getting plea, I forgive you. Otherwise, it is rot. . . . Suppose families *are* separated! They know the law; there ought not to be permitted any other immigrant of any sort in America!

Under date of March 9, La Guardia responded:

> I am sure you want to be fair, and you would not criticize me so savagely if you had all the facts before you. My protest was absolutely justified, and the Speaker of the House acknowledged it, because we adjourned thereafter, and the bill was taken up on the following day.
>
> The bill had no reference at all to the deportation of undesirable citizens. My whole fight was to permit parents of American citizens, who can establish that they are coming to join children who are able to take care of them, to come within the limits of the existing laws. The proposed bill, which I am opposing, would have cut off these aged parents of citizens.

My opposition was against the procedure. . . . There was an understanding that the bill would be called up in due course—which means that it would have had opportunity to offer an amendment. . . . Instead, the bill was called up late in the evening under suspension of the rules. That means that no amendment could be offered; and it did not even leave an opportunity to explain the situation to the House.

Now, I am sure you would not want to abuse me to the extent of your letter, for simply seeking to invoke proper parliamentary procedure for the intelligent consideration of a bill which affects human beings. . . . I mean, that upon reflection, you will not want to connect me with a corrupt Tammany. . . . I received very little encouragement or help from a large number of citizens who are now clamoring for a clean-up of our city administration, when I ran for Mayor, and opposed Tammany tactics and Jimmy Walker!

It is just as easy (may I be permitted to say) to criticize a public official as to obtain the *reason* for his conduct by a simple inquiry without having recourse to insults and abuse.

There were so many things to do.

During these last two years of the Hoover Administration, the indefatigable New Yorker became a sort of Congressional whirling dervish, spinning so rapidly from one issue to another that it was difficult even for his enemies to pin him down. The chronicle of his interests is bewildering as usual.

During this period, he concerned himself with labor conditions in a veterans' hospital, the universal draft in time of war, a pardon for Tom Mooney, Prohibition, the sales tax, banking and stock brokerage practice, the bonus, and Hoover's eviction of the bonus army. Each of these constituted a major interest to which he devoted a great deal of time.

Typical of his entire legislative career, was the vigor with which he threw himself into an investigation of labor conditions at Veterans' Hospital 81 in New York. He was aroused by the discovery that officials were making use of private, fee-charging employment agencies to secure help. La Guardia did not rest until he had forced the Veterans' Bureau to interfere and put a stop to this practice.

As usual, he was flaunting his pacifism for all the world to see. On January 16, 1931, he lost his fight to force the government to discontinue financial support for Reserve Officers' Training Corps units in non-military schools, and on May 20, he went before the War Policies Commission with his own recipe for putting a stop to war.

This included conscription of all man power and materials without compensation, together with a "moratorium to stop all issuance of currency, take over all industry and put all citizens on a ration basis." He added that "any temporizing with this proposition will defeat its purpose."

The resolution urging Governor James Rolph of California to pardon Tom Mooney bore La Guardia's name, but was defeated on February 23, 1932, in the House Judiciary Committee by a single vote.

The war-time flyer opposed the payment of the bonus, but sharply criticized President Hoover's handling of the bonus seekers congregated in Washington. He opened the attack on the bonus on April 20, terming it inflationary and charged that it discriminated against the great mass of the unemployed.

La Guardia knew he was playing with political dynamite when he took the floor against the bonus, with an election scarcely six months away. His friends tried to persuade him to keep quiet but their advice was ignored. As usual, the Major remained true to his own conscience. However, he struck back bitterly at Hoover in July, after the latter had called out troops to disperse the bonus army. "Soup is cheaper than tear bombs," commented La Guardia succinctly.

All these were of lesser importance, however, compared to the major achievements which signalized La Guardia's seventh Congressional term. These achievements were three in number; the revival of the Prohibition fight, the banking investigation, and the struggle against the sales tax.

The defeat of the sales tax was one of the outstanding achievements of his career. It constituted a political miracle and greatly increased the national stature of the courageous Congressman.

Fiorello La Guardia defeated the sales tax almost single-handed—and did it against the organized opposition of a powerful Administration which was determined to put it over.

The Republican leadership, desperately seeking funds with which to combat the depression, was determined to force the $1,000,000,000 tax program through the House. There was little opposition when the steam roller started but La Guardia tossed a monkey wrench into its cogs almost immediately. He raised the standard of revolt, pleading the cause of the ultimate consumer upon whom he said the tax would fall. He worked night and day, rallying his colleagues to his support and to the amazement of veteran political observers, he succeeded in his fight.

"He does not rise to speak," wrote one correspondent in the middle of the sales tax fight. "He bounces. He puts tremendous energy into his oratory, bouncing around, crouching, rising on his toes and swinging his arms.

"He stands above five feet six and weighs about 165 pounds. His complexion is decidedly swarthy, his hair is black. He wears dark blue clothes and black or blue ties. His eyes are brown."

Naturally, he aroused bitter opposition. The *Chicago Tribune* made him the target of an editorial which declared: "La Guardia who is an alien in mind and spirit from Americanism, has no loyalty to our form of government and shows every indication that he is willing to destroy it."

La Guardia took the floor on March 24, 1932 on a point of personal privilege to discuss this editorial. He began:

> Mr. Speaker: There are only two things that a poor man has in this country. They are his honor and his love and loyalty to his country.

Gentlemen, I believe in the freedom of the press. I believe in free speech. I am often, and naturally, attacked and criticized and very often misrepresented because of the active attitude I take on many issues in this House.

I do not complain. I realize it is a part of our work, but I do resent and I protest an attack of this kind, inspired to create passion and prejudice and animosity in order to becloud the real issue—that of taxation—before the House.

The sales tax campaign had been a brilliant and spectacular achievement, but of far greater social significance was the victory which finally closed his long campaign for anti-injunction legislation to protect the rights of labor. The Norris-La Guardia act wrote his name indelibly upon the industrial history of the nation and in later years the Major grew to regard it as perhaps his most constructive contribution to his country.

La Guardia was a liberal by instinct—and that instinct had long before led him to the side of Senator Norris, the beloved Nebraskan, whose integrity was almost universally acknowledged. He had succeeded to the leadership of the Senate Progressives after La Follette's death and La Guardia cheerfully yielded his allegiance. In the House, the Major's leadership of the little group of Progressives had frequently resulted in his functioning as Norris' lieutenant and ally.

This alliance now bore fruit in the anti-injunction measure.

Throughout his public career, the New York crusader had championed the cause of labor—and for years he had struggled against the steadily increasing use of injunctions in the restraint of labor union activities.

His friends knew how keenly La Guardia felt upon the subject. He could not discuss it without flying into a red rage. He declared that labor's right to organize had been frequently checkmated by court orders which were absolutely indefensible.

The Norris-La Guardia act had been born in Norris' office several terms before. The sponsors had consulted fellow Pro-

"A professor at Columbia." The Mayor consults his new Comptroller, Dr. Joseph McGoldrick, at a 1934 Board of Estimate meeting.

"His back to the wall." Mayor La Guardia leaving the Episcopal Cathedral of
Saint John the Divine with Police Captain Harten, his aide, just after the Tammany come-back of 1935.

gressives in both Houses as well as many labor leaders and experts. Among the latter was Edward Keating, Editor of *Labor*.

As finally perfected, it applied to Federal Courts and provided; 1—the outlawing of the famous "yellow dog contract" under the terms of which some employers had bound their employees to refrain from joining outside labor unions; 2—the restriction of anti-labor injunctions; 3—the guaranteeing of a jury trial in cases where it was charged a contempt had been committed outside the immediate presence of the court.

Norris had forced the measure through the Senate by a vote of 75 to 5—but it was the New York legislator who led the battle in the lower House. His knowledge of parliamentary procedure proved invaluable as he evaded one trick after another and finally forced it to a roll call. His colleagues who had repeatedly buried it in the past did not dare go on record against it. It passed 362 to 14. President Hoover signed it on March 23.

Turning from this successful campaign, the busy Congressman next took on the Wall Street bankers en masse. He produced a national sensation, when on April 25, he had a trunk full of evidence lugged into the hearing-room of the Senate Banking and Currency Committee, and produced documents to prove that New York financiers bribed financial writers. Openly charging that banks and brokers had paid out more than a quarter of a million dollars to the financial experts of some of the country's leading newspapers, La Guardia produced canceled checks to back up his statement.

It proved to be a final political bombshell before the election of 1932.

Returning to New York the harassed legislator set about attending to his political fences. And then there came a letter from his old Congressional opponent, William D. Upshaw, who had just been nominated for President on the Prohibition ticket. Upshaw's epistle is significant, among other things, in that it reveals the respect and affection with which even some of La Guardia's bitterest foes regarded him.

Legal Address—Atlanta, Ga.
Residence Address—17 Coleman Ave., Asheville, N. C.
August 13, 1932.

Hon. Fiorella H. La Guardia,
Member Congress,
New York, N. Y.

My Dear Old Colleague:

Once upon a time, not many months ago, you were
kind enough to say that you would debate the Wet and
Dry question with me at any point that would not require too long an absence from Congress, which was
then in session. But now that Congress is not in session,
I am hoping that you will agree not only to one debate
(whose proceeds you generously said you would gladly
turn over to me, after all your expenses were paid) but I
hope you will agree to at least a week of combats—four
or five in number with proceeds divided—one-third each
between the two debaters and possibly the Crusaders,
who seem anxious to stir up all the "wet devilment" possible. The Crusaders in Chicago have agreed to handle a
series of at least twelve debates in the Chicago area, but
they write me that it is very hard to get an outstanding
debater (and I cannot afford, as Presidential Nominee
of the Prohibition Party to take on just any cross-roads
lawyer who wants a fight), but their trouble is to find an
outstanding man who will debate, who is not now a candidate for re-election;—even if you are a candidate, I am
sure the wetter you would seem to your constituents the
bigger your majority would be.

I am sure, if you would consent to go to Chicago for
about one week you could line your pockets with a
comfortable addition to your personal campaign expenses and it would be just as legitimate as it would be
for you to try a law case and collect a fee during your
vacation.

Personally, "old man," the same conditions, of which
I told you, when I saw you last, *still are the same,* and
you would be showing real friendship to your old colleague, who has always appreciated the personal side of
our relations, if you would put yourself at the disposal

of the Chicago Crusaders who are now seeking to line up this series of debates.

Let me have your reaction by first mail.

With delightful memories of our old fellowship in Congress, and hoping that our paths and swords will cross "with both of us at the crossing," I am,

Cordially yours,
(Signed)   William D. Upshaw.

The disgusted La Guardia, who never did enthuse over misspelled versions of his given name, decided he had too many things to do to grant the request of his "dear old colleague." He realized that he wasn't going to be anybody's colleague unless he settled down to a real fight to hold his district. La Guardia could see the bottom dropping out of the Republican barometer.

CHAPTER XX

THE CRUSADER, UNHORSED, REMOUNTS

THE approach of the 1932 campaign found the persistent reformer in just about the most uncomfortable position of his career. He bore the Republican label and its mere possession was a manifest handicap in the face of the gathering Democratic landslide.

Furthermore, his Republicanism brought him no assistance from the party machinery. It was openly whispered in Washington that President Hoover would be glad to see the Harlem gadfly eliminated, and the entire national leadership was sullenly smarting under the sting of the sales tax defeat. Neither was the State Republican organization inclined to give him aid and comfort, the coolness existing between him and State Chairman W. Kingsland Macy having been a matter of open newspaper comment.

Worse than that—he had openly broken with the county leaders—over—strangely enough—a dinner invitation.

It had not been an ordinary dinner. It was the banquet given by the New York County Republican Committee to Leader Sam Koenig, at the National Republican Club on May 11, 1931. La Guardia wasn't invited. The fact that he was the only G.O.P. Congressman in the county made the omission particularly noticeable. Aroused by the snub, he canceled a speaking engagement at a Republican clubhouse and threatened to bolt the party organization.

All these things contributed to make Congressman La Guardia's 1932 battle for re-election a single-handed affair. Undaunted, he mobilized the Ghibonnes again, and marched out to battle, with Marcantonio and Corsi as his lieutenants.

Of course, nobody could take the Republican nomination away from him in his own district, and he was sure of his place on the ballot.

He disassociated himself as completely as possible from the National Campaign, conducting his own fight from the little store at the corner of 106th Street and Madison Avenue. This headquarters was staffed with volunteers from all over New York—Liberals, mostly, attracted by his progressive record.

A fantastic campaign episode resulted from this fact.

Among the Liberals volunteering their assistance was a young author who had just produced a biography of Governor Franklin D. Roosevelt. Since it was being used as a campaign textbook by the Democratic leaders, the Congressman welcomed the support of a recruit thus identified with the Liberal wing of the Democratic party. He invited the gentleman to call at his headquarters.

The young man pushed his way into the store on a very busy evening at the height of the campaign. The place was jammed with enthusiastic Ghibonnes, volunteer workers and the usual hangers-on. In the middle of the tumult sat the Major and Marie, endeavoring to bring order out of chaos.

The newest volunteer finally reached the desk and introduced himself. Springing up, the candidate shook hands warmly and invited Mr. Allen to accompany him to a meeting at which the Congressman was already overdue. They fought their way out of the store, piled into a car, and whirled away to a Ghibonne rally. There, the reception of the candidate assumed riot-like proportions. In the attendant confusion, the volunteer became separated from his host and was left stranded on the floor while the latter was escorted to the platform. La Guardia missed his guest and looked vainly about for him. He failed to locate the tall, young man in the worn trench coat.

The candidate had barely begun his speech when a heckler, planted by Tammany, arose with a question. The Ghibonnes growled a sullen warning, but their idol waved them to silence. (Unfortunately, the heckler was also a tall, young man wearing an old trench coat, and the Major had mistaken him for the newest volunteer.)

Thinking that his young ally did not realize that the question was embarrassing, La Guardia answered it patiently and continued his speech. A few minutes later, the heckler bobbed up once more. Again he was received with perfect courtesy by the candidate whose speech he was interrupting, but the third time was too much.

The Major proceeded to dispose of this astonishingly stupid supporter with characteristic efficiency. Striding to the front of the platform, he invited the interrupter to come forward and repeat his lines from the stage, "where the people can hear you."

The astonished Tammanyite came forward hesitantly. He had expected to be thrown out and La Guardia's cordial reception had dumfounded him. His amazement increased when the candidate extended his hand, pulled him up on the platform, faced him about, and introduced him to the audience with a resounding, "Folks, you should listen to this young man. He is one of the keenest political analysts it has ever been my pleasure to meet. He understands politics fully, and I am proud to present him to this audience."

There was a roar of applause which the dumfounded heckler found almost unbelievable, but the worst of his nightmarish experience was yet to come. With open mouth and staring eyes, he heard himself described as a friend of Governor Roosevelt, a prominent Democrat and the author of a well-known book. After another round of applause, he was shoved into a front seat on the platform and given the most flattering attention by members of the candidate's party.

La Guardia, during the course of his speech, turned to the dizzy heckler, again and again, beseeching his approval of a point just made. By this time, the poor Tiger henchman was so thoroughly cowed, that he could only nod emphatic agreement—and the episode ended with the Tammany heckler enthusiastically leading the La Guardia applause.

The campaign increased with bitterness as election approached. Tammany had nominated J. J. Lanzetta in another effort to split the Italian vote, defying the advice of some of its older heads who had urged the organization to let La Guardia alone. As the approaching Democratic landslide gathered force, it became evident that Lanzetta had a real chance to win.

Some of the Ghibonnes frankly admitted that they had been guilty of a major error when they permitted the Tammany organization to register a number of "floaters" while La Guardia was in Washington. They had been assured that the illegal voters would be used only in an inter-Tammany leadership fight. Now the fear grew that they might help to defeat La Guardia.

Harlem rang with the contest. During the last fortnight, it developed into a real—and literal—battle. Bricks hurled from tenement roofs broke up two La Guardia meetings on October 25, 1932, and casualties were carted off to the hospital. One man received a fractured skull during a fracas at 113th Street and Madison Avenue—and awoke to explain that he had been knocked out with the handle wrenched from a baby's go-cart.

The Major fought desperately. He openly charged that Tammany was using the city's unemployment funds to buy votes in his district—a charge which Commissioner of Public Welfare Frank J. Taylor eloquently denied.

When the votes were counted, Lanzetta had won by a margin of 1200.

Next day there was wild jubilation in Tammany Hall.

The Democratic sweep was complete. The Tiger wasn't vitally concerned with the victory of President Roosevelt and Governor Herbert H. Lehman, but it rejoiced exceedingly

over that of its city-wide ticket. Surrogate John P. O'Brien
was in City Hall and the Board of Aldermen was overwhelmingly one-sided. The leaders decided that they had been unduly frightened by the repercussions arising from the La
Guardia blast of 1929.

They had been greatly concerned for a while—especially
when Ex-Judge Samuel Seabury, appointed by the Appellate
Division to investigate the Magistrates Courts, had brought
Mayor Walker's Administration under fire. They had faced a
growing panic when Walker resigned and fled to Europe during the middle of the resultant hearing conducted by Roosevelt. Some of the Tigers—Cassandra Cubs—had professed to see
the handwriting on the wall—but all their fears had been unfounded.

La Guardia—the source of all their grief—had been whipped
at last. For the first time in eighteen years they had defeated
him in open combat on his own ground. There was high rejoicing in their Hall.

The crusader had been unhorsed.

It was a bitter blow to his friends—and they included some
of his bitterest political foes. His desk was buried by a deluge
of letters and telegrams from men and women in all walks of
life. They came from politicians, labor leaders, American Le-
gionnaires and hundreds of the simple poor. And they all
grieved over his defeat.

The announcement that he might get a recount brought another flood of messages a few weeks later. And typical of these
communications was a hastily typed note from Mrs. E. D.
Prendergast, Director of the State Women's Christian Temperance Union, with which he had fought for so many years.

Dear Friend:

You see I AM interested in something beside the DRY
Cause—I am very much pleased you will have a re-count
in your district with a very good chance that you have
won your seat after all. I most earnestly hope so. Also

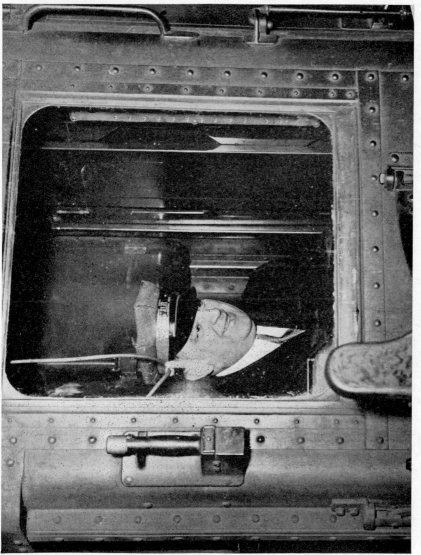

"Labor was gently reminded . . ." The Mayor takes the controls at the opening of a new subway line in the spring of 1936.

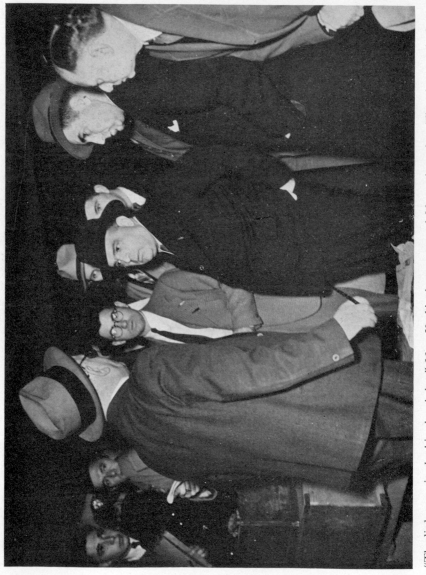

"The little man in the big slouch hat." New York's short-tempered Mayor in action. The photograph shows his clash with a Tammany election official at the polls in 1937.

that the several District Leaders conniving with Tammany to put you out will be brought to justice. . . .

That election, as far as this city was concerned, was a farce and a disgrace. We are having so many holdups that it would seem to me martial law could be proclaimed and this city run by Federal troops till the gangsters are got under control.

"Little Corporal," can't you do it? With every good wish you come out victorious, always your friend, sincerely

(Signed)   Evie D. Prendergast.

And scrawled at the bottom was a parting "Do Vote as *Dry* as you can!"

Yes, even his opponents grieved over his defeat.

La Guardia himself was heartbroken—for a week.

During that week his misery was pitiful. He spent the evening of the day after election with friends and blinked suspiciously as he described the things he had hoped to do in Congress. Marie—as always—encouraged him but without result. He felt the defeat too keenly.

"It's no use," he said, "they got me at last. I am too old to start over and they have wrecked my political career. I'm going to get a little place in the country and settle down and raise chickens."

"It's only a temporary set-back," his host encouraged. "You will be back in Congress in 1934. They only licked you by an eyelash in the midst of a landslide."

Fiorello La Guardia shook his head despondently.

"It wouldn't do any good," he replied. "I might go back to Congress—but I would be starting all over again. You know the power of a Representative depends upon the amount of seniority he has acquired. I have forfeited all mine. I would have to begin all over to try to work myself up to a chairmanship. It would take too many years—and I am too old."

Yes, La Guardia was heartbroken—for a week.

Then he snatched his broken sword and staggered back into the arena.

One week after election he renewed his conflict. He announced that he would call a mass meeting of Tammany foes and he hired the Town Hall for it. The date was set for November 28, 1932.

Tammany Hall resounded with ponderous belly laughter next day. That fellow, La Guardia, was at it again. He didn't know enough to keep his trap shut even when he was licked— and what a farce his anti-Tammany mass meeting in Town Hall turned out to be. There were only 400 people present— 400 crack-brained reformers—400 crackpots led by a lame duck, declaring war on an organization that had polled more than a million votes for John P. O'Brien.

It had been a rather pitiful spectacle—rather pitiful, yet dramatic, when the battered crusader walked out on to that vacant stage and faced the half-empty hall. That little audience seemed to offer such inadequate material for the beginning of a new crusade. Yet it rallied to the flaming eloquence which had electrified the Italian masses after Caporetto. They came out of their seats cheering when he reached his peroration: "You can't start a few weeks before election and beat professional politicians who have been crooked for a hundred years."

That was his text—as well as his climax, and when the meeting ended, he distributed signature cards in the lobby. They bore the title, "Non-partisan Committee for the Revision of the Election Laws," and the signers dedicated themselves to the new crusade against the high-riding Tiger chieftains.

Then La Guardia went home to Harlem to prepare to function as a lame duck Congressman in the final session.

He went out in a blaze of glory.

It was unbelievable, but thoroughly in keeping with his whole unbelievable career.

The lame duck Congressman—defeated for re-election and

repudiated by his constituency—during the last ninety-day period, became the most important member of the House of Representatives. He was chosen by President-elect Franklin D. Roosevelt to guide New Deal legislation through the House.

The choice was really made by Professor A. A. Berle Jr., a member of the soon-to-be publicized Brain Trust, who left his chair in Columbia University to go down to Washington and look for a lieutenant. Roosevelt told Berle to select a Congressman to sponsor the Farm and Railroad Bankruptcy Law.

The crisis of 1932 had inspired the President-elect to an unusual action. He had decided to get his own reform program under way at once and to attempt the passage of basic legislation in the expiring Congress.

So Berle went to Washington and looked up La Guardia— and the two men took to one another from the start. The nervous, thin-lipped, slender pedagogue and the stocky, irascible legislator promptly effected an alliance which was to endure far longer than either of them anticipated.

The Major welcomed Berle warmly. He had just finished reading the latter's authoritative work *The Modern Corporation and Private Property*, and was anxious to meet the author. After probing one another's minds, the two men settled down to business. Berle notified his chief that La Guardia was the man they had been seeking.

Representative La Guardia therefore strode back into the halls of Congress in the closing days of his career, as the recognized and accredited agent of the President-elect. He not only fought through the Railroad Bankruptcy and Reorganization measure, as well as the Farm and Home Mortgage Relief bill, but he went on to sponsor legislation for the protection of minority bond holders. It was regarded as La Guardia's final public service.

Of course, he couldn't pass from the stage without putting on one last show. It was staged on December 9, when he paralyzed the hearing conducted by the Ways and Means Committee on the beer bill. The most famous Wet in America denounced a committee of brewers to their faces and ordered them out of Washington.

Waving his arms and shouting, La Guardia blew up with his old-time vigor. He waded into the hearing when representatives of the brewers finished testifying. Accusing them of being "up to their old pre-Prohibition tricks," he shouted that, "The quicker the brewers and distillers get out of Washington, the better off the anti-Prohibition movement will be." He then went on to say "The brewers must be divorced from the Wet movement," declaring that unless this was done, the passage of the beer bill would kill all hope of eventual repeal.

The session ended—the new Administration took office—and La Guardia returned to civil life.

He told friends that he was through with politics. He and Marie intended to settle down and enjoy life. He would practice law with the hope that some day he might acquire a position as an instructor in a law school.

In the meantime, however, he accepted an appointment as impartial arbitrator of a clothing manufacturers union and moved into the Times Square headquarters of that organization. It paid a reasonably good salary and the La Guardias rented a summer cottage at Westport, Connecticut.

They adopted the first of the two children who were to complete the family and settled down for a happy summer. The Major commuted between his New York office and the Westport cottage where Marie and little Jean enjoyed the sun and sand. It was a very happy period for the La Guardias.

The crusader had turned his back on the arena—but his fanaticism persisted as ever. It was demonstrated by a friend who dropped into his office that Spring and found Fiorello wrestling with his income tax return. The latter endeavored to assist in its preparation and quickly pointed out that La

Guardia had failed to credit himself with the usual exemptions to which he was entitled.

"But I can't take them," wailed La Guardia.

"Why not?"

"Because I helped to pass the law that created those exemptions. It would not be fair for me to benefit by the provisions of an exemption that I helped to put into the law."

And no argument could shake his conviction.

La Guardia was out of politics—but he could not keep his mind away from the subject. The sneers of a triumphant Tammany had bitten deeper than any one realized and the cagy political chief of the Ghibonnes began to consider the possibility of revenge. Unlike most observers he decided there might be a real chance to overthrow Tammany in the approaching Mayoralty election of 1933. That hope was based upon an unexpected phenomenon of the preceding year.

Tammany had elected Surrogate John P. O'Brien to finish out Jimmy Walker's term. O'Brien had received 1,056,115 votes against 443,901 for Lewis Pounds, Republican. But what gave La Guardia hope was the fact that 241,899 independent voters had taken the trouble to write the name of Joseph V. McKee in on the voting machines.

McKee had been acting Mayor during the period between Walker and O'Brien. In that capacity he had fought frequently with Tammany leaders and had been just as frequently mentioned as a reform candidate for Mayor.

The McKee candidacy had been rejected by his county leader, Edward J. Flynn of the Bronx, and the latter had gone along with his colleagues in support of O'Brien. Nevertheless, the McKee vote caused a wrinkle to appear in the brow of the lawyer-politician pondering the figures in the office of the clothing spongers association.

He decided in the Spring of 1933 that the McKee vote represented a protest against Tammany and that if almost a quarter of a million people took the trouble to write in McKee's name, the reform movement might have prospects of success.

La Guardia had repeatedly demonstrated that, unlike most reformers, he was a practical politician as well. Now he proceeded to exhibit a real mastery of the delicate art. He wanted to head an anti-Tammany ticket himself; therefore, he nominated Ex-Governor Alfred E. Smith for the post.

On May 10, he issued a statement outlining a complete "Fusion" ticket, composed of what he described as anti-Tammany elements. It was headed by Smith, and included Socialist Norman Thomas for Aldermanic President, Republican Robert Moses for Comptroller, Ex-Mayor John F. Hylan for Borough President of Queens, Mayor John P. O'Brien for Surrogate and a host of prominent Independents for other offices.

This La Guardia ticket was a masterpiece of political maneuvering. There was no possibility of Smith and O'Brien accepting places in the ranks of Tammany foemen. Both were intensely loyal to the organization. But the ticket illustrated the strength of a Fusion movement and familiarized the public with the idea.

Furthermore, Moses was one of the strongest potential Republican contenders for the nomination and the La Guardia slate relegated him to an inferior position, thus illustrating what the Major regarded as his most valuable place in the picture. Furthermore, La Guardia added a whipcracker to his statement. This afterthought was the comment that unless Smith accepted the Fusion nomination, he, La Guardia, would be forced to take the place himself.

That statement jarred the politicians severely. Republican leaders discovered overnight that their pet headache was still in evidence. They began considering ways and means of heading him off. Moses exhibited no enthusiasm for the task and they finally concentrated upon Major-General John F. O'Ryan as the G.O.P. white hope against La Guardia. State Chairman Macy swung in behind him, as did also the State

Chamber of Commerce and the newly formed City Party. It began to look as if O'Ryan would walk off with the Republican nomination at least, and there was no hope for a La Guardia-Fusion movement without the Republican contingent.

The Major retaliated in masterly fashion. He enlisted the support of Ex-Judge Samuel Seabury.

Seabury was Reform personified. He it was who had followed the trail first indicated by La Guardia in 1929 to its successful conclusion. He had ripped the lid off Tammany corruption and furnished the evidence which drove James J. Walker from office. The white-haired, ministerial Seabury was above reproach and he had no political ambitions. His blessing was far more effective than that of any professional politician.

And La Guardia sold himself to Seabury—as effectively as he had done in the case of Berle. The aristocratic old gentleman with the colonial ancestry enrolled beneath the banner of the son of the Italian immigrant, and he went into the final conference of the reform elements prepared to do battle for his candidate.

That meeting was held on August 4 at the City Club under the chairmanship of Charles C. Burlingham, former president of the New York State Bar Association. There were ten other members present. Besides Seabury and Burlingham, they included James Finnegan, a Brooklyn reform Democrat, J. G. L. Molloy of the Knickerbocker (Manhattan reform) Democrats, Maurice Davidson, Chairman of the City Party, William J. Schieffelin of the Citizens Union, Joseph M. Price of the Independent Fusion Committee, President J. Barstow Smull of the New York State Chamber of Commerce, Kingsland Macy representing the Republicans, and Berle who was there as La Guardia's spokesman.

They battled for six hours before Seabury finally put his man over. The final vote was nine to two with Smull and

Price walking out in a huff and refusing to make it unanimous. Seabury's victory was partially due to the fact that General O'Ryan finally offered to withdraw in the interests of harmony.

That night La Guardia sat on the back steps of the Westport cottage with a single friend and pensively studied the summer sky. "You know, I've really got a chance this time," he said. "There's a little more unrest in New York than Tammany believes." Then they got up and strolled across lots to the near-by Windels home where the two old friends laid down the first outline of the coming campaign.

Next day, La Guardia reappeared upon the New York political scene. Once more he was the anti-Tammany candidate for Mayor—and beneath the banner of reform he galloped back into the fray.

The crusader, unhorsed, had remounted.

The candidate played his political cards almost perfectly from the very beginning—and he was favored by the fact that Tammany still sneered. The Democratic politicians had been highly amused by the split in the Fusion ranks and the struggle between La Guardia and O'Ryan. They continued to laugh as the campaign got under way.

La Guardia stole a march on them almost at once. He issued another public statement offering to withdraw from the race if McKee would accept the Fusion nomination, at the same time rejecting Flynn's leadership. There was no possibility of McKee accepting the same generous offer—and La Guardia knew it. McKee did not really want to run and he wasn't the type to indulge in any such desperate gamble as that involved in breaking with Flynn. He had been Flynn's man throughout his political career.

Nevertheless, the offer placed La Guardia in a strategic position. It enabled him to denounce any later McKee candidacy as that of a Tammany stooge attempting to split the reform vote. This proved a most effective argument when the Bronxite finally decided to enter the race.

McKee was no stooge, however. He later became the spearhead of Boss Flynn's dramatic attempt to seize the Democratic leadership of the city. It was a genuine raid and one which almost succeeded.

The battle lines on the 1933 campaign developed slowly. It started out as a simple contest between La Guardia and the old-time foe. Tammany Hall, the Democratic organization of New York County, had as usual dictated the Democratic ticket to the other four counties. Tammany Boss, John F. Curry, had renominated the thoroughly well-meaning and definitely honest John P. O'Brien. Boss John McCooey, of Brooklyn, had been permitted to name the candidate for Comptroller while Boss Flynn was given the Aldermanic President.

There had been murmurs from the Bronx—and threats to run McKee in the primary but they didn't really worry Tammany. Its leaders had listened to the same story the preceding year.

The strange new currents forecast by the Major actually existed, however, and they came to light in the Democratic primary. They were revealed by the victory of Frank J. Prial, Independent candidate for Comptroller. He defeated the regular organization's candidate. The Tiger chieftains were frankly shocked but glibly explained their first fright away. They pointed out that Prial was the acknowledged leader of New York City's Civil Service employees and had always commanded a vast personal following. McKee did not enter the Primary and O'Brien took the Democratic nomination by default.

Meanwhile, La Guardia dictated the choice of his own running mates on the Fusion ticket. He selected Major Arthur B. Cunningham, a prominent Queens County banker, for Comptroller and Bernard S. Deutsch, Bronx social worker, for Aldermanic President. Deutsch was Jewish and Cunningham a Catholic, circumstances which helped to balance the Fusion city-wide ticket.

The campaign began as a contest between La Guardia and O'Brien—but there was unrest in the Bronx.

Flynn leaders could scarcely believe their eyes when they received the reports of their first midsummer canvass. The precinct workers reported an almost unbelievable sentiment for La Guardia. Whole families hitherto devoted to the Democratic cause openly announced their intention of voting for the Major. The Italian sections were wild with enthusiasm.

When they totaled up the various district reports, Flynn's leaders realized that they faced a crisis. The Bronx was out of hand. Its voters were disgusted with Tammany. They wanted reform, and La Guardia was the only reformer in sight.

Flynn went into a huddle with his closest advisors. The latter included Supreme Court Justice Stephen Callaghan, Collector of the Port Harry Durning and Postmaster Albert Goldman, and out of that conference came the decision to risk a desperate gamble.

"They want a reformer," said the Bronx leaders, "and if we don't give 'em one, we'll lose our whole county ticket." That was serious.

The defeat of the city-wide ticket, as far as the Bronx was concerned, meant the loss of only a handful of jobs in the Aldermanic President's office—but the defeat of the county ticket meant the loss of hundreds of jobs, including a Borough President, a District Attorney, a Sheriff, a Register, a County Clerk and several judges.

"They won't vote for any ticket headed by O'Brien," his advisors told Flynn. "You'll have to give 'em Joe McKee. That way we'll be reformers, too, and we can save the county ticket."

Flynn hesitated at first but finally decided to risk the gamble. Running McKee independently meant a definite break with the other four county organizations and splitting the Democratic Party from top to bottom. It was a desperate measure but Flynn decided to adopt it, and once committed to the move, he hoisted the banner of the New Deal and led a daring raid against Manhattan. He tried to wrest the city leadership from Tammany Hall.

Flynn almost succeeded. He created a new political party overnight and christened it the Recovery Party. He nominated McKee for Mayor and proclaimed him as the champion of President Roosevelt's doctrines. He proudly pointed to the presence of Postmaster General James A. Farley in the front rank of the raiding party as a testimonial of the President's blessing and he contracted alliances with dissatisfied district leaders in every one of the other four counties.

When the McKee bandwagon began rolling a half dozen of these leaders swarmed aboard. They staged an open rebellion against the Curry-McCooey coalition and enrolled beneath the Flynn banner. It was the greatest rebellion in Tammany's history—and the leaders were stunned for a space.

Then—with bitter cries of "traitor," the regular organization went into action against McKee. Now it was La Guardia's turn to laugh. His little tiff with O'Ryan, which had inspired such merriment in the Hall, was a mere Summer breeze in comparison to the hurricane aroused by the McKee-O'Brien brawl.

The Major conducted a typical La Guardia whirlwind campaign. Marie came down to the Paramount Building where headquarters had been installed and took charge as before. Once more the same old supporters rallied around; Windels, Harry Andrews, Edgar Bromberger, Corsi, Espresso and even Letter Carrier Gugenhan, still as devoted as in 1914. In addition, there were a number of unexpected recruits attracted by the Major's glamour. They were brisk young bluebloods from Park Avenue with Social Register names and an amazing willingness to fight. Two of them—Clendenin J. Ryan and Allan Stuyvesant united with Bromberger to form the Fusioneers.

The Fusioneers constituted a new force in politics. It enlisted 5,000 burly young men who announced that they proposed to see that La Guardia voters were not molested at the polls. These warlike young men included in addition to the Park Avenue bluebloods such awe compelling names as those of Tony Canzoneri and a whole bevy of Italian prizefighters.

The Fusioneers made elaborate plans for election day. Squads of them were distributed at strategic points throughout those districts in which Tammany thugs predominated. Each squad was provided with a high-powered car donated for the day. Scouts were to watch and telephone the Fusioneers headquarters whenever it seemed advisable. These calls were to be relayed to the combat squads.

This system grew out of La Guardia's familiarity with Tammany's tactics. He knew that in many lower East Side sections it was customary for thugs and gangsters to congregate in the doors of polling places effectively blocking all passage. They gave way willingly enough at a word from a Democratic election captain—but this word was given only when a Tammany voter approached.

It was impossible for any one else to reach the voting machine without shouldering his way through the group of roughs. Any attempt to crowd through them always resulted in an attack which usually sent the independent voter to the hospital. These tactics had been responsible for overwhelming Tammany majorities in these districts for many years.

The Fusioneers planned to escort non-Tammany voters through these thugs—and the escorts were to be composed impartially of the prizefighters and the Park Avenue-ites.

(As a matter of fact, the Fusioneers proved 100 percent effective on election day—although the casualty lists were unexpectedly long. Before that hectic day was over, young Stuyvesant went to a hospital with a broken jaw and many of his colleagues bore similar marks. The vote was cast under their protection, however.)

There was another unusual recruit. Into Headquarters one afternoon strolled a New York City patrolman in uniform. He was a burly Irish cop and he announced that he was anxious to work for "the little guy." A member of the staff took him in hand.

"Why are you so enthusiastic about the Major?"

"It's this way," began the volunteer. "I ain't seen him since he was Aldermanic President—and that's twelve years ago, but I'll never forget what he did for me.

"I was new on the force in those days and I had a beat down on 14th Street. One evening a couple of thugs threw a brick through the window of a jewelry store, grabbed all the stuff they could and got away. A crowd collected fast.

"I never had a chance to get the robbers but I phoned the station house and then I stood in front of the broken window to keep the crowd back. There was a lot of jewelry in there that the robbers hadn't had time to grab and I knew it was my job to protect what was left until help come. The crowd kept pushing closer and closer and I was pretty busy trying to keep them away. And suddenly, this little, dark-complected fellow pushes his way through the crowd right up behind the window.

"I shouldn't have done it, but I had a lot on my mind and I grabs him by the shoulder and tosses him back into the crowd and I snarls at him, "Get back there, you Guinea barber!"

"Well, nothing happened until the next day when I got orders to report to the President of the Board of Aldermen. I went down to City Hall, marched into his office and saluted. Mister, I almost died in my tracks. The guy behind the desk was the same little dark-complected fellow I'd shoved around the night before. When I recognized Mr. La Guardia I figured I was done for.

"I stood there with my knees shaking while he looks me over and when he finally spoke, his voice was cold as ice.

" 'Officer,' he says, 'I sent for you to give you an opportunity of seeing just what a Guinea barber looks like at close range.'

"I couldn't say anything except 'Yes, sir.' I couldn't think of anything to say and then he hands me a sealed envelope addressed to the Police Commissioner, and he tells me to take it back to Headquarters and present it in person. I was scared stiff but I had to do it.

"And, Mister, when the Commissioner opened the letter, he read it to me. And there wasn't a word about me calling him that name or even shoving him around. He told the Commissioner that I had done a swell job protecting that broken window and he recommended me for promotion.

"I'll do anything I can for that little guy."

Despite the efforts of the Fusioneers, things grew blacker as the campaign progressed. It began to look like a McKee landslide and there was no surer indication of disaster than the sudden cessation of contributions to the Fusion Campaign Fund. La Guardia and his running mates were unable to raise any funds at all. The Major was broke as usual—and had borrowed $600.00 for his own personal campaign expenses. Finally, the situation became so desperate that there was no money available to pay the headquarters rent.

At this crisis, one Fusion worker brought in a check for $20,000.00 as a contribution from a public utilities corporation, but the candidate refused to accept it.

There was a brief and bitter exchange in the Major's private office in the Paramount Building Campaign Headquarters. Grouped about a long table were the members of the general staff and the candidate. Everybody present knew that the situation was desperate.

"I won't touch it," shrilled La Guardia, pounding the table. "I have never put myself under obligation to a public utility yet—and I won't do it now. They are just trying to play both ends against the middle. They don't really think I can win but they would like to be in a position to remind me of the favor if the miracle should happen. Send the check back. I won't touch it."

"But, Major," urged one advisor, "we need it so badly. Why can't we use it now and return the money later after some more contributions come in?"

The Major exploded.

He rejected that suggestion with such profane eloquence that the window shades smoked. When he concluded there was no doubt in anybody's mind that the utility check would be returned. But the conference wasn't ended yet.

"Then what will we do about the headquarters' rent?" queried the original speaker triumphantly. "There's no money in the treasury."

The Major laughed.

"We'll evacuate headquarters," he snapped. "I don't need a desk anyhow. We'll move out of headquarters and I'll run this campaign from the tail end of a truck. Furthermore, I'll borrow the truck."

The conference dissolved amid the sighs of the more material-minded.

It wasn't necessary to evacuate headquarters, however. One of the Park Avenue recruits stepped in and guaranteed the rent at the last minute.

He was a young man just out of Princeton, with a fresh face and an engaging manner. He didn't have a cent to his name at that time—but that name was compelling. The landlord was perfectly willing to accept the pledge of Clendenin, the grandson of Thomas Fortune Ryan, in lieu of cash. It was another victory for the Fusioneers.

During the first half of October, the experts agreed that McKee was making a runaway race of it. It was Berle who first checked him. The scene was Cooper Union. The time, the evening of October 2.

The Columbia professor threw all the weight of his Brain Trust membership behind the La Guardia candidacy, when he told a cheering audience, "No one without the direct authority of President Roosevelt has the right to attempt to steal his name and prestige and particularly no one, especially a raiding crew, has the right to try to embarrass him by misusing his name as part of a political boarding party."

That was a palpable fling at the McKee candidacy and the

President's continued silence increased its effect. The race tightened up but Flynn's entry remained the odds-on favorite.

Then, on October 14, the Major reached back into his arsenal for a four-year-old bombshell. With the weapon which he had refrained from using in 1929, he blasted the McKee candidacy right off the New York City political map. The bombshell was that 1915 *Catholic World* article to which reference has heretofore been made.

La Guardia proved himself the master politician once more. With consummate artistry, he played his cards in such fashion that McKee received the blame for injecting the religious issue—while La Guardia acquired all the benefit. The Recovery candidate carelessly left an opening and that was enough for the Major.

McKee demanded that La Guardia disown Seabury's attack on Governor Lehman. (The judge had accused the Governor of failing to act when certain crimes were uncovered by the previous Hofstader Inquiry.)

> THE CHARGE IS UTTERLY AND CONTEMPTIBLY FALSE
> AND I DENOUNCE, HERE AND NOW, SAMUEL SEABURY
> FOR MAKING IT. WHAT DO YOU SAY?

Thus, McKee wired La Guardia.

La Guardia's response was the telegram which defeated McKee. It began with the statement that the Major did his own thinking and speaking—and then it called attention to the article containing McKee's criticism of Jewish children. The La Guardia parry ran:

> YOUR SILLY EFFORT TO CREATE A FALSE ISSUE NOW
> THAT THE FLYNN-FARLEY CAMPAIGN HAS BLOWN UP,
> WILL NOT BE TAKEN SERIOUSLY BY ANY ONE IN NEW
> YORK. ARE YOU TRYING TO DRAW A RED HERRING
> ACROSS THE COWARDLY, CONTEMPTIBLE AND UNJUST
> ATTACK THAT YOU HAVE MADE AND PUBLISHED
> AGAINST A GREAT RACE GLORIOUSLY REPRESENTED BY

OUR GOVERNOR? ANSWER THAT, MR. MC KEE, AND
THINK TWICE BEFORE YOU SEND ME ANOTHER TELE-
GRAM. STICK TO THE ISSUE AND EXPLAIN TO THE PEO-
PLE OF THE CITY OF NEW YORK YOUR CONSTANT
SHIFTING AND COLORLESS RECORD AT CITY HALL FOR
SEVEN YEARS.

I CAN READILY UNDERSTAND HOW YOU, OF ALL PEO-
PLE, WOULD CALL UPON A THIRD PERSON TO EXPLAIN
THE STATEMENTS AND THOUGHTS OF ANOTHER PERSON.
YOU ARE ACCUSTOMED TO HAVING EDDIE FLYNN THINK
FOR YOU AND YOU ACT AS HE SAYS.

That focused attention upon McKee's article in which he
had criticized Catholics as well as Jews, but that fact could
not save him. More than one third of New York City's population was Jewish and most political experts agreed that it was
the shifting of this vote which turned the tide toward La
Guardia. McKee's frantic last minute effort to brand him a
Communist got exactly nowhere. It was hamstrung by the
welcome arrival of the conservative Robert Moses in the
Fusion camp.

The campaign drew to a riotous close and in the crashing
confusion, many people missed a significant headline in the
New York Times of October 21. It read: "La Guardia Warns
Republican Rally He Is Non-Partisan—Serves Notice He
Will Go Out of Politics on Taking Hold of City Govern-
ment."

G.O.P. leaders who considered that merely "another campaign statement" were due for a shocking reminder in the near
future.

There was another brisk interchange just at the close of the
campaign. On the Saturday night before election, McKee
made a last minute attack upon La Guardia's integrity. He
charged that his opponent, while a Congressman, had inter-
vened on behalf of a crooked narcotic agent who was later
sent to prison.

The charge was unexpected and created real confusion in Fusion Headquarters. The candidate couldn't even remember the man to whom McKee referred. "I have met so many people during the time I was in Congress, that I don't dare say I don't know this man," he wailed to his distracted advisors. "Of course there is nothing wrong—but some poor devil I befriended may have gone wrong later. I have been searching my files all afternoon and I can't find a thing on this case."

The entire headquarters' staff suspended all other activity and devoted itself to a search for the record covering McKee's unexpected revelations. Voluminous Federal Court records were procured and carefully perused as the afternoon wore on. The tension increased.

It was a brisk young woman lawyer who found the case at last. She sprang up with a cry, "Here it is!"

La Guardia dashed across the room and followed her pointing finger. Then the pair of them united in a shout of laughter.

McKee's bombshell was a boomerang.

La Guardia hurled it back in his teeth at the final rally in the Brooklyn Academy of Music on November 5.

> I will say that I have never in any way intervened on behalf of the convicted narcotic agent, Richard Nash, he began. I have looked up the records in the Nash case and I find that the two character witnesses for the agent in question, were Lester Patterson, candidate for Bronx Sheriff on McKee's ticket, and James W. Brown, Bronx Public Administrator, who is McKee's strong supporter.

The newspapers leaped on that and the narcotic case scandal evaporated.

New York went to the polls on November 7 and elected La Guardia. The final vote was:

La Guardia 858,551
McKee 604,045
O'Brien 586,100

Election evening was stirring and dramatic. The Major and Marie had spent the afternoon with her mother in the Bronx, the candidate taking a nap in the afternoon, but he awoke and they went back to their apartment just before the polls closed.

A few minutes later, the candidate emerged from his door, intending to go down to Seabury's home to receive the returns. He found a flock of reporters on the front step and one of them gave him the returns from his own polling place just around the corner. McKee led by 84 votes.

La Guardia gave a yelp of glee and cried: "I'm elected. I'm in." (He had almost instantaneously translated the proportion of his own usually overwhelmingly hostile precinct into terms of the entire city.) Then he snatched a friend by the arm and cried anxiously, "I didn't say that—I didn't say I was elected? It is too soon to say anything of the kind—I didn't say that, did I?"

It was his only evidence of emotion over the greatest triumph of his life.

The most dramatic episode of that stirring day, however, was yet to occur, and it was almost completely ignored by the newspapers frantically engaged in recording the Fusion victory. Consequently, few persons knew the details of the Major's midnight dash to save his Comptroller.

La Guardia learned of his own victory while he sat with Seabury in the latter's den. They smiled at one another as the glad tidings rolled in. Then the phone rang.

The call came from a newspaper reporter—an intimate friend of the Major—whom the latter had sent over to the Hotel Astor to make sure that everything was ready for the appearance of the victorious candidate at a celebration arranged for the thousands of Fusion campaign workers, and this reporter had stumbled across a threatened disaster in the very moment of triumph.

He had found the upper floors of the Astor jammed with a wildly hilarious throng. Its numbers increased momentarily as the subway trains brought more and more Fusion workers from the outlying boroughs, and in the middle of that jubilant crowd one desperately worried individual was vainly seeking to fight his way into the little diningroom reserved for the candidates.

It was Major Arthur Cunningham, the second man on the Fusion ticket and a "forgotten man" among its cohorts. The tall, slender soldier eagerly snatched the reporter's arm and led him into a corner.

"For God's sake, give me some advice," pleaded the candidate. "I don't know anything about politics. I've just discovered that Tammany Hall is counting me out. They're about to steal my election from me. My lead has dropped from 50,000 to 4,000 in the last hour—and I hear they're holding up the returns from 400 precincts. What *can* I do about it?"

The reporter nodded. "It's an old trick," he replied. "They'll wait until all the other returns are in and then fake the figures for those last 400 precincts. They'll give one of your opponents whatever he needs to beat you out. Then he'll be declared elected—and you can go to court to prove the count was wrong. Maybe you'll win and—maybe you won't. But how did you find out about it?"

"One of my friends from police headquarters called me up and tipped me off," said Cunningham.

"There's only one thing that I see for you to do," said the newspaper man. "That is to get hold of La Guardia at once. He is the only man in New York who can save you now. Remember, he is elected. He has as much authority tonight as he will have the day he is sworn in. Get him over here."

"Where is he?" asked Cunningham.

"Seabury's," responded the reporter.

"I'll phone him."

Information of Cunningham's distress brought La Guardia rushing over to the Astor. He was almost mobbed by his jubilant supporters who brushed his police escort aside at the first rush. Two husky cops fought their way back and held the door when he took refuge in a service pantry. There he was joined by Cunningham and the reporter, and the situation explained to him.

The light of battle sparkled in the dark eyes as he listened. He tossed his head and said simply: "Come on Arthur. I'll go get those 400 precincts for you."

Slipping out the back way, the three men hurried down to La Guardia's car which roared away to Police Headquarters in southern Manhattan.

Down there Tammany Hall still held sway. Up on the top floor the employees of the Tammany controlled Board of Elections were handling the returns. They filled one huge room. The hundreds of workers were seated at tables, or busy at the blackboards upon which the results were posted.

High-ranking police officers, loyal to the Tammany administration which had elevated them, moved about the room. Patrolmen guarded the doors, and seated on a high chair which was perched upon a central table was the director of the entire scene. He was a Tammany henchman busily engaged in snapping out orders, telling his underlings just what precinct should report—and when.

Down there—on the fifth floor of Police Headquarters— Tammany was still supreme. The machine was functioning as of old. Busy Tiger lieutenants chuckled wisely as they worked. Let the crackpot reformers celebrate up in Times Square—the machine was still functioning where it was needed.

Yes—Tammany was very confident. Many of its supporters expected the organization to save control of the Board of Estimate, as well as the Board of Aldermen—while "that lucky little wop" was posturing on the Astor marquee.

Suddenly, an almost visible wave of horror swept across that room.

It was evidenced in the deathly silence which gripped those hundreds of workers. Almost magnetically it seemed, their eyes turned toward the north doorway.

And there stood La Guardia.

He surveyed them slowly. Thoughtfully he teetered up and down on his toes as he studied the man on the central table. He smiled—and it wasn't a friendly smile at all.

The silence was broken by policemen, bowing, scraping and saluting. They surged forward. Captains and Inspectors vied with one another in a fawning contest. "Good morning, Mr. Mayor—Congratulations, Mr. Mayor—Can I help you, Mr. Mayor?" They were almost servile. "They'd better," a headquarters' reporter chuckled, "because to Hell with Tammany. They have to live with this guy for four years and they know it."

The Major went into action in typical La Guardia fashion. He exploded like a bomb.

As he shot into the room, ripping out orders—the startled Tammany leader sprang from his table and ran for the door. La Guardia took his place instantly. He spouted instructions as confidently as if he was already Mayor.

"I want 400 patrolmen mobilized behind headquarters just as fast as they can get here," he rapped.

"Yes—Mr. Mayor," and a Captain ran for the telephone. La Guardia swung to an Inspector.

"Get me 400 patrol wagons," he snapped. "Roll 'em into the alley behind headquarters as fast as God will let you."

"Yes, Mr. Mayor."

"As fast as each patrolman gets here," he continued, "send 'em to one of the 400 precincts in which the count for Comptroller is being help up. Tell 'em to mount guard over that voting machine with drawn gun."

"Yes, Mr. Mayor."

"As fast as the patrol wagons get here, send one of them to each precinct. In every case the cops are to load the voting machine into the patrol wagon and bring it here at once."

"Yes, Mr. Mayor."

There was another instant of stunned silence. It was broken by the Mayor-elect. Tossing his dark locks, he observed sweetly, "By God, I'm going to count those votes for Comptroller myself."

Such was Fiorello La Guardia's introduction to his Police force. It was an effective one. Word of his action spread magically—rippling in whispered tidings across a thousand telephone wires. It ruined the Tammany strategy. Before the first police guard had left the precinct to which he was assigned, the belated returns were coming in.

They flooded headquarters almost simultaneously—with the count for Comptroller from 400 precincts. And as soon as they were totaled, the Mayor-elect turned grinning to his new colleague. "There you are, Arthur," he beamed, "you're elected. Let's all get a drink."

CHAPTER XXI

HIS HONOR, THE MAYOR

THEY celebrated the victory up at La Guardia's that night—
the Major, Marie, her sister Elsie and one reporter friend.
They broke away from the jubilating crowds at last—from the
endless barrage of handshakes, congratulations, felicitations,
"I knew you could do its," and "I voted for you, Major."
Fiorello had insisted on stopping at the Hotel Lexington to
call on General O'Ryan—for the sole purpose of publicly acknowledging his debt to the rival candidate who had stepped
aside, and finally he had made his escape from the bevy of
white ties and low-necked dresses which surrounded him.

Up in the little four-room apartment, overlooking East
109th Street, they celebrated—alone at last. They locked the
door and Fiorello doffed his coat and vest. Then he donned
one of Marie's kitchen aprons and bustled into the kitchen.

And the Mayor-elect cooked dinner on election night.

They sat around the table and glowed over the victory.
They congratulated Fiorello on his triumph and his cooking
impartially—and finally Marie leaned back and smiled at the
ceiling.

"You know what?" observed the new First Lady of New
York. "Do you folks know what I think is the best thing of all
about today's events?"

"Why, Fiorello has won the second most important post in
America," interjected the newspaper man.

"Oh, that's nice," replied Marie. "But the really important
thing is that now we can afford to get a new rug for the living
room. You all know how long I have wanted it."

She wasn't posing. The La Guardias were poor when he
took office. They didn't even own an automobile—because

they couldn't afford one. Fiorello had borrowed spending money to last him during the campaign.

Therefore, his first official action was to cut his own salary from Jimmy Walker's $40,000.00 to $22,500.00.

* * *

And now the job hunters! They swarmed about him in unbelievable numbers—personal friends and politicians, neighbors and old schoolmates, well-wishers and campaign workers—they descended upon him in legions. They overflowed the corridors of the little Broadway office and they waited at the door for him to come home. Some of the wiser ones wrote letters to Marie.

Republican leaders generously volunteered to relieve him of all of this detail work. They submitted lists of the faithful, carefully indicating the jobs and salaries to which each worker's merit entitled him. A lot of Fusion potential politicians did likewise.

And La Guardia broke their hearts.

He took Marie for a brief vacation in order to recuperate from the campaign and they spent two weeks cruising in the Caribbean Sea before taking a plane home from Panama. They were the guests of Frank A. Tichenor, publisher of the *New Outlook* magazine, and New York began to get acquainted with the explosive potentialities of its new Mayor while he was still at sea.

Tichenor was rash enough to nominate a couple of gentlemen to be Police Commissioner as he strolled with reporters along the deck—and when La Guardia heard about his host's indiscretion, he went into a blazing rage which provoked headlines all over Manhattan.

"You can't justify it. It's all wrong," he shouted—and then dashed off a message for the newspapers at home. It read, "No justification for Police Commissioner story. I gave no statement. Said nothing concerning subject. Utterly groundless."

Back in Manhattan the Mayor-elect cleared the decks for

action and began preparations for the first Reform Administration in twenty years. When he began making his appointments, he shocked the skyscrapers clear down to their foundations. New York had never seen anything quite like it. The Commissioners—or heads of the various city departments—each charged with the spending of millions of dollars—had traditionally been political leaders. Their fat salaries had always gone to reward the faithful. Now La Guardia broke most of the rules of the political game.

He did not break all of them, however. Semi-stunned by the first impact of this Reform Administration, New York was slow to recognize the background of practical politics upon which the new Chief Executive projected his most spectacular achievements.

And they were spectacular. This precedent-shattering Mayor proceeded to appoint a uniformed fire-fighter—Chief John J. McElligott—to be Fire Commissioner, and Tammany reeled at the shock of seeing a man who actually knew how to fight fires in charge of the department. La Guardia went on to appoint non-residents of New York who were experts in their field to take charge of the city prisons and the Health Department. He even persuaded the almost unbelievably efficient Moses to replace five borough park commissioners in a single unified office.

Such appointments were unorthodox. And never before had out-of-town experts been called in to head New York City's departments. The action of the Mayor-elect in requesting the United States Public Health Service to indicate the city with the best public health record in the United States—and the appointment of Dr. John Rice as Health Commissioner because he had won that reputation for New Haven, Connecticut, was without precedent. So was the selection of Austin H. McCormick to head the City Prison System because he had made a brilliant record in charge of the Federal Penitentiary at Chillicothe, Ohio.

New York was so dazed by these appointments that there

was no criticism of others which would have been regarded as purely political if made by any one else. Of course, La Guardia required Frederick J. H. Kracke to resign as Republican Leader of Brooklyn before accepting an appointment as Commissioner of Plant and Structures. There was no doubt that the appointment of a county boss to public office by any other Mayor would have brought wails of anguish from the reformers, but Kracke's designation was drowned out by the chorus of praise for the Independent appointments.

Even his friends admitted that the Mayor-elect selected O'Ryan for Police Commissioner in payment of his political debt. They pointed out, however, that O'Ryan was a capable soldier and that there had been a string tied to his appointment. That string was the promotion of Captain Lewis Valentine, then commanding the 4th Avenue Station in Brooklyn, to be Chief Inspector of the New York Police Force.

Valentine's name was almost as well known as O'Ryan's. It had been frequently featured in the headlines during a long career in which he had acquired a reputation as a courageous reformer. This reputation was usually regarded as responsible for much of the trouble which had marked his police career. Valentine had worked his way up from a pavement-pounding patrolman to an inspectorship. He had been reduced to the command of a police station following a series of gambling raids on Tammany clubs. At any rate, Captain Valentine was not popular with Tammany—and that was enough for La Guardia. He directed O'Ryan to place Brooklyn's trouble-making cop in command of the uniformed force.

The new Mayor was sworn in just as the New Year exploded with its usual wild tumult in Manhattan. He took the oath before Justice Philip McCook in Seabury's drawing-room. It was Seabury's party. The white-haired reformer had made all the arrangements and the Mayor-elect graciously bowed to the wishes of the man to whom he owed so much.

The guests were mostly Seabury's friends and members of the new Administration. Among them were Windels who was to be Corporation Counsel and Berle designated as City Chamberlain. At La Guardia's request, five of his own personal friends were present. They included Piccirilli, two reporters and the latters' wives.

* * *

On the morning of January 1, 1934—exactly twelve years and one day after he had been driven from the city service—Fiorello La Guardia dashed up the front steps of New York's City Hall once more. He fought his way through a welcoming crowd which packed the big central corridor and darted a hasty glance toward the office of the Aldermanic President which he had once occupied. This time, however, he turned to the left toward the Mayoralty suite at the west end of the building where John O'Brien was waiting to turn over the helm of the city government. The Major had reached the goal which he had set for himself in 1920.

As soon as the ceremonies were over the new Mayor bustled reporters, photographers and spectators out of the private office, ensconsed himself in the big chair, summoned a platoon of stenographers and went to work. Reaching for a pen, he dived into the city's business with a dynamic energy which never faltered through the ensuing years. The human dynamo thus galvanized into action worked at unbelievable speed.

In the beginning, he burdened himself with a mass of detail that would have submerged an ordinary executive. He attended personally to huge stacks of mail, working his secretaries in relays. From the very first day he proceeded to give his personal attention to minor matters throughout the hundreds of municipal bureaus and departments. For months on end he worked like a demon sticking to his desk from early morning until late at night. He would break away only to descend unannounced on some city office, sweep through it in a tornado of reorganization and vanish amid sighs of relief from the confounded staff.

He had the nation's biggest city dizzy within a week. Brigades of bewildered reporters were unable to keep up with his chameleon mind. Their confused queries irritated him from the beginning. He did not attempt to conceal that irritation.

He was too busy. During those amazing first two months, he plunged into a bitter fight with the Governor, clashed with the Board of Aldermen, took the offensive against the vast Tri-Boro Bridge Authority, quarreled with his Police Commissioner, became involved with the biggest taxi strike in New York history, went to war with the racketeers and shattered precedents on every hand.

New York could not keep up with its spectacular Chief Executive. One day he was haranguing strikers from the running-board of his official car and the next, donning judicial robes to lock up slot machine racketeers whom the judges refused to hold. A little later he might be smashing down doors at the head of a police raiding party. And already there were stories of the irascible temper which frequently erupted within the private office. New York had never encountered such a Chief Executive.

City editors almost went crazy trying to keep up with the rapid sweep of events. Platoons of police marched on to the property of the Brooklyn Ash Removal Company and seized its five plants before La Guardia had been in office a week. The Mayor thus defied an injunction secured by that concern. A little later his subordinates staged a spectacular raid on the Welfare Island Penitentiary and recaptured it from the gangster convicts who had controlled that penal institution during the Tammany regime.

The new Mayor lost his first major engagement—that with Governor Lehman and the State Legislature. On his first day in office, he demanded dictatorial powers to save the city from bankruptcy. Although his request was backed by the Fusion Board of Estimate in which he controlled 13 of the 16 votes, Lehman refused the request. Fourteen weeks elapsed before they worked out a compromise as a result of which the City Administration was authorized to institute a series of payless furloughs which enabled the Mayor to balance the budget he had inherited from Tammany.

He continued his surprise inspections, bobbing up unexpectedly all over the city. On January 15, he came storming into the Municipal Building at nine o'clock in the morning and dashed from one office to another, while underlings frantically telephoned their missing superiors that the Big Boss was on the rampage. It was a salutary lesson frequently repeated in the ensuing years.

One month later, he stormed into Harlem Prison and fired a civilian cook because he found a trusty preparing lunch in the latter's absence. Before he departed he almost took the quaking prison apart. The Major flew into a rage when he found two small boys imprisoned there, each held in $25,000 bail as material witnesses in a murder case. He forced attendants to unlock their cells and transfer them to the Children's Society.

The same day, La Guardia spectacularly reminded his city that the law authorized its Chief Executive to sit as a magistrate. A Federal Judge had blocked his drive on slot machines by issuing an injunction ordering the police to keep hands off such machines when "not actually being used for gambling."

The Mayor suddenly appeared in the West 100th Street Police Station, established a temporary court there and took the bench. "This is a gambling machine and not even a Federal Judge can make it anything else," he snapped, holding the possessor for trial. One week later he repeated that performance in the Brooklyn, Gates Avenue Station. He held both defendants for Special Sessions.

"This will serve notice to owners, operators, racketeers and other riffraff who run this racket that they will enjoy no comfort," declared the Mayor-Magistrate. "This game is mechanical larceny. Players do not get a gambler's chance. Only a moron or imbecile could get a thrill out of watching these sure thing devices take his money."

And before he was through he smashed the slot machine

ring which had been operating in the metropolis for years.

Another typical performance was his unexpected descent on a lower East Side Relief Station. Investigating a complaint contained in an anonymous letter, the Mayor stopped off to see for himself on the morning of May 15. He left his car a block away and went and joined the line of applicants.

He found the personnel lounging about and the policeman on duty daydreaming. The latter's coat was unbuttoned and a carefree, lackadaisical air brooded over the place. Only one stenographer was interviewing the waiting applicants while a dozen others sat at idle typewriters. The little man in the big slouch hat waited—patient and unrecognized—until he had seen enough. Then he pushed through the crowd toward the head of the line until his way was barred by a brusque attendant.

"Where the Hell do you think you're going?" barked the latter.

La Guardia went into action like a cyclone. He seized the man by the shoulders, whirled him about and sent him spinning into the crowd. A second employee rushed forward and received the same treatment. By this time he had reached the rail and a cigar-smoking, derby-hatted individual came swooping down vengefully on the intruder.

He too received short shrift. The Mayor struck the cigar from his mouth with one swift blow and his hat with another.

"Take off your hat when you speak to a citizen," rasped His Honor, and vaulted the inner railing. Then, at last, he was recognized by the dumfounded attendants and a sudden silence descended.

Invading the office of the director, La Guardia blew up when he found that gentleman missing. He ordered a secretary to telephone a summons to Welfare Commissioner William Hodson at once. Emerging from the private office, His Honor bawled out the policeman for his slovenliness and snatched up a high stool which he placed inside the railing.

Perched on it, the Chief Executive took out his watch and

barked, "Let me see how fast you can clear up this crowd of applicants." The bureau flew into action. Word spread through the adjoining offices that the Boss was on the job and the activity was epidemic.

The Mayor had arrived at 9:16 A.M. By 9:37 the entire crowd of applicants had been interviewed and hustled out. They lined up and gave a cheer for His Honor before they left.

A few minutes later Hodson arrived. The attendants clustered about the two men, confessing their misdeeds and pleading for mercy. Several were ordered stricken from the city pay roll.

"You wait here, Bill," directed the Mayor, "until your director gets here. If he doesn't have a good excuse for his absence, he's fired, and by good excuse I mean a doctor's certificate that he was ill this morning."

He hurried out but paused in the doorway as an afterthought struck him. Pointing to the cigar-smoking individual of the derby hat, the Mayor growled:

"Oh, yes, Bill. There's another S. of a B. that has no job."

Then he hurried back to his car and resumed his trip to City Hall.

That kind of thing went on for four years before there was any opportunity to evaluate public reaction. Most of these performances resulted from the dramatic reflexes of a highly emotional nature; others were doubtless due to an undeniable talent for the spectacular. (It was too much to expect the Congressman who had waved pork chops in the House and made beer on the steps of the Capitol to pass up all the theatrical opportunities offered by his command of the Police and Fire Departments.)

Without a warrant he smashed down the door of a Brooklyn private home at the head of a police posse and he rode to work in a Battalion Chief's red fire wagon. He snatched the baton from an orchestra leader at a Central Park concert and with it beat time to popping flashlights. He donned fire hat

384

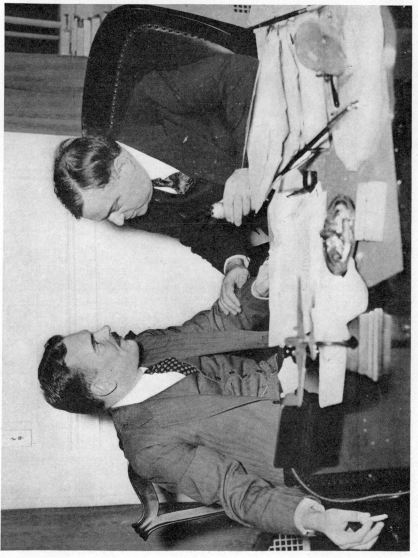

"An invaluable reinforcement." Mayor La Guardia with District Attorney-elect Thomas E. Dewey on the morning after their 1937 victory.

The Mayor and his son, Eric, in the summer of 1937.

and raincoat and responded to alarms with Commissioner Mc-Elligott.

And the people ate it up. Less spectacular but none the less effective was his steady drive toward a cleaner and non-partisan form of government. Bit by bit he pushed the almost bankrupt city toward solvency even at the cost of imposing that same kind of sales tax against which he had fought so bitterly in Congress. He was doing things—but it wasn't all clear sailing.

La Guardia was a dictator from the day he took office—and that caused most of the trouble. He proceeded to browbeat his subordinates in the same fashion in which he had always bulldozed his little office force. That meant shrieking, screaming and cursing at them—frequently when others were present. It was no rarity for the Chief Executive to hurl his pen on the floor and launch into a bitter tirade against the head of some great city department.

He had grown accustomed to the use of such tactics in the past. For years the fiery reformer had been surrounded by worshipful young crusaders who didn't dare resent that kind of treatment. Now it was different. Men of larger calibre who didn't know and love him were quick to resent such treatment.

Most of them concealed it—and merely endeavored to avoid precipitating such scenes. Some—like Moses—fought back energetically. They made a surprising discovery.

"You can't talk to me that way, Fiorello," made much more rapid progress in his regard than an obsequious, "I'm sorry, Mr. Mayor." Moses stood for no nonsense, fought La Guardia time after time—and never ceased to be his friend. In fact, the Mayor defied the whole National Administration with its deadly relief control weapon, in order to protect Moses' Tri-Boro Bridge Authority job.

There was similar strife with O'Ryan—but the two men had much less in common. There was friction between them almost from the beginning. O'Ryan resented the Mayor's interference with his administration of the Police Department and he had little sympathy with La Guardia's refusal to authorize the use of force during some riotous labor troubles.

The two men just couldn't get along. The brusque soldier took occasion to announce—in midwinter—that his patrolmen would not be permitted to doff their heavy uniform coats when summer came. The Mayor later went over the Commissioner's head and authorized the cops to do just that. (It is significant that the busy Mayor took time to examine samples of the shirts to be worn by the officers and to dictate the kind of buttons they should bear. Concern with such trivial details was typical of the way he ran his office.)

O'Ryan had made his announcement public and La Guardia over-ruled him just as publicly. There were headlines in the newspapers. The friction increased as the weeks went by.

Finally, O'Ryan exploded and on September 24—after less than nine months in office—the Police Commissioner resigned. He accompanied his resignation with a public statement in which he accused the Mayor of interfering "with the conduct and discipline of the Police Department," and in connection with strikes of encouraging "the Communists and other vicious elements of the city to exploit these occasions for their own ends." O'Ryan maintained that the Chief Executive had over-ridden the rights of the general public.

It was neither the first time that the Mayor had been, nor the last time that he would be, accused of sympathy with the Communists. That accusation seemed to burst out almost automatically from the lips of all of his critics—except the Communists themselves. *They* usually accused him of being a traitor to the working class and frequently picketed City Hall against him.

In fact, the Communists were much more bitter against him in those days than the men who accused him of being one of them. The Reds almost created a riot at Lewisohn Stadium on the night of June 25, 1934, when they sent an organized cheering section to a concert of the Philharmonic Orchestra.

Mayor La Guardia is a yellow dog! Mayor La Guardia is a yellow dog! Mayor La Guardia is a yellow dog!

Thus the Communists chanted their chorus, throwing back at the Mayor, an epithet which he had applied to leaders of a Red riot at City Hall. Champions of the Mayor rushed to attack his insulters but he took personal charge of the police and directed them to "keep the aisles clear." So tremendous was the ovation from the audience of 15,000 that the Reds finally gave up in despair.

As the months wore on and the Mayor continued working desperately long hours under an almost unbelievable tension, his always quick temper frayed more and more. He snarled at his best friends, lashed out savagely at well-meaning critics and fought desperately with avowed foemen. It was during this period that his feud with "Room 9" developed. "Room 9" was the press room at City Hall, and the newspaper men were very quick to resent what they regarded as the Mayor's attempt to dictate to them. And when he committed journalism's major political crime and went over their heads to complain to city editors about individual reporters, war was declared in earnest.

It started out as a very bitter conflict. The City Hall reporters accused the Mayor of being childish and he counterclaimed that they were discourteous. They pointed to the fact that he refused to inspect the old William's Bridge Reservoir on May the 11, 1934, if any reporter was permitted to accept the invitation of Aldermanic President Deutsch to accompany the party. (As a result, the parade consisted of one official and three empty cars.) He replied by accusing them of "getting drinks on the cuff from politicians."

Two journalistic friends who attempted to pour oil on the troubled waters found the Mayor hurt and angry. He was utterly bewildered when they presumed to criticize *his* conduct.

"Major," asked one, "did you really ask one managing editor to fire his City Hall reporter?"

"Damn right, I did," snapped La Guardia. "He wrote lies about me."

The mere remembrance of the incident inflamed the Mayor. His voice trembled with rage as he went into detail explaining how in addition, this particular reporter had spat upon the rug in the Mayor's private office during a press conference.

"That's why I stopped all press conferences," rapped the Mayor. "I'll never hold another."

But he was instantly disarmed when one of his critics responded: "Isn't that in keeping with the La Guardia tradition —a fitting performance for the man who always fought for the under-dog, to use the prestige of the second most powerful office in this country to get the job of a forty-dollar-a-week reporter? Won't that be something for your children to boast about?"

The Major gazed at his critic in stark horror.

"Good God," he whispered, "I never thought about it that way."

He wasn't quite so hostile to the reporters after that—though he became intimate with only a few. He continued to be exceedingly sensitive to newspaper criticism and often flew into a rage over what he regarded as misstatements, but generally he got along famously with the photographers. He won their admiration because of his cheerful co-operation and this admiration grew into a real liking on both sides.

The Mayor became a popular and honored guest at their professional functions and the picture men reciprocated by manufacturing an elaborate set of albums containing photographs of his official activities which they presented to him.

It took years for the breach with "Room 9" to heal—and the feud with certain individual reporters never terminated— but conditions gradually improved. Part of the credit for the improvement must be given to the Mayor but even more to his fanatically devoted secretary, Lester Stone. Stone, a former reporter, worked night and day with his erstwhile colleagues trying to straighten things out.

He succeeded so well that when the La Guardias adopted another youngster—three-year-old Eric—in the Spring of 1934, the reporters generally respected the Mayor's wishes and the event received practically no publicity.

*   *   *

As the months went by, La Guardia developed his own system of administration. He was forced to work it out for himself—almost from the beginning. He learned by trial and error. New York's new Mayor assumed office with practically no large scale executive experience. For twelve years he had directed nothing more complicated than a small personal staff. Now—practically overnight—he became the executive head of a mammoth municipal corporation; a corporation with 140,-000 employees. He directed the expenditure of six hundred million dollars annually, and he stepped into this position at a time when the vast institution was being reorganized from top to bottom.

He taught himself to operate this gigantic municipal machine—and to do it efficiently.

He made his mistakes in the beginning—but revealed an invaluable capacity to benefit by them. Before his first term was half over the Mayor himself realized that he was devoting far too much time to insignificant details. Out of this realization grew the conception of a Deputy Mayor—a lieutenant who might relieve him of a great mass of such annoyances. (And when the office was finally established, he appointed that same Henry Curran who had defeated him for the Mayoralty nomination in 1921.)

Likewise came a gradual change in his system of supervision. The original version was peculiarly his own.

Its mainspring was jealousy.

In the beginning, jealousy of each other was one of the principal characteristics exhibited by the members of his personal staff. These subordinates were wildly envious of each other's access to the Chief. If he did not promote the inter-office feuds which sprang up as a result, he certainly did nothing to check them. Before many months elapsed, most of the members of his personal entourage were bitterly antagonistic to each other. Angry subordinates continually poured complaints against colleagues and superiors into the Mayor's ear. Cliques and factions sprang up.

They existed for many months—persisting throughout most of his first administration. Gradually, however, he ceased to grant so ready a hearing to this kind of complaint and the situation improved. A certain amount of competition, however, was never eliminated.

Gradually his associates fell into three circles—a trio of rings circulating around the despot in City Hall. Closest was the group of men he respected and to whose advice he would listen and upon which he would occasionally act. They included the trusted Windels, Berle, Seabury, the veteran Charles C. Burlingham and George Z. Medalie.

Revolving just outside their orbit was a group of younger men—fanatically devoted subordinates who occasionally suffered almost brutal humiliation and abuse from their leader but repaid it with the warmest devotion. With most of them he stood *in loco parentis*, occasionally giving them fatherly advice or long paternal lectures. This group constituted his most frequently used lieutenants. It included Stone, later Assistant Budget Director, Paul J. Kern, whom he made President of the Civil Service Commission, Deputy Commissioner of Correction David Marcus, Maurice Postley, Secretary of the Board of Education, Deputy Police Commissioners Harold Fowler and Byrnes MacDonald, and Clendenin Ryan Jr.

In the outer orbit circulated a group of men whom he liked and whose work he respected. They were individuals who devoted more time to their jobs than they did to cultivating the Mayor. Typical of this group were Valentine who succeeded O'Ryan as Police Commissioner, McElligott and Moses.

"A man who actually knew how to fight fires." The Mayor and his Fire Commissioner watch an early morning blaze.—(*Courtesy Associated Press*)

"Life . . . centered around the youngsters." The Mayor instructs his household in military drill. The youngsters include a nephew, his own children, a niece, and the son of the La Guardia cook.

These groups circulated in orbits which centered at City Hall. Very few of them were permitted to intrude upon his home life. That was sacred. The little circle of the pre-Mayoral days was not permitted to expand perceptibly—although there was far less time available to spend with his old time friends. Piccirilli remained a frequent visitor but many of the others dropped away.

Life in the six room apartment centered around the youngsters. The cares of State were banished at the door and replaced by problems brought from kindergarten. The Mayor of New York seldom walked through that door. It remained the happy home of "the Major and Marie."

She seldom accompanied him to official ceremonies—and then only when he insisted. On such rare occasions she deliberately sought to remain in the background. Often the quiet little lady beaming proudly on the side lines was unrecognized.

One such occasion was an open air dance contest staged in Central Park by a New York newspaper that first summer. The Mayor accepted an invitation to preside and Marie influenced by her love of music came along.

It was a beautiful evening and the audience proved larger than any one had anticipated. Tens of thousands of New Yorkers poured into the Mall and overflowed the section reserved for spectators. Even before the honor guests arrived the tens had become hundreds of thousands and the crowd was completely out of hand.

Pressed on by the curious multitude on the outlying edges, the helpless horde about the bandstand pushed irresistibly forward. It trampled down ropes, broke through the thin police lines, overflowed the dance platform and became an inert, frightened mass of humanity.

Panic was already threatening when the Mayor drove up. Instantly he took command.

Leaping from the car, he asked a near-by patrolman to look after his wife and then bored his way toward the center.

Somehow he fought his way through, arriving at the band-stand with torn and disheveled clothing.

Swiftly he began snapping out orders to the anxious police officers in charge. He was very explicit.

"Send somebody to the nearest telephone," he rapped. "Order out the reserves and get a couple of emergency squads as fast as God will let you. We've got to break this thing up before it gets out of hand. Tell the reserves to start working on the fringes of the crowd. They are not to try to fight their way into the center. Tell them to start pulling people away at the outer edges and send them to the rear. Break it up from the outside. I'll do what I can."

He turned to a group of colored youngsters from Harlem. "Can you boys dance?"

"Yas, suh, Mr. Mayor."

Their shining eyes were proof of their enthusiasm. He laughed cheerfully.

"You wriggle your way out of here and go up and start jigging, away off yonder by the fountain. I'll come over and watch you as soon as I get things cleared away here. There isn't going to be any contest."

He struggled up to the platform and seized the loud-speaker. As soon as he was recognized, the whole park roared applause.

Quietly he explained that the contest had been postponed and would be held later. He begged the people to go home and as soon as the pressure about the platform lessened, he began urging the spectators to leave the shaky structure. Bit by bit the situation was relieved.

Turning about he was horrified to catch a glimpse of Marie already perched in the packed bandstand near by. She had re-fused to remain at the car. Ignoring the pleas of her police escort, she had struggled through behind him. Marie had rec-ognized the danger and followed her husband determinedly. She didn't propose to be separated from him at such a time.

Hours elapsed before the crowd broke up. During all that time, the Mayor struggled through the crowd begging, urging and commanding. That night he won the respect and admiration of the police force. High-ranking officials, experts in crowd psychology, gave him unstinting praise for preventing a panic which might have resulted in a real disaster.

When it was over the Mayor was a wreck. Perspiration stained his white summer suit and his face was streaked with grime. He didn't look like the Chief Executive of a great city.

Finally he packed Marie into a friend's car and they started home. And then he saw the old woman.

Weeping hysterically, she stood beside a driveway and waved at the passing automobiles. Two or three cars stopped beside her and then drove on. Instantly the Major directed his friend to pull up beside her. He leaned out with a cheerful query. "What's the matter, Madam?" She responded with a torrent of Italian.

The Mayor sprang from the car, took her by the arm and reassured her in her own language. After she had quieted down and told her story, he turned back to his host.

"This lady speaks no English. She is a stranger here. It's her first visit to New York. She is the mother of one of the contestants and she comes from Plainfield, New Jersey. She lost her family in the crowd and she's terribly frightened. If you don't mind, I'm going to put her in the car and take her over to the Arsenal police station."

With extreme courtesy he escorted her to the car and seated himself beside her. As soon as he had done so, he spoke warningly.

"I don't want any of you to address me by my title. This poor woman speaks no English but she may happen to know that particular word. She is very grateful for my assistance and I am afraid she would become somewhat emotional if she suspected just who I am."

The car drove on and the Mayor busied himself with entertaining the stranger.

When he ushered her into the police station, the place was a bedlam. It was over-run by busy officers still working desperately to clear away the crowd in the near-by park. The harassed lieutenant in charge never dreamed that the disheveled, grimy, individual before him was his superior.

Courteously La Guardia explained the difficulty and waited for the lieutenant to take charge. The latter snapped irritably, "My God, what do you expect me to do with her? There's hundreds of old women lost in that mob."

The Mayor answered gently.

"There are many things which you can do, Lieutenant, if you are familiar with your duty. You can notify the Missing Persons Bureau; you can notify the Plainfield police in case her family reports her absence, and you can even broadcast to the police in the park just where she is to be found so that they can send her relatives to her if an appeal is made to them."

The busy policeman exploded irritably.

"Say, just who in hell do you think you are, telling me how to run my job?"

The bedraggled little man before the desk smiled. He almost cooed his response.

"Personally, Lieutenant, I am a person of no importance, but—(and the voice grew suddenly tense)—the job I happen to hold is Mayor of the City of New York—and damn you, Lieutenant, I want to see my police force function."

The policeman collapsed like a pricked balloon. He dropped his pen and stared at the visitor as if he had seen a ghost.

"My God," whispered the Lieutenant, "I was just thinking you looked kind of like him."

Thereupon the Mayor of the City of New York got his wish. He "saw" his Police Department function—promptly, energetically and efficiently. Anxious cops ran to bring a chair for the lady from Plainfield. A glass of water was quickly produced, telephones began buzzing—and the Major remained until he saw the frightened visitor restored to the arms of her family.

That episode, too, was typical of His Honor, the Mayor.

CHAPTER XXII

THE ROUT OF TAMMANY

"It's in the bag."

The Mayor of New York smiled reassuringly and patted his anxious friend on the shoulder. There was more than a hint of patronage in his tone.

"It's in the bag," he repeated. "I tell you we have got this outfit licked. McGoldrick can't lose. I've got the people behind me. Don't you worry."

"But even so," protested the lieutenant, "It doesn't seem right for you to go chasing off to Wisconsin in the middle of the campaign on which so much depends."

"What do you mean—so much depends?" snapped the Mayor. "There's only three votes in the Board of Estimate even if we should lose—which we can't—we'd still control the Board of Estimate by 10 to 6."

"You will—if Palma and Harvey stand fast," came the rejoinder. "If they should vote with Tammany, you'd be sunk."

"Nonsense," laughed His Honor. "You're seeing ghosts, and anyway McGoldrick can't lose. It's in the bag, I tell you."

That conversation was typical of the overconfidence which almost gave New York back to Tammany. Flushed with victory and already a little dizzy from the chorus of gathering yes men, the Mayor lost his grip on the Board of Estimate before his first term was half over.

Fate proved unkind. The brilliant Cunningham died from a heart attack on May 9, scarcely five months after the new administration had taken office. The soldier financier had been a tower of strength to the Mayor and his close advisor. His unexpected death was a bitter blow and Tammany rallied instantly prepared to battle for the Comptroller's three votes in the Board of Estimate.

The Board of Estimate consisted of the Mayor and seven other city officers. Its importance was due to the fact that it was the upper house of New York's municipal legislature.

Under the old charter New York City had a government which resembled the national government at Washington. There was a Mayor and two houses of the legislature instead of a President and two houses of Congress. The Board of Estimate was the upper house corresponding to the United States Senate, while the Board of Aldermen occupied the same place in the city setup that the House of Representatives constitutes in Congress. All New York City laws including appropriations had to be passed by both houses and then approved or vetoed by the Mayor.

The Mayor acts not only as Chief Executive but sits as a member of the upper house. He casts three votes in the Board of Estimate. The Comptroller and Aldermanic President also have three votes each, while the Borough Presidents of Manhattan and Brooklyn cast two votes each. The Borough Presidents of the Bronx, Queens and Richmond each possess a single vote.

Republican leaders swarmed about His Honor, each with a candidate guaranteed to win the special election which would select Cunningham's successor. It was up to the Chief Executive to appoint a man to fill the office until November and everybody agreed that the Mayor's choice would be the Fusion candidate.

La Guardia defied the political camp followers as well as their chieftains. He refused even to talk to the Republican State Chairman when he found the latter waiting at his door one evening—and he demonstrated his complete independence by appointing a novice in politics. He selected Dr. Joseph McGoldrick, a professor of government at Columbia University, whom Cunningham had drafted as expert advisor. The college professor was a jovial, pudgy little bachelor who promptly revealed an unexpected talent for practical politics. His financial ability was unquestioned.

The Mayor seemed to be still dizzy from the effects of his own victory. For the first time in years, the wily Ghibonne Chieftain exhibited no political sagacity. He could not be persuaded that McGoldrick was in danger; that Tammany was still a menace.

La Guardia refused to face the fact that he was a minority mayor. He had seemingly sold himself the idea that he would have received all the McKee votes if the latter had not run. Consequently, His Honor labored under the delusion that he then commanded the support of a vast majority of his constituents. It required a major disaster to wake him up.

Serenely confident that his endorsement meant McGoldrick's election, La Guardia went blithely off to the Middle West to campaign for his friend, La Follette, leaving the professor to carry on his own campaign.

It was bitter. The five Democratic organizations had united behind Frank J. Taylor, a veteran of Brooklyn and a former Commissioner of Public Welfare. They waged a typical Tammany campaign in his behalf. McGoldrick, practically unassisted by his chief, fought desperately—and almost won.

The Mayor refused to admit the possibility of his Comptroller's defeat until the night before election. That evening he talked matters over with a friendly political reporter in the Advertising Club bar.

"How does it look?" asked His Honor.

"It's neck and neck," replied his friend. "If McGoldrick wins, he wins by an eyelash."

La Guardia gestured for silence and stared at the ceiling for a long time. He seemed to be gazing into the future. At last he spoke.

"If you're right," he said, "we're facing a real disaster. If this election is at all close, it means McGoldrick is licked. If I lose my Comptroller, Tammany will stage a comeback. In that case, you're going to see one hell of a fight."

Next day; a stunning shock.

McGoldrick lost.

La Guardia was right. The vote was very close. Taylor won 831,390 to 815,561.

It was a terrible blow. La Guardia still controlled the Board of Estimate 10 to 6, but already Borough Presidents George U. Harvey of Queens and Joseph Palma of Staten Island had shown signs of a willingness to bolt. Tammany controlled the Board of Aldermen, too.

There was great rejoicing down at the Hall. Old timers sagely observed that no reform administration had ever yet succeeded itself in the history of New York City. "La Guardia was just a flash in the pan," they observed. "We've still got the machine and the votes. We'll toss him out in 1937 and write the whole thing off to experience."

Most observers agreed with them.

The shock seemed to bring La Guardia to his senses. Finally he faced the fact that his supporters still numbered less than 900,000 out of the city's voting population of more than 2,200,000. Finally he realized that he had not yet sold himself to the great mass of McKee's Independent followers. That was a stunning realization.

He had repeatedly declared that he wanted no second term; that he considered himself a one-term mayor whose mission was to disinfect the cesspools of municipal corruption and then step aside. This decision had been based upon his belief that Tammany had received a mortal wound.

Now, the potential corpse was showing a disturbing activity. La Guardia began to realize that the crusade to which he had devoted most of his life, was yet unfinished; the ancient foe still on his feet.

Furiously La Guardia returned to the attack. Mercilessly he renewed the assault upon the Tiger and the latter's allies. Anxiously he urged Paul Blanshard, the Socialist reformer whom he had appointed Commissioner of Accounts, to go out and get the goods on Tammany.

Blanshard needed little urging. As head of the Municipal Department of Investigation, he possessed the power of subpoena and he used it wickedly. At his elbow stood Special Counsel, Irving Ben Cooper, another reform champion who had won his spurs in the Seabury Investigation. They started looking for filth in the Tiger's den—and discovered plenty of it.

La Guardia attacked all along the line. He sent Valentine into action against the gangsters who had constituted Tammany's shock troops and threw "Big Mike" Fiaschetti into the fray as a deputy commissioner to clean them out of the public markets. (Big Mike, a retired police captain who had won an Italian knighthood for smashing the Black Hand, worked without gloves and proved unbelievably efficient. He was inspired by an almost religious devotion to his idol, the Mayor.)

La Guardia attacked all along the line. He gave prompt and hearty co-operation to Thomas E. Dewey, the youthful Special Prosecutor appointed by Governor Lehman to clean out the racketeers whom the Mayor also regarded as Tammany allies. Valentine received blanket orders to work with Dewey at all times.

The results were impressive. During the ensuing three years one scandal after another was raked out and laid bare to the gaze of an astonished public. New York was horrified to learn of graft and brutality among the aged inmates of the municipal charitable institutions; it watched breathless as Dewey convicted three score racketeers and it could scarcely believe the results of Blanshard's activities.

These results *were* impressive. They included 94 public officials who either were removed or resigned under fire and the prosecution and punishment of 119 private citizens. Criminal indictments were returned against 28 public officials and 20 of them were convicted, while 86 private citizens were indicted and 75 of them convicted.

As these results piled up, a lot of Independent Democrats began to observe publicly that "this La Guardia fellow" was a pretty healthy influence and they guessed they might have been mistaken about him.

The Mayor promptly proceeded to mobilize this public sentiment behind a permanent reform program. He trotted out a couple of proposals which were calculated to strike at the very foundation of Tammany's strength. One was a recommendation for a new City Charter and the other to consolidate the various offices which were duplicated among the five counties.

Tammany was slow to recognize the peril involved in these flank attacks. The Tiger leaders agreed that there was little danger of either proposal getting anywhere and they refused to get excited. Their appointees filled every one of the 834 county offices involved and two-thirds of the 65 Aldermanic seats which would be abolished by the new charter. Tammany, however, did not worry. It was cockily confident following the Taylor victory.

It didn't even fret when its obstreperous opponent managed to get a county office reorganization constitutional amendment through the Legislature for submission to the voters at the 1935 election. That amendment for which La Guardia was campaigning so ardently merely authorized the municipal assembly to pass legislation consolidating those offices. Tammany did not think it would pass—but even if it did the Tiger still controlled the lower house of that municipal assembly (the Board of Aldermen) by 20 to 1. The leaders were justifiably confident that no embarrassing measure would emerge from that body. They were sure they had La Guardia on the run.

There was a little uncertainty about the situation in Brooklyn. Young Dr. McGoldrick had bobbed up again as a Republican candidate for District Attorney and was making a commotion about a forgotten murder case which was embarrassing a number of the faithful. Ordinarily that would have been a matter for jest except for the fact that the ubiquitous professor had carried Brooklyn when he ran against Taylor.

The organization therefore exerted unusual efforts to re-elect William F. X. Geoghan.

McGoldrick was handicapped by an evident rift in the ranks of reform. The Mayor once more failed to exert himself on behalf of his former Comptroller. (Insiders whispered that the fiery Chief Executive was punishing his ex-ally for failure to follow his advice during the preliminary manoeuvers for the nomination.)

Election day brought another organization victory. McGoldrick went down to a disastrous defeat and the Tammany allies elected 62 Aldermen. In the ensuing celebration most of the Tiger cubs ignored the fact that La Guardia's county office amendment had won. They had no fear of any reorganization which needed the approval of their Board of Aldermen.

Within the month they captured the Board of Estimate, too.

Fate struck once more. Deutsch died November 21.

Timothy J. Sullivan, Majority Leader of the Board of Aldermen, automatically succeeded to the Aldermanic Presidency and its three votes in the upper house. Before his term was half over, the Mayor had seen his 13 to 3 majority in the Board of Estimate dwindle to a 7 to 9 minority. Almost before he realized it, La Guardia had lost control of the city government. Tammany and its allies controlled both houses of the municipal legislature.

When a little later, Harvey and Palma began voting with the Tammany majority, the Mayor found himself with his back to the wall. Only Ingersoll remained loyal and they could muster only 5 votes between them.

The Fusion crusade seemed doomed. A resilient, optimistic Tammany was on the march once more. The greatest political machine in the country was set for revenge.

And down at City Hall, a harassed Mayor took counsel with himself.

Politically he was "on the spot"—but it was no new position for him. He had spent most of his legislative life as a member of a hopeless minority and experience had taught him just which cogwheels of a majority steam roller offered the best target for a hand-wrought monkey wrench. La Guardia settled down to fight Tammany in the Board of Estimate as he had fought Tories in the House of Representatives.

And his intention to retire in 1937 vanished like an icicle in a blast furnace.

The Major prepared for another battle to the death.

He had one magnificent asset; his knowledge of dirty politics.

Never before had a reformer been re-elected as Mayor of New York—but never before had Tammany encountered a reformer who knew all the ins and outs of its own dirty game.

Early in 1936, then Fiorello La Guardia faced the realization that he must fight for his political life when his first term expired. Deliberately he prepared to do so. Deliberately he began trimming his sails to the political winds and occasionally he permitted his gaze to wander from that nonpartisanship ideal which previously had seemed to be the guiding star of his administration.

The Mayor began to play practical politics—and he was a master at the game.

The papers printed pictures showing the Mayor with a Republican leader and the latter's personally sponsored appointee. Such photographs aroused considerable interest in organization ranks. Later appointments were "politically balanced" in that they gave recognition to various creeds and races. As a result, the Mayor's neglected fences began to look considerably stronger.

Then he planned and carried out an astounding larceny. When nobody was looking, he stole an entire political party.

The Democrats thought they had it nailed down safely. They had filed a claim on the fledgling American Labor Party almost as soon as it was born. They lined it up for President Roosevelt and Governor Lehman in 1936. Democratic chieftains beamed approvingly upon this precocious youngster when it turned in 250,000 votes.

They never dreamed a potential kidnaper was crouching in the northwest corner of City Hall.

The American Labor Party was a Democratic creation—and Tammany's ally—until La Guardia walked off with it when its sponsors' backs were turned. He planted the brilliant young Kern in its General Staff as soon as it began to take shape and Kern began building fences even before the 1936 campaign got under way. Before it was over, he had a dozen lines of communication leading into City Hall.

The Labor Party was something new in New York politics. Its foundation consisted of an alliance of labor unions, the most important of which were the garment workers, those same garment workers for whom La Guardia had fought back in 1913. They mobilized behind Sidney Hillman, David Dubinsky and Luigi Antonini. They received the blessing of John L. Lewis, Chairman of the Committee for Industrial Organization.

The Mayor beamed approvingly upon the new party—and carefully restrained himself to a minor role in the Presidential Election of 1936. He supported Roosevelt but most of his campaigning took place in Nebraska. Responding to the appeal of an old ally, the New York Mayor went out and took the stump for Norris. La Guardia's sentimental soul was thrilled by the silver-haired veteran's independent candidacy and he joined the group of Liberals mobilized in his behalf. Among them were young La Follette, Wheeler, Nye and Shipstead.

Back in New York, the Mayor came out for the President at a big Labor Party meeting and then campaigned for his new charter—which was coming up at last. The rank and file of Tammany did not know much about the measure but they distrusted it for two reasons; McGoldrick had helped to write it and La Guardia was for it. The organization passed the word to turn thumbs down. It also opposed another newfangled idea which the Mayor was urging—some sort of novel voting scheme called "Proportional Representation."

Tammany shared the glory of the Roosevelt landslide. It was much more pleased, however, by the election of William F. Brunner to fill out Deutsch's term. Brunner had swamped Alderman Newbold Morris, the Republican nominee, and definitely nailed down those essential three votes in the Board of Estimate.

Tiger chieftains spoke patronizingly of the new labor party and the one quarter of a million votes which it had given the Democratic ticket. Then they settled down and began the usual scramble for next year's Mayoralty nomination.

And while they were scrambling—La Guardia stole the labor party.

He passed the word—and his representatives got busy in the unions. Labor was gently reminded that it had received unusual treatment from the Fusion Mayor. "Peaceful picketing" had been interpreted very liberally by La Guardia and policemen on strike duty deprived of their clubs. There were references to the Norris-La Guardia Act and the Mayor's long labor record; reminders of his trips to Albany to plead for the Child Labor Amendment, etc. The unions lined up behind him before Tammany even thought about the possibility.

The Mayoralty Campaign of 1937 was planned at "Summer City Hall." This was an old Park Department mansion located at College Point in Queens, to which the Mayor removed his office force to avoid the summer heat of downtown Manhattan. There he summoned his most trusted advisors and outlined his program—all the while ostentatiously proclaiming that he would wage no campaign and accept a nomination only if it were pressed upon him.

Nobody was greatly surprised when it was so pressed. George Z. Medalie took care of that. Early in the Summer, he lined up 1,000 leading citizens. They all went out to College Point and begged the Mayor to run again. Graciously the Chief Executive appeared upon the veranda, beamed at everybody and tossed his sombrero into the ring.

Then he went back into his office and remained there throughout his most unique campaign. He broke all the rules. He established no headquarters. He appointed no campaign manager. He solicited no contributions. He seldom bothered to make speeches. New York beheld the dumfounding spectacle of a Mayor too busy with his official duties to stage the usual pre-election show.

His hand, however, was never really far from the throttle. He always found time to confer with his principal supporters. They included Windels, Hillman, Ben Howe of the City Fusion Party and Kenneth Simpson.

And Simpson outguessed La Guardia.

Kenneth Simpson was a newcomer on the political horizon. He had succeeded to the virtually worthless position of Manhattan Republican Leader. This big man with a bushy, red moustache and a great booming voice was a successful lawyer who had reluctantly taken command of New York County's crippled G. O. P. organization. It was so weak that most politicians dismissed it with a laugh. It had polled less than 175,000 out of 691,000 Republican votes the preceding Autumn. Now Simpson proceeded to put this battered machine into the race.

It was one of the five Republican county organizations. La Guardia realized he needed the G. O. P. nomination which, after all, was worth some 600,000 votes. He soon discovered that Simpson was the only one of the five county leaders who seemed inclined to give it to him. The Brooklyn and Bronx organizations were definitely hostile, while Queens and Richmond evinced little enthusiasm.

An amazing amount of political maneuvering went on behind the scenes with this Republican nomination as the stake. La Guardia proceeded on the theory that the G. O. P. must ultimately reconcile itself to him because no other anti-Tammany candidate would have a chance to win. Therefore, he went ahead arranging a slate of running mates which would appeal to both the Laborites and the Republicans.

He reckoned without Kenneth Simpson.

The new Republican boss staged one of the most successful political *coups d'etat* which New York had seen in years. The driver of the battered G. O. P. machine calmly nominated the rest of the city-wide ticket and forced it down La Guardia's throat. Without warning, one evening he called in the reporters and presented to them two Republican anti-Tammany candidates as Mayor La Guardia's running mates. The dumfounded reporters found themselves face to face with Dr. McGoldrick whom Simpson had chosen for Comptroller and young Mr. Newbold Morris, selected for President of the new Council, provided for in the equally new charter.

His Honor was enraged by Simpson's stolen march and publicly denounced the action. Simpson knew that La Guardia had his own candidates for both offices but he also knew that he had caught the Mayor napping. The Republican leader sat tight. He had not yet played his ace. That was a public endorsement of La Guardia as the organization candidate. Without such backing both men knew the Mayor would find it difficult to win the Republican Primary and La Guardia had to have that Republican nomination.

The Mayor countered by a concealed threat. His ace was his possible refusal to run in the Republican primary. He knew that unless he headed Simpson's ticket, the Republican organization would be helpless. The two men bluffed each other for a week but finally they came to terms. La Guardia met Simpson at a City College concert and agreed to accept the slate.

The leaders of the new Labor Party were equally furious but found themselves caught in the same trap with the Chief Executive. They finally gave up their hope of dictating one of the city-wide candidates.

Midsummer found La Guardia carefully maneuvering for the Republican Primary endorsement. Simpson's support was not sufficient. It was necessary to line up the G. O. P. organization in one of the larger counties. Boss John Knewitz of the Bronx was furiously opposed to the Mayor. There was no hope there. Leaders of the Queens organization which supported Harvey were prepared to drive a hard bargain. Brooklyn seemed to offer the best opportunity and the Mayor turned the problem over to his friend Windels.

The Corporation Counsel faced a difficult situation. John Crews, the Brooklyn leader, remained ostentatiously neutral in the face of a bitterly hostile faction headed by Jacob Livingston.

Livingston was a veteran Republican politician who occupied a very strategic position as one of the four members of the City Board of Elections. He controlled a great deal of patronage. He exerted all his influence against the Mayor.

Most of the Brooklyn leaders lined up behind Livingston. They were still raging over La Guardia's failure to permit them to name his appointees to office. He had further aroused their anger by publicly referring to their followers as "club house loafers." They offered a united front against Windels.

The Corporation Counsel delivered the goods—but he went through a near riot in order to accomplish it.

What was probably the major victory of La Guardia's 1937 campaign was won in an ante-room of Brooklyn's Kismet Temple on the night of July 29. There Windels and his lieutenants finally sat down at a table with the leaders of the Livingston forces. They caucused while the auditorium was slowly filling with the 3,000 members of the Kings County Republican Committee.

It was the culmination of Livingston's eight-year fight against La Guardia. Everybody knew that the Elections' Commissioner intended to force through a resolution publicly repudiating the Mayor. Most of the experts believed that the passage of this resolution would defeat him in the primary, deprive him of the Republican nomination and thus insure his defeat.

There was no doubt that most of the leaders around that table hated the Mayor. They were torn between their anxiety to punish him and their desire for a Republican victory. They listened dourly as Windels presented the case for His Honor.

Livingston's followers were obdurate until the Corporation Counsel played his trump. It was the public endorsement of La Guardia by the Manhattan G. O. P. organization. "I've just talked with Kenneth Simpson," said Windels. "Manhattan will support the Mayor. If you don't come along we'll go into the Primary and battle it out. You may whip us but you'll split the Republican Party and wreck your own organization in the battle."

It was a compelling argument and it converted some of the Brooklyn leaders. Livingston and his lieutenants, however, remained obdurate. Among them were other men who hated La Guardia bitterly. They were perfectly willing to wreck their party if they could ruin his career in so doing.

The conference dragged on while the impatient committeemen waited for their leaders to appear and finally Windels engineered a compromise.

It was a happy solution to all their troubles—because each side thought it was putting something over on the other. They agreed to refer the question of a Republican nominee for Mayor back to the 23 Brooklyn district organizations. Livingston's followers were satisfied because they *knew* that they controlled two-thirds of the Republican commiteemen. They were sure that they could crush La Guardia either in the central committee or in the district organizations.

Windels knew better. He had carefully analyzed the make-up of each of the 23 organizations. He knew that La Guardia had no chance at all in 11 districts but the cagy Corporation Counsel had managed to line up a narrow majority in each of the remaining 12 districts. Windels knew that his 1,000 votes were so distributed as to give him control of 12 districts while the 2,000 anti-La Guardia votes were concentrated in 11 districts.

Windels accepted this compromise because it was the best he could do. His opponents accepted it because they did not realize how it would work out. And being the stronger party, they dictated terms. They insisted that they were to be permitted to denounce the Mayor to their hearts content; that they could say anything they pleased about him and there would be no attempt to choke them off by parliamentary procedure. Windels agreed to everything merely insisting that Livingston himself should open the meeting by introducing the resolution which referred the nomination back to the district clubs.

Windels and his lieutenants saved La Guardia there in that back room—but even so the victory almost escaped them at the last minute.

The meeting proved to be packed with La Guardia's foes. They outnumbered his supporters by more than two to one. Windels' speech was drowned out by a storm of hisses. Livingston's attack upon the Mayor provoked wild demonstrations. Windels began to look worried. It was evident that if the opposition broke the agreement they could pass their resolution with ease. Some of the Livingston leaders decided to stampede the committee. They seemed certain of success.

Then the La Guardia luck prevailed.

One of his most ardent opponents launched an attack which backfired all over the hall. She was Miss Grace Lease, a district co-leader, and the rafters were ringing with applause for her vitriolic denunciation of the Mayor. Enthusiastically she perorated:

"I don't know whom we want for Mayor—but I do know whom we don't want. That is the man in City Hall today. Sooner than support him—I am willing to tie up with Tammany Hall."

There was an instant of stunned silence. After all, her hearers were Republicans—and hatred of the Tiger was bred into their bones. They were not prepared to go that far.

And in that momentary silence, a swarthy Italian committeeman sprang upon his chair and shrilled, "Tammany sell out."

The phrase caught. Instantly a 1,000 La Guardia supporters began chanting it in unison. Windels' lieutenants grasped their opportunity. They quickly organized cheering sections. The chant, punctuated by boos and hisses, went on endlessly. It swamped the woman's effort to explain. It finally drove her from the platform. The mocking chorus drowned the voice of every speaker who attempted to follow her. The disgusted anti-La Guardia leaders saw their opportunity vanish.

Nobody else was permitted to address that meeting. Crews finally ruled that the resolution referring the mayoralty candidacy which Livingston introduced according to agreement had been carried. He then adjourned the meeting.

John Crews and Paul Windels had saved La Guardia's Republican nomination.

The campaign proceeded. Simpson bestowed his official blessing and began a gallant fight on behalf of La Guardia. Accompanied by McGoldrick and Morris he stormed about the city speaking in Republican Clubs in all five boroughs. Never before had a county leader invaded other counties, but the bull-throated Manhattan chieftain broke all the rules. Everywhere he preached his gospel, "Half a loaf is better than no loaf at all."

He received an invaluable reinforcement. La Guardia enlisted the racket-crushing Thomas E. Dewey as a candidate for District Attorney in Manhattan. Dewey temporized for long weeks but finally agreed to run. Irving Ben Cooper who had received the original G. O. P. endorsement generously stepped aside.

The youthful Dewey was a regular Republican—and the hero of his entire party. He joined Simpson in the latter's canvass of Republican Clubs. Gradually they won support among the professional politicians.

Meanwhile, there was equal friction in the ranks of the opposition. The five Democratic county leaders were unable to get together. As the Summer wore on they bickered endlessly among themselves over the Democratic slate. Confident of victory, they were already scrambling for the spoils and finally they split once more.

It wasn't Flynn this time. The Bronx boss had learned his lesson in 1933. Tammany, however, insisted on dictating the candidate for Mayor. Boss James J. Dooling rose from his deathbed to veto the choice of the other four leaders.

Once an acceptable compromise loomed when they all agreed on Senator Robert F. Wagner. La Guardia's one-time Congressional ally flatly refused to lend himself to the scheme. Despite the most powerful political pressure, Wagner rejected the nomination. The threatened split became inevitable.

Dooling finally designated Wagner's running mate, Senator Royal S. Copeland for first place. The other four Democratic leaders united on Grover Whalen who had been Walker's Police Commissioner. They were prepared to fight it out in the Primary—and Dooling then offered La Guardia's Republican opposition a rallying point by entering Copeland in the G. O. P. Primary, too.

Tammany prepared for a bitter battle but suddenly discovered it was facing a revolt in its own ranks. Half a dozen powerful district leaders headed by James J. Hines, United States Marshal John Kelley and James Torrens quit the reservation to support the other four leaders.

Whalen's backers were greatly disturbed by the first reports from their precinct captains. The latter reported that they could not hold their lines. A great mass movement for La Guardia seemed under way. Everywhere the story was the same. Voters who had been loyal to the organization for years were in open rebellion. The Italians wanted La Guardia, the Jews were enthused by his frequent denunciations of Hitler and the German Nazis.

There was a hasty conference of the four leaders—and then they attempted a *coup d'etat* in their turn. They withdrew Whalen and substituted Jeremiah T. Mahoney. Mahoney was a Tammany district leader but he possessed an equally good anti-Nazi record. He too had denounced Hitler and as President of the American Athletic Union, had opposed American participation in the Berlin Olympics.

Both parties went swirling into the primaries with Copeland denouncing Mahoney and La Guardia impartially. When, on September 16, the votes were counted, the Senator was swamped by both opponents. La Guardia and Mahoney prepared for the final struggle.

It was hectic and bitter. The nation watched as Tammany swung in behind the Democratic candidate, and Mahoney, like Copeland, made Communism his principle issue. Once more the Mayor was denounced as a Red. Once more he ignored the charge, limiting himself in his few speeches to the discussion of the record of his Administration. Once more he announced his political independence.

"There's only one issue in this campaign," he repeated again and again. "I make no promises. If you like my kind of administration, you can have four more years of it."

Of course, the Mayor did not permit his idealism to handicap his sense of political timing. He enraged his Labor Party supporters when he made a deal with Harvey. The Queens President had bolted the Fusion ranks early in the administration. Palma of Staten Island had followed his example. Both were marked for punishment but the Mayor decided he might need them. His Liberal followers were deeply grieved to behold him championing both before the campaign ended. La Guardia ignored their protests, however. He knew what he was doing.

The Mayor was driving a four-horse team—and none of his chargers were especially fond of the others. He was directing the campaign and commanding the support of, 1—silk stocking Republicans; 2—New Deal Democrats; 3—Union labor; and 4—assorted Liberals. He was campaigning under four emblems, those of the Republican Party, the American Labor Party, City Fusion Party and the Progressive Party.

The Progressive Party was the personal organization of

former Water Commissioner Maurice Davidson. It consisted mostly of his personal following and polled only 28,000 votes. The other three were more important, however.

La Guardia conferred with their leaders frequently but apart. He would dismiss Simpson and Crews to receive Antonini and Alex Rose of the Labor Party who would in turn be followed by Ben Howe. Howe's City Fusion group contained a weird assortment of Liberals but there were 160,000 of them and they had to be considered.

The Mayor continued to exhibit his fanatic honesty. None of his subordinates was permitted, with his knowledge, to do any campaign work during office hours. Each was frequently reminded that he must not use city stationery or stamps for political purposes. Stone was forced to install a separately staffed office and to work there at night in order to direct and synchronize the Mayor's publicity. In this work he was assisted by Maurice G. Postley and Tax Commissioner Joseph Lilly, one-time Scripps-Howard veteran political writer.

The battle centered on the labor vote. Tammany attempted to counter La Guardia's capture of the American Labor emblem by the organization of a rival group. It was christened the Trades Union Party and political analysts agreed that the result of the election depended upon the outcome of the struggle between the two labor factions. La Guardia was sure of the Republicans and Liberals. If he could hold labor he was safe.

Tammany refused to read the handwriting on the wall when the American Labor Party packed Madison Square Garden to overflowing the week before election. One union local after another marched into the Garden bearing La Guardia's banners. They staged a wild demonstration when the smiling descendant of Gouverneur Morris addressed them as "Fellow Communists."

New York went to the polls on November 2—and La Guardia's labor ranks held. Mahoney's Trades Union group received 7,163 votes while the Labor Party polled 482,459 for La Guardia. That told the story. The total count was:

La Guardia 1,344,016
Mahoney 889,591

It was a complete rout.

When the crushed and broken Tiger crept out of the storm cellar next morning, there was debris on every hand. The bedraggled cat could scarcely believe his eyes. He had lost everything.

The first reform Mayor ever re-elected had polled more votes than any other man who ever held the office. He had carried every county and completely wrecked the machines in four of the five counties. He had swept to victory McGoldrick and Morris and four of the five Borough Presidents. He controlled the Board of Estimate 15 to 1. The organization had lost control of the new City Council which was evenly divided with Morris holding the balance of power. Dewey had been elected District Attorney.

It was the end of everything.

Even the county offices seemed doomed. La Guardia had both houses of the municipal legislature. The Tammany Tiger had been kicked to death by the victim it had tortured so long.

On January 1, 1938, the survivors of the little group that had gathered to see the Major sworn in four years before, re-assembled in the Seabury parlor. They applauded as the Mayor once more faced Justice McCook and repeated his oath of office. Flashlights illuminated the scene.

Back behind a sofa, peering tiptoe over the shoulders of the intervening spectators, stood a little blonde lady. She was beaming.

It was Marie.

CHAPTER XXIII

"I'D RATHER BE CANDID . . ."

THE second smashing victory over Tammany Hall automatically focused the national spotlight on the Mayor of New York. Almost overnight he became a member of that select group which the country regards as potential presidential possibilities. And a lot of ambitious politicos began sporting labels, each of which read:

"I'm the ORIGINAL La Guardia man."

The Major grinned a little and said nothing. Nobody was able to read his mind. Neither by word nor gesture did he indicate any ambition to go higher—but he wouldn't have been human if he hadn't played with the idea at times. And certainly he didn't cloister himself in order to avoid the public gaze.

Rather, he permitted his public duties to take him on rather frequent excursions into other sections of the country. He explained that he was fighting the battles of Agriculture because its prosperity was so closely linked to that of the industry of his own city. But the battle for Agriculture made a lot of friends for its champion in distant reaches.

New York's Mayor made it clear that he wasn't running for anything during those early months of his second term. But, as always, he kept his eyes and ears open. And there was no keener political intellect in the country, when it came to evaluating public opinion and reactions.

Many of his friends were already pressing him to play for the presidency, but there was no doubt in anybody's mind that he would make up his own mind when the time came. It was also evident that the impressions he had gathered on his western speaking trips would assist him in arriving at a decision.

The Mayor was in no hurry to make up his mind. "I have a contract with the people of New York City, which still has almost four years to run," he told a cheering audience at Wichita Falls, Tex., late in April, after an introduction which had again mentioned him as a White House possibility. "And after I get through making this speech, I won't have any friends left at all."

He went on to explain that in his opinion Government relief payments could no more continue indefinitely than they could stop suddenly. And he continued with a striking slogan in which there was so much truth that it wasn't even funny:

"I'd rather be candid than a candidate."

Nevertheless, it was evident that another phase of the Mayor's career was drawing to a close, and friends and foes watched anxiously to see what the next—and probably final—phase would reveal. Analysts considered seven possibilities.

1—There was the Presidency. It was a distinct possibility, yet political experts regarded it as highly improbable. La Guardia's chance at the White House seemed to lie in the hope that a voluble public demand might force the politicians to give him a nomination. This possibility was discounted by the experts.

They pointed out that election is far less difficult than nomination; that nominations are almost always controlled by professional politicians and that no such politician would tolerate La Guardia for an instant. It was clear that nothing short of a public uprising could force them to accept him.

There were some indications that such an uprising might be taking shape. New York's Mayor was receiving tremendous ovations throughout the Southwest and West. All kinds and conditions of people were rallying to his standard. In fact, it was an ancient chief of the Cheyenne Indians, wrinkled, old Wolf Tooth, bowed with the weight of 80 years, who first nominated the son of the Italian immigrant for President. The nomination was made in the Indian tongue, during a ceremony at Guthrie, Okla., on April 22, when La Guardia was initiated into the Cheyenne-Arapahoe tribe and solemnly christened Chief Rising Cloud.

Other Westerners, with paler faces, went whooping aboard the La Guardia band-wagon in those early days and great masses of the common people turned out to see and cheer for the simple man of the people, the fellow-Southwesterner, who had risen to first place in the distant metropolis. Indications of their feeling were manifold.

It was demonstrated when the little village of Muenster, Texas, sent automobile patrols out to the main highways that skirted their community and flagged down the speeding motorcycle escort that was rushing the Eastern visitor cross-country to catch a train. They pleaded so eloquently for a glimpse of him that he turned back and spent two whole minutes in the town, while its residents cheered him to the echo.

Professional politicians anxiously weighed the meaning of such episodes, trying to decide whether they were inspired by simple curiosity or by real love and admiration. Much of La Guardia's future was to depend upon the answer at which they arrived.

Of course, the wiseacres did not completely discount the possibility that some group of hard-bitten professionals might not decide to salvage some late-appearing hopeless situation, by nominating the uncontrollable candidate and riding to victory on his popularity. Nor did they overlook the even more doubtful possibility of a third-party movement which might perform an overnight miracle.

His friends did not expect La Guardia to bid for any such support. They thought, however, that he might at some psychological moment announce a personal platform and his willingness to accept a nomination from any group that would endorse the platform. There was some hope that this might result in a national Fusion coalition with hopes for ultimate victory.

2—Then there was the Vice Presidency. This was generally regarded as a much more distinct probability than was the White House. It was not difficult to visualize a political situation in which one of the major parties might find it advisable to balance the National ticket by nominating an Eastern Liberal for second place. La Guardia was bound to appeal to either party in such a case. He was the outstanding Liberal in the East and the possessor of an amazing amount of support beyond the Mississippi River. The experts conceded him a real chance at the Vice Presidency.

3—The Cabinet. New York's Mayor had been mentioned frequently for a place in President Roosevelt's Cabinet before he entered City Hall and there were those who expected him to receive such an appointment at the end of his first term. La Guardia was generally regarded as exceptionally well qualified for the post of Secretary of Labor although he had also been mentioned to head the War Department.

These circumstances indicated the possibility that the head of a later Liberal Administration might recognize his indebtedness to the Major for the latter's support by giving him a Cabinet place. It was one of the possibilities which could not be ignored.

4—The United States Senate. This was the career which La Guardia most earnestly desired. He had had his eye upon the upper house for many years and had frequently observed that he thought he could be both happy and useful in the Senate. La Guardia was especially attracted by the length of the six-year term which would obviate the necessity of the expensive recurring biennial campaign which had handicapped his work in the House. "You can't get anything done," he observed, "when you have to spend half your time running for re-election."

Unfortunately the Major might expect to encounter considerable difficulty in securing a nomination from either of the major parties. The Republican leaders of upstate New York had no use for him whatever. They had even refused Simpson's urgent request that he be nominated as one of the fifteen delegates-at-large to the 1938 Constitutional Convention.

Furthermore, the friends of the public utilities corporations exerted great weight in upstate Republican councils and they couldn't tolerate a candidate so opposed to their very existence. Under the circumstances, a Republican nomination for the Senate seemed out of the question.

Equally impossible was a Democratic nomination because of the influence which Tammany Hall still exerted in State conventions. La Guardia had almost kicked the tiger to death in New York City and optimistic indeed would have been the Fusionist who might have expected the bedraggled Tammany to assist him to further heights.

La Guardia's best chance for the Senate therefore seemed to lie in the growing labor movement with the possibility that the Labor Party might secure control of one of the greater organizations.

5—Governor of New York. The situation with regard to the Governorship was much the same as that concerning a seat in the Senate. The only difference was that the La Guardia opponents in both parties were even more determined to keep him out of the seat at Albany. The Chief Executive of the State controls far more patronage than a United States Senator and both parties had long ago learned to distrust the Major in the matter of the disposition of jobs. They didn't want him in Albany at any price.

6—A third term as Mayor. This was possibly the easiest road of all. With his mastery of politics and the control of the City Administration for two terms, the Mayor was regarded as politically unbeatable should he choose to run again. His friends believed that he might reconcile himself to such a course if, as seemed probable, he was unable to carry into effect all the reforms he had in mind during his eight years in office and he was not in the meantime summoned to public service in some other capacity. This course was regarded as probable only if nothing better offered.

7—Congress. There was ample precedent for his return to The House in the example set by President John Quincy Adams which had made a deep impression upon La Guardia. The Major actually *liked* his service in the House. He enjoyed the hurly-burly and there was no doubt that he would have preferred it to retirement. He was very popular in the old district where the Ghibonnes remained a mighty power. Friends doubted however if he would willingly step down to the old level. They considered it more probable that he would shoot for the moon.

*   *   *

What he will do no one can predict.

INDEX